Difference and Sameness as Modes of Integration

Integration and Conflict Studies
Published in Association with the Max Planck Institute for Social Anthropology, Halle/Saale

Series Editor: Günther Schlee, Director of the Department of Integration and Conflict at the Max Planck Institute for Social Anthropology

Editorial Board: Brian Donahoe (Max Planck Institute for Social Anthropology), John Eidson (Max Planck Institute for Social Anthropology), Peter Finke (University of Zurich), Joachim Görlich (Max Planck Institute for Social Anthropology), Jacqueline Knörr (Max Planck Institute for Social Anthropology), Bettina Mann (Max Planck Institute for Social Anthropology), Stephen Reyna (Max Planck Institute for Social Anthropology)

Assisted by: Cornelia Schnepel and Viktoria Zeng (Max Planck Institute for Social Anthropology)

The objective of the Max Planck Institute for Social Anthropology is to advance anthropological fieldwork and enhance theory building. 'Integration' and 'Conflict', the central themes of this series, are major concerns of the contemporary social sciences and of significant interest to the general public. They have also been among the main research areas of the institute since its foundation. Bringing together international experts, *Integration and Conflict Studies* includes both monographs and edited volumes, and offers a forum for studies that contribute to a better understanding of processes of identification and inter-group relations.

For a full volume listing, please see back matter

Difference and Sameness as Modes of Integration

Anthropological Perspectives on Ethnicity and Religion

Edited by Günther Schlee and Alexander Horstmann

berghahn
NEW YORK • OXFORD
www.berghahnbooks.com

First published in 2018 by
Berghahn Books
www.berghahnbooks.com

© 2018, 2020 Günther Schlee and Alexander Horstmann
First paperback edition published in 2020

Library of Congress Cataloging-in-Publication Data
A C.I.P. cataloging record is available from the Library of Congress

British Library Cataloguing in Publication Data
A catalogue record for this book is available from the British Library

ISBN 978-1-78533-715-4 (hardback)
ISBN 978-1-78920-765-1 (paperback)
ISBN 978-1-78533-716-1 (ebook)

Contents

Illustrations

Figures

Tables

Introduction

Difference and Sameness as Modes of Integration

Günther Schlee

Some Research Questions

Refugees from war zones, forced migration for economic reasons, ecological disasters and the globalization of production chains, finance and trade, have led to a phenomenon, most prevalent in large cities, that is no longer called diversity but 'superdiversity' (Vertovec 2007). Political responses vary from the celebration of diversity to xenophobic backlash and the justification of violent attacks against migrants. Intermediate positions are frequent. Immigration and the resulting diversity are described in ambiguous terms and regarded as a cause of worry. With how much diversity can a 'host' society cope?

Many states in Africa and Asia, which have not gone through the homogenization processes characterizing (to varying degrees) historical developments in Western European nation-states, have mottos such as 'unity in diversity'; and, in attempts to achieve this goal, they experiment with various models of federalism. These examples also ensure that the question of when and how integration depends on sameness, or when and how it requires difference or a combination of both will remain on the table for some time. As such questions play a role in many violent conflicts, they are matters not just of academic interest but of life and death.

In discussing modes of societal integration from different continents and historical periods, contributors to this volume describe social orders that are based on diversity, rather than merely tolerating or coping with it. However, other forms of integration require assimilation resulting in sameness along a core dimension of social identity, or so their proponents claim.

The theme of coming to terms with diversity looms large in discourses of day-to-day politics (e.g. debates about the integration of refugee, 'parallel cultures', secularism and politicized religion); but it also has a philosophical dimension, or implications for our ideas about being human and about the conditions required for realizing our full human potential. Do we have innate mechanisms for recognizing strangers and rejecting or mistrusting them? Are monolingualism, consistent systems of values and cultural homogeneity the best conditions for our intellectual and emotional development? Or are we adapted to diversity from the earliest stages of the development of our species onwards? According to Levinson (2006), we have an 'interaction engine'. When we meet speakers of another language or people who use signs other than speech, such as the hearing-impaired, we start looking for clues for decoding communicative behaviour immediately, and, if we do not find a code, we develop one spontaneously through interaction. Large states with just one national language seem to be exceptional, when viewed on a larger historical scale. In rural Africa, even illiterate people tend to speak a handful of languages, which may even be unrelated to one another. This may be closer to the normal state of humankind. Why else should we all have the capacity to learn more than one language? The environment in response to which such a capacity developed must have been polyglot. How has this problem been dealt with so far?

Somewhat paradoxically, both difference and sameness are frequently used to explain societal cohesion and forms of political integration. Much has been written about the often violent homogenization processes that led to the emergence of modern nation-states, starting in Europe. In the classic example, France, religious minorities like the Albigensians and the Huguenots had to be massacred or expelled, because they impeded attempts to create a homogeneous nation by religious criteria. Even in the nineteenth century, the transformation of 'Peasants into Frenchmen' (Weber 1976) was still underway, and the homogenization massacres[1] of the twentieth century may trump even the forced conversions and burnings at the stake of suspected dissenters in the early modern period. Some modern nation-states have come into being through unification, that is, by integrating smaller units into a larger whole, while others have come into being through the disintegration of larger entities. Irrespective of these different histories, however, modern nation-states seem to require a higher degree of cultural sameness than other political entities, including some of earlier periods.

The kind of homogeneity that is required by the homogenizing agency changes from place to place and from one historical period to another. Religious prosecution of 'heretics' has, of course, a long tradition in Europe and beyond; and, later, unifying the language was an important part of the 'nation' state project. Some of us might recall their grandparents telling stories about how they were beaten at school for speaking Breton or Low German or some other language that had not made it to an official status. However, homogenization of some traits combines easily with differentiation of other traits. For example, people who have the idea that they and their co-citizens should all adhere to the same religion and speak the same language might still advocate strongly differentiated gender roles. In fact, these convictions seem to combine frequently in conservative mind sets. Whatever the content of homogenizing efforts, however, all homogenizing policies seem to share one general point: that, for successful integration, the people to be integrated need to be the same along important lines of classification.

It should be noted that the concept 'integration' in this volume, especially in combination with adjectives like 'successful' (which have a normative ring: one should be integrated, one should integrate oneself), is sociocentric. It takes up a political discourse and a sociological perspective (in asking 'what keeps society together?'). We should not forget that, for many people who are not regarded as well integrated by others, this lack of integration is no problem at all. Some people love to sit alone in their gardens, others prefer a dog for company, and yet others spend their days and nights in front of a computer screen, communicating, but with whom? Real people, invented persons, machines? In this volume, the focus is not on individual psychological configurations, and we do not adopt a normative perspective on integration. It is not a 'must' to integrate into your local community, or any other community, if you are happy otherwise. It is not even a 'must' to be happy. We take up a political and a sociological discourse on integration, and our discussion remains immanent to the social domain, although we are well aware that one can look at human beings from many other perspectives than sociocentric and sociological ones.

In comparative perspective, Alexander Horstmann and I theorized some time ago (Horstmann and Schlee 2001) that a principle diametrically opposed to assimilation and homogenization, namely 'integration through difference', has obvious advantages, such as the reduction of competition. There seem to be conditions under which ethnically heterogeneous societies and political units can be internally peaceful and remain relatively stable over long periods of time.

There is a great deal of variation: in the recent processes of globalization of the nation-state model, some nation-states have incorporated significant levels of ethnic heterogeneity, while others have remained fairly homogeneous or, as late-comers among nation-states, are still struggling to achieve a higher degree of national unity along cultural lines.

While nation-states show great variation in their degree of ethnic heterogeneity, empires are always ethnically heterogeneous. In fact, ethnic heterogeneity is intrinsic to empires, in contrast to nation-states. I cannot really think of an empire with no ethnic or ethnicized distinction, at least between the rulers and the ruled; and very often empires comprise great ethnic diversity, which they tend to use for organizational purposes. Generally, the examination of different kinds of reasoning about sameness – or identity – and difference is the key to studying various forms of social and political integration, and this approach seems especially fitting in the comparative study of empires.

Table 0.1   Four-field table

	Good for integration	Bad for integration
Sameness	A	D
Difference	B	C

Theories that stress the importance of difference for social cohesion or systemic integration[2] implicitly or explicitly assume that sameness has disruptive effects, while those ascribing an integrative value to sameness assume the same disruptive effects for difference. We can thus arrange the arguments in a four-field table, with 'sameness' and 'difference' on one axis and their integrative value ('good' or 'bad' for integration) on the other.

The alphabetical order of the capital letters in the four fields, which proceeds counter-clockwise, does not have a deeper meaning. It just produces a kind of table of contents for the subsequent pages, i.e. it reflects the order of the following subchapters. In viewing this four-field table, one should keep in mind that, according to what has just been explained, some pairs of types are not mutually exclusive. A and C could have been collapsed into one, because people who think that sameness is good for integration also tend to think that difference is bad for it. A similar argument can be made about B and D. Still, many popular convictions stress one aspect or the other (e.g. they stress how bad differences are, without concluding that uniformity should be sought). Therefore, for present purposes, it makes sense to distinguish four different types of theory.

In the following, I consider popular assumptions in the same way as scholarly theories. When I mention those who have proposed sociological theories, I risk doing injustice to them by simplifying their positions. Durkheim, for example, has produced an extensive oeuvre rich in inspiration, and there is extensive secondary literature about him. If, here, I merely allude to his distinction between 'mechanical' and 'organic solidarity' (Durkheim 1998 [1893]), I am attempting neither to claim originality nor to do justice to Durkheim. I just do what most authors do when they refer to Durkheim, that is, I cite only those aspects of his works that seem useful with regard to my themes. My aim, in the following paragraphs, is not to make a contribution to the history of sociology or anthropology. All I want to achieve is a typology of arguments. In this typology, one can also include the perceptions of scholarly theories by a wider readership (i.e. vulgarizations of those theories) or any ideas that people have about sameness or difference, and their significance for integration, irrespective of the origin of these ideas. After an overview of such ideas, we shall ask ourselves how to move on from there.

Sameness as a Mode of Integration (A)

Examples that fit into field A of our graph abound. That people need to become like us in order to belong to us is so widespread an assumption that one could easily fill a book by listing its occurrences. In the field of sociological theories, those concerning 'assimilation' and 'acculturation' find their place here (Park 1930; Redfield, Linton and Herskovits 1936). Similarly, theories of socialization seek to explain how young people learn a culture, that is, the norms and values of their seniors and peers, whom they then come to resemble. The concept of culture itself seems to imply internal homogeneity and external distinction, and that is what sceptics criticize. In one definition, culture is the sum of what one needs to learn to become a competent member of a particular group, the bearers of that culture. Note that 'culture' in this sentence is used in two slightly different senses. In its first occurrence, it refers to a kind of competence, namely acquired knowledge and skills, as distinct from the genetically inherited ones (or the learned, rather than the genetic, components of complex forms of behaviour); and, in its second occurrence, it is the defining criterion of a bounded group of people, 'a' culture. Where there is one culture there are also many cultures, and that is where the critics come in. Many people dislike the conception of cultures as distinct, quantifiable units, and there are good arguments for this critical position. Nevertheless, many critics of 'culture(s)', in this sense, find the term hard to avoid.

What is uncontested is that sharing a 'culture' presupposes the acquisition of a form of sameness, including ways of organizing difference. (A simple example for sameness in the organization of difference would be that an uncle is different, even maintaining a different structural position from his nephew, but the two might share a way of organizing their difference, i.e. ideas about how uncles should treat nephews and vice versa.) You acquire culture by learning[3] – no problem so far. And then you become like the other bearers of this culture – and here the problems arise, as the singular of the particular, i.e. a specific culture, implies the plurality of bounded units, i.e. cultures, which are hard to pin down in empirical reality.

Cultural relativism,[4] in its extreme form (which may be a caricature created by its critics), assumes a world of mutually non-comprehensible ('incommensurable') but internally homogeneous 'cultures'. If one were to take this assumption seriously, full humanity would have to be mediated by successful socialization into one such culture, resulting in full membership in it, which would, in turn, entail incomprehension of other cultures. The counter-argument – that one would have to overcome one's restriction to one such culture (to the extent that such mutually unintelligible cultures exist) in order to become fully human in a more universal sense – is also possible.

If one observes debates in the media about the integration of migrants in (post-)industrial societies, one can distinguish between arguments for the rejection and the acceptance of migrants. Arguments for rejection stress real or imagined religious or cultural differences. Arguments in favour of immigration often accept a degree of difference, sometimes even valuing it as a potential enrichment of the society in question. Usually, however, arguments in favour of accepting immigrants include requirements that the immigrants become like members of the 'host' society in a number of ways. Acquisition of the national language is one such requirement, while others include accepting core values (minimal consensus) such as democracy and tolerance of other groups, or, going beyond that, postulating that people have to identify with and to be proud of a constitutional order that transcends the cultures and religions of particular groups (constitutional patriotism) would be another such requirement. The underlying assumption in all cases is that a degree of sameness is a prerequisite of integration (see Pautz 2005 for a critical review of such a debate, the '*Leitkultur*' debate in Germany).

Difference as a Mode of Integration (B)

The obvious starting point for a discussion of difference and its role in society is Durkheim's 'organic solidarity'. He juxtaposes the 'mechanical' solidarity of 'segmentary' societies with the 'organic' solidarity of 'advanced' societies. The former is based on similarities or sameness, the latter on differences. While 'mechanical' is a metaphor which can be easily traced to physics and technology, both 'segmentary' and 'organic' are biological metaphors. If you cut a worm in the middle, both halves may crawl away in different directions. The cut may heal; indeed, the products of the cut heal in two separate places as two separate worms recover from a stressful separation. This is possible because a worm consists of segments that are all alike. Each of them contains everything that is essential to wormishness.[5] If you do the same thing with a mammal, with heart and lungs ending up in one half, the guts and the liver in the other, both parts die. The reason for this is that organs do not replace each other; rather, they differ and stand in a complementary relationship to each other. The human body is one of the oldest metaphors (the other one being the ship) for state and society. We use this metaphor constantly. Anthropologists speak of 'corporate' groups.[6] 'Corporations', 'corporate America', the 'organs' of the state, the 'body politic', et cetera, are very much part of common English. The metaphor was there long before Durkheim, but it is Durkheim's merit to have spelt it out and thought it through.

The functioning of vital organs is a condition of the survival of complex organisms. Individual organisms are units for selection (though, admittedly, not the only ones) and healthy organisms characterized by a well 'organized' interplay of organs live longer and have more offspring than those whose internal interplay does not unroll so smoothly. The evolution of complex organisms, which in spite of their complexity function remarkably well, is therefore not a surprise from an evolutionary perspective. Humility, of course, demands that we acknowledge immediately that many things in the biosphere are still far beyond human engineering capacities and that admiration and curiosity are the appropriate attitudes toward our fellow organisms. What I mean to say is that, in principle, the emergence of complex forms does not present a problem to the evolutionary paradigm. (As long, of course, as the complex forms have some advantage for survival and reproduction. Comparison between organisms living at the same time shows that simple forms may also do quite well and sometimes live on while complex organisms go extinct.) As entire organisms are units of selection, the functionality of each single organ in the context of the whole becomes an adaptive feature and enhances fitness (in the biological sense of number of surviving progeny). Selection here favours functionality. As we transfer the concepts of 'part', 'whole' and 'functions' to society, however, they very soon turn out to be quite problematic. What is the whole? Of what is a part a part? Why should a part care about being functional for the whole? Or, if no intentions are involved, by which mechanism is this achieved? What is the unit of selection in the evolution of society or societies?

Durkheim's position may be called 'proto-functionalist' or 'functionalist *avant la lettre*'. It is an answer to the question 'what keeps society together?' This may appear to be a difficult question,[7] but it is not as difficult as the next one. The more difficult question is 'how did that, which keeps society together, come about?' Whatever it is that causes societal cohesion, it must have evolved. Have societies with more cohesion survived while the ones with more disruptive internal dynamics have ceased to exist? Has cohesion, whatever its mechanisms are, evolved through variation and selection among distinct societies? Apart from being loaded with the burden of having to define what 'a society' is and which 'societies' present different cases and units of selection, there are other reasons not to pursue this type of question.

So far all answers to this question, which takes entire systems as its starting point, have been unsatisfactory. To base an evolutionary model of cultural development on system selection is not very convincing because such processes would require enormous periods of time.

In the 1970s, ecologically oriented neo-functionalists[8] tried to explain the functional interplay internal to 'cultures' and 'societies' by system selection. Their theory implied the following: those social orders that did not work well have disappeared. Members of the surviving societies are not aware of the functional aspects of their beliefs and practices. If they had been, this might even have been detrimental. A morality based on religion only works if people believe in religion and not just in its instrumentality or functionality. People who explain religion by saying that it is good for society if people (preferably others) believe in it might not be the strongest believers and strongest holders of religion based moralities.

For those theorists, the functioning of the system requires that its parts worked unconsciously. Conscious processes such as social engineering (or simply sitting together to organize things so that they work better) play a negligible role in this kind of theory. But the costs of evolution would be high. Entire systems would have to die out and new ones would have to come into being. How many millennia this would take is not specified by these theorists. I am not aware that they even asked the question.

For a better explanation of social change, including the emergence of 'coherence' or 'integration', we need a theory that fits historical timeframes such as years, decades or centuries, and does not demand spans of time of the order of magnitude of biological evolution in order to fit historical timeframes; we need to get down to smaller units of selection with shorter lives.

I suggest that the decisions taken by individuals are suitable units of this kind. If we suspect that we have taken a wrong decision and become aware of alternatives, we may reject a decision and replace it by another one within a second or a day. How to get from the decisions of many individuals to the change of social systems is another problem, known as the micro/macro problem. I do not claim to have solved it. I just claim that we cannot get around it. We cannot just remain at the level of systems, nor can we remain at the level of individual action. Any theory about societal processes (the emergence of coherence, integration, conflict or social change) demands that we link the actor's perspective with the system perspective.

The actor's perspective offers some insight about the emergence of difference and the evolution of complementary relations on higher levels of aggregation and organization. In fact, actors do at least partly differentiate themselves from each other, sometimes intentionally.[9] They may actively strive to avoid competition or demands for the redistribution of acquired wealth. A relevant theorem in this context is the trader's dilemma. This theorem has been developed on the basis of empirical examples of traders in rural areas remote from state control. It is about making arrangements with one's customers in the absence of mediation by third parties (the state might be out of reach or be perceived as hostile).

What Evers and Schrader (1994) have called the trader's dilemma is this: if the trader defines himself too much as a foreigner, he risks his life; if he becomes too much a local person, he loses his profit. Tradespeople of foreign descent always live on the edge between these two forms of failure. They have to be foreign enough not to be obliged to grant credit. Rural societies in many parts of the world are characterized by an ethos of equality and redistribution. The household with many children will delegate workers to those where older people predominate. Everybody who works is fed, and those who cannot work anymore are fed, too. If measurements of the productivity of an individual household are represented on a graph, the result is a jagged curve; but if consumption is measured, one sees, instead, a series of flat waves approaching a horizontal line, for the redistribution of consumables causes the fluctuations of production to be evened out. Risks such as illness, pests and hailstorms are counterbalanced this way. If someone is too rich, in spite of redistribution, they must not show their wealth. Otherwise they might be suspected of witchcraft or malicious magic: they are said to have the souls of their victims work in their fields during the nights, or the like. They are said to appropriate the vital energy of others, who, in turn, are tired when they awake in the morning or even become ill and die. Rural societies ensure that no individual stands out. If a member of a local peasant ethnic group opens a shop, he or she cannot evade the demands of general solidarity and the constraints of redistribution. He or she must grant credit, at least until the next harvest, and that harvest might not be good. Bankruptcy is only a few months away. The constantly repeating fate of rural shops in local hands can be summarized in the lyrics of a verse I saw on a wall in a rural shop in Kenya:

God made Man.
Man made money.
Money made many men mad.

To avert these obligations, one must mark a separation between the traders and the local population or at least define trade as a separate sphere, distinct (some would say 'disembedded') from ordinary social life and freed from its norms. If traders are, initially, too similar to members of the local population, they sometimes convert to other religions or sects in order to create this difference.

The trader of foreign descent, or the one who has had the opportunity to define himself as belonging to a distinct category of people to whom norms of redistribution do not apply, is able to evade the constraints of redistribution and does not need to listen to tough luck stories: 'Your problem'. In Indian shops in East Africa, there are frequently printed pictures on the walls which express the shopkeepers' philosophy. One such picture shows a fat Englishman in old-fashioned tails that are way too tight. Sitting on an overflowing money chest with his belly bulging over his belt, he wears a big grin under his top hat. The caption is: 'I sold for cash'. On the picture next to this one, a gaunt figure in rags is displayed over the caption: 'I sold for credit'. On the same wall, a little further away, there is a framed motto: 'Do not mix friendship with business'.

But not-belonging and being 'foreign' also entails risks. Under Idi Amin, the Indians were expelled from Uganda. The action was disastrous for the country's economy, but it was very popular, supported by the angry masses. There are abundant examples, from all around the world, of violence against tradespeople from minority groups – of murder up to the scale of genocide, robbery and arson. To the degree that they dissociate themselves from the society of the majority, traders are also excluded from the larger community of solidarity and protection.

If the foreignness is not to evoke hostility, it has to be counterbalanced by a certain degree of charity. That is why minorities that are successful in business often practice ostentatious generosity. For example, the Aga Khan hospitals and other social institutions might have contributed a lot to the acceptance of members of the Isma'iliyya sect in many parts of the world.[10] In this way, interethnic relations constantly need to rebalance social distance.

It is not only in the case of traders and their customers that interethnic and interreligious relationships may often be understood in terms of the management of distance among social groups. Keeping the right distance is often an important aspect of interethnic relations. To take another example in which trade plays a role (but not with regard to specialized traders), in what is now Kenya, Maasai warriors took a hands-off approach to Kikuyu farmwives who came to them with trade goods, even in time of war.

Trade, which is often a product and a cause of occupational differentiation among neighbouring ethnic groups (there may be feedback loops between the two), contributes to the integration of a wider regional system. Let us, therefore, have a look at some examples of trans-ethnic trade.

Among the Maasai and the Kikuyu in pre-colonial Kenya, the differentiation of occupational niches was incomplete. The nomadic Maasai (to be exact, only certain groups of Maasai living in close proximity to the Kikuyu) raised cattle in the plains of the Rift Valley. The Kikuyu had withdrawn to the wooded highlands and cleared fields there. Kikuyu and Maasai, therefore, occupied separate ecological and economic niches as farmers and herders. The Kikuyu, however, continued to keep cattle, despite the fact that the Maasai believed that God had given all cattle to them. Insofar as they occupied the same or similar economic niches, they competed; but where their economic niches were distinct, they exchanged goods.

The relation between Kikuyu and Maasai was characterized by latent war and concurrent trade. The Kikuyu had an age-group system that was copied, in part, from the Maasai, who had probably developed it under East Cushitic influence. Age-group systems spread because they allow communities to expand, filling continuous areas. They are effective instruments for recruiting whole units of young men for raids on neighbouring ethnic groups. The latter are then forced by this to develop the same kind of organization, either to defend themselves or to create a balance between robbing and being robbed. (Incidentally, this is how early states spread, too.) The age-grade units of the Maasai and the Kikuyu raided each other's cattle and took every opportunity to kill men and boys among the enemy and to capture girls as well. At the same time, there was a kind of market peace for the women (Muriuki 1974: 86; Middleton 1979: 20). Kikuyu women could wander to the lowlands, undisturbed, with their crops in baskets, which were held by a strap across the forehead, to exchange them for animal products, and Maasai women could come from the opposite direction, undisturbed, with gourds of milk.

To summarize our contemplations about sameness and difference in the field of trade: trade between the Kikuyu and the Maasai was an exchange of products between producers. Other forms of interethnic relations involve professional traders, that is, people who specialize in buying and selling, without producing themselves. In surprisingly many cases, traders are of foreign descent (Stichweh 1992). This is not quite a universal phenomenon, but there are considerably more traders of foreign descent than tailors or policemen, not to mention farmers. This may have to do with the 'Trader's Dilemma'. The Phoenicians in the ancient Mediterranean, the Jews in medieval Europe, the Chinese in South East Asia, Hausa and Lebanese in West Africa (Peleikis 2003), the Greeks in Sudan, and Yemeni and Somali in Kenya and Tanzania are all examples of tradespeople who are ethnically different from most of their customers. The historic circumstances which made them become traders are different for each of these examples. However, there seem to be generally applicable factors which favour traders and their customers belonging to different ethnic groups, for this pattern is a frequent one, and it often survives for long periods of time. The trader's dilemma reproduces difference, and the market peace, and all kinds of norms and rules protecting trade, to some extent (sadly not in all cases at all times) guarantee peace between people who – even if they are not specialized traders – tend to be different at least to the extent that they produce different things.

Difference as an Obstacle to Integration (C)

In recent contributions to conflict theory, 'identity-based conflicts' has become a popular catchword. Usually, it is contrasted with 'resource-based conflicts' and accompanied by the claim that 'identity-based conflicts' are much more bitter and tend to be more violent than those based on 'resources', which can be solved by negotiations and peaceful sharing.[11] There is a basic flaw to this line of reasoning. The definition of 'identities' or the study of 'identification' aims at answering questions starting with 'who', while the resource issue addresses the question 'about what'. Who-questions (e.g. who sides with whom against whom, along which lines of identification, religious, ethnic or whatever) need to be asked in the analysis of any conflict, and the same is true for the question 'about what' (e.g. water, oil, jobs, political representation, etc.). 'Identity' and 'resources' are not qualifiers of different kinds of conflict but different aspects of all conflicts (Schlee 2009: 572).

In the context of theories that regard difference as an obstacle to integration, we can state that people who talk about 'identity-based conflicts' tend to regard difference, as such, as an obstacle.[12] Popular usages of the term 'difference' suggest that there is a widespread implicit conviction that differences are a cause of conflict. In phrases such as 'people work out their differences', 'difference' is used as a euphemism for 'quarrel' or 'dispute'.

Modernization theories tended to imply that, with the formation of modern nation-states, ethnic, dialectal and cultural differences would go away. Starting with Glazer and Moynihan, there is a newer strand of literature which states that, in a number of cases, ethnic differences had not simply gone away, as modernization theorists had expected. The 'melting pot' had not produced a homogeneous alloy (Glazer and Moynihan 1963). In the 1970s, the resurgence of ethnic politics was noted in Western societies, where they were supposed to have disappeared (Esman 1977). Brass (1985) gives a broad overview of the literature on this topic. The common element of the different strands of this literature is that diversity, or cultural differences, are assumed to be a force which is antagonistic to shared statehood and peaceful integration. The various analyses differ only in the importance they attribute to such differences as persisting or re-emerging elements of the social and political landscape. That is, they share the same theoretical assumptions but differ in their perception of the empirical reality. Class is discussed at great length, as authors ask whether class is the real issue, while ethnicity is simply 'false consciousness', or whether ethnicity is something real, which can aggravate class conflict (Brass 1985: 20). In both cases, cultural difference is an inhibiting factor for the advancement of society. Some authors attributed a potentially very disruptive character to these differences and predicted the disintegration of the Soviet Union and Yugoslavia long before it occurred (Brass 1985: 85).

This leads us to the literature about 'ancient hatreds' (Kaplan 1996; see Bringa 2005 and Besteman 2005 for a critique). Of course, to attribute ethnic violence simply to primordial sentiments and historical continuity (which is often constructed by taking leaps over epochs that display discontinuities) neglects all contemporary factors, such as political and economic incentives and outside intervention (Schlee 2008a: 6f). Of all examples of 'Type C' approaches reviewed briefly in this section, the 'ancient hatreds' literature makes the most direct link (or takes the shortest shortcut) in linking difference to disintegration and violence.

Sameness as an Obstacle to Integration (D)

Type D theories, which imply that sameness is an obstacle to integration, are mirror images of type B theories, which stress the integrative aspects of difference. Still there are some theories that put the emphasis on the disruptive effects of closeness and sameness rather than on integration through difference, although both ways of stating the problem lead to the same conclusions.

There is no category of people with which we share more of what defines us than our full siblings. We share with them as many genes as with our parents or children; we are of the same generation – in the case of multiple births, even the same age; and, in roughly fifty per cent of the cases, we are of the same gender.

Still 'sibling rivalry' is a phrase of wide currency because it refers to a common phenomenon. Students of animal behaviour, as well as anthropologists, use it frequently. Sibling rivalry takes the form of a deadly scramble when there are more piglets than the sow has teats. Milder forms, which many of us can observe in our own families, are teasing and boasting among children. Siblings tend to compete for the same resources, whether material ones or immaterial ones such as the love of their parents. In a large proportion of humankind, for which the provisioning of basic nutrients is precarious, close birth spacing may reduce the chances of survival of individual children significantly. The competition is about food, and what is at stake is survival. Where people can afford to have more complex needs than to fill their bellies, sibling rivalry is about parental attention and support, rank or position in peer groups, inheritance or succession. From the Book of Genesis onwards, the literature of the world abounds with examples.

It has often been observed that minimal differences are often emphasized in negative evaluation of others, especially in cases of manifest or latent hostility. Middle-middle class people denigrate lower-middle class people, lower-middle class people denigrate upper-lower class people, and so on. Discrimination is directed against members of adjacent classes (Fox 2004: 119). While little of what is said in such a context may reflect good taste, many would consider it to be more reprehensible to talk in a depreciating way about someone far below oneself on the commonly perceived social scale than about someone closer to one's own social position. A person in an elevated and secure social position might not feel the need to deplore the lack of style or the rude manners of the classes engaged in manual labour, and, if he or she did so, it might be perceived as arrogant and even vulgar.

The principle of the minimal difference applies not only to class but to all axes of social identification. The sound of a language unrelated to our own and which we have never heard before may elicit few emotions in us apart from, maybe, friendly curiosity. It may also be experienced as completely unfamiliar and even non-human, if it is compared to animal sounds. It is mostly neighbouring dialects, often so close to our own that we understand them, which invite a different kind of evaluation. They are interpreted in strongly value-laden, even moral, terms and may be perceived as sounding arrogant, pretentious, harsh, inarticulate, sloppy or boorish. Or take religion. Protestants tend to direct their suspicions about idolatry and latent polytheism (in the guise of saint worship) against Catholics. Hindus, to whom the same kind of criticism may apply, are often not found in the immediate vicinity, so the rejection is more strongly, and with more serious consequence, articulated against the close other than against the distant other.[13]

Class and dialect distinctions are relevant within a language community (e.g. Labov 2006); speakers of other languages would hardly understand what these minimal differences are all about. On similarly low levels of difference, we struggle about the correct interpretation of our own religious heritage. Tolerance is more easily applied to adherents of other religions than to the ones of the 'wrong' interpretations of our own. Sometimes, a discourse about language really is about language, just as one about religion may really be about religion. In many cases, however, we discover when we examine the social context that these discourses are about people who are in many ways too close to us, so close that they may be viewed as competitors for positions or other resources. The emphasis on the minimal difference articulates the rivalry 'within': within a political system, within a certain segment of the job market, within an intellectual community, etc. It has as much to do with sameness as with difference.

The Interplay of Difference and Sameness in Processes of Social Integration

To get beyond this four-field table, which roughly classifies existing social theories and popular assumptions about the significance of difference and sameness for social integration, we need to look at real life situations. In real life, sameness and difference are not simply 'good' or 'bad' for integration; rather, processes of integration are characterized by the complex interplay of both sameness and difference. One comes to terms with differences. They may be a factor in the peaceful division of labour, but at the same time their disruptive potential must be bridled. Ways of handling differences, of dealing with this disruptive potential, may, for example, involve fostering interaction in some contexts, such as the market, and avoiding it in others.

Real and self-styled peacemakers can be heard to give two kinds of advice which are the opposite of each other. They may encourage or discourage interaction. A couple with a strained relationship may be advised 'to put everything on the table', 'to discuss everything' and 'to do more things together'. On the other hand, marriages in societies in which there are clearly distinct male and female spheres and spouses interact little, and that only in clearly defined roles, may be quite peaceful if not harmonious. At the level of groups, including ethnic groups and nations, one can find the same contradictions.

How much interaction there should be, for the sake of peace, between macro-groups perceived as different is a time-honoured question. Living in a world of emerging warlike nation-states, classic political theorists discussed how to achieve peace among different groups or polities. Rousseau proposed economic self-sufficiency and isolation. The less interaction there is, the less can go wrong. The probability of war is reduced (Joas 2000: 55). Others held just the opposite view, proposing the multiplication of links between the potential rivals and enemies. Kant suggested constitutional arrangements and contracts, an eighteenth-century premonition of the EU; and Adam Smith saw trade as a means of peaceful integration (ibid.: 56).

If one wants to take up such lines of reasoning today, one can no longer simply assume that the differences among states or groups are naturally given. One has to discuss the construction of cultural difference, which is closely interwoven with the different forms of interaction, peaceful or hostile, that one wants to study.

Rather than treating this problem as one of minimizing or maximizing interaction, one may more fruitfully treat it as one of optimization. How can one reap as many advantages of interaction as possible without incurring too many of the costs and risks associated with it?

Another way to look at the same problem is to pose the question of how social distance is handled. If you want to rule over someone, you need at least some social distance, which has to do with a postulated difference. In a situation of total familiarity and equality, there can be no rule of one over another. On the other hand, a degree of identification and some feeling of closeness between rulers and ruled reduce the costs of rule by reducing the necessity of monitoring, control and violent oppression. So here, as is often the case in life, we find the optimal solution to be somewhere in the middle. If, in a Machiavellian fashion, we want to teach how to rule (which is not my primary concern), we can tell those who aspire to rule neither to be too close to nor too distant from the ones they want to rule. The optimal social distance is in-between.

Yet another approach to the same basic problem is that taken by Kraft, Lüdtke and Martschukat (2010: 10ff.) in their introduction to a recent volume presenting new perspectives on colonialism. They juxtapose perceptions of clearly marked boundaries between colonizer and colonized, premised on total otherness, with stories about everyday life in which this boundary was blurred. In complex settings marked by apparent paradoxes – e.g. the coexistence, in a given relationship, of exploitation and paternalistic benevolence or the claims of colonizers that colonial subjects are racially inferior and, simultaneously, amenable to elevation by a civilizing mission – difference is constantly renegotiated.

What the Present Volume Contributes to our Understanding of Difference and Sameness as Modes of Integration

In the following overview, rather than just summarizing the contributions to this volume, I take the liberty of grouping them into blocks of twos or threes according to which general themes they address, from my perspective, at the risk of foregrounding things which were in the background and vice versa. The emphasis of the authors may differ from mine and will only become clear if the reader turns to the respective chapters. I will also part from the usual practice of giving an editor's overview of a volume by occasionally referring to literature published elsewhere.

Interethnic Communication and Social Distance

The first contribution to this volume, the one by Pfaff-Czarnecka on Nepal, deals with caste. The second, by Ruf on Mauritania, deals with caste-like divisions like that between the warrior class (*hassân*) or the scholar class (*zwâya*) and with the hereditary stigma of being of slave descent. The privileged position given to caste in this volume is not coincidental. The model case of a caste system, the Indian caste system, can be seen as an example of a specific kind of meta-ethnic system.[14] It is known that its genesis is due to the circumstance that initially horizontally aligned ethnic groups were integrated into a vertical hierarchy of castes according to ritual criteria. In this volume, Pfaff-Czarnecka shows how the Hindu caste system in Nepal functions as an encompassing vertical structure that even incorporates non-Hindu groups into its middle ranks.

Apart from being an interesting case for theories about difference and sameness in processes of social integration, caste is also interesting in the context of political morality and 'anthropological projects' such as 'cosmopolitanism'.[15] It is one of those social phenomena from which it is difficult to maintain analytical distance. It contradicts Western concepts of liberty and equality, and it may be irreconcilable with those human rights that some claim are or should be universally valid.[16] Readers may expect us to point an accusing finger at the caste system, saying that, unlike botanists who classify plants, social scientists, who are also members of human society, cannot simply classify social forms without taking sides against those which do not correspond to their core values as citizens. Hierarchy, refusal of commensality or refusal to touch certain categories of co-citizens for fear of pollution, occupational specialization by birth and other features of Indian caste thinking are hard to reconcile with liberal Western values, and expectations that one should condemn them as a matter of course are hard to avoid. The intrusion of such moral imperatives, understandable or even inevitable as it is, can, of course, also obstruct a more detached, scientific perspective, which tries to find out how things work and claims the liberty to postpone moral judgements for a while. Such a position would have to acknowledge that the Indian caste system has been an instrument of relatively peaceful integration over long periods of its history, changing in many ways but preserving some basic features, and that its durability does not rely on the continuous use of open violence. One may, of course, find 'structural' or latent forms of violence in it, and there is no need to idealize or to romanticize it. Nor do ethnographers have to carry cultural relativism to the point of feeling obliged to like what they write about. Sharma (1994), for example, writes about the Indian caste system and is very critical of it. But critics of caste might also acknowledge that what strikes the observer of the Indian caste system as remarkable is the relatively high level of heterogeneity in combination with the relatively low level of physical violence. In some respects, Pfaff-Czarnecka's account is reminiscent of Leach's description of ethnic diversity and interethnic systems of communication using visible signs of differentiation in highland Burma (Leach 1954). The Nepalese are well versed in reading such signs. In addition to aspects of costume and jewellery that indicate marital status or ethnic and caste association, the animals in the compound give indications of what their owners can eat and, thus, of their caste.

Being able to classify one another and having access to a common meta-culture of symbols of subordination and difference is a very limited form of commonality. There does not need to be more commonality than that existing between old enemies, practiced opponents in warfare. Even these have a common repertoire of threats, of tactics and strategies learned from the opponent, common forms of propaganda and iconographies of violence that mirror one another down to the finest of details – except that the positive and negative valences are reversed: Y has a negative attitude toward Z, just as Z has toward Y. Therefore, understanding one another is not necessarily the same as getting along.

In Nepal it is not friendship or enmity but distance that is the most important factor in mediating relations among different groups. The hierarchical order, based on requirements that people of low status avoid those of high status, has long served to create distance and prevent friction among castes. But fairly recently, people of lower rank have begun to question it and to consider the symbols associated with them to be demeaning. Thus, a 'victim' status has been created and used for ethnic mobilization. But as long as distance and the accentuation of difference are maintained, caste systems can apparently remain stable for long periods of time.

These findings about Nepal resonate with observations about other parts of the Indian subcontinent. With reference to a village in South India, Münster (2007) states that he found it to be a back-to-back rather than a face-to-face community. The village as a social unit for him appears to be a colonial construct.[17]

Recently, the Nepalese caste system and the political order based on it have come under pressure. In terms of sameness and difference, we can read Pfaff-Czarnecka's findings in her contribution to this volume in the following way: the Government has gone too far in the direction of 'integration through sameness'. High-caste Hindu symbolism and the Nepalese language had come to dominate the public sphere to such an extent that other ethnicities were excluded. Their languages and religious practices played no public role at the national level. In response to this exclusion, members of the lower castes have mobilized and re-introduced their ethnic symbols and practices, which were still thriving in the private sphere, and in some local settings, into the public sphere and the national framework.

It may be useful to dwell on the Indian caste system a bit longer, since further down we will come across the problem of whether we can apply it to Africa or to certain types of interethnic relations in Africa.

One problem with 'caste' is the range of the application of this concept. In his examination of problems and possibilities encountered in the formulation of cross-culturally applicable terminologies, Jensen (1999: 66; my translation) takes 'caste' as an example of a term that has often been used in comparative studies, but which fails time and again to shed light on what it is meant to describe: '[T]he social contexts, for example, in African societies [are. . .] so different and provide little opportunity for comparative analysis with Hindu society, such that a rendering of the term caste that goes beyond the associations with the latter can serve no purpose'. Although the term is of Portuguese origin – which means that it has already gone through one process of cultural transfer – it has experienced such a reduction to the Indian case that, in today's usage, it is only applicable there. Some do not find it very useful even there. 'Are there castes in India?' (*Y a-t-il des castes aux Indes?*) is the title of an old essay by Meillassoux (1977 [1973]: 277–311). He thinks that class is the more important category and that caste is just an ideological screen (for a critique cf. Barnett et al. 1976). But on some general level of client-like relationships, he does perceive similarities to West Africa. Jensen defines caste in broad terms which may enable scholars to apply the concept outside India. He notes that the elements of endogamy and vocational specialization have been central in previous attempts to use the term in non-Indian cultures. Endogamy may need some specifications. In India, women may frequently marry 'up' (hypergamy), while other rules of endogamy might strictly entail marriage within the ethnic, sub-ethnic or status group (isogamy, endogamy in all gender configurations). So, those forms of marriage which transcend caste divisions also clearly imply the idea of hierarchy. In Jensen's definition, hierarchy and the distinction between status and power – so prominent in analyses of the Indian caste system (Dumont 1979 [1966]) – no longer play a role. The comparison between Indian and non-Indian 'caste systems' suffers from the incongruence that, outside India, the hierarchical relationships between 'castes' are often not accepted equally by all parties involved, as they are in India, at least in principle. There may be disagreement in the middle range as to which caste is actually higher or lower than the other (Dumont 1979 [1966]: 21, 110f; 1980: 57, 81) and in recent times class, secular convictions, notions of race and 'ethnic-like' units which have come about by interregional and vertical amalgamation of sub-castes have provided alternative choices to identification to notions of caste based on descent and ritual purity (Barnett 1977), but at least the basic notion of status difference between the four varnas seems to have been and continues to be accepted by many Indians since Vedic times. In cases in which the concept of caste has been used in Africa, sometimes agreement about the hierarchical order is reported (e.g. Haberland 1993), but often no such agreement can be found (e.g. Amborn 2009).

Occasionally, one finds signs that a caste system with the characteristics postulated for India (division of religious and ruling functions, association of ritual purity and status) exists outside of India. Bali for example, is considered 'Hindu' for good reason, despite the fact that the Indian influences date back 1500 or more years. Howe (1987: 141) must, nevertheless, admit that having worked out these similarities, the basis for his comparison of caste in Bali and India is crumbling, precisely because of the question of their hierarchical arrangement. Priests, kings and ascetics may very well be separate ideals, each of which forms the foundation for parallel hierarchies based on completely different value criteria, namely the standards of holiness, royalty and self-control.

Quigley (1997) would prefer to abstain from linear, ladder-like models of hierarchy completely. These models disguise the fact that the Brahmans and the Untouchables may have more in common with one another than with the other castes and thus do not form opposite poles to one another. According to him, numerous ethnographic observations speak against such a model: 'To resolve these disputes arbitrarily . . . by squeezing castes into an artificial vertical line where each caste is higher or lower than every other is simply to violate ethnographic reality' (Quigley 1997: 115). Quigley himself prefers a model of concentric circles in which proximity to the king or to the locally dominating caste is the basis for status. Status differences do exist but not on a single scale since the centre can be approached from different sides, depending on one's function at court (or wherever the ritual focus may be) (ibid.: 116). Such circular models have also been considered for Bali, where categories of 'centre versus periphery' also find their analogy in 'high vs. low' status (Parkin 1987: 59, referring to Hobart 1978).

But some status difference accepted by the higher and the lower alike needs to be there in one form or another, or else it would be difficult to speak of castes at all, even if other defining criteria are met.

We shall come back to ethnicity and caste below, in connection with Diallo's contribution. One aspect often attributed to caste systems, namely conflict avoidance, or at least conflict regulation through the creation of economic niches and the differentiation of rights, rather than the separation of territories, can also be found in other case studies in this book.

As the ethnographic examples in this volume have been chosen to illustrate theoretical ideas, it does not matter whether they are up-to-date in political history or other day-to-day matters. I have grouped them in this introduction according to the comparative lines which occurred to me, and the order of the chapters follows these lines. Other readers may see other connections between them. In fact, this is what the 'mission' of this publication is all about: it provides pieces for comparative games, and like chess pieces, these can be put into many different configurations. I have avoided grouping these chapters regionally or by time period, because whether a given chapter deals with Africa or Asia or with historical or recent data is irrelevant to the points I want to make about difference and sameness. Indeed, one of the chapters goes as far back as Chinggis Khan, several of them refer to the colonial period and others have their 'ethnographic present' in the 1990s or the 2000s. So now I move on from social distance in the context of economic exchange to economic and social inequalities.

Economic Differentiation and Social Hierarchies

The chapter by Ruf shows that after the abolition of slavery, the free and freed populations of Mauritania did not form separate segments; rather, they continued to be interdependent parts of society. People who had been freed oriented themselves on the model of the free, imitating them as closely as possible. The elevated status of members of the free population is confirmed by the fact that the freed never really manage to get it right. The freed measure themselves on the scale of the free; or, to use an equestrian metaphor, members of the two groups run in the same race, but with different handicaps. An exception to this seems to be the field of music, where (as in the Americas) slaves and ex-slaves have developed particular forms, appreciated by others but regarded as different from their own. Ruf in this context speaks of 'equality within difference'.

To a degree, the difference between free and freed in Mauritanian society may be described in the idioms of 'white' and 'black'. Since, however, so-called 'blacks' include both the descendants of ex-slaves and members of other low-status groups with no history of slavery, the two dichotomies are not quite congruent. Both 'blacks' and 'whites' are part of a Mauritanian society whose major characteristic is the Hassaniyya dialect of Arabic. Only on the next higher taxonomic level does one find the distinction between Mauritanians and non-Mauritanians, the latter of whom include the 'other blacks', that is, the West Africans from the societies from which the Mauritanian ex-slaves originated. But, as Ruf explains, members of the freed Mauritanian population are no longer able to return to their countries of origin, due to the loss of their genealogies and their past.

The wives of the Senegalese *tirailleurs* who were stationed in Mauritania during the colonial period provide a case study of the consequences of the return of ex-slaves, or the descendants of slaves, to their African regions of origin. When these women returned to Senegal with their husbands, they found that they could not escape the stigma of slavery. Their husbands were in no way ignorant of the institution of slavery, and they treated the ex-slaves in their polygynous households as second class wives (Ruf 1999: 191, citing McDougall 1988). 'Back to the roots' is thus no escape from slavery, since there is not a single country in West Africa where having once been a slave, or having slaves as ancestors, is not stigmatized. The only chance for ex-slaves to really be free is among groups to which they belong by descent. But patrilineal descent is tied to marriage, which was denied to slaves. Therefore, the full reintegration of the descendants of slaves in their societies of origins is only possible among groups with matrilineal descent, as among the Ashanti (Fortes 1969: 147). But even this possibility depends on continuity of genealogical knowledge.

Thus, the freed, including both those who were freed individually and those who were freed merely as a function of state law, have no other option than to compete for status with other Mauritanians on a Mauritanian scale of values. More often than not, this leads to a denial or a reinterpretation of the past rather than to pride in their past and its higher valuation.

Ruf's findings relate to the issue of social distance and its strategic use, discussed above, while pointing to gender-specific differences. For a male slave, spatial distance and a specialization different from that of his master may be the keys to asserting a sphere of agency of his own and to achieving a degree of social advancement. For example, a male slave in a pastoralist society may practice gardening in an oasis, while his master roams about, returning to the oasis only periodically. Or, if a male slave is close to his master, he often performs the same kinds of tasks, for example those associated with herding. This, too, may have a liberating effect, relatively speaking. For female slaves, however, the key to advancement is closeness to the master. By giving birth to his child, she can be freed and rise in status. But working closely with the mistress in the domestic sphere is no help at all, for the mistress usually gives detailed orders, assigning tasks that are clearly distinct from her own. As Ruf notes, '[w]omen working under these conditions reproduced their dissimilarity from the free women'. Thus, work may have a liberating effect for men, who either work independently of their masters at distinct tasks or together with their masters at common tasks. Women's work does not have this effect, both because of their spatial closeness to their mistresses and because of the different kinds of tasks that they perform.

In this inescapable closeness between a female slave and her mistress, indirect kinship between the two can come about. By suckling her mistress's children, the slave woman becomes milk-mother of the latter's children. Therefore, her own children, irrespective of who begot them (the master may have had sexual access to her, but her own children may also stem from a slave marriage), become milk-siblings of the children of her mistress. So, in spite of all the continuously marked and reproduced differences, a free woman might have had to accept her closest helper and continuous companion, her female slave, as a co-mother of her own children, the mother of the milk-siblings of her own children – a relationship considered so close in Islam that it precludes intermarriage and sexual relations. This makes the female slave the mistress's potential rival for the favours of her husband and maybe even a potential cowife – a dense relationship indeed.

Competition seems to be the key to explaining the difference between being the slave of a 'warrior' and being the slave of a 'scholar', the two gross categories within 'white' Mauritanian society (a bit caste-like, but without a clear hierarchy). In Mauritania, unlike other Islamic countries, there is no tradition of religious scholars of slave status. Scholarship was the capital of the 'scholars' among the free, and they kept it for themselves.

Men of Mauritania, who were, originally, pastoralist warriors, have many tasks for their slaves that prevent them from becoming competitors in their own preferred fields of activity. The slaves are cultivators and craftsmen. Therefore, the proportion of slaves is relatively low in the deserts of the nomadic north; and there is a higher proportion of slaves in the south, where water is more readily available, where there are more fixed settlements, and where nomadic trajectories are shorter, so that pastoralists can network more easily with sedentary populations, including their own dependents.

Ruf's description of Mauritania resonates with the literature about nomadic Arabs in the Sudan, where slaves were frequently freed and incorporated into Arab descent groups, though often as lower-status members with less wealth (Cunnison 1966: 80 about Humr Baggara). Alternatively, freed slaves in Sudan became clients of wealthy and leading personalities, strengthening their power base (Asad 1970: 174 about Kababish). The literature stresses the close ties, based on loyalty, between patron and client (Asad 1970: 190ff.). The relationship of a herd owner to his herder, be he a slave or freeman, cannot be based on brute force. To let someone move around freely with all the wealth one owns on the hoof requires trust, and a relationship that is familial in character, regardless of the herder's origins. Therefore, nomads do not have much use for kinds of slavery based purely on enforcing ownership.

In describing the situation of ex-slaves, including their continued dependence on their former masters in the more sedentary settings of the south, Ruf openly takes sides with the ex-slaves, without denying his own egalitarian ethos, be it of 'western' origin or not.

There follows a chapter by Schlee with the title 'Identification with the State and Identifications by the State'. This chapter marks a shift of emphasis as the argument of the book unrolls, since the state plays a greater role in the chapters following it than in the chapters preceding it. In northern Ivory Coast, the case described in the chapter by Diallo, the state identifies with urban people and favours pastoralists as providers of meat for urban markets. The chapter by Grätz about northern Benin shows statehood and shared citizenship as forces competing with other offers of identification.

In northern Ivory Coast, too, we find an ethnic division of labour with each group characterized by corresponding rights and skills. The Senufo are farmers who are also masters of the earth, authorizing settlement on it or withholding authorization, as the case may be. The Malinke are merchants. And the Fulbe are hired herders or independent pastoralists, who are consulted when the Senufo have problems with the few cattle they themselves own, at least in those cases where they are not maintained by Fulbe herders or given over to the care of Fulbe pastoralists (cf. Diallo, Guichard and Schlee 2000). As Muslims, the Fulbe do not have to deal with the local divinities which are so essential for the relationship of the farmers to the earth they cultivate. In a way, this is a mirror-image of what Ruf describes in his chapter on Mauritania, where it is precisely the people with the greatest longevity and a higher standing as Muslims who have to meet the higher and more rigid ritual requirements.

Thus far, the relationship between the Senufo and the Fulbe is a complementary one, and one would therefore assume that it is a peaceful one as well; but it is prejudiced by the damage caused by the Fulbe cattle to the crops and to the harvest stored in the fields. The Senufo hunting associations take drastic retribution, and the Fulbe would undoubtedly be much weaker in this conflict if they did not have state forces on their side. The urban elites in the south of the country have a vested interest in a secure supply of beef, and through their political influence they ensure a continued Fulbe presence in the rural areas. In Ghana similar conflicts of interest between farmers and urbanites have on occasion led to the expulsion of the Fulbe back to Burkina Faso (see Tonah 1993: 127ff.). Thus, the state or its constituent parts always have a role to play in interethnic systems, not only as an external factor but also as a factor that has incorporated ethnic forces or even as an instrument of ethnically defined interest groups.

Diallo cites Fulbe living among Bobo and Bwa as cases of acceptance into farming societies. The newcomers then become part of 'a ritual division of duties that becomes the basis for a close interdependence'. The creation of ritual interdependence resonates with what I have found in the *Gada* systems of different ethnic groups in Northeast Africa, likewise in a relatively egalitarian setting (Schlee 1998).

Taking up the earlier discussion of caste systems (above), in many ways differences rather than similarities prevail between what Diallo describes and caste systems like the one described by Pfaff-Czarnecka. Ethnic relations in northern Ivory Coast may, when viewed from the outside, be considered almost egalitarian. However, the actors themselves may very well maintain a hierarchical view of their society, more often than not with hierarchies in which their own respective ethnic group retains the highest position in the scale of importance; but it is in no way possible to speak of a single universally accepted hierarchy. A further West African example is the town of Tanguiéta in northern Benin, subject of the chapter by Grätz (see also Grätz 2006). Northern Benin is geographically part of the Sudanic zone and, thus, of a belt of extreme ethnic and linguistic differentiation. Grätz describes heterogeneity and commonality on several levels. He describes a great variety of linguistic differences and heterogeneous origins within larger socio-economic categories (farming ethnic groups, trader ethnic groups, civil servants). Cross-cutting these internal differences are several connecting elements such as discourses of autochthony among the farmers, the colonial stereotyping that places all farmers in a single category, the 'culture of the Zongo' (in the traders' quarter) and two linguae francae (Hausa and Dendi) among the traders. Again, pastoralism is represented by the Fulbe.[18] Due to their association with different economic specializations, these larger categories stand in a complementary relationship to one another. These various modes of identification, and the ways in which they are subject to change, are studied by Grätz in contexts of local, regional and state political action.

Grätz describes the internal integration of the different groups and the wider categories into which they are amalgamated as 'distinct moral places'. These moral places become part of a wider whole by an '(unwritten) contractual relationship between them'. In social and cultural terms this wider integration is limited. It is limited to the political sphere, and, even there, the wider unity is fragile. Due to economic differentiation, there is one more sphere of interaction: the market. This may remind us of Furnivall's (1944) classical study of plural society in colonial Malaya, where he found largely separate groups interacting only at certain nodal points.[19] From another angle, Grätz's chapter invites comparison with that by Pfaff-Czarnecka. He shows that the contrast between places for the consumption of alcoholic beverages and snack bars or coffee houses distinguishes non-Muslims from Muslims in northern Benin, just as practices regarding food and domestic animals are indicators of caste in Nepal.

Grätz has a processual view of social identities, reminiscent of the theory of path dependence: apparently insignificant events trigger irreversible processes, leading to dramatic effects, by limiting future choices. He calls this amplification. The amalgamation of farming groups, on the one hand, and the Muslim trader groups (the Zongo), on the other, widens the units of inclusion and exclusion, while politicization – the fact that the cultural and economic distinctions become the basis of political alliances – further amplifies these identities by giving them new functions and new meanings.

These amalgamated social categories within Tangietà, each of which comprises a myriad of original ethnic groups and local origins, also make sense in terms of the 'information economics of identification', a way of thinking about identity which requires further development (for a beginning see Schlee 2010): how much can a social identity cost? Obviously, acquiring the right to an attractive social identity, which comes with an exclusive status and economic privileges or political power, is worth a greater effort than a less attractive one; but all activities with all identities have a price tag. When it comes to acquiring, shedding, communicating, foregrounding or hiding an identity, or using an identity to advertise one's goods and services, or checking whether the identity claim of another person is justified or not – all of this requires that one make a certain amount of communicative effort or persuasion (costs)[20] and also leads to a greater or lesser material or moral reward (benefit). Complex, highly fragmented or little known identities do not make sense in many contexts. The costs of communicating them are too high and the rewards are too low. The middle-range identifications described by Grätz which combine (and obscure) sub-identities and establish some simple equations (e.g. all traders are Muslims and all butchers are Hausa or convert to that ethnic identity) may be quite plausible constructs from such a perspective.

These forms of identification can be traced to the colonial period. This opens another dimension of comparison, this time within the present volume: in which ways are such classifications shaped within political systems and by them and what are the causes of their persistence? Hansen and Kaiser (below) deal with the persistence of Soviet categories in the post-Soviet sphere, and Schlee (below) discusses the role of ethnic classifications in empires.

Transnational Relations and Cross-Border Ethnicities

Just like the flow of commodities, economic networks and ethnic as well as religious loyalties cut across national borders. Moving back to Asia, we find that changes have occurred on a dramatic scale since the demise of the Soviet Union, but also that a Soviet or post-Soviet identification linking Central Asia to Russia has persisted until the present, alongside other macro-identifications. The trade networks of the 1990s, examined by Kaiser (2001), run straight through the Turkic language areas and beyond, along the Great Silk Road. For this reason, Menashri (1998) has published an edited volume dealing with this region entitled *Central Asia Meets the Middle East*. Following Bennigsen and Broxup (1984), Menashri differentiates three levels of identification among Central Asian Muslims, 'Sub-national, that is by clan or tribe; supra-national, whether religious (Islamic) or ethnic (Turkic); and national':

> Central Asian Muslims tend to discount national consciousness as a 'Soviet creation forced upon the population' in order to divide the Muslim territories and ensure Russian control. By contrast, they claim, the sub-national and supra-national are 'deeply rooted in the culture' of the region. In spite of all Soviet efforts, they are cutting across the Soviet imposed national divisions. (Menashri 1998: 5)

Despite a wide-ranging and encompassing identification with the Islamic world and with other non-Uzbek speakers of Turkic languages (cf., Finke 2014), the citizens of Tashkent do not live in an exclusively Turkic-Islamic world, but have integrated ethnic Others on a smaller scale. The Russian language, if not Russian people, informs the jargon of petty trade and the Korean market, which is indeed populated by Koreans, and where products from South Korea and also from Europe and Japan are sold. In Central Asia, there is a substantial, now mostly Russian-speaking, Korean population, the elderly members of which were sent there forcibly from the Russian Far East during the Stalinist period.

Religious and linguistic forms of identification cut across national borders and are factors in the development of transnational space. Not only are Turkish-speaking teachers of Islam from Germany present (Kaiser 2001), but also Turkish-German companies, active as contractors and investors. Other (i.e. non-Turkish) German companies, as well as the German labour market, benefit indirectly (and often unknowingly) from the transnational activities in these ethnically influenced sectors. A German-Turkish transnational space has spread into Central Asia (Faist 2000). The Russian advertisements and signs in Istanbul, where Russian is used as a lingua franca even among speakers of Turkic languages (Kaiser 2001), are thus mirrored by Turkish and Germany-Turkish influences in Central Asia.

More recently, Kaiser has widened his geographical horizon and extended his period of observation. In their contribution to the present volume, Hansen and Kaiser describe how and why pan-Turkic identification has not quite played the role some people expected it to play in the 1990s. Instead, they find that a post-Soviet identity is remarkably persistent, not only in Central Asia but also in the Baltic states, Belarus, Ukraine and Moldova, and the Caucasus. They speak of 'transsociational figurations' in the entire space of the former Soviet republics. These appear to represent transcontinuities, that is, continuities which survive a system change. Among the features that have persisted since Soviet times are ways of understanding ethnicity and interacting with members of other ethnic groups. These are at work both within the Russian federation and beyond it, informing new nationalisms and their role in relation to other nationalisms. What is shared here is not ethnicity, of course, but the meta-ethnic level, the way people recognize or perceive each other's ethnicity or nationality and interact accordingly (Schlee 2008a: 10). These ways of organizing ethnicities and interacting in a pluri-ethnic framework may have some roots in pre-Soviet times, in the Russian Empire, which already undertook the 'standardisation of its ethnic-cultural diversity' (Schorkowitz 2015: 8).

Another shared feature which, as Hansen and Kaiser show, has survived the Soviet Union in its former space is a culture of informality. There appear to be practical considerations and material incentives attached to the continuation of Soviet cultural practices which help people to cope with and to circumvent bureaucracy. Trade within the post-Soviet space makes up a considerable proportion of the trade of the successor states of the Soviet Union, and bureaucracy continues to make trade and other aspects of life difficult, necessitating creative solutions.

As we have seen, trade seems to contribute to the maintenance of – even an emphasis on – ethnic differences, instead of blurring them (Evers and Schrader 1994). Thus, besides identities and postulated kinship in relationships that are maintained over long distances, we find marked differences in the immediate vicinity and in the closest space of interaction. This is the case not only in Central

Asian cities; rather, we may be following, here, a trail of apparent paradoxes that are, in fact, basic principles of social organization.

'Difference' and 'identity' are terms that refer to one another. What we mean by 'identity' is nothing other than the absence of difference, that is, being the same with regard to a particular dimension of characteristics or a complex of features. There are enough gurus and modern medicine men who deal with the 'deeper' psychological and existential connotations of this term, and we can leave those aspects to them. That there is no propensity to violence (or any other specific emotional load) in identity as such, and that identity and difference can be played out in quite different ways, is illustrated by Horstmann's contribution on Southern Thailand. While the conflict in Patani has developed into a most violent one in which local Buddhists are pitted against local Muslims, ritual exchange based on cultural tradition (and ancestor worship, in particular) takes place 100 miles north of Patani in the Songkhla Lake region. Horstmann's contribution also demonstrates the occasional, somewhat paradoxical, intertwining of identity and difference. In the multi-confessional communities, Ban Tamot and Ban Hua Chang, world religion is indigenized by the agency of the villagers, and in turn, Southern Thai culture adapts certain elements from world religion.

In a way that is reminiscent of Tule's description of Keo society in Flores, eastern Indonesia (Tule 2004), the religious systems of southern Thailand are shaped by their interaction, which also links them to deeply-rooted local beliefs. Here, Buddhism and Islam share a cosmology, based on the continuing relationship of the living and the dead, and common values, which allow for inter-religious marriage and conversion from one religion to the other. Conversion to Islam is, however, a formal affair, while conversion to Buddhism does not require any formal ritual.

The refugee crisis of 2015, in which Muslims from Myanmar fled by boat to Malaysia and Indonesia or perished attempting to do so, shows that some Southeast Asian states have become identified with the religions dominant in them – Myanmar and Thailand with Buddhism, Malaysia and Indonesia with Islam – no matter how much modernist, secular-minded elites and human rights champions within these states and world-wide may regret such an identification.

From Ethnic Dyads to Multi-Ethnic Empires

Further considerations of a rather fundamental nature are raised by the next contribution (Schlee), which compares three interethnic dyads: Anywaa and Nuer in Ethiopia, Maasai and Kamba in Kenya, and Buryat/Evenki in the Russian Federation. These examples illustrate a third form of interaction, beyond hostility or peaceful coexistence, namely, uneasy coexistence with limited interaction. In her chapter, discussed briefly above, Pfaff-Czarnecka also emphasizes the importance of limited interaction and mere coexistence in certain settings. She discusses precautions showing 'that rules of maintaining distance can make coexistence of people of different status groups possible'. From Mutie (2003, 2013),[21] Schlee's source on relations between the Maasai and Kamba, we now learn that in this setting as well, where, in contrast to Nepal, integration into a vertical hierarchy is not the issue, social distance and mere coexistence play significant roles. Cultural difference need not serve either to justify rejection or hostility or to provide the basis for complementarity and peaceful interaction. It can also be left to stand by itself: One can agree to be different, one can limit interaction to certain nodal points, and one can live alongside others looking most of the time the other way.

The final chapter, again by Schlee, takes the reader back to some of the regions (Central Asia/Turkey) already visited by Kaiser (2001) and Hansen and Kaiser in this volume. But the chapter has an even wider scope, including India and parts of Africa, and refers to earlier historical eras. While Hansen and Kaiser's focus is on the time since the fall of socialism, when different parts of the world opened up to each other and some identifications widened or were even globalized, this chapter discusses social formations which precede both socialism and modern nationalism. It goes back all the way to Tamerlane and Chinggis Khan and draws a line from there to later, early modern and modern forms of rule. It looks at how difference and sameness are handled in a specific political formation, namely empires. Empires can be studied in their interconnection in history. The Qipchak Uzbeks, for example, played a role in Tamerlane's empire and in the Moghul Empire in India; what is more, they were an important ethnic component of the Mameluks in Egypt. And of course there are the ubiquitous British, who changed roles over time, acting first as allies and then as mercenaries, advisors or vassals of local rulers, and, finally, as the rulers of these rulers. Empires succeed each other in history, they provide models for each other, or they compete with each other and make war; or they do all of this at the same time. Apart from that, they can, to a degree, be treated as separate cases and compared. The question of how empires – or, more generally, systems of rule – are derived and learn from their predecessors is hardly touched here; rather, it must remain a presumably inexhaustible topic for future research. Schlee focuses, instead, on the ways in which empires exploit sameness and difference as structural principles, with the aim of specifying particular types and contributing to the development of a typology.

What all empires share, almost like a defining feature, is that they are ethnically heterogeneous. Building on cultural homogeneity or wishing to bring about such homogeneity is a characteristic of the nation-state, not necessarily of the empire. So, obviously, handling difference is a necessary skill for empire builders. Rhetorically, difference is a justification for empire; and, from a system perspective, difference is the glue that keeps empires together. But sameness also plays a role. A rather pervasive pattern seems to be that homogenizing forces are at work in creating a ruling stratum, while the groups over whom the rule extends have to differ from the rulers and may differ from each other too.

Some of the questions posed in Schlee's chapter on 'Identification with the State and Identifications by the State' – namely 'who is the state?', 'who identifies with the state?', 'in whose interest does the state act?' – can also be addressed to empires. Some of the earlier nomadic empires of the Eurasian steppe may have been purely predatory. Every summer, armies went from oasis to oasis and from city to city, demanding tribute. Tribute was paid to avert destruction. The tax payers (if that is the appropriate term at this low level of regularity and regulation) had no reason to identify with such predatory empires except in the rhetoric of submission. Presumably, such states or empires, in terms of identification, recruitment, exclusion and inclusion, have closely followed the logic of the 'gang of robbers' model (Tilly 1985; Schlee 2008a: 26).

When it comes to the colonial empires of European powers, there is more than one additional twist to the question 'who is the state?'. In the early phase of colonialism, private companies such as the Dutch East India Company, the British East India Company, the British South Africa Company, and the Niger Company[22] collected taxes and waged war just like states. This 'early phase' cannot be fixed on a global timescale. British colonialism, for example, was over in much of North America before it reached its peak in India and from there expanded to East Africa. These companies, which are characteristic of the early phase, often legitimized their activities by acting on behalf, by claiming to act on behalf, or by being allies, of local rulers. The British East India Company, for example, maintained the fiction of being agents and tax-collectors of the Moghul Empire. In fact, as time progressed, local rulers, only nominally vassals of the Grand Moghul, often were just puppets of Company rule. And, later, the Grand Moghul suffered the same fate. So, in fact, statehood was vested in the Company, not in the empty shells of Moghul rule.

To stay with the British example: what was the relationship between 'The Company' and Britain? The Company was licensed by the government. That is the formal aspect. But did it act on behalf and in the interest of the government? (A recursive question, because one can continue the line of questions by asking on whose behalf the government acted.) Government, in Britain, was in the hands of the aristocracy. Well into the phase of industrialization and global political and commercial expansion, what counted for both status and power in England was land (agricultural estates in England) and titles. The company agents who made quick money in India had a problem with their social identity. They desperately wanted to belong to this aristocracy, and this aristocracy vehemently (to the extent that English aristocrats can be vehement) rejected them as *nouveaux riches* who had acquired their fortunes by dubious means. (From the aristocratic perspective, proper wealth was based on chasing English farmers off their land to acquire huge estates, not by causing famines in India by over-taxation of Indian peasants or by acquiring war spoils there at the expense of their Indian equivalents, the Indian nobility.) So, the 'nabobs', the company agents who had become rich in India, tried to invest their fortunes in land in England, in buying titles and marrying into good families.

An 'agent' is expected to act in the interest of his 'principal' (Coleman 1990: 145–74). Did the Company agents act in the interest of the Company? One can ask the same set of questions of a state-like company (one that wages wars and collects taxes) as one can of the state: who was the Company? That is, from which parts of the population were the Company personnel recruited? With whom did the Company identify? Who identifies with the Company? Who were the allies of the Company, that is, who was outside of the Company but engaged in reciprocal relations with it?

Rather than going through these questions one by one, we may refer the reader to the work of historians (Darwin 2013; Dirks 2006; Fergusson 2004; Wild 2001). In the present context, it may suffice to say that there were problems of identification and divergence of interests between the personnel of the Company and its shareholders, because the former tended to declare the best business as their private business and to view the lavish gifts from Indian rulers, meant to grease their relationship with the Company, as private possessions. Company interests were not necessarily British interests. The military adventures of the Company were a potential drain on the state budget, because they might lead to the military involvement of the Crown. In terms of class, the nabobs were as alien to the working class[23] as they were to the aristocracy and to those parts of the middle classes that sided with the missionaries in their endeavour to Christianize the 'pagans' and to 'lift' them to higher levels of humanity – which is quite a different agenda from instrumentalizing differences in order to justify and implement the rule of the British over the Indians. For the Company and its officers, issues of identification were as complex in Britain as they were in India.

In his contribution to this volume, however, Schlee focuses on the interethnic relationships between rulers and the ruled in conquered territories, and leaves problems of identification in colonial 'motherlands' across the sea largely aside.

Günther Schlee is one of the Founding Directors of the Max Planck Institute for Social Anthropology in Halle, Germany. Prior to this appointment he was Professor of Social Anthropology at the University of Bielefeld. He conducted fieldwork in Kenya, Ethiopia and Sudan. His publications include *Identities on the Move: Clanship and Pastoralism in Northern Kenya* (Manchester University Press, 1989), *How Enemies Are Made: Towards a Theory of Ethnic and Religious Conflict* (Berghahn Books, 2008) and *Pastoralism and Politics* (with Abdullahi A. Shongolo, James Currey, 2012).

Notes

1. I use this phrase as a combined reference to 'genocide', 'ethnic cleansing', killings of religious dissenters and all forms of mass violence aimed at producing a more homogenous social setting along ethnic or religious lines of identification, mostly more similar to the perpetrators of such mass violence.
2. Cohesion (which evokes solidarities and togetherness) is not the same thing as integration. Here, we use 'integration' not in the sense of politicians or social workers who want to achieve something and for whom the term is laden with a positive value, but in the sense of system theory. When something becomes an element of a system, it is integrated into that system. Much of our work on how humans aggregate has had a focus on identification and alliances (e.g. Schlee 2008a; Eidson et al. 2017), and is all about agency and choice. People adopt, foreground or deny one or the other collective identity in response to incentives. In other words, we have frequently taken the individual as the starting point of our analysis. In the present volume, we start more often from larger aggregates. For example, how do empires, in contrast to nation-states, comprise and link the parts which constitute them? This has nothing to do with deep convictions or loyalty to schools of thought. We have not converted from *Handlungstheorie* to *Systemtheorie*. We simply hope that changes of perspectives and combinations of perspective might offer new insights. Sometimes, the choice between individuals or systems or larger aggregates as a starting point is determined by our sources. Often historical or ethnographic accounts do not tell us a lot about individuals, in particular ordinary individuals.
3. Some anthropologists feel they are doing this. By becoming fluent in another language and acquiring the habits of one's surroundings one can be accepted by a group as one of them. People might make great and very generous efforts to explain away the fact that the anthropologist still looks different, in terms of pigmentation or whatever it may be. As a former stranger one may even have had to think more about 'culture' as one learns it, and one may be able to explain it in ways the people who have grown up in it and acquired it through early habituation have never thought about but find quite interesting. Other anthropologists prefer to mystify what they study and present 'culture' as something one can never really penetrate unless one has grown up in it. These different attitudes may correlate with linguistic skills and other kinds of intellectual performance.
4. For a critique of relativism, see Jarvie (1984).
5. A hobby fisherwoman among the commentators, who has harmed many worms in her life by using them as bait, warns me against using 'wormishness', because not all worms or worm segments recover from such an injury and because there are differences among various worm species. Anthropologists always find exceptions, as does this commentator. Nevertheless, with these qualifications, the worm might be allowed to stand as an example of the segmentary principle.
6. Zitelmann (1999) explores some of the ideological load of this concept.
7. The difficulties include defining what is kept together (society, a particular society, within which limits?), the definition of a coherent or undisrupted (ideal) state of such an entity as a backdrop against which disruptive forces can be identified, the identification of forces of cohesion/disruption, and the measurement of cohesion and disruption (the effects of these forces).
8. See Harris (1974) for an example.
9. Some authors regard self-reflection as the specific feature which makes us human. In practice, some people are clearer and more explicit about their motivations than others.

10. Cf., Aga Khan Development Network. (Retrieved 24 April 2013 from www.akdn.org.)
11. See Rothman (2000) for a theory that makes a basic distinction between identity-based conflicts and resource- or interest-based ones and advocates different strategies for dealing with each. See Schlee (2009) for a critique of this kind of reasoning.
12. Note that 'theories' is used here in a rather value-free way. We do not discuss whether the statements in question need to meet a standard of scholarliness to deserve the name 'theory'.
13. To balance the picture, the reciprocal element, the Catholic dislike of Protestants, also needs to be voiced. A German woman from the Catholic south once told me how, many years ago, she wanted to familiarize her father with her intention to marry her present husband, an Arab. It took her father some time to swallow that his future son-in-law was an Arab, but he managed to contain himself. He expected him to be a Muslim and was about to accept even that with a sigh. He only blew his top when his daughter told him that the young man was a Lutheran. 'How dare you!'
14. See Schlee (2008a: 10) for an explanation of the term 'meta-ethnic'.
15. Nigel Rapport (2012), in a volume which is pertinent to our subject because it also deals with narrower and wider identifications, speaks about the 'cosmopolitan project' both in politics and in academia, and he leaves no doubt that cosmopolitanism is also his project. The present author shares the political sympathies of Rapport, but this volume does not have a 'project' in that sense. It wants to describe the world as it is, without having to take a moral position at every junction. This attitude does not exclude the hope that a better understanding of how things are interconnected may also be of help in changing them. The normative element in Rapport's writing is justified, and anthropology does have a role in setting political aims and making moral judgements; but these things are not in the foreground of our present exercise. Here, we want to explain empirical givens rather than critiquing them.
16. 'Hindu caste is based on fundamentally different presuppositions from individualistic Western philosophy and cannot be understood if viewed through Western Eyes' (Banton 1992: 74).
17. Münster's book is quite unusual as it combines a 'village study' with a 'postcolonial' perspective, since the two normally stand for quite different fashions and periods in the writings about India. See Berger (2012) for a history of these fashions.
18. For collections on Fulbe and their integration into the market and wider society, see Bourgeot (1999), Botte, Boutrais and Schmitz (1999), Diallo and Schlee (2000).
19. For a critique of Furnivall, see Banton (2015: 73f).
20. Other costs of identification (identity work, investing in identity), which are sometimes monetary, may include the acquisition of formal qualifications or status symbols, investments in building up a reputation or getting rid of a negative identification, or research into the identity claims of others to ascertain or dismantle them, to cite only a few examples.
21. Pius Mutie sadly passed away on 23 October 2013 at the age of only 45 years.
22. The British East India Company, modelled after the Dutch East India Company, seems to have served as a model for the later establishment of such companies in Africa (Fergusson 2004: 228).
23. Fergusson (2004: 283) summarizes sources contemporary with the high time of British Imperialism, the turn of the twentieth century, as describing Imperialism as 'a rip-off: paid for by British taxpayers, fought for by British soldiers', it benefitted 'only a tiny elite of fat-cat-millionaires'.

Chapter 1

Distances and Hierarchies

The Struggle over Ethnic Symbols in Nepal's Public Spaces

Joanna Pfaff-Czarnecka

Introduction

Culture can build bridges or erect insuperable barriers. Which option is chosen largely depends on the social context within which persons – more or less consciously – make their decisions. Such decisions, for instance, exert great influence on the attitudes towards people considered to be 'different' – because they belong to a different ethnic group or caste, for example. In the event of conflicts, in particular, the tendency to emphasize differences increases. Barriers are erected by symbols which point to the increasing importance of social distance. A common choice is to pursue strategies of avoiding each other; another possibility is to express differences in the language of hierarchy.

However, strategically significant symbols can gain new meanings within comparatively short periods of time (Elwert 1997). Their interpretations change, and there is a tendency for additional connotations to develop. Four issues are of particular interest in this context. First, we must ask in which kinds of situations of societal change – for instance, in which phases of ethnic mobilization – does the readiness to critically examine symbols increase in order to influence public opinion. Second, it is of interest which symbols are particularly well suited to be challenged by political opponents. Third, these can be studied advantageously against the background of an analysis of the cultural repertoires used by the members of a national society. Finally, we should examine the intersection of public spheres on different levels – local, national, global.

Ethnicity, therefore, is a complex matter. In times of ethnic mobilization, the activists and their followers have a choice of numerous cultural and religious elements to fall back on if they attempt to express their displeasure and if they want to present their visions and projects publicly. Among the elements which are particularly 'suitable' for public presentations are religious symbols, rituals and customs, historical events remembered through public festivals, as well as those elements declared 'national treasures' like language, clothing or customs. All of these elements can be stressed as positive values – or may undergo transvaluation, that is, acquire connotations considered negative in a particular context. The latter occurs in particular when the cultural elements of the dominant group, which used to form the core of national unity, are emphasized in phases of ethnic mobilization as symbols of oppression by the minorities. Corresponding examples are not hard to find: if a society has to use a language which is pre-determined as 'national' in public space, and at the same time the languages of ethnic minorities are systematically ignored, then the probability of ethnic activists selecting language politics as the scene of their disputes with the predominance of the majority group rises. Other arenas of struggle include national holidays, which ritualize political power (cf. Pfaff-Czarnecka 1998). It is a frequently used pattern in the 'politics of reaction' (Hirschman 1992) to direct ethnic mobilization against national symbols: 'ethnic' versus 'national', 'diversity' versus 'unity', 'equality' versus 'hierarchy', 'back-to-the-roots' movements versus cultural influence 'from the outside'.[1] In the following, processes of ethnicization in Nepal, which in this context includes, amongst other things, reactions to historical processes of integration of ethnic populations into the hierarchic state structure, will be examined with regard to this position.

Ethnic Minorities in the Nepalese State Structure

From the middle of the eighteenth century, extensive social transformations have taken place in the territory of present-day Nepal.[2] With the military expansion of the Gorkha empire (beginning in 1744), a forcible 'unification' took place in the territory of the Nepalese state, in the course of which around sixty political units – including a great number of ethnic groups and Hindu castes – were joined together into one political structure. Among the Hindu rulers of Nepal a social order crystallized, which concentrated political and economic power largely – but not exclusively – in the hands of high-caste Hindu groups. The social inequality was structured according to norms of Hindu hierarchy that the first civil legislation (Muluki Ain) defined in 1854. This civil code prescribed a 'national' caste order – with the so-called 'twice-born' Hindu castes on top, the low ('untouchable') Hindus on the bottom, and the 'ethnic groups' in the middle ranks.[3] This legislation not only prescribed the relative status of the collective units, but also to a large extent regulated mutual relations. It defined penalties, rights and obligations according to the group's position within the hierarchical structure.

Table 1.1   The 'national' caste hierarchy of Nepal in 1854

---

1. Caste group of the 'Wearers of the Holy Cord' (*tāgādhārī*)
2. Caste group of the 'Non-enslavable Alcohol-Drinkers' (*nāmāsinyā mātwālī*)
3. Caste group of the 'Enslavable Alcohol-Drinkers' (*māsinyā mātwāli*)
4. Impure, but 'touchable' castes (*pāni nācālnyā choi chito hālnunāpārnyā*)
5. Untouchable castes (*pāni nācālnyā choi chito hālnupārnyā*)

Source: Höfer (1979: 45).

Between 1951 and 1990, and in particular since the early 1960s, the political opinions of the rulers about what constituted the Nepalese nation changed. On the basis of the hierarchical caste order, which was de jure largely abolished in 1963, but de facto continued to exist, the rulers endeavoured to link the process of nation-building to the idea of modernization. If the former system had divided the population into hierarchically arranged castes, at the same time it expressed the diversity of and the differences between the population groups. The imperative of modernization, however, meant that attempts were made to emphasize national unity by banishing all features of ethnic diversity – religious as well as linguistic – from the public repertoire (for a classic example for exclusion, see Schlee and Werner 1996a). Anything ethnic was regarded as outdated, entirely according to the thesis of dualism. The idea of progress in official rhetoric assumed national unity, which forced the language (Nepali), religion (Hinduism) and the customs (clothing, rituals, etc.) of high-caste Hindus upon the society as a whole. The state 'belonged to' the high-caste Hindus.

In the context of bloody communal disturbances in the spring of 1990, the Nepalese monarch Sri Panc Birendra Bir Brikram Shah Dev found himself compelled to give up some of his political prerogatives and to proclaim a constitution which embodied the separation of powers in a multi-party system and granted the population extensive civic and political rights. Only one year earlier, hardly anyone in Nepal had dared to dream of the country obtaining a constitution which would embody the nation as a 'multi-ethnic, multilingual, democratic, independent, indivisible, sovereign, Hindu, and Constitutional Monarchical kingdom' (Art. 4). The movement of 1990 – driven by diverse social representatives – has given minority matters a tremendous impetus. The Nepalese population today makes use in particular of the freedom of speech and of assembly through a large number of newly founded ethnic organizations who articulate their concerns in public. Their actions have contributed considerably to the differentiation of the public sphere in that communication media have appeared (newspapers and radio stations in several national languages), numerous cultural projects have been established (for instance the ethnographic museum), and broad discussions – also within the political committees – have been initiated. The debates concern internal matters of individual ethnic groups and they touch on questions of mutual relations: political representation of ethnic organizations, claims concerning financial contributions from the state, reparations for past injustice or the change of societal balances of power.[4]

The last point in particular contains potential for conflict.[5] Ethnic activists link their demand for a cultural re-definition of national unity with the claim for more political participation, and – as a consequence – for a larger share in the social surplus (and in external financial contributions from development partners). A great number of the activists consider their chances too small to represent their matters in the framework of party politics. Rather, representation in the Upper House of Parliament on the basis of ethnic organization is demanded: quota systems and – in the most extreme version – the division of the country into autonomous ethnic areas. A great political explosive force is contained in the demand for collective regulations which would restrict the resources of power of high-caste Hindu élites to a considerable extent. Forms of collective recognition usually require a new national census, on the basis of the proportions of minorities and majorities can or have to be rearranged. The demands of several political leaders to establish autonomous ethnic areas seem to be particularly problematic. In view of the fact that the peoples of Nepal are intermixed in their daily lives, the socially explosive force of this request is obvious.

In Nepal there is no population group constituting a majority. The high-caste Hindus are the largest group, amounting to 30 per cent (the low castes come to around 10 per cent), while the ethnic groups make up little more than 40 per cent. Among them are the Magar (c. 7.2 per cent), the Newar (c. 6 per cent) and the Tamang (c. 5.5 per cent).

This chapter does not claim to provide an analysis of ethnic relations and ethnic conflicts in Nepal. These have been documented elsewhere.[6] Rather, it describes the politics of identity, which presently mobilize a significant proportion of social forces in the context of ethnic mobilization. It goes without saying that the politics of minorities and representation directly touch on the question of the basis of national unity and in addition show a strong local component. Internal debates among the ethnic activists, partly carried on in the Nepalese villages seemingly far away from the national centre, today cannot be kept isolated from public discussions. Important arguments and ideologies arise within the frameworks of different public spaces. While ethnic introspections are an important 'ingredient' of political communication, they cannot be comprehended without knowledge of the contexts of the extensive cultural change in Nepal. Three remarks come to mind in this context:

1. The focus of this chapter on cultural repertoires from which members of ethnic groups supply their cultural manifestations follows the constructivistic approach (cf. especially Calhoun 1994, and Schlee in his introduction to this volume). Individuals as well as groups, according to my line of

Table 1.2   Classification of 59 Official Janajatis by NEFIN and NFDIN (2004)

Region	Classification of Indigenous Nationalities				
	Endangered	Highly Marginalized	Marginalized	Disadvantaged	Advantaged
Mountain (18)		Shiyar (Chumba) c. 1,000 Shingsawa (Lhomi, Karbhote) c. 2,000 Thudam c. 200	Bhote (Bhotiya) 19,261 (0.08%) Dolpo c. 20,000 Larke (Nupriba) c. 4,000 Lhopa (Mustang) c. 5,000 Mugali (Mugu) 10-12, 000 Topkegola (Dhokpya) 2-3,000 Walung 1,448 (0.01%)	Barhagaule (Bargaule) c. 2,000 Byansi (Sauka, Byasi, Rang) 2,103 (0.01%) Chairotan (Tamang Thakali, Panchgaule) c. 200 Marphali Thakali (Puntan, Punel) c. 2,000 Sherpa 154,622 (0.68%) Tangbe (Tangbedani) c. 400 Tingaule Thakali (Yhulkosompaimhi) c. 1,500	Thakali 12,973 (0.06%)
Hill (24)	Bankariya 44 Hayu 1,821 (0.01%) Kusbadiya 552 (0.00%) Kusunda 162 (0.00%) Lapcha (Lapcha, Rong) 3,660 (0.02%) Surel 149	Baramu 7,383 (0.03%) Chepang 52,237 (0.23%) Thami (Thangmi) 22,999 (0.10%)	Bhujel 117,568 (0.52%) Dura 5,169 (0.02%) Pahari 11,505 (0.06%) Phree (Free)?? Sunuwar 95,254 (0.42%) Tamang 1,282,304 (5.64%)	Chantyal 9,814 (0.04%) Gurung (Tamu) 543,571 (2.39%) Jirel 5,316 (0.02%) Limbu (Yakthung) 359,379 (1.58%) Magar 1,622,421 (7.14%) Rai 635,151 (2.79%) Yakkha (Dewan) 17,003 (0.07%) Yolmo (Helambu) 579 (0.00%)	Newar 1,245,232 (5.48%)
Inner Tarai (7)	Raji 2,399 (0.01%) Raute 658 (0.00%)	Bote 7,969 (0.04%) Danuwar 53,229 (0.23%) Majhi (Bhumar) 72,614 (0.32%)	Darai 14,859 (0.07%) Kumal 99,389 (0.44%)		

Table 1.2   (continued)

Region	Classification of Indigenous Nationalities				
	Endangered	Highly Marginalized	Marginalized	Disadvantaged	Advantaged
Tarai (10)	Kisan (Kuntum) 2,876 (0.01%) Meche (Bodo) 3,763 (0.02%)	Dhanuk (Rajbanshi, Khumu) 188,150 (0.83%) Dhungar/ Ghangar/ Jhangad/ Dhangad 41,764 (0.18%) Santhal (Satar) 42,698 (0.19%)	Dhimal 19,537 (0.09%) Gangai 31,318 (0.14%) Rajbanshi (Koch) 97,241 (0.43%) Tajpuriya 13,250 (0.06%) Tharu 1,533,879 (6.75%)		
Total	10	12	20	15	2

Sources: Adapted from Gellner and Karki (2007: 368–69).

Notes: The figures and percentages cited (which are the percentage of the total Nepali population of 22,736,934) were provided courtesy of Professor Sant Bahadur Gurung, director of NFDIN (National Foundation for Development of Indigenous Nationalities) until 2006: these follow the 2001 census. Where there is no percentage this means that the group was not a category recognized by the 2001 census; thus the figures are either unknown or are based on an estimate (note that in some cases, e.g. Yolmo, the ethnic label is not widely recognized or accepted in the region, and therefore the figures are much lower than might be expected: thus while only 579 people returned 'Yolmo' as their ethnicity, 3,986 recorded that they spoke 'Yolmo').

argumentation, can at a given point in time particularly emphasize specific values or signs from the existing cultural repertoire, or repress them in favour of other values or signs. I counter the essentialist views of what-has-always-been-there, or of what is the basis of the identity of individuals and groups and cannot be negotiated, with the well-known 'truths' of the social sciences: the constant readiness of human beings to invent traditions (Hobsbawm and Ranger 1983), and the fact that communities tend to be 'imagined' (Anderson 1983). An arbitrary 'switching', however, is not possible (Elwert 1997). Cultural re-orientations necessarily have to be meaningful in their respective context – for even the politics of reaction (Hirschman 1992), which shatter the supposedly natural values and norms, follow existing cultural repertoires, more, they seem to be fed by them.

Adopting a position against essentialism, however, in no way means that the large emotional content of ethnic affiliation can be left out of the equation. Kinship, language and religion for many people form the crucial basis of their self-perception. The references of critical researchers proceeding comparatively and pointing to the constructed character of identities relying on these elements are often in conflict with their investigated actors' claims to their truth – to the correct version only accessible to themselves.[7] For even if primordial conditions are constructions,[8] the force of primordial attachments is strong – as paradoxical as this may sound. In view of the enormous pertinence of ethnic mobilization it is necessary to examine why essentialist identities are still, maybe even increasingly, evoked vehemently today.[9]

2. The second remark refers to the types of cultural dynamics on which I will concentrate. It is important to distinguish two phenomena. Ethnological literature on Nepal contains numerous examples of which elements of culture and religion have been adopted from the Hindus by members of ethnic groups in Nepal in the course of the past two hundred years.[10] The spectrum of adoptions ranges from conversion to Hinduism (for instance expressed by the use of Brahmin priests on ritual occasions) to modifications in kinship systems (for instance abandonment of marriage to cross-cousins) to the learning of new productive techniques (for instance turning to agriculture). Such changes happen more or less unconsciously and are to be regarded as adaptation strategies to a changing environment, which take place largely unnoticed over long periods of time.

   Forms of cultural mobilization in times of radical societal changes are an entirely different category. The more flexible and hybrid (Werbner 1997) the local realities are, the more drastic the programmatic rejection of or turning to a 'correct version' of what the members of an ethnic group, in their struggle for recognition, consider the authentic view of their own identity. In moments like this, the language of ethnicity seeks unambiguity and large contexts: Hinduism versus Buddhism, hierarchy versus equality. In addition, systems of classification are contrasted (cf. Macfarlane 1997 and below). The politics of identity usually fall back upon clear agendas: differences and uniqueness are increasingly emphasized when the correct versions of ethnic identity reach the public; additionally, those politics are strengthened, are directed towards the recognition of collective rights – be it in the form of political representation in the Upper House, or in the form of political autonomy – and require delimitation.

3. Finally, the politics of identity have to be considered in the field of tension between 'private' and 'public'. Ethnic mobilization is usually aimed at making the 'private' public. In Nepal, members of ethnic groups look back upon a long tradition of tolerance of state jurisdiction towards their own cultural and religious forms.[11] Whom one married, which language one spoke, which belief one practised was regarded as one's personal affair. At the same time, however, these ethnic elements were largely banished from public life. Only Nepali, the language of the powerful groups (i.e. high-caste Hindus) was permitted in schools, in the mass media or in administration. Conversions

from Hinduism were prohibited. Official rhetoric, claiming national unity, blatantly denied the fact that Nepalese society shows enormous cultural diversity. The politics of social recognition, as they are presently taking place in Nepal, seek a connection between ethnic introspections and public exhibition. They are not only about re-defining national cohesion, but about demonstrating publicly that cultural politics are directly connected to other politics aiming at the redistribution of resources in a society. Since cultural politics are so closely linked to institutional and procedural forms, cultural-religious matters cannot be forced back from the public sphere, nor can they be understood without stating that the 'struggle over the state' (Wimmer 1995) is an important basis for their development. I will, as mentioned above, leave the 'struggle over the state' out of the account in this short examination, but the discussion of cultural politics always has to be considered in this context.

Unfortunately, there are only a few studies documenting the forms of 'coexistence' of the diverse population groups in Nepal – on a national level as well as in local contexts. Hence there is a great lack of analyses of signs which used to regulate interaction in everyday life as well as for special (ritual) matters. Until 1990, the official rhetoric as well as numerous scientific publications presented Nepal as an example of interethnic harmony instead of as a complex social structure characterized by a precarious and partly antipathy-charged coexistence of groups struggling for power. This multi-ethnic situation was often referred to as a 'garden in which a hundred wildflowers have bloomed, for centuries' (Sharma 1992).

Until the year 1990 the – mainly Western – social anthropologists analysed Nepal's ethnic groups without referring to the potential for conflict in the disputes with each other and with Hindu groups; after 1990, however, the focus of anthropological research changed drastically. Since then, analyses of ethnic processes involved in the drawing of borders and of the outbreak of conflicts have increased in number for at least two reasons.

The first reason lies in the new political climate, in which the studies in the social sciences are now carried out. For until the late 1980s, Nepal's responsible persons actively prevented any investigation of the social potential for conflict, in particular those having an ethnic component. The second reason is the actual increase of 'open' conflicts since the 'revolution' of 1990. Ethnic displeasure and conflicts had been detected before 1990, but the success of the political movement, which led to extensive political reforms, virtually opened Pandora's box of ethnic displeasure expressed in the national public. Strong symbols play an important part in these processes, expressing the protest, the feeling of injustice and the alternative visions of what personal goals are and how national unity is to be imagined. Ethnic movements are particularly intent on giving expression to the unity of one's own ethnic group and at the same time their different nature and their social distance towards other groups, especially towards those groups whose symbols dominate. In nearly all Nepalese ethnic groups we observe processes of reconsidering 'their own' cultural values, deciding on those features on which unity is based, cultivating their own culture and making its uniqueness visible, can be observed. Obviously, such processes do not always take place without internal conflicts (cf. especially Gellner et al. 1997).

The fact that the illusion of Nepal as a place of ethnic harmony could be destroyed so rapidly calls into question the quality of ethnographic research in Nepal's society (the author by no means regards herself as an exception). On the other hand, the mentioned changes can partly be analysed in the light of Scott's concept of moral economy (1976). Scott is known to have given warnings not to take specific representations at face value. Not infrequently, members of ethnic groups – although numerous ethnic leaders would vehemently contest this statement today – actively took part in displaying pictures of communal peace, for within certain constellations of power it is advisable to express consent to the order in force and to the language of symbols supporting it. Only when the political constellations change do the supposedly – or actually, but for a limited length of time – recognized symbols become the focus of attention. The mere fact that a cultural feature could be associated with political power can make it a symbol of oppression which is publicly fought against. Later I will concentrate on such recent examples. But before I deal with the current cultural struggles, I consider it useful to sketch out the forms of symbolization in interethnic interactions in Nepal.

Hierarchy, Difference, Distance: The Language of Signs in a Multi-Ethnic Local Society in Central Nepal

Belkot is a central Nepalese multi-caste village representative in this context of large parts of Nepal's hill area. Most of the signs used and perceived by residents in their everyday interactions belong to the category of what Bloch calls 'what goes without saying' (1992). Hardly noticed consciously, the signs meeting local requirements of differentiation and maintaining distance were, for a long time, part of the hidden agenda of interethnic encounters.[12] Presently, however, processes are starting which make these signs the focus of public perception. Ethnic and low-caste activists are engaged in investigating the forms of interaction and the signs used in this process. Some of these signs are now interpreted as symbols of oppression or as inadequate representations of local cohesion.

Particular attention in this context is directed towards the language of hierarchy. It is hardly surprising that a local microcosm, which for centuries has been dominated by Hindu values and norms, has learned to express social differences and distances in an idiom of domination and subordination. Life in Nepalese villages, where several castes and ethnic groups live close together, is strongly semiotized. Numerous signs are used as symbols of social order. In addition, visitors can gather information about the relative status of the persons involved in encounters from certain situations. Until ten years ago, signs of this kind seemed to be natural and obligatory. For instance, status differences in clothing and in the construction of the farms were clearly visible. Some forms of conduct also informed unambiguously about status. Other messages were rather more hidden or were only in retrospect interpreted as part of the language of hierarchy.

Among the particularly visible signs is the outward appearance of persons. The Nepalese are very accomplished in 'reading' signs expressed in clothing or jewellery. In everyday life, these messages are hardly taken into account, for one knows the other and nobody has to rely on additional information. Foreigners, however, entering the village territory immediately become subject to closer examination. If the outward appearance is not unambiguous, the respective person's position is directly inquired after. It is not only the caste or ethnic affiliation that is significant, but also marital status. In the case of women, this can hardly be concealed. A widow is not permitted to wear colourful clothing or the necklace (*pote*) brides receive at their wedding. For this reason, unmarried women also stand out clearly: not only are they strictly denied the wearing of the *pote*, but they usually do not wear gold jewellery, which widows again are allowed to wear. Their ears and noses are already pierced and the holes are equipped with small studs, so that the brides are able to put on gold jewellery in the course of their wedding. The decoration of the forehead is permitted to all women. Widows, however, are only allowed to wear metal *tikas*, which means they – unlike unmarried and married women – have to abstain from colourful ornaments. Only a married woman wears the red powder (*sindur*), the quintessential symbol of being married, in the parting of her hair.

Other features indicate ethnic or caste affiliation. In central Nepal, members of high castes – unlike those of low castes – wear no black clothing (the men's black waistcoat being an exception). There, the female and male members of ethnic groups in the majority wear the same clothing as the high-caste Hindus (although women of the Newar ethnic group do not have nose jewellery). Occasionally one can find people of the Tamang ethnic group in their traditional costume, which is made of wool and has a special cut. In the district capital it was repeatedly observed, before 1990, that civil servants teased Tamang people dressed according to old traditions.

Different signs are used depending on whether the interactions occur in public or private space. In the private sphere, the treatment of guests is strongly regimented. Guests visiting the houses of high-caste Hindus are either asked to enter or are received outside. Outside, anyone is permitted to stay on the veranda. If there are several visitors, however, the low-caste persons (the so-called 'untouchables') have to leave. Those invited into the kitchen for a meal may – provided they have the same caste status – eat together with the host near the fire, where the rice is prepared, which is particularly susceptible to ritual pollution. People of lower status have to stay in the area usually allocated to uninitiated children of the household. Still lower (but 'touchable') persons are provided with food far from the fire, almost on the threshold. The outward appearance of the farmhouses (Brahmins conceal the entrances to their houses from the random glances of passers-by), the livestock kept there (until a few years ago, only animals were kept which were allowed – again, according to caste status – to be eaten by the owners themselves), the existence of sacred plants and religious insignia can all be read as signs either indicating the caste status of the household members or presenting precautions taken to distance oneself from neighbours of another group.

In public situations – around the temples, in offices, schools and shops – it is also obligatory to keep to the rules of interaction mainly determined by the regulations of ritual purity. Those rules are particularly strict in places where food is served. The rules of segregation have to be strictly obeyed, for a person belonging to a higher caste must not be touched while taking food. For an outsider the alterations in the spatial arrangement are hardly visible, but as soon as even just tea is served, people move away from each other. A distance of around 20 cm is sufficient to keep to the rules of ritual purity. The behaviour towards persons of low, i.e. so-called 'untouchable' castes is pronounced: not only must members of this group always stay outside a tea-shop, but tea is served to them in special containers not used by anyone else (also cf. Bluestain 1977). Occasionally they receive their tea in normal glasses, but they have to wash them themselves. The smoking of cigarettes and water-pipes offers clear indications about the relative status of the persons involved: since saliva is regarded as very polluting, a cigarette can only be passed from a person of higher status to one of lower status – until it ends at the feet of an untouchable. In case of the water-pipe (*hookah*), who is permitted to use which part of whose pipe is precisely prescribed.

Rituals present a broad field for expression of differences and distances. Usually, on the occasion of rituals the spatial arrangement is precisely predetermined. Only certain persons are allowed to go to places particularly susceptible to ritual pollution. The relative status of persons is expressed by bows and by the exchange of ritual signs and gifts. Specific rules exist for the distribution of sacred food. Furthermore, the status differences become obvious during meals. Only holders of the highest status can actually do the cooking for groups consisting of different castes, thus frequently Brahmins. The high-caste Hindus have to eat in the ritually purified area, and members of other castes may eat only after or behind them. The 'untouchable' musicians (Damai-caste), without whom hardly any ritual can be performed, are tightly segregated during meals, for even a glance from an untouchable is sufficient to ritually pollute a Brahmin eating rice.

Specific ritual occasions make further precautions necessary. The Brahmins and members of the Magar ethnic group living in close proximity in Belkot have special agreements regarding the use of the shared water source. In everyday life, there is no need for special regulations. But when the Magar slaughter pigs and eat the meat on the occasion of rituals – the consumption of pork is strictly prohibited to the Brahmins – then the use of the common water source is denied them. Usually drinking-water is stored in big containers for this purpose. To wash themselves, the Magar then use other springs. These precautions show that rules of maintaining distance can make the coexistence of people of different status groups possible. As such, this agreement is not a sign. A few years ago, however, the Magar decided to 'read' this, in their eyes, rather troublesome regulation as a sign of the – for themselves disadvantageous – difference in power.

The status differences become very visible in Belkot on the occasion of the *Dasai* festival (also called *Durga Puja*), during which most of the residents are connected by the requirements of ritual division of labour, and at the same time are separated by the imperative of maintaining distance. *Dasai* – the way it used to be celebrated in Belkot until a decade ago – consists of an elaborate ritual sequence including different protagonists. Among them are:

– several priests, who in the course of this ten-day festivity have to perform different tasks;
– the local persons in power/rulers, who appear in person on the tenth day;
– the Magar specialists responsible for the ritual killing of animals (*upasye*);
– the village leader responsible for co-ordination (*naike* – from the ethnic group of the Newar);
– the Damai-musicians and others.

The *Dasai* activities in Belkot largely correspond to the pan-Hindu pattern of the *Durga-Puja* festival. But they, on the other hand, include some local peculiarities and some meanings added to the ritual corpus (cf. for example Krauskopff and Lecomte-Tilouine 1996; Pfaff-Czarnecka 1998, 2012).

Neither the complete ritual nor the details can be reported here, but the above-mentioned cooperation of ritual specialists should be pointed out. Until a decade ago, *Dasai* could be celebrated in Belkot as a festival emphasizing local unity and the special meaning of Belkot within the ritual geography of Nepal. Furthermore, members of different population groups were able to use this event to express their own meanings on the occasion of certain rituals, e.g. the head priest could ritually closely relate the deity of his own lineage to the *Durga* goddess and thus emphasize the special position of his own lineage within the village structure.

Furthermore, on the occasion of this festival the ritual arrangement of different population groups and their representatives is revealed. For on the tenth day a subtly developed display of the respective status of the residents takes place. In this context, it is the political power rather than the caste status that is of significance: this was, however, exclusively concentrated in the hands of high-caste Hindus until about 1990. On the morning of the tenth day a male goat is sacrificed. Its head is placed on a dish and deposited in the sanctuary. The Brahmins assemble and read from the holy script of *Devi-Mahatmya*. The residents gather in the ritual grounds of the temple. In the sanctuary, the head priest venerates the objects symbolizing the *Durga* goddess. After that, the ritual objects, including the goat's head, are carried outside. Now the head priest sticks a ritual marking (*tika*) on the village chief's forehead. Then follows an elaborate exchange of *tika* and bows between the priests and dignitaries. After that, the village chief remains at the centre of events and the village residents approach him in order to receive a *tika*, to bow to him and to present him with a gift. The particular political significance of the *Dasai* festival used to lie precisely in the fact that until about 1990, all village residents were obliged to appear before the village chief on this occasion and to pay their respects in a hierarchically prescribed sequence. As I want to explain in the following section, *Dasai* in Belkot today is regarded as a ritual of power expressing the political and ritual dominance of high-caste Hindus over a large portion of the ethnic population.

New Perspectives on Supposedly Established Signs

The forms of interaction just described and the signs employed have become a focus of attention for ethnic and low-caste activists for more than ten years now. What used to be interpreted as the result of extensive processes of acculturation currently presents itself in a new perspective. Many elements considered normal, or even natural, over long periods of time, and declared a cultural means of guaranteeing social cohesion by the dominant groups, are now becoming objects of a detailed examination usually resulting in criticism and disapproval. Nepal is no longer regarded as a place where peaceful ethnic coexistence is fostered, but rather a place where fierce cultural debates are carried out and where struggles of representation break out. Signs, which until ten to fifteen years ago seemed to be incontestable, are now regarded as symbols of oppression, of subordination or as symbols of forced cultural take-overs – at least in the view of ethnic and low-caste activists.

The *Dasai* festivals of the past years illustrate the incipient change in perceptions. In 1986, that is prior to the political change of 1990, the newly elected village chief of Belkot stayed away from the celebrations. This man, the first village chief from among the Tamang ethnic group, and his supporters explained their non-attendance and their refusal to make a contribution to the celebration with the fact that *Dasai* was a symbol for the subjugation of ethnic minorities. In 1986 and in the years to follow during his term of office (the next elections were won by a Brahmin again), the village secretary from the high caste of the Chetri represented the 'political power'. Many village residents continued to appear on the tenth day of the celebration in order to give proof of their loyalty, but the village peace from then on remained disturbed.

It is remarkable that the open-minded political leaders from the Tamang ethnic group started to denounce signs of Hindu dominance immediately after they had won the election, instead of taking the opportunity to be honoured in the centre of power themselves – to which they would have been perfectly entitled. The young generation of Tamang in particular took part in this kind of expression of displeasure. *Dasai* was from then on regarded as a symbol of dominance of the Hindu rulers – with the Nepalese king at the head of the regime – and their clients, who maintained the power in the village societies.

According to the reports of the Tamang leaders, the participation of actors in earlier *Dasai* celebrations used to be an expression of their religious feelings. Furthermore, the secular power could be supported religiously. The local population had for many decades been required to make known this fact by showing their subordination. The dignitaries present – the civil servants, the priests and the influential families – regarded the *Dasai* festival as a means to show their loyalty and at the same time demonstrate their own proximity to power, in being the first to be admitted on the tenth day to bow to the local ruler. The local population of the lower ranks had to wait. Their presence could be read as a tacit recognition of this social order. Everyone was obliged to attend, to bow and to look – in short, to provide the populace for the celebrations. For one was not only invited, but compelled to appear, and in addition one was required to take part in forming a ritual order by having to observe the rules of domination and subordination and of distance maintenance. The presence of lower ranks at a correct distance only showed the significance of the persons at the forefront of the celebrations in a favourable light.

While the high-caste people's representatives – who after 1962 were no longer appointed, but elected – used the traditional ritual form to emphasize their own status, the Tamang leaders now made efforts to stop entirely the *Dasai* festival. During the late 1980s the Tamang of Belkot took the conscious decision to abolish this symbol of power completely. This was also the case when they acquired political power and could have used this ritual for expressing their political supremacy. But by emphasizing the fact that *Dasai* not only supported a rigid political order, but also gave expression to the ethnic inferiority of minorities within Hindu caste structure, the intention was rather to boycott this entire ritual complex. It is remarkable that this strong gesture represented an attempt to fight a tradition more than two hundred years old, during which Hindu dominance had extended at the expense of ethnic minorities. It should be added that during the 1980s ethnic protests against the *Dasai* festival took place in other parts of the country as well, mainly by religious movements (cf. Paul 1989), where non-Hindu activists endeavoured to stop animal sacrifice and to perform purification rites which were to cleanse Nepal of sins weighing on the kingdom through the sacrifices (see also Hangen 2005).

The mobilization against *Dasai* is not an isolated phenomenon. In large parts of Nepal conflicts broke out more and more often, shattering cultural and religious certainties. Some examples for this: members of low Hindu castes increasingly resist the custom of being segregated in tea shops and of having to wash their dishes themselves.[13] Residents of many villages are also attributing growing symbolic value to dress, as they are increasingly wearing traditional costumes again, which not only demonstrate their recollection of their own ethnic culture, but also their efforts to boost local craftsmanship. All over Nepal efforts can be observed which I call 'exodus out of South Asia'. The term refers to the deliberate turning away of the ethnic population from Hinduism and the cultural forms derived from it. This turning away takes place in two ways: first, by endeavouring to remove Hindu influence from their own customs and emphasizing more clearly the non-Hindu elements; and secondly by holding discourses which unambiguously protest against Nepalese ethnic groups being regarded as a component of the pan-Hindu world of South Asia. In the second case it is obvious that the ethnic activists following this line of argument are partly oriented to ethnological research. The most important characteristic of these processes is the implementation of reforms intended to remove Hindu influence from ethnic customs. Macfarlane's report (1997) about the activities of the Gurung ethnic group on this matter is of particular interest.[14] His report is concentrated especially on two fields currently regarded as particularly important by the Gurung. First, he deals with the rising interest in chronicles documenting the history of ethnic groups, and secondly he reveals a new perspective on the personal social structure and its portrayal in the academic public. Both efforts are closely connected, because they are also thought of as criticism of Brahmin practices, which today are blamed for the distortion of their own customs by the Gurung – a criticism that has been adopted uncritically by some researchers, who are relying too much on the activists' information. In this respect, the Gurung activists participate in the trend generally to be observed in Nepal of accusing the Brahmin priests of forging ethnic chronicles (*vamsavalis*). Furthermore, the Brahmins are said to have actively contributed to a hierarchical portrayal of ethnic cultures (for instance in ethnological studies), although these – according to the general tenor – are in reality of an egalitarian nature.

On 13 March 1992, Professor Macfarlane received a fax in his office in Cambridge (England) from Pokhara (Western Nepal), signed by Gurung activists. This letter informed Macfarlane of the fact that on the occasion of a national meeting of Gurung several resolutions had been passed, in particular that

1. the history of the Gurung had up until now been written and distorted by Brahmins;

2. there are no higher or lower ranked clans of the Gurung;
3. the traditional Gurung priests are the *pachyu* (Bön) and the *klabri* (Bön); the Buddhist *lamas*, however, were not part of this until later.

Several aspects are of special interest here. In this period of time, the Gurung very clearly oppose the idea that they are not organized along egalitarian lines. The activists support this statement among other things with the comment that in their culture marriage to both a patrilineal and a matrilineal cross-cousin is permitted. The 'exodus out of South Asia' is expressed in the revision of the chronicles. The activists insist that they migrated to Nepal not from India, but from Mongolia, where they had adopted the *Bön* religion. Of further interest is the mutual relationship between the activists and the (foreign) researchers. One reason why Macfarlane and his wife Sarah Harrisson received this fax was that both were at the time translating Pignède's monograph about the Gurung from French into English. The activists accused Pignède of having analysed their culture from a South Asian perspective. This had resulted in a Brahmin perspective being applied to the Gurung. The activists emphasized that Pignède was a student of Dumont who had viewed all of South Asia through the prism of Hinduism and its values and norms (see also Dumont 1979).

Comparing the current efforts of Gurung activists with my above description of signs used in everyday interactions, two considerations come to mind. First, it becomes obvious that many practices critically examined today were not a public issue only two decades ago. Certainly, private criticism occurred or resentments increased, but people shied away from making such matters public. One might think there were no open conflicts carried out prior to 1990. But a statement like this should be taken with caution. Did they not exist? Or was it maybe rather the case that social anthropologists of Western as well as Nepalese provenance simply did not notice them, did not even want to notice them (cf. Dahal 1993)? After all, some conflicts were documented: my own report of the conflict regarding the *Dasai* festival, the film *Makai*, as well as Paul's observations regarding the Buddhists' negative attitude towards animal sacrifice. But in view of the innumerable efforts of ethnic mobilization after 1990, these early observations seem quite scanty.

A second remark refers to the new accentuation in the perception of what is culture and what is the meaning of individual symbols. What seemed to be regarded as natural until a decade ago has now presently acquired new connotations. Signs hardly noticed in former times now appear as new and significant means in identity politics. What I have described above as a 'pattern of peaceful coexistence' from today's perspective seems to be a naive description of specific patterns of how the rulers maintained the hegemonic claim of high-caste Hindus and forced the local societies to observe their rules. Today, however, signs provide weapons in the contested arenas. A certain uniformity of ethnic reform movements, which can be observed all over Nepal and which all follow a similar pattern, cannot be overlooked: the rediscovery of ethnic chronicles, 'back-to-the-roots' movements as well as an emphasis on equality in public portrayals of one's own group.

Cultural Production, Reforms, Reactions and the Role of International Publics in these Efforts

Why are ethnic activists willing to examine the symbols used critically? Ethnic mobilization in Nepal is gaining increasing significance, and ethnicity – at least during the initial phases of mobilization – is always accompanied by symbolic struggles (Pfaff-Czarnecka et al. 2007). The more suitable a sign is for symbolizing internal cohesion and at the same time marking a difference, the greater the probability for this sign to be used in the politics of representation. A strategic significance is allocated to signs which at the same time point to (positively) the group cohesion and (negatively) the differentiation from the Other. Furthermore, symbols are particularly effective if they are available to a broad public.[15] The questions of change in the use of signs and of the laws governing new orientations therefore directly touch on the processes of ethnic mobilization.

The readiness to review passed-on cultural repertoires of the national society – to return to the question initially asked – as well as the insistent demands of ethnic activists to make ethnic symbolism increasingly visible in public, are indicators for ethnic mobilization being a recent societal phenomenon in Nepal. Whether cultural politics will also have precedence in the future, or whether activists will increasingly concentrate on other social resources, will depend on whether satisfying cultural compromise solutions can be found (Wimmer 1995) and whether activists will be able to mobilize their supporters for struggles of distribution. For the cultural gains of ground in public space will not be able to stem ethnic displeasure. Presently, it is mainly cultural and religious matters, however, which are characterizing ethnic mobilization.

It is still not possible today to predict in what way the extensive efforts of ethnic activists to influence the politics of identity will lead to a new understanding of Nepal's national unity. The growing interest in one's own personal culture, the search for one's own personal origin and for the 'correct' version, the new cultural projects (like the endeavours to find scripts for ethnic languages not written down as yet), the public debates on culture in general and national culture in particular, the cultural comparisons and cultural competitions are in part to be seen as reactions to the previous disregard for the minority cultures as well as to the former attempts of the rulers to stem ethnic diversity in Nepal; they can be regarded in part as tactical manoeuvres, and in part also as a new sphere of action of the intelligentsia in dealing with the roots of one's community.

It should have become clear which kinds of symbols are particularly susceptible to challenge in Nepal today: the displeasure of ethnic activists is aimed at the
dominance of Hinduism, especially at rites and customs of high-caste Hindus.
Pointing at this strong cultural-religious 'backlash' by using the above-mentioned
examples, however, is not meant to imply that the entire Nepalese society is
engaged in reformatory projects which can be reduced to a simple formula of
rejection of Hinduism towards an ethnic solidarity. We do not presently know
enough about the status that the politics of reaction towards the Hindu predominance have in large parts of the country. It cannot be denied, for instance, that
important trends of protest, among which I class particularly the Maoist movement escalating in many Nepalese districts 1996 and 2006, cannot be attributed
to ethnic displeasure; it rather buttressed ethnic mobilization. Other conflicts are
carried on within the context of formal election campaigns, which in Nepal take
place beyond ethnic borders. Therefore, caution is advisable when it comes to
assessing the widespread impact of ethnic reactions to Hindu hegemony. Ethnic
struggles are vehemently fought in the centre of the country, where firstly the
ethnic activists are directly confronted with their lack of access to state resources,
particularly to significant positions in politics and administration, secondly they
have already created a strong public, and thirdly they are able to carry out their
projects in coordination with activists from other groups, as difficult as this coordination may be.

It is only due to extensive efforts towards cooperation, for instance, that it
is possible to build a museum in Kathmandu, in which all peoples of Nepal are
represented. The new censuses attach great importance to ethnic affiliation which
is also the result of the united endeavours of different activists and organizations,
who partly make their public appearance individually, and partly are represented
by NEFIN (formerly NEFEN – the Nepal Federation of Nationalities). The
foundation of an umbrella organization is an important indicator for the fact
that the individual ethnic organizations had to realize early on that they could
only gain ground from the dominant groups by joint actions. For the Nepalese
ethnic groups, the low-castes and the minority religions have founded dozens of
small organizations with only a few members, among the most well-known of
which are the Nepal Magar Association, the Nepal Tamang Association, Thakali
Services Committee, Nepal Sherpa Association, and the Newar Language Joint
Committee (see Whelpton, Gellner and Pfaff-Czarnecka 2008).[16] Their activities are expressed in the public in manifold ways, and the mere fact that ethnic
matters are negotiated publicly and that there is an increasing number of press
products and radio stations called into being by ethnic organizations gives expression to the new openness.

In order to understand the current forms of symbolization it is important to refer to the public nature of the debates. The highly discontinuous processes of Nepalese democratization and the efforts regarding social development

constitute important structural conditions in this context. The new constitution, having come into force only half a year after the bloody disturbances of spring 1990 (on 9 November 1990), embodies extensive political and civic rights, of which the Nepalese minorities indeed make regular use. The demand for more participation – in the context of party politics and the increasingly dense networks of civil society – is reflected for instance in the debates on social objectives, which today are not only held in different languages and with an emphasis on different attitudes of value, but precisely contain the demand for promotion of this ethnic diversity. The differentiation of cultural politics is regarded by the activists both as an indicator of and the condition for the ethnic population to be able to increasingly participate in societal decision making and redistribution.

Nevertheless, the question of the extent of the impact of these efforts arises in view of the increasing presence of ethnic matters in the Nepalese public. What proportion of the ethnic population is actually involved in cultural politics? To what extent do farmers in remote valleys of the Himalayas know the objectives their self-appointed leaders assert and claim? Usually it is teachers and experienced 'opinion leaders' familiar with the formation of opinion and with current values in the national, sometimes the international public, who formulate and communicate local objectives and who participate in adjusting symbols so that they can be 'read and understood by wide audiences. It is therefore even less surprising that most ethnic activists employ similar methods, so that, for instance, the writing of chronicles is all of a sudden generally widespread in most ethnic movements.

As soon as the debates on cultural forms are held publicly, there is an increasing risk of cultural peculiarities getting lost due to the 'translation' for the public. With regard to the question of what is in fact the correct version of their own culture or religion, ethnic activists are currently involved in sometimes highly conflictual internal discussions. Old (many priests) and new élites (many teachers) for instance argue about whether the blood sacrifices performed in some shamanistic practices are still compatible with the requirements of modern times. Ramble (1997) documents that many activists regard shamanism without blood sacrifice as a progressive attitude. Other members of the same ethnic group regard the blood sacrifice as precisely the essence of the ritual. Thus, the majority of the debates on the cultural content flare up between purists and reformers.

Not infrequently the search for cultural distinction, towards which the ethnic introspections are oriented, paradoxically results in an adjustment to other minorities and to the national environment. Not only do different activists proceed in accordance with well-known patterns, but also the delimitation towards formerly valid values and norms, which are revolted against, can result in the origin of a we-group. A national arena is occupied by role models to whose messages activists are susceptible. Whenever activists of a group have successfully adopted a measure, the probability of other activists following increases.

Furthermore, it is of course advantageous for all minorities to participate in common projects: be that the foundation of a National Museum of Minorities or a new census intended to establish the proportions which could be decisive in the future for possible quota systems. The mobilization against Hindu predominance – like the compulsory use of Sanskrit in schools – provides an important basis around which the numerous ethnic and religious minorities in Nepal unite.

Finally, for an understanding of ethnic mobilization it is of significance to know at whom the messages are aimed. The public currently forming in Nepal is a contested social field. The existence of a great diversity of organizations and opinions must not obscure the fact that Nepal's new pluralism is characterized by inequalities. Public spaces are dominated by forces capable of preventing actors from making their issues and contents public. The control of political agendas is strongly contested (see also Lukes 1974: 21ff.). This is not altered in Nepal by the fact that the Nepalese public is not only defined by national interests but also by international actors and their matters. Rather, the international actors – the experts on development cooperation (cf. Burkert 1997), the international capital, the tourists, the Western religious disciples – are also involved in formulating objectives and introducing internationally accepted values.

The current debates on the superior role of certain ethnic groups still have a special standing within the process of social development initiated by the Nepalese social anthropologist Dor Bahadur Bista. Dor Bista triggered a medium-sized earthquake in 1991, when in his book *Fatalism and Development* he advocated the thesis that Hindus, with their egoistic and fatalistic attitudes, were not capable of boosting Nepal's development. This role, according to Bista, had to fall to the numerous non-Hindu ethnic groups, who showed a strong cooperative spirit. Bista's argumentation and the controversies provoked by it show that collective identities have become a resource, in spite of or maybe even because of the vagueness of the concept. Having communal forms is prestigious.

Through international and national actors meeting and favouring specific values in mutual negotiations, signal effects are frequently created. Since the early 1990s, values like community, equality, small-scaleness and locality have been apportioned particularly positive connotations. In short, the development discourse and the Western dream of authenticity rate highly precisely those elements the Nepalese minorities have to offer in their self-representations. The fact that the public production of meanings is subject to such complex processes of opinion formation and provides manifold cultural repertoires is surprising – probably not only for the Western researchers, but also for the members of Nepalese ethnic groups, who are positioning themselves anew.

Joanna Pfaff-Czarnecka is Professor for Social Anthropology at Bielefeld University, Germany, co-director of the Centre for Interdisciplinary Research

(ZiF) at Bielefeld University and Senate member of the German Research Foundation. She has been a visiting Fellow and Professor at the Universities of Oxford, Tokyo and Jawaharlal Nehru University in New Delhi. Her fields of interest are ethnicity, democratization, political communication, belonging and global students. She is co-editor of *Nationalism and Ethnicity in Nepal* (Vajra Publication, 2008) and *Facing Globalization in the Himalayas: Belonging and the Politics of the Self* (Sage, 2014).

Notes

This chapter was written in the year 2000 and it reflects on the first decade of Nepalese ethnic groups' cultural self-assertion, that began in 1990. The new, translated version of this text does not take into consideration what has taken place since 2000. It is therefore silent on the scope and the dynamics of ethnic activism in the recent years. Ethnic activism continues to engage in identity politics and has become significantly more assertive, with many activists demanding state's restructuring in order to establish ethnic autonomous regions and advocating the realization of minority rights. Ethnic activists have been struggling, along other societal groups, to overthrow the monarchic system and to bring an end to Nepal's being a Hindu state. Also, it is beyond the scope of this chapter to thematize the Maoist resurrection that has impacted ethnic activism in manifold ways. Some additional references were included for further reading.

1. Hirschman on this subject (1992: 17): 'Once we contemplate this protracted and perilous seesawing of action and reaction, we come to appreciate more than ever the profound wisdom of Whitehead's well-known observation, "The major advances in civilisation are processes which all but wreck the societies in which they occur"'.
2. These processes have been comprehensively documented. For general historical accounts, see Regmi (1972, 1978); on government measures in view of ethnic diversity, see Burghart (1984); on the embodiment of the 'national caste hierarchy', see Höfer (1979); and on the extensive transformations in the relations between Nepalese ethnic groups and Hindu groups, as well as on cultural change as a consequence of these processes, see Pfaff-Czarnecka (1989, 1997, 1999).
3. The differentiation between 'Hindu population' and 'ethnic groups' is based on Nepalese custom. Among the most important ethnic groups of Nepal are the Newar, Magar, Gurung, Tamang, Limbu, Rai, Thakali, etc. – cf. Gellner, Pfaff-Czarnecka and Whelpton (1997).
4. Activists of several ethnic groups claim that their estates, which they held and cultivated on the communal basis, had been transferred to high-caste owners through cunning and trickery (see, e.g. Krämer 1996: 217ff.).
5. The Nepalese cultural anthropologist Bhattachan (1995: 92) paints a pessimistic picture: 'Indigenous ethnic groups are federating themselves to challenge continuing monopoly of the ruling class in national political, social, cultural, and economic resources. Similarly, Madhesiyas are raising their voice against the hill people's domination, and the Dalits are fighting against continuing social discrimination by high-caste groups. . . . Also, the rise of Hindu fundamentalist groups in India, such as Shiv Sena, has fuelled Hindu-Muslim conflicts in the Terai, and Hindu-Buddhist and Hindu-Christian conflicts are slowly brewing up. Given the continuing and rising social and economic inequality, the Nepalese people now fear that Nepal may be on the verge of witnessing ethnic conflict(s) in near future as a part of the process of globalisation'.

6. Cf. for instance Bhattachan (1995, 1996, 1998); Gellner (1999a, 1999b); Gellner et al. (1997); Krämer (1996); Pfaff-Czarnecka (1997, 1998, 1999).

7. The social anthropologist Bhattachan (1998: 112f.) provides impressive evidence for this conflict in his review of our book on nationalism and ethnicity in Nepal (cf. Gellner et al. 1997): 'I myself being a Thakali, a member of the National Committee for Development of Nationalities representing the Nepal Federation of Nationalities (NEFEN) and a faculty member of the Department of Sociology and Anthropology from its inception in 1981, who was trained in sociology in a Western school, I must frankly say that my reactions and analyses about the book under review would be multiple – partly from an academic perspective, partly from an advocacy perspective and partly from an ethnic activist perspective. In other words, I will primarily rely on reason, logic and rationality, but also emotion . . . our ethnic demands are not just about economic and political gains. Our demands are also for the recognition of our very existence, our histories, cultures and religions'.

8. Cf. Geertz (1973: 259), who has repeatedly and mistakenly been accused of primordiality: 'By a primordial attachment is meant one that stems from the "givens" more precisely, as culture is inevitably involved in such matters, the assumed "givens" – of social existence: immediate contiguity and kin connection mainly, but beyond them the givenness that stems from being born into a particular religious community, speaking a particular language, or even a dialect of a language, and following particular social practices. These congruities of blood, speech, custom, and so on, are seen to have an ineffable, and at times overpowering, coerciveness in and of themselves'.

9. Calhoun (1994: 17) in this context points to a change in feminism, which is of interest for research in ethnicity. Some feminists increasingly think it a practicable option 'to risk essentialism': 'At its simplest, the argument suggests that where a particular category of identity has been repressed, delegitimated or devalued in dominant discourses, a vital response may be to claim value for all those labelled by that category, thus implicitly invoking it in an essentialist way'.

10. For a survey of the most important adoptions, see Pfaff-Czarnecka (1997). At the same time, the 'ethnic influence' on Nepalese Hinduism must not be neglected.

11. An important exception is the ban of the levirate, embodied in the Nepalese civil legislation of 1854 with regard to the groups practising this type of marriage.

12. I rely mainly on my own survey; cf. above all Pfaff-Czarnecka (1989).

13. A conflict of this kind, which erupted in another central Nepalese village, was documented in the film *Review of Makai* by Garlinski and Bieri (1991).

14. In comparison see also Krämer (1996), Campbell (1997), Gaenszle (1997) and Russell (1997).

15. The most famous sign of the last decades is probably the lettering of the Polish movement of Solidarnosc.

16. A more detailed listing, including Nepalese names as well, can be found in Krämer (1996: 390f.).

Chapter 2

Identity through Difference

Ambivalences of the Social Integration of Mauritania's Former Slaves

Urs Peter Ruf

The relation between slave and master holds a special fascination. It is commonly understood to be synonymous with what seems to be the most archaic exploitation of humans by humans. This associative content of the term slavery does not fade in view of the fact that this institution is considered to have been overcome long ago. On the contrary, the supposed historical distance contributes to making slavery seem even more exotic. By becoming the *ultima ratio* of inhumanity and the expression of a total institution of exploitation, the concept of slavery attains an essential meaning for any society which considers itself a modern one: it describes its counter-image. From this perspective it becomes comprehensible why present forms of strong dependence are often compared with slavery. All too blatant examples of a systematic combination of inhuman living conditions with economic exploitation and personal dependency relationships, which are by no means in the process of becoming extinct in the age of globalization, are denounced as modern forms of slavery and as slavery-like conditions, particularly by human rights groups.[1] Against this background of slavery as conceived by the media, and given its recontextualization, reports about continuing slavery in our time are explosive stuff. According to numerous media and human rights groups, the purchase and sale of human beings and life without personal freedom is, in some countries, a fact of the present, not of the past.

Two countries are at the centre of such accusations: Sudan and Mauritania. However, the two cases differ. The government of Sudan is explicitly reproached for at least tolerating the enslavement of inhabitants of the southern part of the country (especially women and children), if not indeed using this as an instrument of terror in the context of the civil war dividing the country.[2] The roles of victims and culprits seem to be allocated clearly: marauding Arabic-Islamic troops and militia pillage and kidnap people in the south of the country, which is inhabited by adherents of indigenous religions and Christians. In particular, this last circumstance, a seemingly convincing proof for Huntington's thesis (1993) of Islam's bloody borders, provides Sudan with a great deal of attention in the media.

In Mauritania, the borders between slaves and masters conform less to this pattern of interpretation. The area of the Western Sahel has been almost completely Islamized for centuries. Running straight through modern Mauritania, the border between Northern, Arabic and sub-Saharan, black Africa cannot therefore be presented as a border between Islam and non-Islam. In this respect, this is a much less useful example for the supposedly warlike character of Islam and the issue of slavery in Mauritania appears to meet with much less interest in comparison to Sudan, at least in the Western European context.[3]

What then is behind these accusations of continual slavery in Mauritania? To outline this with regard to history and the present is one purpose of this chapter. I will also examine how the drawing of strict social borders within Mauritanian society has promoted integration and the development of identity.

The Past and Present of Slavery in Mauritania

'An Arab must indeed be poor not to own at least one Negro slave', wrote Saugnier (Saugnier and Brisson 1969 [1792]: 99), summing up the importance of slavery among the nomadic Moors. He knew what he was talking about, for he himself had been made a slave for about three months after being stranded on the West Saharan coast in 1784.[4] Therefore, there is some reason to believe that among the nomadic inhabitants of the Western Sahara, slavery was similarly widespread and was practised for centuries, while a number of sources show this was the case among the sedentary populations on both 'shores' of the Sahara as well as of the sub-Saharan region.[5]

To supplement their diet, the pastoral nomads were in need of agricultural products, especially grain. These they obtained by trading, for instance in exchange for fossil salt mined in the Sahara by slaves or tributaries, or for various animal husbandry products. At the same time, their high degree of mobility gave them military superiority over sedentary populations. For this reason they were able to extend their territorial control as far as the agricultural regions of the savannah. This way, reciprocal forms of exchange between farmers and herders could be converted into hierarchical relations. Apart from collecting tributes from free sedentary groups, their political dominance allowed them to settle slaves of their own who, although living and operating quite autonomously in economic terms, were obliged to leave a share of their agrarian production to their masters (cf. Baier and Lovejoy 1977; McDougall 1985a: 18).[6]

The diffusion of slaves from the trans-Saharan trade in human beings – probably already flourishing prior to the tenth century – into pastoral-nomadic society, as well as the establishment of agricultural branches inhabited by slaves in favoured areas of their own territory and in the northern frontier areas of the Sahel, cannot, however, by itself explain the large proportion of slaves in the population of the Western Sahara in the past and partly still in the present. A more careful evaluation of the demography of slavery and, based on that, of the tasks and social positions of slaves in Moorish society will help to provide some initial insights.

The Demography of Slavery

Although exact data for the pre-colonial period does not exist, the reports from this time suggest the existence of a great number of slaves. Census data, collected by the colonial administration from the beginning of the twentieth century, allows for deeper insight into this issue. According to this, in 1957 the proportion of slaves (*'abîd*) and manumitted slaves (*harâtîn*) among a small group of Ideybussât nomadizing in the arid north and specializing in camel herding was 11 per cent as opposed to 80 per cent among a group of Awlâd Mbarek, who are almost completely sedentarized.[7] This data implies that there used to be a considerable difference with regard to the demographic importance of the *sûdân*, i.e. the slaves and manumitted slaves, among Moorish tribes. These differences must be attributed mainly to differing economic specialization. While highly mobile nomadic pastoralists kept comparatively few slaves, the latter sometimes even represented the majority in those tribal groups living in areas with predominantly agricultural use. Ideal-typical representatives of both constellations, however, are and were relatively rare. The majority of the Moors specialized in herding cattle, as well as goats and sheep, not least because close to the river Senegal, but also on the Plateau of Tagant *tabûrit*, a disease transmitted by mosquitoes and similar to sleeping sickness prevented the keeping of camels (cf. Toupet 1958: 81). Instead of the erratic pasture-seeking migrations typical of nomadism centring on camel herding, the lives of the vast majority of Moorish nomads were mainly governed by the strategies needed when utilizing much smaller areas and by fixed transhumance routes. Occasionally, the cultivation of millet and sorghum even reversed the priorities with regard to mobility and sedentariness (cf. Bonte 1986; Ruf 1995: 128f.).

In areas with comparable forms of land use, a relatively homogenous picture emerges from various statistics, according to which the proportion of *sûdân* in the total Moorish population comes to approximately one third. In the area of Assaba, for instance, 32 per cent of the total population were recorded as *sûdân* in 1950 (cf. Munier 1952: 40), and in the subdivision of Moudjéria they made up 33 per cent of all tribes on average, according to the official statistics of 1950.[8]

These figures from regions which at that time were still mainly pastoral-nomadic are nonetheless much lower than those of the official national estimate of 1965, which for the last time presented population data divided into status groups. According to this, the proportion of slaves and *harâtîn* among the total Moorish population amounted to as much as 43 per cent (cf. documentation of the results of the SEDES study in Davis 1997: 96). This data provides a good indicator of the numerical ratio of *bidhân* and *sûdân*, i.e. white and black Moors;[9] a number of details providing a deeper insight into the practice of Moorish slavery will be discussed in the following.

Subtle Differences: Slaves of Warriors and Slaves of Scholars

An essential criterion for the differentiation of the slave proportion in individual tribal groups in the above-mentioned statistics from Moudjéria is membership in the warrior class (*hassân*) or the scholar class (*zwâya*). Within the tribal federation of the Abakak (warriors), from among whom the emirate of Tagant was led, the proportion of slaves only comes to approximately 26 per cent, while among the maraboutic Tarkoz it is 39 per cent, and among some other tribes of this region much higher still. This difference reflects the difference in politico-economic structuring of both of these groups of tribes. In pre-colonial Moorish society, the warriors exercised territorial and political control. Their military potential enabled them to protect the tribes or groups of scholars and tributaries to a certain extent from the raids of other tribes – a service in return for which they demanded special privileges or tributes. The scholars formed the counter-pole to the warriors' power. They were considerably superior in numbers, controlled land ownership beyond the spiritual sphere and were the backbone of the Moorish pastoral and trading economy (cf. Bonte 1988: 175).

Although the differentiation into warriors and scholars describes more or less pronounced orientations of the tribal groups rather than a categorical contrast (there are a number of tribes which can be classified as belonging to both groups, as well as cases of status change), these differences are essential for an understanding of the development of different contexts of slavery in Moorish society. The warriors were far less involved in productive activities, which persistently influenced the spectrum of jobs that were delegated to slaves. Apart from the tasks of herding and watering livestock, slaves were also in great demand as foot soldiers in conflicts and as confidants of their masters. A comparable advancement to influential positions was more difficult for the slaves of the scholars. For their masters, the economic profit to be derived from the unfree labour was clearly the main concern. At the same time, the symbolic distance between scholars and slaves was more profound than between warriors and slaves. To this day it is accepted only with great difficulty by a large number of *bidhân* that *sûdân*, i.e. slaves, and manumitted slaves (*harâtîn*), can be leaders of prayers. Until a few years ago, they were denied access to prayer in a big mosque in the centre of the capital of Nouakchott. Only strong protests by *sûdân* made the Imams of the mosque finally give way (interview with Mahmoud, *hartâni*, in Brhane 2000: 230).

The rise of a slave to spiritual greatness and leadership in view of these circumstances required a miracle – and these are legendary. Mohammed Khairat was accused by his master of having secretly milked a camel while herding and therefore of having stolen his master's milk. The slave defended himself against this accusation by having the camel foal speak and tell the master that it suckled the milk from his mother. While the holiness of the slave was thus proved, in the legend woven around Mohammed Khairat, the circumstances of his rise to the status of free person remain closely linked to the ideology of the masters. After all, Mohammed Khairat's special abilities resulted from his unlawful enslavement, for while his mother was an old slave, his father was a *Shurfa* (a descendant of the Prophet) who passed this status on to his son (cf. Brhane 1997: 127ff.).

Another obstacle to the social advancement of slaves is the fact that mystically-based holiness is only one cornerstone of the self-conception of the Moorish scholar (*zwâya*). Although it is of central significance, mysticism is supplemented by knowledge of Islam and of the sciences based upon it, obtained and certified during long years of study. For social outsiders like slaves, access to this source of complementary symbolic capital, controlled by a comparatively small circle of *zwâya*, had to remain closed (cf. El Hamel 1999: 77f., 81; Clark 1998: 105f.).[10] It was not until recent decades that individual *sûdân* succeeded in obtaining access to the traditional Koranic education. Unlike other Islamic societies, for instance Morocco (cf. Ennaji 1994: 52), there are no known cases of slaves becoming respected Islamic scholars in the Moorish cultural area. While in some cases slaves of *zwâya* managed whole lines of business in place of their masters and were able, in this context, to gain a certain measure of respect (cf. McDougall 1985b: 111), their possible entry into the central identity-creating domain of the scholars seems to have been placed under an absolute taboo.[11]

The highlighted differences show that not only were the options for gaining more respect from their masters distributed unequally among slaves of warriors and slaves of scholars, but that the interest of the two leading social groups in unfree labour was led by different rationales. Within the narrow limits set on the accumulation of wealth in a pastoral-nomadic society, the use of slaves was one possibility for the scholars to have a larger number of workers at their disposal beyond those of their own household and to diversify productive activities into different sectors. Apart from herding the livestock, slaves could cultivate date palms and gardens in the oases, plant millet, collect gum arabic and perform work in the caravan trade. This way, they contributed considerably to the wealth of their masters. Although the slaves frequently replaced or at least relieved members of their masters' family with their work, observations of scholars' slaves being treated worse than slaves of the warriors indicate that the scholars were much more apt to exploit unfree labour than were the warriors (cf. Caillié 1830: 102; Ould Ahmed 1983: 29).[12]

These different motivational situations of warriors and scholars can be observed even today. It is less common, for example, for former slaves of scholars to have had the status of *hâratîn* for generations, compared to the former slaves of warriors. Correspondingly, more formal liberations of slaves have taken place in the scholars' milieu in recent times. While some of these releases take place without services required in return, there are still a considerable number of cases where slaves commit themselves to certain payments or work. Differences also manifest themselves in today's relations between scholars on the one hand and warriors on the other hand, and individual *harâtîn* and slaves. While among the scholars it is customary for the free to lease their land to former slaves or other members of this group on fixed, lease-like terms (usually in return for half the harvest), no such arrangements can be found among wealthy land owners of warrior status. Instead, services are rendered by the land users to the land owners in a seemingly voluntary fashion, for instance by helping to bring in the harvest. Without questioning the patron's position of power, the clients from among the *sûdân* have the opportunity to take part in the legal appropriation of land much like free persons in a complementary relationship, i.e. freely considering what would constitute an adequate service in return, and thus demonstrating their ability to act honourably and in a socially appropriate manner (cf. Ruf 1999: 120ff., 250f.).

The Feminity of Enslavement

Apart from the different practices of slavery among warriors and scholars, it was gender which decisively shaped the experience of enslavement in Moorish society. As with other slave-holding societies in Africa, a preference for female slaves can be discerned from the available sources in the case of Moorish society. In the whole of West Africa, as well as north of the Sahara, they were traded at usually much higher prices and were in greater demand than male slaves, who in turn were the preferred goods of transatlantic slave traders. While these complementary gender preferences of the slave-holders on the African and American continents stimulated the dynamics of slave hunting and the slave trade in Africa, these opposing orientations of the two practices of slavery raise the question of the different natures of these types of slavery. The plantations in the south of the USA in particular have become a symbol for a kind of slavery in which the rational, immediate exploitation of human labour was wickedly combined with the logic of profit maximization in the context of a production for the world market. Faithful to their patriarchal views, according to which men are most suited to hard, manual work, the plantation owners of the New World sought strong young men as slave labourers (cf. Lovejoy 1989: 381ff.).[13]

The reasons given for the structure of demand for female and male slaves on the African continent are less conclusive. In many societies these coincide with a social ideology wherein women, and not men, bear the main burden of everyday work, particularly in agriculture (cf. Lachenmann 1992: 76f.). Women therefore were not *per se* considered weaker and less fit for hard work than men, but on the contrary, were seen as more experienced workers in many areas. Nevertheless, it remains doubtful whether higher productivity can generally be attributed to female slaves than to male ones, as Meillassoux (1986) suggests, nor is it clear whether the strong demand for them was primarily motivated by this criterion, while other aspects, like the exploitation of their sexuality and of the reproductive capacities of slaves, were of no importance (cf. Klein 1983). The different proportion of women and men among slaves in various African societies gives a clue to another rationale. The more the use of slaves was concentrated on production, the more the proportion of women among the slave population became equal to that of men (cf. Cooper 1977: 221f.; Hanson 1990: 212).

While more precise data on the number of slaves purchased by Moorish nomads as well as on the gender proportions within these groups is unobtainable for the pre-colonial era, the census data from the 'Subdivision Moudjéria' of 1950, arranged according to gender and age, provides an instructive picture of the composition of the enslaved and the manumitted population: 58 per cent of those classified as 'black Moors', i.e. *sûdân*, were women.[14] This result is even more amazing as it describes the situation almost fifty years after the beginning of French colonization of the region and therefore towards the end of the slave trade.[15] The uneven distribution according to gender can therefore – assuming a biological reproduction of the slave population – be attributed only to a small extent to the Moorish masters' preference for the purchase of female slaves. Rather, this result points to an already manifest migration of men slaves and *harâtîn* away from the rural area. Here they made use of an opportunity to escape from their dependence, which was obviously only seldom available to female slaves.[16] The fact that women had to overcome much greater difficulties than men in freeing themselves from slavery is also confirmed by an analysis of the statuses of the heads of households in ten villages of the Achram-Diouk region in central Mauritania conducted in 1996: among those still called slaves, the proportion of women amounts to 68 per cent, while the gender ratio in other social groups is largely balanced.

One reason for the reluctance of masters to grant female slaves their freedom or let them pay for it can be located in the constitution of Moorish slavery. While among the free, descent and thus status membership is structured in patrilineal fashion, this does not apply to slaves. Here, status is decided by 'the womb', i.e. the child of a slave also becomes a slave. This is different again in relationships between white Moors and female slaves, where children take on the status of their fathers. However, this only applies unreservedly to the issue of a marriage between a white Moor and a female slave. In the case of a concubinage or a secret relationship, the children obtained their father's status only if he recognized them as legitimate. Contrary to concubinage, marriage – and thus the release – of female slaves by white Moors was quite a common practice in Moorish society and therefore provided an important opportunity for social advancement available to female slaves (a number of famous personalities, such as for example the last officially recognized emir of Tagant, were sons of slaves).

This partial permeability of the borderline between free and enslaved does not call into question the difference marked by it and considered fundamental. Rather, the integration of female slaves into the kinship system of their masters demonstrates the special significance of the patrilinear compared with matrilineal filiation. The practice of marriage between white Moors and female slaves not only provides the slaves with an opportunity for social advancement, but at the same time affects the balance of power between genders among the *bidhân* to the women's disadvantage.[17] While it is precisely the lack of their own social attributes that made the integration of female slaves into the kinship system of the *bidhân* possible, this societal deprivation caused male slaves to be excluded from any paternity in a social sense. Marriages between slaves are possible according to Islamic law and were practised in some cases in Moorish society, but the arrangements concerning the principles of descent among slaves remained untouched by this; after all, this would have affected the property rights of the masters over the children of their own female slaves. The situation for *harâtîn* was similar. Although they had obtained the status of free persons, they could only seldom become fathers according to the model of white Moorish men. This could only be done if their wives had the same status as they did, i.e. if they were *hartâni-yya*. Owing to the preferences of the masters already described, however, this was rarely the case. But if those men married a female slave, they, unlike white Moors, seldom had enough possessions to buy their wife's freedom, and as a consequence, the woman – together with her children – remained the property of her master or mistress.[18]

Maintaining slave status for women and liberating men with comparative generosity was not a contradiction in terms, but for the Moorish slave-holders indeed complemented each other advantageously. Liberating the men released the masters from their obligations regarding the maintenance of these slaves, and retaining slave status for women not only secured the rights of the masters to their person and labour, but also to their descendants. After all, the children of female slaves became the last source of new slaves after the end of the slave trade. Against this background, it is hardly surprising that the gradual '*hartâni*fication' of the Wadi Tidjikja, by way of contractual liberations which turned slaves into dependent tenants, is only stated for the male unfree part of the population (cf. Ould Khalifa 1991: 282ff.). Unlike male slaves, who achieved social advancement by increasing the distance between them and their masters, female slaves pursuing similar goals had very few options besides tying themselves more closely to their masters. This paradox is a basic characteristic of Moorish slavery and is to be analysed in the following.

The Differential Effect of Desocialization

By being denied integration into kinship relations, men and women slaves experience a profound desocialization. Not only were they snatched from their home and their family by enslavement, but they were also unable to establish new, fully adequate kinship relations in the slave-holding society: this is characteristic of the situation of Moorish slaves, as it is for their fellow sufferers in other societies.[19] This experience of social deprivation is even more serious in societies in which kinship relations are an essential means of localizing the individual in societal and political space, or in which social and political relations are interpreted mainly as articulations of kinship. It is in this sense that slaves in Moorish society experienced their 'social death' (Patterson 1982) and became permanent 'social outsiders' (Finley 1968: 308).

No matter how great the gulf between the free and the enslaved was, the different ideological constructs could never conceal the fact that difference and equality in this context are inseparably linked. In order to be able to derive any profit at all from his slave, the master must have recourse to his human characteristics. There is no work without the slave making use of his intelligence, no communication between slave and master without the establishment of a common language, no power of one over the other without the mediating force of an ideology which legitimizes inequality.

Thus the everyday life of slaves and masters presents itself as one full of contradictions. Far from being spatially separated by master house and slave hut, they live in the same camp, if not in the same tent in immediate contact and in each other's constant presence; the differentiation between slave and master had therefore to be (re-)produced continually. Areas of conflict developed, when the production of the symbolic difference between masters and slaves all too obviously contradicted the fundamental structures of the society of the free Moors. So the maintenance of a largely gender-segregated structuring of space, for instance, collided with a practice of slavery which ignored sexuality and with it the sociability of the slaves.

The perception of the tent as the domain of the free women and of the world beyond these borders as the living space of the freemen during the day, i.e. the constituting of spaces mutually exclusively characterized as masculine and feminine, reflects the localization of activities considered gender-specific in Moorish society. According to this, women mostly take on activities to be performed in the tent or at least close to it. They process wool and milk, cook, gather firewood and under certain circumstances they fetch water too. Men, by contrast, are above all supposed to take care of livestock, and attend to things like trade and warfare, and possibly agricultural work.

Yet the division of tasks between men and women is by no means absolute. If, for example, the fetching of water conflicts with another, more important task of women due to the great amount of time needed to walk to a faraway watering place, then it is done by men.[20] Thus, the watering place cannot clearly be defined as a locality of women's or men's work. This means that the borders between spaces influenced by gender are not inflexible, but vary according to specific circumstances. A well can therefore appear as part of the camp and thus be of the inner and intimate sphere occupied by women, as well as a place outside these borders, frequented by men as part of their responsibilities. Conversely, there are male activities which are not only localized in the camp, but directly inside the tent. The administration of the emirs, for instance, apart from extensive travelling and possibly military actions, also included a representative presence in their own camps. In particular, the work of the scholars required them to stay in the tent so as to be protected from wind and sun. While most members of this profession limited their intellectual activity to early mornings and evenings, and were able to perform pastoral tasks during the day,[21] this case shows that the gender division of labour and space did not simply transform tent and camp into places which were inaccessible for men during the day. Rather, it was essential to carry out distinctive practices in diverse localities. While women gathered in order to perform activities like the preparation of millet-couscous together, men could meet in the same camp in the tents deserted at these times without risking being held up to ridicule as an appendage to the women.[22] Analogous to this is the hospitality towards visitors. Instead of the borderline between the male and female space being between tents, in this case it runs within the tent, where the front, which is turned to the light and therefore to the public, is differentiated from the back, which is more shaded and thus protected from indiscreet gazes (cf. Caratini 1989: 111ff.).

The specific function of slaves in this context was to free their mistresses and their masters from a multitude of work obligations. Restrictions came about essentially where tasks were only reluctantly delegated to slaves because of their high degree of responsibility or low possibilities of control, for instance the herding of camels. This structuring of slave labour as mainly externally determinated and not responsible, as well as the necessity of observing the intimacy of male and female spaces, had far-reaching consequences. Male slaves could only in certain cases take on the work of free women or work in close proximity to them. Although they were not regarded as analogous to free men, their gender was taken into account in the societal construction of their work area. In spite of the frequently exercised denial of the social gender of slaves, it was taken into account if connected with their localization in the work process. The general exclusion of male slaves from the tent and camp area became necessary from the free women's point of view, since in their community and their activities they would have been exposed to the men's view. In turn the male slaves from the free men's point of view would have had a privilege, had they been granted free access to the female localities.[23]

Although male slaves were sometimes enlisted for tasks like pounding millet which was clearly women's work, usually they were spared the systematic denial of their social gender by the nature of their work. This denial of gender attributes concerned female slaves much more. They primarily worked in the camp or its surroundings and were therefore responsible mainly for activities connected to the household, yet their labour was also used for tasks beyond this framework. In their life stories, slaves repeatedly report this and emphasize that they were forced to do all kinds of work, no matter whether this was breast-feeding the babies of their mistresses and masters or herding livestock.

Because of the conflict inherent in the gender-specific structuring of slave labour, the question of which work a female or male slave had to take on became a debate essentially about the nature of the dependency relationship. The slaves' work and tasks mirrored the respect of the masters for their slaves gender and thus to which extent slaves were respected as social beings. While for male slaves it was relatively easy to occupy fields of work that would not be dishonourable for free men either, and in these fields make themselves quite irreplaceable by the acquisition of special qualifications, such as the cultivation of palm groves or the herding of livestock, a comparable strategy of professionalization was well nigh impossible for female slaves. The reasons for this are on the one hand the structure of housework, including a multitude of activities requiring a comparatively low specific qualification, and on the other hand the fact that female slaves performed a large part of their work under the direct supervision of their mistresses. Unlike male slaves, who were able to evade direct control through spatial distance of their activity from their masters, female slaves achieved little autonomy in the conception and execution of their work. On the contrary, their work was alienated to a particularly high degree, because it was often determined to the smallest detail by their mistresses. The image of the slave performing her work reluctantly but being unable to articulate her own will, in the end performing it, has become a formative stereotype of the oral traditions of white, free Moors with regard to their female, but not their male slaves (cf. Tauzin 1993: 71ff.).

Female slaves working under these conditions reproduced their difference from the free women. This was due to the women slaves being compelled to follow the meticulous instructions of their mistresses and to free the latter from almost any physical activity. No matter how close the slaves got to their mistresses while working, the symbolic distance between free and enslaved women remained due to the physical separation of work into its intellectual and its practical component, even if the slaves were spared from performing typically male tasks. While male slaves were able to present themselves as equal to free men in certain fields and to receive acknowledgement for this, female slaves experienced their work as a manifestation of their dissimilarity and thus inferiority to free women. However, a female slave could gain recognition as a social person and therefore recognition of her femininity in a different field.

The close contact between mistress and female slave was not limited to the immediate reproduction of the symbolism of dissimilarity. Apart from the commands and endless tasks, female slaves could also establish intimacy in dealing with their mistresses. This becomes particularly obvious where female slaves performed socially relevant tasks for their mistresses. Frequently, female slaves breast-fed their masters' children, as a consequence of which relations of milk-kinship developed between female slave and free child corresponding to those which existed among the free regarding extent and social consequences (free contact with the other sex and marriage ban analogous to blood-related siblings). With regard to their own children, they were essentially only considered biological mothers and in their social function were replaced to a great extent by their masters, whereas female slaves were connected to the free children they had fed by social ties. Furthermore, the milk-kinship not only established relations between 'milk-mother' and 'milk-child', but made those free and slave children fed at the same breast milk-brothers and milk-sisters as well. The integration of female slaves in social relationships with their masters was thus extended to the next generation, where the shared experience of the intimacy of milk-kinship formed a peculiar amalgam with the perception of the opposing roles of master and slave.

The sexuality of the female slaves, however, was not only a way of producing intimacy with their mistress. It could also be used to the contrary to court the favour of free men in direct competition with the free women. On the one hand, female slaves were victims of sexual violence and exploitation by free men; on the other hand, however, they found a comparatively safe option for social advancement in Moorish society through a relationship with, and particularly in a marriage to, a free man. Marriages of this kind required the female slave to be formally manumitted, and thus to receive a status she could not lose even in the event of a future divorce. Children resulting from these marriages took on their father's status and could assert this in practice in most cases – in spite of a number of ambivalences resulting from their mother's descent. Occasionally, this form of descent was said to have specific qualities: children of free men and former female slaves inherited either the good qualities of both parents combined (physical strength and intellect), or their negative aspects.

These fundamentally different options for achieving improved social integration available to female and male slaves in the slave-holding society resulted in diverse strategies in pursuit of their respective interests. Female slaves looked to the innermost level of Moorish society, the nuclear family, whereas in striving for greater autonomy male slaves moved at the peripheries of their masters' sphere of influence. The creation of long-term relationships between male and female slaves was impeded by this power relation and the spatial segregation resulting from it. The limited mobility granted to female slaves by their mistresses and masters forced the male slaves to settle with them, if they wanted to live in the same place as their spouse. If their pastoral-nomadic masters gave up living in the vicinity, for instance in the same camp, this usually meant separation for the slave couple. The essential point of reference of social integration for the female as well as for the male slave remained the hierarchical relationship to the family of their mistress or master, and not their respective partner. If necessary, a certain amount of security and support could be expected from the masters rather than from an equally poor partner (cf. Oxby 1978: 193ff.).[24]

Support for the economic development of West Africa's French colonies starting after World War II led to the increased availability of wage labour and, particularly for male slaves and manumitted slaves, this opened up options for increased economic independence. This reduced the dependence of the *sûdân* on their former masters. As they were able to live largely autonomously, and to meet the costs of living for their families through their income from migration and wage labour, these slaves began to accept less and less situations in which they had to act as appendages to the families of their wives' masters. Female slaves on the other hand, of whom only a few were able to effectively benefit from these options of social acknowledgement by the white Moors, likewise tried to reduce their services to their mistresses and masters. Usually they succeeded in a gradual way, thereby avoiding open confrontation. So, for instance, their presence in their masters' household could be limited to certain seasons, when the mistresses had a particular need for domestic labour. Another possibility was to send their daughters as their representatives to the masters and thus be free themselves to stay with their own family.

The Uniting Force of Difference

The structures and practices described here show how the differentiation of female and male slaves and their descendants on the one hand, and free born members of Moorish society on the other hand, was produced and maintained. This difference, however, is by no means absolute, but rather strangely ambivalent. The opposing features of slave labour show this paradox clearly. They are based equally on the dehumanization and desocialization of slaves and on the renunciation of their human capacities, which form the basis for labour. Besides the difference between 'commanding' and 'obeying', the relation between master and slave also includes an element of similarity. The practice of delegating work to the slave is necessarily linked to the establishment of a communicative structure connecting slave and master, and is based on shared social and human capacities. The development not only of a specific division of labour between slaves and masters, but also of forms of labour typical of masters and slaves can be regarded as yet another means of emphasizing a fundamental difference between slave and master. The greater the dissimilarities between the models of the working capacities of slaves and masters – for instance, by attributing intellectual and controlling faculties to the master and physical abilities to the slave – the more obscured the balance of power, on which this difference was based, became.[25]

A comparable constellation was formed by the social identifications of slaves and masters. Because the ideology of the masters developed the conception of their own self as a positive counter-image to the supposed character of the slaves, the frameworks constituting the positions of slave and master become entangled. The localization of these two poles in a social hierarchy is contradictory to the framework of fundamental and irreconcilable difference stated at the beginning. It is this tension-charged relationship – in the ideology of slavery as well as in its practice – which creates interfaces and contacts, making possible forms of identification which exceed the postulated borders of personal freedom and enslavement. How this difference between the inclusion and exclusion of slaves is expressed in detail will be clarified in the following.

The Dynamics of the Borderline 'Free/Enslaved'

Slavery originates in an act of violence. Only through their violent enslavement do human beings become objects to be sold and purchased in a seemingly legitimate way which is analogous to other goods in slave trade. Meillassoux (1986: 68ff.) pointed out that an essential part of the production of slaves is the reinforcement of depersonalization and desocialization connected to the violent separation of individuals from their social and family relations. The transport of the slaves to frequently far away destinations created a spatial distance impeding their escape and return. At the same time, the structure of the trade, into which numerous middlemen were usually integrated, caused an effective erasure of the knowledge of local origin and individual features of the slaves still manifest at the beginning of the chain of transaction. This process of depersonalization of the slaves, who could not speak for themselves, furthered the initial enslavement and was essential in transforming the slaves into a faceless article and thus making them easily consumable goods.[26]

Thus embodying the stranger, the difference between the free and the slaves takes the shape of a borderline between the inside and the outside of society. Because of the presence of the slaves, the foreign Other no longer only exists on the outer interface of society and its social surroundings, but can be experienced in the very centre of it. As a result of this, a special dynamic of identification and differentiation develops (James 1988: 133f.; Barth 1969a). The description of the features of the slaves' foreignness promotes the homogenizing of their own group, i.e. the society of the masters. Only through the immediate opposition of 'free' and 'unfree' do these attributes of personal status obtain their full meaning. By defining mutually exclusive attributes of the slaves and the free, the enslaving society enters a process of profound transformation. Analogous to the domestication of the slaves, the masters go through a process of socialization into their role. The distance between master and slave is not only produced by the disparagement of the slave, but also by the raising of the master. This constant process of self-portraying and self-disciplining occasionally opens up space to allow slaves the gradual approach to the social ideal of the free. Positive definitions of the master's identity allow slaves to develop practices which purposefully transgress the border between 'free' and 'unfree' and in addition to demonstrate the human identity of slave and master while respecting their social differences.

A succinct example for such a social practice of slaves is their singing, which can most closely be compared to gospels. Because they were largely excluded from religious practices by their masters, and because their own religiousness was not recognized (although the instruction of their slaves in religion was one of the duties imposed on the slave-holders by Islam), the slaves of Mauritania developed a specific form of music: the *meddh*. This *sprechgesang* (form of chanting), accompanied by a big drum, praised the Prophet. The production of the *meddh* is profoundly different from classical Moorish music. Forming a separate endogamous group in Moorish society,[27] the *iggâwan* (griots) essentially produce a modal music, dominated by the harp (*ârdîn*) and the lute (*tidinît*), and sometimes accompanied by singing and drumming. The *meddh* on the other hand, mainly sung by women, consists exclusively of song which alternates between leading voice and choir, as well as the rhythm of the drum and the clapping of the audience. While dancing is not part in classical Moorish music and is at best indicated while sitting by movement of arms and legs, the very presentation of *meddh* is inconceivable without accompanying dance. In the course of the performance, usually lasting for hours late into the night and early morning, this dance takes on ecstatic features (cf. Ould Mohand 1993; Guignard 1975).[28]

The essential features of the *meddh* and of traditional Moorish music as described here show their contrasting nature, in spite of certain mutual influences. The two different types of Moorish music reflect the difference of the norms regulating the conduct of *sûdân* and *bidhân*. While the music of the *sûdân* is directly connected to expressive dance leading to trance and therefore to a loss of self-control, the ideal of Moorish socialization demands demonstrative control of emotions, among other things by exercising restraint in abandoning oneself to music. At the same time, the music of the *sûdân* breaks the pattern of a stereotypical reproduction of cultural difference. By taking up a topic constitutive of the society of the masters – praising the Prophet – and combining it with imported traditions of rhythm and song, the *meddh* creates a specific amalgam superior even to classical Moorish music in one respect. Orthodox supporters of the Malikite school of Islam, which is widespread in Mauritania, disapprove of the stringed instruments used by the *iggawân* and categorize them as *harâm*. The *meddh* is classified as belonging to the pure, however, and does not belong to the category of 'music'. By virtue of its content and in spite of being a means of entertainment for the *sûdân*, it is regarded as particularly worthy by orthodox supporters of Islam. The religious practices of the free and the unfree still differ, but in this perspective they do not appear to relate to each other hierarchically, but rather complementarily. The hierarchy of slaves and former slaves and masters is at certain points replaced by a horizontal social structure which gives the impression of equality within difference.

This reversal of the valuation of one aspect of slave culture and master culture shows that the identification of the *sûdân* with their former masters' society or with features of their identity could well become effective. Comparable to the gospel songs of American slaves, the development of a separate form of musical entertainment would hardly have been possible without borrowing from the culture of the masters. Masters could hardly suppress *sûdân* music because of its religious significance. If the *sûdân* still had to be discriminated against due to their ignorance of the essential duties of a believer, for which ultimately their masters were to blame, the custom of the *meddh* nevertheless foregrounded their professing Islam and thus their aspirations towards equality with the *bidhân*. The gradual weakening of the immediate balance of power between master and slave during the past decades has finally resulted in slaves and former slaves being able to realize these claims more and more effectively, and in the specific religious value of their cultural practices being recognized even by orthodox Islamic scholars.

While representatives of the group of the masters stress the cultural common grounds of slaves and former slaves in changed socio-economic surroundings, the *meddh* became a medium for the presentation of difference for those who began to fight openly against the continuous social and economic discrimination. For political agitation and the creation of a collective identity of slaves and former slaves, the *meddh* was evoked as part of the authentic cultural tradition of this group. The form and presentation remained unchanged, but the texts were replaced by ones which, by following Mao's little red book in spirit and content, clearly indicated what kind of break the authors anticipated between former masters and slaves (cf. Brhane 1997: 225).

Incorporation and Integration

In view of the often massive desocialization and humiliation experienced by the *sûdân*, i.e. slaves as well as manumitted slaves (*harâtîn*), in Moorish society, which continues to this day in the form of social and economic discrimination, the question of the motivation for their strong identification with the society of their masters arises. In contrast to the point of view held by Miers and Kopytoff

(1977), the practices of slavery in Mauritania and the long lasting disputes concerning its abolishment prove that there is virtually no organic integration of slaves into the society of their masters. The different forms of dependency ensuing from slavery and kinship relations do not constitute a continuum. Rather, the successes achieved by slaves on their way to a stronger integration into the community of the free are rooted essentially in their own ability to integrate. In effect, the strategies of the slaves are based on building bridges between the social worlds, which make sustainable social connections between the free and enslaved possible. The reactions of the masters and mistresses to these efforts were ambivalent. Improvements for the slaves could be attained in a number of cases. However, achievement as enhanced freedom of action and respectful treatment of slaves often remained tied to conditions that could easily be cancelled. If a slave-holder died, his heirs became the owners of his slaves, could deal with them at their own discretion and were not bound by the practices of their predecessor (a fact which could work to the benefit as well as the disadvantage of the slaves concerned). For the slave-holders who felt obligated to their slaves, this situation created a problem. Their own descendants' interest in the possession of as many slaves as possible contradicted their own obligation towards their slaves.

Until today conflicts are sparked off at this point. Slaves present themselves as *harâtîn*, citing verbal promises of manumission which their master is said to have given prior to his death, while the descendants of the slave-owners deny such components of their legacy. Several slave-holders resorted to a legal trick in order to avoid the obvious dilemma. They declared their slaves *hubs*, i.e. they transferred their slaves to a kind of foundation, the components of which were indivisible and could not be sold by the joint heirs. As a result of this, slave communities or families could no longer be shared out between individual heirs as was custom in accordance with the division of inheritance practised in Islamic law.

The possibility for slaves to be officially manumitted by their masters and thus to achieve the status of a *harâtîn* can be considered the strongest argument for the possibility of real integration of slaves into Moorish society. Indeed, the Koran recommends the manumission of slaves and links this act to advantages for the slave-holders, who in this way can obtain absolution from their sins as well as generally demonstrate their charitableness (cf. Lewis 1990: 6). In spite of these incentives, the number of manumitted slaves remained minimal until the beginning of the twentieth century, when the French colonization of Mauritania started. Around 1910, the proportion of *harâtîn* among the dependent population in the region of the Adrar was approximately 1 to 2 per cent; in the 1950s, however, it had increased to 50 per cent (McDougall 1988: 378, Note 26). Apart from the chances of being manumitted, which improved drastically only in the twentieth century and from which men can still benefit much more easily than women, to become *harâtîn* by no means meant obtaining a status comparable to that of the free born. Although the *harâtîn* had rights and duties analogous to their former masters' (participation in collective payments of the tribes, right to property and family), they remained socially downgraded. As former slaves they could not trace their descent back to tribe members, but only to slavery.

It is this ambivalence of the *harâtîn* status which has made the term the focus of dispute about the place of former slaves in Moorish society. *Harâtîn* is today commonly used as a euphemism for all dependent classes (no matter whether these were formally manumitted or not) and thus the emphasis is on the fact that they used to be slaves. Conversely, there are numerous discourses from among the *harâtîn* which deny any direct connection of this status to pre-ceding enslavement, and instead lay claim to dependent but free ancestors. In view of the existence of comparatively independent groups who are also called *harâtîn*, several pieces of evidence indicate that such assertions have a realistic core to them (cf. Ba 1932: 118f., Note 1). Therefore, there is reason to assume that the term *harâtîn* has not always denoted 'manumitted slave' as clearly as has been propagated in recent times (cf. Ould Hamidoun 1952: 49), but that this is a result of the discursive forms of self-description and description by others of masters and slaves.[29] The increasing tendency for a dichotomous description of Moorish society as regards black and white is not least contradicted by the *harâtîn*, who by their own manumission or their descent from *harâtîn* assert a difference between themselves and the slaves. This protest against this form of levelling social hierarchy emphasizes that the borderline between the free and the unfree still exists between slaves and *harâtîn*, and thus not between *bidhân* and *sûdân*. The inflationary use of the term *harâtîn* and its being claimed by formally non-manumitted slaves ultimately dilutes the social prestige so often laboriously gained – and to this day indeed often bought – by 'real' *harâtîn*.[30]

Conclusion

The process of the social integration of former slaves and masters in Moorish society is characterized by profound ambivalences to the present day. On the one hand, the *sûdân* are becoming a part of the society of their former masters, i.e. the *bidhân*; on the other hand a number of separating and usually discriminatory social and economic features continue to exist. In this respect, the ideology of the masters, according to which the slaves are not equal members of Moorish society but appear in it merely as incorporated strangers, seems to remain undisputed. Added to the emphasis on the foreignness between slave and master, however, is the factor of the gradual cultural assimilation of the slaves. The balance of these two tendencies has undergone decisive change during the twentieth century. While slaves in past centuries were indeed often 'strangers' in the first generation due to a high mortality rate and the continuous import of new slaves, this defi-nitely changed after the end of the slave trade. The growing assimilation, to which there was no alternative for the majority of the slaves, promoted the change of the fragile balance of difference and identity between slaves and masters. Because of the increasing cultural competencies of the slaves, of the gradual formation of slave communities, and most of all the growing economic autonomy of many slaves, the fields of articulation of the slave/master relation shifted. Emancipatory discourses became widespread and questioned the subordination of the *sûdân* in the hierarchy of Moorish society. If, in spite of harshest criticism of the master -mentality and discrimination, the majority of these discourses do not propagate a fundamental rejection of the society of the masters, this is on the one hand the result of a manifest assimilation of the former slaves. On the other hand, even decades after Mauritanian independence, there are no workable alternative patterns of identification. The recollection of roots of their own, i.e. the descent from several sub-Saharan ethnic groups, propagated by some *sûdân*, has little attraction. The members of the different black African ethnic groups settling in Mauritania are still discriminated against by the state apparatus, which is dominated by the Moors. Furthermore, slavery was not only common among the Moors, but also in nearly all other ethnic groups of the region. The stigmatization of slaves, not only of one's own society but also those of others, is therefore a general phenomenon and not one restricted to a single ethnic group. In view of these factors, the poor response by the bulk of *sûdân* striving for an immediate improvement of their social and economic situation to discourses propagating ethnic authenticity is not very surprising. What remains is the continuation of the dispute as to the place of the *sûdân* in Moorish society. This is about handling features of identity and difference creatively and flexibly in changing contexts. Through these 'pluritactical identifications' (cf. Schlee and Werner 1996: 11ff.), it is possible to use the contradictions of Moorish society – in the form of the opposition of inclusion and exclusion of the ex-slaves – productively.

Urs Peter Ruf studied sociology at the University of Bielefeld where he focused on methods of empirical analysis and social change in modern Mauritanian society. His PhD thesis, entitled 'Ending Slavery' (1999), is a detailed study of past and present dependency among the strata of Moorish society. Currently, he works as IT consultant at Technologieberatungsstelle (TBS NRW e.V.) for work councils and enterprises as well as trade unions and ministries on management systems, data protection, demographic change and flexible working hours. His publications include 'Unternehmen in NRW werden Demografie-Aktiv', in *Qualitätssicherung in der Demografieberatung* (Bundesanstalt für Arbeitsschutz und Arbeitsmedizin, Bertelsmann Verlag, 2011), 'Den demografischen Wandel gestalten: Vom Werkzeugkasten zur betriebsindividuellen Lösung' (co-author), in *Corporate Responsibility 2013: Demographischer Wandel – Zukunft verantwortungsvoll gestalten* (AmCham Germany and F.A.Z.-Institute, Frankfurt am Main).

Notes

1. Paradigmatic of this type of argumentation is the way in which Anti-Slavery International presents itself (http://www.antislavery.org/english/). Although it addresses the question of the persistence of slavery (the Anti-Slavery Award 1988 went to the Mauritanian human rights activist Professor Cheikh Saad Bouh Kamara; also cf. Mercer 1982), the main focus of its work today is 'modern slavery': child labour, interest serfdom, sexual exploitation of children and trade in women.

2. *Slave Hunters in Sudan*, a film by Stefan Schaaf, *German Südwestfunk*, 1988. All recent popular publications on this issue appear to be based on one single source: Christian Solidarity International (CSI), recently renamed Christian Solidarity Worldwide (cf. http://www.csw.org.uk/home.htm). Initial information about the revitalization of personal dependency relationships in Sudan, however, came out of the country itself and presented the problem in a much more subtly differentiated manner (cf. De Waal 1997).

3. This restriction does not apply to the USA, where a distinction between Black Africans as victims and 'Arabs' as culprits is sufficient to evoke reminiscences of the history of slavery in their own country. Nevertheless, the reactions on the part of the African Americans are by no means consistently negative, since within the black section of the population there are Christians, Muslims and Jews and correspondingly different affinities for countries like Sudan and Mauritania (cf. Gregory 1996).

4. Mr Saugnier regained his freedom after one of his successive owners brought him to Goulimine (Southern Morocco), where there was an intermediary who identified ship-wrecked persons on behalf of the French consul and negotiated for their freedom (cf. Barbier 1984: 30).

5. Ibn Hawqal, who in 947–951 travelled the Maghrib, reports the significant trade with slaves (mainly girls and women) from Sudan (cf. Ibn Hawqal in Levtzion and Hopkins 1981: 47). Al-Bakri (who died in 1094) describes the desired qualities of the women slaves of Awdaghust (then the most important commercial centre on the southern edge of the Western Sahara, whose economic activities were closely connected to those of the nomadic inhabitants of the region), and notes that some inhabitants of the city owned thousands of slaves (cf. Al-Bakri Hawqal in Levtzion and Hopkins 1981: 68). It can therefore be assumed that the intensive oasis farming in Awdaghust was essentially based on the work of slaves imported from the Sudan (cf. McDougall 1985a: 12).

6. The territorial expansion of the pastoral nomads of the Sahara far into agriculturally cultivated areas of the savannah was particularly distinctive in the case of the Tuareg. A description of their rule from the point of view of the subjugated can be found in Sardan (1976). Among the Moors, there was a comparable difference in power especially between the emirate of Trarza and the region of the Waalo in modern Senegal, as well as between the region of the Brakna emirate and adjoining areas to the South (Barry 1972: 199; Taylor 1996: 47ff.).

7. Commandant de Cercle du Hodh, I. Bastouil, Aioun el Atrouss, 25 May 1959: *Étude sur la population noire dans la subdivision d'Aioun el Atrouss*: 2, document of the Archives Nationales de Mauritanie (no reference number), kindly put at my disposal by Meskerem Brhane.

8. Data from *Rapport politique, année 1950, Tableau de population, TOM de la Mauritanie, Cercle du Tagant, Subdivision de Moudjéria*; this document was kindly put at my disposal by Roger Botte and recorded in Ruf (1999: 118).

9. The meaning of 'white' and 'black' contained in the terms *bidhân* and *sûdân* is a social feature of distinction. Numerous Moors of noble descent have very dark skin, whereas certain members of the *sûdân* are of light colour.

10. Unlike in the northern African societies influenced by urban culture, the training in mystic practices of Islam in the form of Sufism and the training in diverse disciplines of Islam were not separated in the learned circles of Moorish society, but were all equally taught in the Koran schools (cf. El Hamel 1999: 79f.).

11. The élite of the *zwâya* was by no means generally beyond the reach of social climbers. It was conditional, however, as the case of the famous Shaikh Siddiya al-Kabîr proves, on one's reputation as a scholar and as a mystic developing equally (cf. Ould Cheikh 1991).

12. Hamès (1979) was the first to formulate the thesis that the import of slaves helped to compensate for the latent lack of workers within pastoral-nomadic society, and that certain parts within the scholars strata were able to profit from this development following the growth in trade with gum arabic (eighteenth-nineteenth century) and further intensified the hierarchical structuring of society.

13. This trend increased during the nineteenth century, when the slave trade was gradually brought to an end by means of politics, the supply of slaves dwindled and thus immediate cost-benefit calculations gained importance in the purchase of slaves (cf. Lovejoy 1989: 383).

14. Data from *Rapport politique, année 1950, Tableau de population, TOM de la Mauritanie, Cercle du Tagant, Subdivision de Moudjéria*; this document was kindly put at my disposal by Roger Botte and recorded in Ruf (1999: 128).

15. Unlike in other parts of West Africa, where slavery was for a long time officially tolerated by the French colonial authorities, in Mauritania measures to stop slave raids and organized slave trade were comparatively effective (cf. Roberts 1988).

16. For female slaves, escaping usually meant leaving at least some of their children with their masters. Cases of slaves demanding to have their children handed over by their former masters keep Mauritanian courts occupied to this day, and the outcome is often uncertain (cf. S.O.S Esclaves/Mauritania, 1999, http://www.achpr.org/communications/decision/198.97/, last accessed 24 May 2016).

17. Women have great influence in Moorish society in spite of its patriarchal structure. This female power can be seen as originating in the special position of women in nomadic societies, where they often used to run the household on their own while the men were away, and in the former, matrilineal kinship structure in the Western Sahara (cf. Cleaveland 1995: 40ff.; Tauzin 1984).

18. Even today, masters exert a significant influence on their female slaves. I was able to personally record a case in which in the late 1980s masters forbade a slave to follow her husband to a new place of residence with her children (cf. Ruf 1999: 47ff.).

19. Kinship relations among slaves in the south of the United States, where, unlike in Africa, the slave population reproduced themselves, were also negated by the social practices of the masters. By addressing and recording slaves exclusively by their first names, there is no way, apart from oral traditions, to reconstruct family structures (cf. Walsh 1997: 4).

20. What is decisive for the assignment of an activity according to gender in this case does not seem to be its degree of hardship, i.e. the physical strain. Rather, considerations of time management and availability are crucial in individual situations. During the 1992 drought, for instance, when donkeys used as draught animals had already died, only young women could be observed fetching water from a village well thirty metres deep.

In another village, in which there were still draught and transport animals available, the work was done by men.

21. According to Caillé's observations in the first half of the nineteenth century, lessons in the well-attended nomadic Koran schools were limited to those times of day (cf. Caillé 1830: 89). Teachers (in some cases, especially for the instruction of girls, there were also female teachers) as well as pupils were thus able to use the remainder of the day for tasks of everyday life.

22. Bourdieu (1972: 50) paradigmatically analysed the differentiation of female and male spaces and patterns of behaviour for the Kabyle society of Algeria: 'Celui qui demeure trop à la maison pendant le jour est suspect ou ridicule: c'est "l'homme de la maison", comme on dit du gêneur qui reste parmi les femmes et qui "couve á la maison comme une poule dans son nid". L'homme qui se respecte doit se donner à voir, se placer sans cesse sous le regard des autres, les affronter, faire face (*qabel*)'. ('Those, who stay at home during the day too often and for too long, arouse suspicion or make a fool of themselves: he is "the man in the house", as the trouble-maker is called, who stays among the women and "broods at home like the hen in the nest". A man who takes a pride in himself must show himself, must constantly face the looks of the others, stand up to them, face them [qabel]'.)

23. In the traditions of the Prophet Mohammed it is also reported that male slaves are excluded from the women's spaces by the commandment of seclusion. One way in which the free as well as the unfree could overcome this barrier was the establishment of a milk-kinship (cf. Conte 1991: 78f.; Ruf 1999: 83–89).

24. Support in old age by the master was by no means certain for slaves. If a slave was manumitted, which happened more frequently at an advanced age, the master was not obliged to further contribute to the material livelihood of his former slave. Some slaves covered themselves against this risk by purchasing slaves of their own, whose work was to secure their own living in old age, or, in societies practising polygamy, they tried to obtain this security by marrying a second woman (cf. Klein 1983: 80–84).

25. The stereotypes, imposed on black slaves in the context of Islamic slavery and slavery in the south of the USA are amazingly similar. In both cases, black skin colour was equated with ugliness and the slaves were said to have a foul smell, a capacity for hard physical work, and a fondness for music (cf. Brown 1993: 665f.).

26. In accordance with Islamic jurisdiction, only the enslavement of unbelievers is legitimate in a Holy War. Only these and their descendants can be held in slavery, but not persons professing Islam at the time of their enslavement (cf. Barbour and Jacobs 1985). Since this stipulation did not receive any significant attention during the slave raids in the strongly Islamized Sahelian and sub-Sahelian region, but served well to soothe the conscience of the purchasers, the erasure of the knowledge of the slaves' denomination was an essential part of their transformation into goods.

27. Like in other West African societies, the *iggawân* sang of the glory of the great warriors (*hassân*) and preserved their traditions. The scholars (*zwâya*), however, despised the *iggawân*, as both groups were active in transmitting knowledge of the past. This separation, which was never total due to the liking of most Moors for music, is currently becoming less significant, and *iggawân* are invited to accompany ceremonial events by members of the warrior and scholar class equally and partly also by former slaves and *harâtîn*.

28. There are parallels between the *meddh* of the Moorish slaves and ritual practices of several other slave communities coming from sub-Saharan Africa in Morocco, Algeria and Sudan. Here, elements of non-Islamic obsessive cults obviously mix with those of mystic

Islam and result in independent cultural practices, in which dance, ecstasy and obsession play a central role (cf. Hunwick 1992: 28f.; Makris 1996).

29. The term *harâtîn* in different societies of North Western Africa is used to refer to groups of low social esteem situated between the free and the slaves. The etymology of the word is unknown (cf. Colin 1960). A detailed study of the relation of *harâtîn* and *shurfa* in an oasis in the South of Morocco can be found in Ensel (1998).

30. In the region of the Adrar, individual *harâtîn* possess documents of manumission up to 200 years old. These persons often had responsible functions as intimates of the tribe leaders and emirs (Pierre Bonte, personal communication). It seems reasonable to assume that these persons considered the difference between themselves and slaves greater than that between themselves and a great number of free Moors. In the Achram-Diouk region I was able to record a number of cases in which slaves to this day pay considerable sums to their former masters for a formal manumission.

Chapter 3

Identification with the State and Identifications by the State

Günther Schlee

While the two preceding chapters (Pfaff-Czarnecka and Ruf) have had a focus on distinctions which have to do with caste and caste-like differences in social status and economic role, the four chapters which follow (Diallo, Grätz, Hansen and Kaiser, and Horstmann) in different ways all underline the role of the state in the field of sameness and difference. The collective identities they discuss can be distinguished as more or less closely associated with the state or even as identities which – mostly from the perspective of others – cannot or should not be integrated and become fully part of the state project. In the contribution of Hansen and Kaiser, even a defunct state, the Soviet Union, is attributed a great role for collective identification. It may therefore be appropriate to reflect on identification with the state and identifications by the state at this stage in the progress of our volume. Apart from outlining some general considerations which aim at inviting theorizing on these issues, the present chapter also somewhat widens the geographical range of our discussion. As the following chapters are on West Africa and different parts of Eurasia, the circumstance that I get my examples from Northeast Africa may serve this purpose.

Universal Citizenship Versus More or Less 'Real' Citizens

In many parts of the world, ethnic and religious criteria seem to be used to distinguish between different kinds of citizens. Some citizens are somehow more prototypical citizens, while others are discriminated against because they do not exhibit the 'right' features.

Let me take the example of the Sudan (from Schlee 2013). When, after the construction of the Aswan High Dam, Lake Nasser, straddling the border with

Egypt, was filled from 1958 to 1971, the lands of Nubian farmers were flooded. On the Sudanese side of the boundary, the farmers around Halfa were affected. They were compensated with a huge new irrigation scheme below the Khashm al Girba dam in the Eastern Sudan, where the settlement of New Halfa was founded. Farmers got compensation for their lost land and could continue to be farmers elsewhere (Sørbø 1985). In 2013, the heightening of the Blue Nile dam at Roseiris was completed. It is located 1,000 kilometres south of Lake Nasser near the border with what, since 2011, is a separate 'nation'-state, South Sudan, and also with Ethiopia. As the reservoir behind the new dam filled up, it expanded to cover a huge surface, since it is located on a flat alluvial plain. It soon became clear that many farmers would not be compensated with land elsewhere, though there might be some money and some residential plots. Large tracts of land along the new coastline have been given not to displaced farmers but to big companies. Politicians praise this 'development' because it will create employment for local people. One might ask how much employment for former farmers turned into labourers modern mechanized agriculture actually provides; but the more important question in this context of 'identification' is why it seems to be unquestioned that the Blue Nile farmers can be turned into labourers, while in the earlier case further north, near the Egyptian border, farmers were compensated with land and continued to be farmers. Maybe in the 1960s and 1970s populations were smaller than they are today, and resource competition was less fierce. But one also may suspect that the Sudanese government (if one can construct the continuity of such an institution across the many regime changes which have occurred since 1970) regards the Nubians as 'real' Sudanese (after all, most northern Sudanese are descended from Nubians, whatever else their Arabized genealogies claim), while the farmers south of Roseiris are regarded as 'Southerners', 'Ethiopians', 'Chadians' and 'West Africans', according to their various local and ethnic origins.[1] Identification might be at work here. The decision makers feel closer to the northerners. This may or not have to do with material rewards from those included in a broader identification. Government representatives may have thought that the Nubians would support them politically and may have suspected the people south of Roseiris of SPLM (Sudan People's Liberation Movement) sympathies anyhow. Differences in skin colour, real and imagined, covered by a rich terminology from 'brown' and 'red' to 'green' and 'blue', are also a significant factor for social identification in the Sudan, a country where racialism is by no means unknown.

It is perfectly consistent with common sense reasoning to expect governments (given that they do discriminate, which, from a normative perspective, of course they should not) to discriminate in favour of people who are like themselves. But it is not clear that the leading strata in state and society always identify with people who are more like themselves. They may also have an ideal of 'the people', a vision of how the people should be, which they themselves reflect only to a degree. The murderously racialist Nazi regime which criminalized many forms of interethnic marriages (then called 'interracial' because the reasoning behind it was based on [misconceived] biology rather than culture) not only tolerated but actually encouraged intermarriage with Scandinavians who were regarded as more purely 'nordic' and somehow superior breeding stock to the garden-variety Germans like themselves (or the present author).[2] From a rational choice perspective, which would assume that actors favour themselves and those close to themselves, this can be seen as a racialism which overshoots its aim: it does not favour the racialists themselves but those who exhibit the features by which they define themselves in a more extreme form.

Sudanese elites stress their Arab origins which they equate with lighter skin colour. This equation is, of course, debatable. Sudanese who are critical of it point out that the ancestry of the modern Egyptians mostly consists of *firac uun* (literally 'pharaos', meaning people who lived in Egypt already in pharaonic times). One might also point to Greeks, Romans, Turks and others to explain the phenotype of modern Egyptians. Be that as it may, from the perspective of some Sudanese, the Egyptians represent more purely the light-skinned ideal to which they themselves aspire.

In spite of intensified competition for land between Sudanese, according to the *Daily News*, Egypt, 13 December 2014, the Sudanese government offered 10,000 acres of irrigable land to small-scale Egyptian farmers. According to all other sources the area involved is 100,000 acres. The reasons given were all about unity ('Sudan and Egypt are one country') and development ('the great [farming] experience of the Egyptian farmers').[3] If one knows the everyday ethnic nationalism and racialism (indicators: role of skin colour on the marriage market, abusive language, employment opportunities) which prevail among the 'proper' Sudanese, one suspects that the hidden agenda behind this measure is upgrading the people. So this would be a case of non-acceptance of one's own group and the wish to change it into something else. The described policies proclaim and act on behalf of a collective identity to which the actors belong only to a degree and which is more purely represented by others. It is an identification which has its centre of gravity elsewhere.

Up to this point, in this volume we have mostly considered entire countries, regions or 'societies' as a mosaic of peoples or other collectivities, such as religious groups, and we have examined to what extent and in which cases difference or sameness are the forces which hold the stones of the mosaic together. In other words, a pervasive concern of our discussion has been: what keeps society together, and what are the roles of sameness and difference in achieving this effect? We can also describe the Sudan in terms of large categories and groupness. The government of the Sudan proclaims the Arabic Islamic Civilization (ath-Thaqaafat ul-ᶜArabiyyat ul-Islaamiyya) as its cultural ideal. Groups that are Arabic but not Muslim (e.g. the Copts), or Muslim but not of Arabic descent, are somehow not prototypical Sudanese. The latter – Muslims of non-Arab descent – may in fact make up the majority of the population, but many of them have managed to claim Arab genealogies and to get away with it. But from the preceding paragraphs, it has already become clear that more is involved than the cultural semantics of high-level societal segmentation. If one looks at government not as an institutional abstraction but as people, as a collection of individuals who share – and groups that share – characteristics that play a role in their ability to rule over the rest, one can see that individual interests and individual agency are involved in more than one way. While 'society' is an abstraction and does not want or do anything, the people who make up the government are indeed endowed with intentions and agency.

Identification in the Shape of Concentric Circles

People in power, like people in general, tend to act in their own individual interests. Their decisions often look as if they were based on careful cost-benefit analysis. There are, however, many ways to avoid hard thinking. One can adopt habitual solutions or accept the advice of others. Also, our intuitions and feelings tend to guide us towards decisions which are good for us. Our brains are the result of biological evolution, and they do a lot of cost-benefit calculations for us without our being aware of it. They tell us to avoid pain, to fill our bellies, to find the right mate, to look for friends who may be useful and many other things we do not need to think a lot about. Our brains are cost-benefit calculators which are permanently switched on, irrespective of whether we (i.e. our subjective selves, our lived experience, our awareness, the film in our minds) record it or not.

But only the most basic models of rational choice are strictly individual. We may also strategize for others (calculating their costs and their benefits rather than ours) for a fixed reward. In that case we are the 'agents' of 'principals'. This is by far not the only time we see the world through the eyes of others. Most of us would also consider our families' interests and perspectives when taking important decisions. Where would my children go to school if I accept this interesting job offer in another city? What would my spouse say about having to find a new job/new friends? And so on. In other words, while, in the simplest kind of rational choice model, the individual is the reference point of self-interested cost/benefit analysis, we have to widen our understanding of the reference point when we model real life. We call this widening of the self 'identification' (and have used this concept in roughly this sense all along – see Schlee 2004, 2008a). Identification occurs in degrees. It may be greater than hundred per cent, e.g. with a loved one for whom I would sacrifice myself, as he or she counts more for me than I do myself.[4] Or it may be exactly hundred per cent, the value that I set for myself. Or it may be less than hundred per cent for people whom I include in my cost/benefit calculations but who would lose out if their interest contradicts mine, or who I allow to share my gains but not on equal terms. Typically these wider forms of identification are arranged like concentric circles, with family being close; clan, tribe, neighbourhood and friends being not quite so close; church and nation being yet further out; and humankind being somewhat vague on the horizon.[5] This can, of course, vary from individual to individual, nation being more important for a nationalist and so on. Both narrower and wider identifications, along with expectations of reciprocity characteristic of the 'alliance' type of relationship (discussed in the following paragraphs), can, of course, play a role in a single decision-making process: I do what is good for the clan as long as it does not harm my family or me personally; I forego a bit of my profit to let others, whose help I need, participate; I help my group because I identify with it but also because it is good for my own standing in it or for the marriage prospects of my daughter or whatever. There are no limits to the many ways in which narrower and wider identifications can interplay in influencing the way in which an actor calculates the cost and benefits he or she believes a decision might entail. Here, time frames also come in (Wilk and Cligget 2007: 190–94). My calculations may include my yet unborn children and grandchildren or the descendants of others with whom I identify; or they may be based on perceived short-term benefits only. The latter may be the case in insecure environments, in which more distant future effects of actions are difficult to calculate or in systems with short memories where rewards must be claimed instantly or not at all.

One may object at this point that this theory of identification graded in concentric circles around the actor or actors does not account for constructs of identity which have their centre elsewhere, whose purest or ideal-typical representatives are not like the actors but represent their defining features in a purer form, like in the 'nordic' or 'Arab' ideologies described above. This remains a complication to think about. But in most cases the concentric model around the actor(s) comes pretty close to what we observe on the empirical level. It also has merits in deconstructing claims of government to represent 'the people', 'the nation' or 'the state'.

Identification is not the only reason for being good to others. We are also good towards our allies, but that follows a different logic. Identification is based on sameness, alliance on otherness. A political example can illustrate this: one can only form a coalition with another party, not with one's own. A military alliance can only be with another nation or another fighting force, et cetera.

Alliances can be extended to non-relatives and even non-co-ethnics or non-co-religionists on the basis of 'give and take'. We help our allies not because they are like us but because we expect their help in return. However, reciprocity between allies does not exclude elements of identification. The reciprocal logic of alliances may be supplemented by constructs of similarity (comrades, freedom fighters, former fighters for the same 'just cause', etc.). Such constructs are fragile, however, when the rewards for defection become too high, i.e. when the bones of contention appear more valuable than the preservation of friendship (as the case of Eritrean and the Ethiopian leaders, who were former comrades-in-arms against the Derg regime [1974–1991], but waged war against each other from 1998 to 2000 and have mistrusted each other ever since, illustrates).

One type of relationship in which – by definition – identity between the parties is never given is that discussed by Hechter (2013) in his book *Alien Rule*. This comparative study ranges from military occupation and corporate take-overs to university departments in receivership, international organizations that interfere in what used to be national affairs, and empires, a topic which we too address in Chapter 9 of this volume, 'Ruling over Ethnic and Religious Differences'. In the present context (widened identifications versus alliances), we may note that alien rule always comprises an element of alliance, namely the alliance between alien rulers and local collaborators, often also referred to as traitors by members of their own groups.

Just as decisions about alliances tend to be guided consciously by strategic considerations, especially the resulting increase in size and strength, so processes of identification seem to be guided, at least in part, and whether consciously or unconsciously, by anticipated group sizes. We can easily appreciate that widening one's identification (e.g. by relaxing the criteria of admission into one's own group) and forming an alliance have the same effect on the size of one's party in a conflict. Both processes (widening identities and forming alliances) increase the size of that party with all the potential advantages (strength) and disadvantages (having to share the loot) – or benefits and costs, for that matter – that this entails (Schlee 2008a: 25–26). Deciding to widen one's identification, as in the case of alliance formation, necessarily involves a larger number of people. Conversely, narrowing one's identification has similar effects to breaking an alliance. One's own party becomes smaller, more exclusive.

Apart from similarities, there are also differences between widening one's own group (identification) and entering into an alliance with another group. Identification may imply reciprocity, but not necessarily. If I identify with my children, in the sense of acting on their behalf for what I perceive to be their benefit, I may be influenced by the consideration that they might help me in my old age. But I might also be sceptical of that and care for them anyhow. On the other hand, an alliance, if it works, is always based on reciprocity, on give-and-take. It is an instrumental relationship. Its extreme form is the one-issue alliance in which I cooperate with people whom I may strongly dislike and with whom I share no common basis for identification, other than one particular shared aim.[6]

Hechter is right to stress the instrumental aspect and the importance of material incentives in the context of alien rule and social relations in general. 'The role that individual incentives play in social outcomes can hardly be overestimated' (Hechter 2013: 141). We share this perspective and our discussion of 'Who is the State' is guided by it.[7]

Who is the State?

These reflections on the significance of identification in calculating interests and taking action lead us to the following question: who is the state? From which parts of the population is the state personnel recruited? With whom does the state identify? Who identifies with the state? Who are the allies of the state, i.e. those who are not part of the ruling elites but who engage in reciprocal relations with them? In case of internal conflict, we can ask the same questions about factions or networks within the state. To get quick (but possibly not very precise) answers, we can pose all these questions to representatives of the state. They would give us expressions of the official state ideology. Possibly, they would claim that the state represents the people. Often, they also claim that their policies are based on values. Here is a list of values that are often invoked by state representatives in alphabetical order: African, American, Asian, Buddhist, Christian, Humanist, Liberal, Islamic, Socialist. Instead of working for the 'people' they might also claim to work for the 'state', in a fiscal sense, to run the state like a successful business and to maximize state income by encouraging overall economic growth and taxing a larger and larger economy.

Closer observation often reveals, however, that governments make economic decisions which benefit neither their people nor the state and which do not reso- nate with any religious beliefs or ideological 'values' worthy of the name. They – and that does not mean some abstract institution but the people actually involved in making decisions – make such decisions if they themselves and those who are close to them benefit from them. Leasing giant fiefdoms of land at cheap rates to foreign investors might be disastrous to the people who live there, and it might be of no benefit to the wider national economy, but it still might be explicable in terms of more narrowly defined interests. Those who make the decisions might receive kickbacks or shares or jobs for friends and family.

'National development' is a catch-phrase almost as good as Christian values or Humanism. Catley, Lind and Scoones (2013), in a book analysing state poli- cies towards pastoralists – which often have the effect of replacing pastoralism by large-scale capitalist forms of food production said to be 'modern' but which are less (!) productive in terms of the overall economy – ask the following question which they immediately answer:

> Why [do] governments seek to replace pastoralism with alternative land uses? An important reason is the interest of governments in raising tax revenue and, more generally, to exert greater control over economic and political life at the margins. By controlling economic activity in the pas- toral margins through resource grabs, ruling regimes are able to capture economic wealth for national development. (Catley, Lind and Scoones 2013: 11)

Are the government decisions regarding pastoralism analysed by Catley, Lind and Scoones really motivated by the desire to promote national development? There is no doubt that ruling regimes are able to capture economic wealth that could be used for national development. But is that what they do? This, of course, is an empirical question and has to be answered state by state and case by case. Sadly, historical evidence suggests that ruling regimes very often do not use tax revenues and wealth 'captured' in other ways for national development but for a costly security apparatus necessitated by their fear of the resistance provoked by their inability or unwillingness to carry out policies that correspond to the interests of broad segments of their citizenship – in other words by the absence of development promoting the wellbeing of large numbers of people. In other cases, public wealth ends up in private pockets of members of the state class – a fate sometimes shared by development money provided by foreign donors. That is, rather than the state investing in development, development money from somewhere else is 'invested' in the personal bank accounts of state officials. The same might happen to money generated by 'resource grabs' (the terms in quotation marks are taken from the passage from Catley et al., quoted above). The long-term land leases to foreign investors in Africa and many 'developing' tropical countries around the world are often so ridiculously cheap that it is hard to explain their economic logic, unless one takes the possibility of kickbacks to those who make these decisions into account.

Wisely, Catley et al. do not describe 'the state' as a monolithic actor, writing, instead, of 'governments' and 'ruling regimes'. Arguably, however, what governments do should be examined with reference to the perceived costs and benefits that particular actions have for the actors who actually decide to carry them out. In the case of collective decisions, each actor has to take into account the perceptions of others, but, if such decisions do not serve his or her own interests, he or she will accept them only to the degree necessary and will try to influence them in the way perceived to be best for himself or herself, considering the options of widening the 'self' by identification as discussed above.

Let us examine a series of assumptions regarding the 'identifications' of governments or of particular state officials, beginning with the normative assumption that the government represents[8] the people and acts in the interest of the people. This would imply that in situations where local self-regulation works well and government intervention is both costly and unnecessary, such a government would limit its own role. In the reality around us, however, few governments behave in this way.

A somewhat more realistic assumption – one that resonates with the statement made by Catley et al., quoted above – is that governments identify not with the people but with the state. To increase the importance and the splendour of the state, state revenue needs to be maximized. Again, there are two screws to turn. One is the rate of taxation, and the other is the kinds of taxes that are levied. The rate of taxation represents an optimization problem, with the highest returns falling somewhere in between two extremes. If taxation is too high, it threatens the life or the productivity of the producers and, thereby, potentially limits taxable production. High taxation also increases the costs of control and, as control always remains incomplete, leads to a rise in tax evasion and outmigration. On the other hand, if taxes are too low, the state foregoes possible income. As to the kinds of taxes, in this model one can assume that the government looks for ways to tax all branches of the economy and should, therefore, be interested in the growth of the overall economy.

To return to the scenario described above, this means that a rational, revenue-maximizing government would refrain from removing key resources from the pastoral sector, if that led to losses that are higher than the gains achieved through alternative forms of land use. If the aim of government policy is maximization of the overall economic output of all sectors, taken together, then such a policy would preserve livestock routes and access to river banks and other watering points wherever the losses to the livestock sector incurred by not doing so would exceed the benefits of competing kinds of use. It would also preserve the open range wherever the disruption to the pastoral sector and the ecological damage done by attempts to practice crop production exceed the benefits of agriculture. This will be the case under marginal conditions where crop production is possible but risky. There, one might obtain a crop one year in two or three, but the yields would be lower than the gains obtained by allowing continued use of these lands by pastoralists, either with regard to the same surface area or considering this area as part of a wider system of which it is a necessary component without which other parts of the surface cannot be effectively used. In all of these cases, a revenue-maximizing government would make careful calculations about what removing a resource from one type of use and transferring it to another would entail for both. Use of that resource would be granted to whichever sector would yield more gain for the overall economy, provided, of course, that this gain is taxable or contributes to the economy in some other way. In the case of mobile livestock production this could be, for example, the production of cheap meat which would help people not to spend all their wages on food so that their incomes can be taxed. Cheap meat could also help to keep the wage levels low enough for the non-food sector of the economy to remain profitable and taxable.

Very often, governments do not behave in this way. Their behaviour cannot be explained by the assumption that they act in the (fiscal) interest of the state. Instead of developing the overall economy and a tax system diversified enough to tap many different sources of revenue, they focus on those sectors where it is easiest to create bottlenecks to siphon off wealth. In such cases, the focus is not on state revenues but on personal income.

When it comes to explaining actual decisions made by holders of state power, their reference in calculating costs and benefits of actions (costs and benefits for whom?) does not seem to be very different from that of ordinary people. Like all healthy people, they want first of all to preserve themselves. When their life is threatened, because of their past crimes or for whatever reason, they fight desperately and cruelly. Only in the impact of their rage do they differ from ordinary people, who have no armed forces under their command. When they become wealthy, they want to become even wealthier, again like ordinary people. That 'resource scarcity' escalates conflict is a myth. Neither governments, government officials, nor pastoralists are ever content with what they have; they always want more of the same, be it power, money or cows. And fights are fought by people with fighting capacity, not by destitute people (see Witsenburg and Zaal 2012). When it comes to sharing wealth, holders of state power do so with their own families and within the wider net of relatives with whom they cooperate (although, if they are of a similar status, relatives can also be dangerous rivals). Here, the logic of identification (on the basis of shared ancestry or similar criteria) interpenetrates with individualistic logic (I help them because they help me).

Seen from the actors' perspective, ethnicity, religion, regional origin, et cetera, may serve as criteria for determining possible allies or as a pool of categories from which one chooses in widening or contracting one's own identification, in response to one's needs in gaining or defending access to resources. Naturally, not all these games of identification can be played out openly, because the actors in question may be exposed to critical observation. Relations among neighbouring groups displaying ethnic and religious differences rarely take this or that course without third parties looking on or actively interfering. Global discourses concerning minority rights, indigenous rights or human rights come into play, but, above all, it is the state which mediates relations among ethnic groups and religious communities. State policies, such as secularism and multiculturalism, often serve – or are supposed to serve – as alternative ways of regulating pluralism, with or without a hidden agenda favouring one or the other group. In some states, ethnicity is forced into the private sphere, while in others the state ignores it, officially, or attempts to overcome it by forcing assimilation. Other states see themselves as federations of ethnic groups, in which only members of the constitutive ethnic groups enjoy full citizenship and, even then, may only be able to exercise their political or economic rights in their respective regions.

States composed of ethnic mosaics are often former colonies. In their internal administrative divisions, they sustain or re-invent forms of ethnic territoriality harking back to the European models that had been transferred to their colonial precursors. Often the model of the nation-state, the 'Westphalian' state or a miniature version of it, appears to be applied rather mechanically. In arid northern Kenya, even pastoral nomads were allocated districts that they could not leave with their herds without special permits. This was detrimental to animal production and, consequently, also to human nutrition and health, because the districts were too small to balance the risks associated with the uneven distribution of rainfall (Schlee with Shongolo 2012: 9, 170; Schlee and Shongolo 2012: 27, 33).

States that make use of ethnic differences to delineate their administrative subdivisions are not all classical post-colonies with European 'motherlands'. Ethiopia expanded in the late nineteenth century to secure for herself territories that would otherwise have been appropriated by rival European powers (Schlee with Shongolo 2012: 2), and it has been accused by its critics of internal, i.e. intra-African colonialism. During Haile Selassie's reign and throughout the socialist period (i.e. until 1991), the administrative structure of Ethiopia followed traffic connections (a reasonable principle given the regional differences in altitude and accessibility) and cross-cut ethnic divisions – perhaps intentionally and systematically with an underlying assimilationist agenda. Since 1991, however, territorial units have been determined with reference to ethnic groups and boundaries. This new order clearly has its terminological roots ('nations, nationalities and peoples') in Stalin's conceptualizations, which were very influential in large parts of the globe (see M. Schatz [2014] on China). The roots of ethnic federalism may lie not only in West European ideas about the nation-state but also in tsarist imperial practices which, in turn, had Mongol precursors. We shall come back to such genealogies of categorizations and systems of rule at the end of this volume.

States categorize people and can have an influence on 'ethnic' identification. On the other hand ethnic groups may use the state as a power resource or an instrument for the exclusion of others from resources. In some cases, where we find a dominating *Staatsvolk*, state and ethnicity may even merge into one and we can speak of an ethnic state, in other cases, political power is based on marked distinctions between the rulers and the ruled along ethnic and religious lines. Political, 'cultural' (ethnic), religious and other identities are connected by loops of influences on each other. Therefore, neither the state nor the ethnic groups can be regarded as prior to the other or more 'real' than the other.[9] Rather than simple relationships of mono-causality, with the state being at the origin of ethnic groups and other collective identities or, vice versa, the latter appropriating, forming and shaping the state, we have a complex interplay of statehood and ethnic and religious identities. Some of the latter may appropriate the state, leaving only second-class citizenship for the rest. Those in power, whether originally recruited along ethnic lines or not, tend to reserve the label 'ethnic' with its multiple rough emic equivalents in the languages of the world, for others, claiming for themselves some higher, universal and rational identity. The subjects have customs, the rulers have law, the subjects have dialects, the rulers have a language, the rulers have a culture or civilization, the subjects have folklore, et cetera. Counter discourses like human rights and minority protection may change this, but only to a degree, because they fall into the same kind of dichotomy: the rulers (in a democracy the representatives of a majority) are the protectors, the minorities need protection, and the minorities have to act in funny ways like painting their bodies or wearing feathers or colourful togas in order to trigger the protective instincts of majority representatives. (Others call this [self-folklorization] 'proudly living out their ethnic cultures'. I have my doubts.) Ethnic identities are defined in political contexts and very often in a top-down way, excluding segments of the population from political power and economic advancement or assigning alternative hierarchies to them which do not lead as high up as mainstream or ruling-minority hierarchies.

Günther Schlee is one of the Founding Directors of the Max Planck Institute for Social Anthropology in Halle, Germany. Prior to this appointment he was Professor of Social Anthropology at the University of Bielefeld. He conducted fieldwork in Kenya, Ethiopia and Sudan. His publications include *Identities on the Move: Clanship and Pastoralism in Northern Kenya* (Manchester University Press, 1989), *How Enemies Are Made: Towards a Theory of Ethnic and Religious Conflict* (Berghahn Books, 2008) and *Pastoralism and Politics* (with Abdullahi A. Shongolo, James Currey, 2012).

Notes

1. For similar distinctions in the neighbouring Gedaref State, see Zahir Musa al-Kareem (2016).
2. See Banton (2015) for an attempt to bring some order into the semantic field race/ethnicity/identity.
3. '10,000 Sudanese acres ready for Egyptian farmers. . .', retrieved 24 December 2014 from www.dailynewsegypt.com/2014/12/13/; also www.africareview.com/News/Sudan-offers-Egypt-farmland and www.news.sudanvisiondaily.com/details.html?rsnpid243584, both retrieved 24 December 2014.
4. Love is often based on contrasts, as in heterosexual love, or it comprises some form of idealization or admiration which implies that one does not feel the same as the loved one but puts her or him in a somewhat exalted position. It is therefore necessary to explain in which sense we can speak of identification in this context. Identification here means that I include the other person in my own cost/benefit calculations as if she or he were me or mine.
5. See Köhler (2016) for such a model of the social world of the WooDaaBe of Niger.
6. Since reality is not replete with extreme forms, one also finds transitional forms between identifications and alliances, as has been clarified elsewhere (Schlee 2008a: 30–33). An alliance may have elements of identification (e.g. a coalition among parties identified as 'conservative' or 'liberal'). On the other hand, a relationship based on a shared identity may also comprise contractual elements, reminiscent of an alliance. A brother will no longer be treated as a brother if he betrays expectations in that relationship persistently. This observation points to an implicit contractual element even in an apparently 'given' relationship. Rather than a clear-cut distinction between 'status' or, in this context, 'identity' and 'contract', there are varying degrees of 'contractuality'.
7. In his causal explanation of the legitimation of rulers, Hechter (2013: 23) cites 'effectiveness', which he opposes to 'identity' (or where they are from) – that is, he emphasizes

'instrumental' explanations at the expense of 'cultural' ones (Hechter 2013: 148). This approach is dichotomizing, and I think that the relationship between individual incentives, in response to effectiveness in the provision of common goods, and identity, like that between instrumental explanations in terms of material incentives and 'culture', are more complex than that. I share Hechter's scepticism of viewing 'culture' as an independent variable, but it does play a role in determining what is perceived to be a common good or an individual incentive (or a resource or a measure of success for that matter). Also 'identity', as we define it, has a lot to do with the legitimacy of rulers. Don't rulers, alien or not, have to identify with the interests of the general public, or some large body of people, to be perceived as legitimate by this larger body? We will continue this discussion in the following footnotes, so as not to disrupt the argument in the main text, which was completed before Hechter's latest book was brought to my attention.

8. A word about the relationship between 'representation' and 'identification' is in order here. Hechter opposes these concepts to one another. In his book *Alien Rule*, he 'extends arguments about political representation to natives and aliens, holding that legitimacy in the contemporary world is largely a function of the effectiveness and fairness of rulers, rather than their identity' (Hechter 2013: 23). In the way we use 'identity' and 'identification' in this volume, they cannot be opposed diametrically to 'representation' in this way. Conceptually (i.e. irrespective of what people referred to by this term do in the real world), a representative is the agent of a principal, the latter being the one or the ones he or she represents. An agent has to act on behalf of the principal; he has to perceive costs and benefits from the perspective of the principal and take his decisions in the interest of the principal. This is very close to our definition of 'identification' which is about widening the self to include others in one's own cost/benefit calculations. The agent, as long as he retains his sanity, will not identify with the principal in the sense of believing himself to be that person; but he certainly has to identify with that person's aims. There are many everyday language expressions for this kind of agent/principal relationship, and more specifically for the relationship between a good ruler and 'his' people. They have to be 'on the same wavelength', he has to be able to 'see through their eyes', and to 'know where the shoe pinches' them. Hechter's discussion of 'effectiveness' and 'legitimacy' is stimulating and invites questions. The legitimacy of a ruler, in practical terms (measured in acceptance and the length of his stay in office), certainly depends to a great extent on his being perceived as efficient by relevant actors, by those who have a voice among the ruled. But how about marginalized people who have no voice? An outside observer might depict the neglect of the interests of these people as a lack of effectiveness on the part of the ruler. (He might then appeal to 'good people', to 'give them a voice' or to practice 'advocacy anthropology'.) But, by definition, the views of those who have 'no voice' do not matter in local power games. Would one then not have to distinguish effectiveness from an observer's perspective from that of a local-actor perspective, something along the lines of the emic/etic distinction?

9. There is a literature which deconstructs statehood. Scott's title, *Seeing like a State* (Scott 1998) suggests that, rather than having thing-like characteristics, as terms such as 'apparatus' or 'institution' suggest, it is more like a way to perceive and a way to act – a language game or a set of behavioural conventions. Indeed, the book is about how states 'read' reality and the blind spots in their reading. Since then, many have followed in Scott's footsteps. Others, like Geertz (1980), with his 'Theatre State', have stressed the performative aspects of statehood. We can no longer pretend to know what the state 'really' is. Statehood is enacted by state-like behaviour. For a recent work in this tradition, see

Sureau (2016) on South Sudan. In some traditions of writing, however, the state seems to have resisted deconstructive efforts much longer than ethnicity or class. Brass (1985), summarizing the literature regarded as pertinent at his time, discusses at great length how states form alliances with ethnic groups or classes, or how states may be captured by such entities. But in any discussion of the relationship between an X and a Y, X and Y remain or are even affirmed as separate entities. Our discussion of identification differs from this perspective. If the state personnel is made up of a specific group of the population, and if the aims of the state approach more and more the aims of that group – in other words, if a state identifies with a group and is identified with it – can we still make out the state as a separate entity 'captured' or 'instrumentalized' by that group?

Chapter 4

Politics of Belonging and Identity Transformations in Northern Côte d'Ivoire and Western Burkina Faso

Youssouf Diallo

Introduction

This chapter deals with the politics of belonging and identity transformations of Fulbe nomadic pastoralists in western Burkina Faso and northern Côte d'Ivoire. It describes historical as well as contemporary aspects of their integration in Bobo-Bwa and Senufo village communities, and discusses the conditions under which some Fulbe have changed their ethnic identity or differentiate themselves from sedentary groups.

Fulbe pastoralists are scattered throughout the savannah belt of West Africa from Senegal to Ethiopia. In contrast to the Sudano-Sahelian zone, which they have inhabited for quite a long time, the movements of Fulbe into the Sudano-Guinean zone are relatively recent. Côte d'Ivoire, which is far from being a unique case in West Africa, is a good example of this. Pastoral migrations to northern Côte d'Ivoire can be ascribed to ecological constraints and political reasons as well.

During the migration, ethnic identity may change with processes of assimilation and differentiation occurring but it is sometimes difficult to discern all the modalities of these two processes. Some authors dealing with the dynamics of ethnic identity distinguish four variant processes of change (Braukämper 1992: 53). Two of them, 'amalgamation' and 'incorporation', are interpreted as basic forms of assimilation. Amalgamation is a process by which two or more groups unite to form a new one; incorporation on the other hand means that one group takes on the identity of another. Differentiation is separated into 'division' and 'proliferation'. Through division, two or more new groups emerge out of one older group without the old identity remaining. There is proliferation when one or more groups emerge out of an older group.

In the processes of assimilation and differentiation, which I will describe by taking up some of the terms just mentioned above, there is a wide range of factors which lead groups or individuals to take on the identity of others but here again it is difficult to discern all the different factors. Quantitative data related to demography, for example, is lacking. That would have enabled us to take into account the number of nomadic pastoralists, the period of their stay in a community and the rhythm of their integration in it. Rather than addressing all these factors, this chapter will concentrate on the discussion on alliances, the religious dimension (Islam), access to land and occupational differentiation, which promote the integration of the Fulbe into sedentary communities.

Pastoralists, Farmers and Traders

The Bobo-Bwa in Burkina Faso and the Senufo in the Côte d'Ivoire are organized into village communities on the fringes of which Fulbe of various clans live. The village is the most relevant unit for all activities. The founding family of a village holds the chieftaincy. The Bobo and the Bwa are similar in their social organization, religion and in their political and ritual life (Capron 1973; Le Moal 1980).

The Senufo populate a wide zone that extends from southwestern Mali to southern Burkina Faso and into Côte d'Ivoire where they constitute the largest ethnic group and are regarded as autochthonous. They are subsistence farmers, but also engaged in cash crop production and grow cotton. The Dyula represent the second largest population in northern Côte d'Ivoire. They constitute, with the Malinke, one of the oldest Muslim groups in the West African savannah where long-distance trade was previously the predominant form of their economic activities. Islamic scholars of both groups contributed to the expansion of Islam across the West African savannah. Because of the competence of the Dyula in long-distance trade and their social prestige, some Senufo adopted their culture and language and changed their ethnic affiliation. Others became traders after being converted to Islam.

State formation and long-distance trade, which were essential for the spread of Islam in Senufo territory, were the two factors of Dyula influence in precolonial West Africa. Small Dyula trading communities settled along the trade routes extending from the Middle Niger in the north to the savannah in the Kola-producing zone in the south. To secure the trade routes, they formed later coalitions with small groups of local warriors and founded the Dyula state of Kong in the eighteenth century. As a result of the development of the political organization of Kong, some Senufo were assimilated by the Dyula. Those subgroups who lived along the trade routes were also subject to Dyula cultural influences because of their ancient cohabitation with Islamized Dyula traders who introduced the art of weaving to the Senufo. In northern Côte d'Ivoire, one can find even today a number of 'Dyula-ized' Senufo along the portion of the ancient trade route that connected Kong and Djenné in today's Mali. These Senufo differ from others in their family organization and the social structures connected therewith. The villages of the 'Dyula-ized' Senufo are divided into quarters called *kabila*, of which each are made up of several families of the same origin. This Dyula lineage-based social organization can also be found in many Senufo villages where one finds several autonomous Dyula quarters.

The Fulbe pastoralists represent the third group in the area under consideration. There is a specific articulation and adaptation of the Fulbe Muslims to the Senufo/Dyula environment. The Senufo territory into which the Fulbe migrated from Burkina Faso over the last three decades covers zones of different population densities. In addition to that, there is another consideration: the different species and breeds of domestic cattle have different ecological adaptations. The most important difference is between the humpbacked zebu cattle (*bos indicus*) introduced in northern Côte d'Ivoire by the Sahelian Fulbe and the humpless breed (*bos taurus*). The tsetse fly remains in this respect the decisive limiting factor for herding the zebu in humid conditions of the Sudano-Guinean zone. This explains why the decision of nomadic pastoralists to settle in a given area primarily depends on local ecological conditions, even if they also take into consideration the availability of natural resources (water, pasture) and access to commercial networks that would allow for the selling of milk.

Identity, Attribution and Self-Identification in a Pluri-ethnic Context

Ethnic identity is a differential identity that can be understood with reference to a wider social context in which individuals and groups define or differentiate themselves from each other. The portion of West African savannah which interests us here is such a context (see also Amselle 1985). The Fulbe pastoralists, the Senufo and the Bobo-Bwa farming communities of northern Côte d'Ivoire and western Burkina Faso were embedded in larger economic networks (Djenné, Tombouctou, Kong) and powerful political formations in the nineteenth century. There were not withdrawn. In this region, crossed by trade routes, an important circulation of individuals or groups existed for ritual, religious or economic reasons. The dynamics of identity are the product of a long history in the course of which different ethnic and professional groups of this region have come into contact with one another and define their identity with respect to kinship relations, descent, residence, religion or occupation. The ethnic terms 'Senufo', 'Fulbe', 'Bambara' and 'Dyula' are all examples of this mode and level of identification.

An important anthropological literature has been devoted to critical analyses of the ethnic terms 'Senufo', 'Dyula' and 'Bambara' (Bazin 1985; Launay 1995; Förster 1997). The term 'Dyula', which describes a cultural as well as an occupational group, also means trader. If, for example, a young Fulbe pastoralist were to change his professional activity from herding to trading, one would say he has become Dyula or he is doing *dyulaya* (that is to say commerce). 'Senufo' is originally a Dyula word that the traders used to describe the 'speakers of the Siena' (i.e. the Senufo language). The French colonial administration later took up the name Senufo. The Senufo call themselves 'Bamana'. There is evidence that this ethnic terminology does not have a pejorative connotation, even if West African Muslims use 'Bamana' or 'Bambara' in a very general way to describe non-Muslims (Bazin 1985; Trimingham 1970).

Division of Labour and Identity Discourses

Besides attribution and self-identification, the examples mentioned above clearly show that ethnic differentiation has cultural, religious and economic dimensions. This is the case again with the Senufo farmers and their Dyula neighbours. Most Dyula people primarily define themselves, and are defined by Senufo, as traders and Muslims (Launay 1982). The Senufo are even today called 'Bamana' ('unbelievers') by the Dyula and the Fulbe. As for the term Fulbe (or Fula), it has an occupational meaning in many farming communities where it is used for those persons whose primary economic activity is herding, irrespective of their actual ethnic belonging. The typical image of Fulbe social identity in West Africa is that of 'keeper of livestock'. But one cannot speak of Fulbe identity without mentioning the role of religion that represents the reference point for the construction of 'Fulbeness'. Islam is an essential element of Fulbe identity and it plays a central role in their daily life. The young begin to practise this religion very early for this reason.

In contrast to outside attribution based on language and religion, the Senufo usually refer to occupational criterion to distinguish themselves from other groups living in their vicinity. In fact, what gives the Senufo a strong self-consciousness of identity vis-à-vis their Dyula and Fulbe neighbours is neither language nor religion but occupational criterion and particularly agriculture. It is with this meaning that the culturally similar blacksmiths minorities use the term 'Senambele' as occupational marker to describe the Senufo farmers. Agriculture remains the most highly valued occupation, although it happened that some Senufo, after their conversion to Islam, adopted the Dyula mode of life and language and changed their ethnic identification.

As we shall see, the emphasis on occupational specialization is also the basis for ethnic differentiation between Senufo and Fulbe. Raising cattle is not valued in Senufo professional ethic (see also Förster 1997). The Senufo do, in fact, consider this economic activity a Fulbe specialization and entrust them with their own cattle so that they can spend more time farming with which they feel intimately connected. The prestige of particularly successful farmers in the local community is one of the values of Senufo society. Such values are also expressed in the work on the fields. Beside the idealized image of self-identification, practical issues play a role: the Senufo territory has belonged to the Ivorian cotton belt since 1962 and is highly integrated into the market economy.

The Fulbe in Northern Côte d'Ivoire

In this section I will describe pastoral movements into northern Côte d'Ivoire, before turning to some modalities of interaction between the Senufo and the Fulbe. During the nineteenth century, a portion of western Burkina Faso called Boobola was under the political influence of the Fulbe chieftaincy of Barani, to which local farmers paid tribute. After the decline of this chieftaincy and the emancipation of the slaves, the Fulbe, deprived of their dependant labour force, returned to their pastoral lifestyle and some of them even took up a nomad existence again. Fulbe from the chieftaincy of Barani were for these reasons the first to move to northern Côte d'Ivoire via Mali. Between 1940 and 1950, cattle-herders from Barani, in search of pastures, moved to the regions of San, Koutiala and Sikasso in Mali. Some of them spent several years in Mali before they settled in Côte d'Ivoire. San and Koutiala are also the most important regions of origin for the Malian Fulbe in present-day Côte d'Ivoire. As mentioned, the first pastoral migrations from Barani occurred in a context of ecological, political and social change that resulted from the liberation of former slaves and their descendants. The migration of the first Fulbe groups was also caused partly by heavy cattle taxation due to the abuse of power by the Barani chiefs. In 1962, after living in Mali for twenty-two years, they penetrated the territory of Côte d'Ivoire.

Subsequent waves of Fulbe immigration into Côte d'Ivoire from southwestern Burkina Faso occurred between 1960 and 1970. Besides the Fulbe families from Barani, one encounters for example members of the Jafunbe clan, primarily in the border region of Ouangolodougou. They belonged to the first pastoral migrations that started to move very early. After a short stop in the region of Orodara, they entered into the Côte d'Ivoire in 1969.

Two other factors later played a crucial role in fostering pastoral migrations in the country. The first was the Ivorian livestock policy that contributed in the 1970s to an increase in pastoral migration from Burkina Faso and Mali. The second factor has been the ensuing development of pastoral economy that has contributed to making northern Côte d'Ivoire attractive for Sahelian Fulbe herders who came to offer their labour to the livestock owners or to find a job on the state farms that have been established here. These migrations were initially undertaken by Fulbe from the provinces of Yatenga in the Mossi region of Burkina Faso and from Mopti in Mali. They moved primarily to the region of Kong (Bernus 1960: 302). Some of these temporary migrants returned to their countries of origin after earning a good wage for several years. Others became permanent hired herders in northern Côte d'Ivoire.

One of the most important pastoral settlements from where the first Fulbe cattle-owners spread then throughout Côte d'Ivoire was Fulabugu ('Residence of Fulbe'), a village located in the district of Tengrela near the border with Mali. Apart from seasonal migrants from southwestern Mali who came regularly to central Côte d'Ivoire, most Fulbe pastoralists were first established in the areas in the north of Boundiali and in the present-day district of Tengréla.

While the nomadic movements up until 1960 were relatively insignificant, between 1961 and 1969 a period of increased immigration set in, which changed considerably from 1970 to 1975. The irregular distribution of Fulbe in the Senufo territory needs to be set in relation to local politics and the special distribution of cattle that can be found in several villages in the northern Côte d'Ivoire.

According to official statistics in 1994, a third of the national herd, which numbered 1.3 million animals, belonged to the Fulbe whose livestock was the source of approximately fifty per cent of the national milk and meat production (Ministère de l'Agriculture 1994). The economic influence held by the Fulbe population in Côte d'Ivoire was significant, but stands in contradiction to their situation as ethnic minority.

In the Fulbe social organization, the camp is the most significant residential unit. Members of the founding family build the core settlement, and are joined by groups from the founding family's home region. All residents of a Fulbe nomadic camp are under the authority of a single leader who is the elder.

The decision to build a camp in a new locality is made by the Fulbe when certain conditions are met. The Fulbe always try first to find out the attitude of local farmers to their presence. Indicative for the finality of a decision to settle is, above all, the building of a mosque. When the social conditions are considered positive, then they hire some of their Senufo neighbours to build for them round huts with straw roofs. The construction of a mosque and the arrival of the imam and a Kuranic teacher indicate the sedentarization of the Fulbe.

The Politics of Belonging and the Reproduction of Social Diversity

The literature on social sciences dealing with ethnicity and nationalism differentiates between two forms of politics of belonging: belonging by nature (i.e. through blood or descent) and belonging by contract (i.e. through will or choice). As we shall see, both conceptions of belonging to community can be found among the Bobo and the Bwa of western Burkina Faso. So, in discussing social identities and the politics of belonging it is necessary to try to understand how village communities organize and structure themselves and how they reproduce social diversity.

The Senufo and the Bobo-Bwa farming societies have developed a form of political organization characterized by the autonomy of village community.

Autonomy does not mean seclusion. In the political configuration of these state-less societies, the village is an open functional unit and the quarter is the immediately relevant frame of reference above the domestic groups. Chieftaincy is here a flexible institution with a collegial character. Power lies in the hands of the elders who collectively hold the office and are situated above the other groups in the village. The Bobo, Bwa or Senufo chief is the oldest man in the oldest generation. He can delegate his power to a quarter chief who has more ritual than political functions and exercises thereby control over a part of the land. In such a case the head of a quarter can utilize the power delegated to him to define the conditions under which others have access to land.

As a general rule, villages' elders assume ritual functions, in the ancestor cult in particular. It is the duty of the Earth priest, who is chosen by the council of elders, to guarantee the safety of the village. Led by him, the elders of the village 'greet' the local divinities or thank them by bringing them sacrifices; the same is done for the ancestors who are then to intervene in their favour so that it will rain or so that an epidemic might spare the village.

The village founding families enjoy the status of being autochthonous and of being the host. In this respect, the Earth priest is equally important for the mediation between newcomers and the divinities of the village. It is the intermediary role that makes the Bobo or Bwa Earth priest one of the central figures for determining and implementing a policy of admission for newcomers and for the allocation of available parcels of land to them. Indeed, the land use system makes provisions for external groups who join the village community or ask for land for cultivation. All except the pastoralists need to meet ritual requirements that enable access to land. There is no contract between farmers and pastoralists, although Fulbe pastoralists must ask the chiefs in the village before setting up their camp. From the point of view of farmers, nomadic pastoralists are not strangers like the others. They do not have a sacred relationship with the Earth and do not adhere to local beliefs based on the ancestor cult because they are Muslims. To gain access to land use rights, the Fulbe are not required to fulfil the same ritual obligations as the farmers.

Oral tradition in Senufo and Bobo-Bwa villages stress their sedentary lifestyle and mention only small-scale residential changes of particular individuals or family groups, which were based for the most part on the search for arable land, hunting games or iron ore. Here, the blacksmiths, griots and hunters were among the most mobile elements. This appears in many narratives about the founding of Bobo villages, where it is often said that a hunter had settled first at the place before being joined later by other members of the previous locality. The movements of the griots were determined by ritual motives (burials). As for the blacksmiths, they were constantly on the move in search of iron, which they need for the production of agricultural tools. Here again, it occurred quite often that they informed the elders of their village of an interesting place to settle.

Although the majority of their residents are farmers who produce foodstuffs and cash crops, Bobo-Bwa and Senufo village communities are made up of many other professional groups. Social diversity is reproduced through the welcoming of groups because they have special technical and professional skills. In the past, the farmers encouraged blacksmiths, with their special technical skills, or farming households possessing new agrarian techniques to settle among them. In addition to blacksmiths, woodcarvers, leatherworkers and pastoralists belong to those groups whose presence contributed to the diversification of the economic and social life of village communities. Cattle-herding being within the competence of the Fulbe, they are allowed to settle so as to encourage them to cooperate and trade. Many Fulbe pastoralists continue to settle in villages at the request of peasant cattle-owners.

Besides occupational specialization and the prohibition on interethnic alliances, locality is relevant in the process of integration and organization of village communities. The respective households live in different quarters but cooperate. They differentiate themselves from each other through origin, patronymic and sometimes language. Some of them maintain special relationships to one another. For example, the Fulbe are prohibited from marrying blacksmiths, griots-musicians and leatherworkers, their 'joking partners'. Such relationships, combining proximity, mutual aid and taboo, are important for conflict avoidance.

Symbols, Discourses and Representations

Pastoralists and farmers are not only in a local situation of competition for resources, but also in a complementary relationship. The most important bases for a complementary relationship between the two groups are the entrustment of herds to the pastoralists and the sale of draught oxen to farmers (Diallo 1996b). This is in accordance with a widespread form of an ethnic division of labour. The Senufo, for example, do not consider themselves as cattle-herders, even if they invest money in cattle. Roussel (1965: 73) has formulated the hypothesis that in the past the Senufo were herders and only later settled to become farmers. As an indicator for the historical practice of herding among the Senufo, he indicates that they wrapped their dead in cattle skins. It is difficult to check whether this is true or not.

The cattle the Senufo possess today are only a form of investment, but they also slaughter a number of them during funerals. Oral tradition on the division of labour between the Senufo and the Fulbe in pre-colonial time is rare. But according to some information, some peasant cattle-owners hired Fulbe and entrusted their cattle to them. Although the presence of the hired herders in certain areas of the northern Côte d'Ivoire goes back a relatively long time, their demographic weight was low. A census taken in the 1950s indicated only 942 Fulbe in the whole region (Holas 1966).

The Fulbe, whether they were hired herders or cattle-owners who settle in the vicinity of villages and agree to be engaged in herding peasants' cattle, dispose of the milk. In return, the farmers can use the dung and, when needed, buy or borrow draught oxen that are bred for that kind of work. The crossbreeds of Fulbe zebu and taurin cattle are much-desired draught breeds. The zebus can pull a plough just as well but the Fulbe do not like selling their zebus for the reasons described below. It is through a good, friendly relationship with the Fulbe that some Senufo purchase a young zebu bull. Others complain about the relationship of Fulbe to zebu.

The zebu plays a role in the Fulbe identity discourse and is tied to geographical, ethnic and religious factors. A myth that refers to the origins of the zebu in Arabia and the specialization of the Fulbe in the breeding of this species provides a good example. According to this myth, four cows and a bull, all of them zebu, came down from heaven after a saint once begged God for help when he had guests but did not know how he was to feed them. After a Fulbe managed to tame the cattle, he drove them across the sea and through Ethiopia to West Africa. While the zebu breed was intended for the Muslims, including the Fulbe, the taurin breed was the creation of the pharaoh into which God breathed life. It was appropriated by 'unbelievers'. The frequency of the colours red and black in the taurin hides was proof of their heathen origin. Those Fulbe who tell this myth and stress the heathen origin of taurin breeds also say that the breeding of the taurin is an economic necessity. The taurin do multiply faster than the zebu since the calves mature more quickly.

From what has been said, it appears that the ownership of the zebus is a relevant criterion of differentiation between the Fulbe and the Senufo. This cattle specie is for the former a source of pride and a symbol of group identity. Despite the ecological limitations on the breeding of zebu in the savannah of Côte d'Ivoire, the Fulbe still insist on maintaining the zebu and expressing their attachment to it. From an identity perspective, the use of the term *na'i pulli* for zebu breeds is interesting since it explains how this species is conceived as a constitutive element of the Fulbe identity. The term *na'i pulli* literally means 'cattle of the Fulbe' and clearly expresses a type of ethnic appropriation of the zebu by the Fulbe.[1] In any case, such discourses serve to mark the existence of two ethnic identities and differences situated at two interrelated levels: Muslim (Fulbe) owners of the zebu opposed to 'pagan' (Senufo) owners of the taurin.

Some of the Fulbe herders, who originally came to keep the cattle for the Senufo farmers, were incorporated into the groups of their hosts and can barely remember their origins. This was a process of complete integration, although the Fulbe did retain their family names. These 'Senufo-ized' Fulbe have all adopted the Dyula language and no longer speak the Fulbe language. Louis Binger, the French explorer who visited part of the region under consideration in the nineteenth century, mentions a similar case of assimilation of Fulbe in the Senufo society. He reported on an encounter with some of these Fulbe in the region of Tengréla, who had adopted the Senufo identity. He speaks of 'black' Fulbe meaning that they had mixed with the Senufo black population, forgotten their language and practised a 'fetishist' religion, but had retained their family names and their 'racial type'.[2] The Fulbe, whose number Binger estimated to be one third of the total population of the village of Fourou, were so assimilated that they were almost not to be recognized as Fulbe since they had not only given up their language but also their herding activities: 'Tattooed like the Senufo, dressed as they are, speaking their language while having completely forgotten their own and having the same occupations as their co-citizens, they are not to be recognized except in some typical traits; they have maintained their straight and narrow nose and their fine limbs, distinctive signs of their race' (Binger 1892: vol. 1, 210).

Despite the inaccuracy of his racial bias, Binger was right in observing the phenomenon of cultural and ethnic assimilation. Some patterns of integration of Fulbe into the Senufo society are still at work, while other factors such as marriage or religious assimilation have lapsed. This suggests that the ethnic distinction between the Fulbe and the Senufo seems to be more rigid than in the past. Religious affiliations, separation of settlements and competition for resources play important roles in processes of differentiation (Diallo 1996a). The major Fulbe groups and subgroups, speakers of the various dialects of Fulfulde, constitute a pastoral community, which is well aware of its particular cultural and economic position. The religious affiliation of the Fulbe as Muslims living in the vicinity of non-Muslim Senufo explains the spatial separation between the two groups. Here, the Fulbe camps are like islands separated from the Senufo communities. The spatial configuration and the ensuing degrees of interaction in everyday life are explained by the relationships to Islam, which reinforces the sense of different community identities. It also appears that ritual provides a sense of belonging to a global community of Muslims. The Fulbe view themselves as being closer to Dyula local communities than to the Senufo who 'do not pray'. They go to the mosques of their Dyula religious counterparts for Friday prayers. They also participate in the Dyula wedding, naming and mourning ceremonies. In the case of the death of a non-Muslim Senufo, the Fulbe will express their condolence only after the burial. This procedure is in accordance with the Islamic rule of conduct.

Over the past three decades, several conflicts have occurred between Senufo farmers and Fulbe pastoralists. Many of these derived from crop damage. The storage of harvests, especially yams and maize, accounts for crop damage, while field deterioration is due to the absence of fences protecting agricultural land. Crop damage takes place during the dry season and it happens more often field deterioration, which occurs in the rainy season.

Environmental degradation is also a matter of concern for some farmers who blame Fulbe pastoralists for land degradation. From the farmers' point of view, the poverty of the soils is due to the fact that cattle trample the earth and grass does not grow (Diallo 1999). In Boundiali the farmers relate the water problems to the movements of Fulbe cattle in their village. In their opinion the drying up of the watering hole is not only due to the watering of the cattle but to the damage they do with their hoofs, causing the water to run off more quickly to lower lying areas away from the village. Thus, the Senufo in certain villages believe that ecological problems can be solved by prohibiting the transhumance of the Fulbe cattle. But this is equivalent to the eviction of the Fulbe from their land. Discontent of local farmers against the position of the local administration for not finding satisfactory solutions to crop damage led some Senufo farmers to find their own solution to the problem by appealing to traditional hunters (*donsow*).

Unlike in Burkina Faso, where the Fulbe have been residing for a longer period of time, they count among the minorities in Côte d'Ivoire. Their presence in this country has become a political issue. After the creation of projects for the development of livestock and herding industries in the 1970s, local elites disapproved of governmental projects being carried out for Fulbe foreigners and excessive privileges being granted to them. The destruction of crops caused by the Fulbe cattle being driven from pasture to pasture amplified the existing controversy. This has been exploited in northern Côte d'Ivoire to persuade the government to evict the Fulbe from the country. Intellectuals, civil servants and politicians from the north did not miss the chance of forcing the government to take a stance. Electoral candidates tried to use the discontent of the farmers to their advantage by promising to solve the problem of crop damage and land degradation by sending the Fulbe back to their lands of origin (Burkina Faso and Mali). The conflicts run counter to the governments' programmes and occasionally led to the emigration of Fulbe from certain regions. The tense ethnic situation has also led to the emigration of many Fulbe from the Côte d'Ivoire. Several pastoralists moved back to Burkina Faso, into the Banfora region, and to Mali.

Changes in the Ethnic Identity of the Fulbe among the Bobo-Bwa

This section examines the case of the Fulbe who were absorbed into the Bobo and Bwa communities and changed their ethnic affiliation. These communities belong to those ethnic groups that are particularly open to influences from the outside world. The feeling of belonging resulting from co-residence (i.e. shared locality) that ties members of groups together irrespective of their ethnic origin is a step towards integration in village communities. Among the Bobo and Bwa live many groups who belong to their community either by virtue of descent, which determines 'natural' relationships to Bobo or Bwa lineages, clans and ethnic group, or by virtue of 'contract'. The Fulbe herders are counted among the second group.

The infiltration of pastoralists into local societies in today's western Burkina Faso was the result of gradual processes instigated in the eighteenth century by small groups coming from the Inner Delta of Niger and looking for pastures. They moved to Bobo, Bwa and Marka village communities. The Yiirlaabe were the most ancient of the Fulbe clans living there; they later assumed the role of host for other pastoral groups. The Yiirlaabe adopted the local languages and mixed with Bobo and Marka local populations through intermarriages. This resulted in their cultural assimilation. There are various interpretations of the meaning of the word *yiirlaabe* related to identity discussions. According to some informants, *yiirlaabe* means 'the disoriented lost ones' and refers to their loss of Fulfulde. The assimilation of the Yiirlaabe into the Marka is also hinted at here. Others interpret *yiirlaabe* as 'brave'. This second interpretation is shared by Mohammadou (1976: 33) who writes that what 'distinguishes the Férôbé Yiirlaabe is their cunning and bravery. All the achievements of the Yiirlaabe were made by arms'.

The Yiirlaabe of western Burkina Faso were anything other than conquerors. According to oral traditions, it was the Sidibe and Sangare who led a victorious uprising as the first political self-assertion of the Fulbe identity and founded the chiefdoms of Barani and Dokui in the early nineteenth century. In Barani, the Sidibe excluded the Yiirlaabe from local political office.

Beyond conquest and supremacy, there exists a policy of recognition and assimilation of strangers in the ethnic milieu of the Bobo and the Bwa. Such a policy comes into play whenever a locality is founded and the most important constituent groups of that village are allocated their place in it. After the founding of a locality, the Bobo founders do not hesitate to encourage other neighbouring relatives or members of the same ethnic group (i.e. Bobo or Bwa) to settle among them and allocate them important ritual functions in the new local community (Le Moal 1990). A process of becoming 'autochthonous' or of rapid assimilation of newcomers is then initiated through a ritual division of duties that becomes the basis for a close interdependence between those groups. The assimilated groups achieve the preferential status of being autochthonous and can no longer leave the village. In this way, the Bobo of Lena (eastern Bobo-Dioulasso) entrusted the Bwa, who came from Poura in the region of Boromo, with the role of the 'custodian of the fetishes'. These Bwa, who founded their quarter in Lena, later became Bobo and adopted the patronym (*Millogo*) from their hosts. Initially, they were blacksmiths who manufactured agricultural equipment and came to the Bobo of Lena to sell or exchange it for cereals. Today, it is no longer possible to differentiate culturally or socially the ancient Bwa from the other Bobo of Lena apart from in terms of their relationship to the assimilated Fulbe with whom they do not enter into marriage relationships. This type of social regulation in which two Bobo groups define themselves in relation to a third, or require the third group to regulate their relationship, is widespread among the Bobo (Le Moal 1980).

Alliance and friendship with the Bobo and Bwa are important themes in Fulbe and Bwa oral traditions (see also Cremer 1924). According to many of these, the Fulbe were invited to settle among the Bobo-Bwa farmers who entrusted them with their cattle. Even today, the Fulbe who wish to settle in a Bobo or a Bwa village are confronted with a contractual formula. This means that they conclude an agreement whereby each household head offers a chicken and millet beer. In Bobo and Bwa villages, the chicken is offered as sacrifice to the ancestors, while the elders consume the beer. In addition, each member of the Fulbe family must pay a symbolic cash amount (5 francs) 'to the masks' who later, during the departure ceremony, are not allowed 'to hit' them. In those villages where there is a totem animal, the Fulbe may be informed of its existence so that they do not kill it should they accidentally encounter it in the bush. After the offering to the ancestors and to the masks and after being informed about the totem animal, the Fulbe become members of the village community.

This specific integration of the Fulbe into the community goes so far that some of them become completely assimilated. As for the change in ethnic Fulbe identity among the Bobo and Bwa, it is the Sangare who are integrated most strongly into the village communities in the regions of Dédougou and Bobo-Dioulasso. In the language of the Fulbe, it is said of this ethnic incorporation that these groups 'entered' those of the Bobo or the Bwa. Burnham (1991: 87; 1996) found the same metaphor used by the Bororo in northern Cameroon, and the metaphor of 'entrance' is widespread even among non-Fulfulde speakers (Schlee 1994a). But in the region that interests us here, those Fulbe who have maintained their identity call the groups that have been assimilated by the Marka, Bobo or Bwa *murube* or *fulamuru*. I have elsewhere explored the semantic field of the term *murunke* as 'he, who pretends something' (Diallo 1997: 102). Actually, the Murube are for other Fulbe people those who do not know 'anything', namely the Fulfulde language, and are said to be ignorant of the Fulbe culture. Those Fulbe who have 'joined' the Bwa, Marka or Bobo are no longer Fulbe, even if they have retained their Fulbe family names. These Fulbe speak the language of the Bwa and are culturally assimilated. They are only recognizable as Fulbe in their family name (Sangare).

Two other examples of the ethnic incorporation of the Sangare Fulbe in the Bobo villages of Baré and Lena can be noted. It is at the request of the Bobo farmers that the Fulbe from Dokui initially settled in the present-day city of Bobo-Dioulasso and later among the Bobo of Baré belonging to the patronymic group Sanu. Several of these Fulbe who today no longer speak Fulfulde are partially assimilated and live in the same quarters as the native population. The Bobo of Baré differentiate between the integrated Fulbe and those that have maintained their 'Fulbeness' by calling the latter *flè pènè* (i.e. 'red Fulbe'). Other Fulbe who live among the Bobo of Baré concluded marriage alliances with them. The children of marriages between Bobo men and Fulbe women are called *fla-si* in Baré.

The terms *fla* or *fula* are the Dyula equivalents of *Fulbe*. The word *si* is also used in the Dyula language (*shiya*, i.e. ethnic group or race) and it is understood by the Bobo in several ways (Le Moal 1980: 61). The term *fla-si* does not actually signify a new ethnic group. In the present case, it refers more to clan identity than to ethnic differentiation. Marriages between *fla-si* and griots or blacksmiths are taboo.

The Fulbe are an endogamy oriented-group. Their religion and nomadic way of life explain the difficulties they have in intermarrying with sedentary farmers. Even so, matrimonial alliances between them and farmers are possible at least for those who have become sedentary. In Baré, marriages between Fulbe men and Bobo women are said to be more harmonious than those between Bobo men and Fulbe women. The problems in a marriage between a Bobo man and a Fulbe woman lie in the Bobo mode of livelihood which is based on agriculture (cf. also Schlee 1994b). Contrary to the Bobo women who are used to work in the fields, the Fulbe women, for whom this kind of work is unusual, hesitate at the idea of marrying a Bobo man. The Bobo think that such a marriage will end in a divorce. The Senufo of Côte d'Ivoire, among whom every woman has to work a field, express such fears in the same manner.

In Lena, east of Bobo-Dioulasso, the circumstances for the shift of the Fulbe from herding to farming are associated with the anti-colonial insurrection in 1915–1916. The Bobo elders relate that the villagers had entrusted their herds to the Sangare Fulbe who for their part entrusted these cattle, along with their own, to other Fulbe. These latter Fulbe seized the opportunity of the insurrection to flee with all the cattle. As a result, the Sangare Fulbe, who had founded their own quarter called *flèta* (i.e. 'the residence of Fulbe'), turned to agriculture. Their assimilation then followed through marriage as well. They became Bobo, took up their patronym Millogo, their culture and language. The *Flèta* take part in the religious and cultural activities of the village in which they have become full members. The prohibition on marrying blacksmiths and the fact that their totem animal is now a monkey are two elements that differentiate them from other Bobo today.

Another group are those individuals who descend from marriages between Fulbe men and Bwa women. They are called Bobo Fula. They can be found in the region of Dédougou. They should not be mistaken with the Sidibe Fulbe of this region, who have been sedentary for quite a long time and all speak the Bwa language, *bwamu*, as a second language. The latter, the Sidibe Fulbe, who are still working as herders, primarily own Taurin cattle. Under the supervision of the herders their herds go into the Lobi region during the dry season transhumance; the whole households do not accompany them.

Summary

The analysis of Fulbe ethnicity includes, in addition to the study of the role of religion and the mode of production, the study of the role of the nation-state which has not been examined here. The aim of this chapter was to discuss different modalities of interethnic relations between the Fulbe, Senufo, Bobo and Bwa in Burkina Faso and Côte d'Ivoire. We have seen that the land of the Senufo and of the Bobo-Bwa was part of the sphere of influence of the Dyula of Kong whose political and economic influence in the whole region has been stressed. Historically, the Fulbe have had a close relationship with the Bobo and Bwa. In northern Côte d'Ivoire, they occupy the same ecological niche as the Senufo and compete for the control of resources. Within the ecological context of the Ivorian savannah, to which the Fulbe economic system has proved to be adaptable, the acquisition and specialization in the breeding of zebu are an expression of their identity. Islam is another important identity factor among the Fulbe.

This chapter has attempted to show that migration and identity are phenomena that are tied to one another. In the long process of expansion, sedentarization and political domination, the Fulbe have sometimes been assimilated here and there. They experienced modifications to their ethnic identity when they mixed to a large degree with sedentary groups. This has occasionally favoured the emergence of new groups. In its totality, the Fulbe identity is tied strongly to economics (raising cattle) and religion (Islam).

Lieutenant-Colonel **Youssouf Diallo** (Dr habil) is cultural advisor at the Center of Operational Communication in Mayen. He was Research Fellow at the Max Planck Institute for Social Anthropology in Halle (Saale), Germany. His research interests include Islam, security politics, cross-cultural communication and development. His publications include *Nomades des espaces interstitiels* (Köppe Verlag, 2008), *L'ethnicité peule dans des contextes nouveaux* (co-editor, Karthala, 2000), *Der wachsende Einfluss des militanten Islam und der Al Qaida in Afrika* (co-author, Österreichische Militärische Zeitschrift, 2012) and *Sicherheitspolitik in Afrika* (German Federal Ministry of Defense, 2014). He has also published widely on military sociology.

Notes

1. The other term used for the zebu is *senooji*. It points to their geographical origins in the Sahel zone (called 'Seeno') from where the Fulbe zebus were introduced into the Ivorian savannah.
2. The opposition of black and white is an oft-found pattern. The Senufo use it to differentiate between the completely assimilated Fulbe from the non-assimilated who maintain their language and their cattle herding practices. The Bobo also distinguish between the transhumant herders, who they call *flè pènè* ('red Fulbe') from those Fulbe who have been assimilated into their midst *flè dungwu* ('black Fulbe').

Chapter 5

Tanguiéta

Identity Processes and Political History in a Small African Town

Tilo Grätz

Introduction

This chapter deals with the constitution of collective identities in the history of the small Beninese town of Tanguiéta. I will primarily explore the conditions for the politicization of social and cultural differences in this region.[1]

Tanguiéta is a provincial community in northwestern Benin and is somewhat typical of similar settlements in the present-day West African savannah. The town is characterized by its history of immigration in waves of migrants of different origin, a growth in area and population since the colonial period, economic, religious, cultural and linguistic heterogeneity and its status as a transportation hub and an administrative and economic centre.

In light of this case study, I will discuss the knowledge existing to date on the constitution of collective identities in West Africa and analyse interethnic relationships in terms of local power differentials in Tanguiéta. I argue that different attempts at a politicization of difference, tied above all to the role of the state and the effectiveness of cultural and political entrepreneurs from the region, were particularly important for the dominant identity processes in Tanguiéta.

I will start with a description of the (larger) socio-economic groups with several levels of integration and exclusion in the region, which, above all, establish distinct moral spaces. Furthermore, I will explore the conditions for their constitution as politically relevant and the conflicting interest groups in the past and present. Finally, I aim at developing a model for an (unwritten) contractual relationship between these groups in Tanguiéta constituting informal conventions, which, nonetheless, are constantly being renegotiated.

Brief Description of the Region Studied

Since the recent administrative reforms (*décentralisation*) in Benin, the community of Tanguiéta (*Commune de Tanguiéta*) has been a municipality, including five urban and rural counties (*arrondissements*; ca. 2,700 residents in the core town and 75,000 in the community altogether, Institut National de la Statistique et de l'Analyse Economique 2014). It is administered by a mayor leading an elected local council (*conseil communal*). The town hosts several state service units and the *Gendarmerie*. Situated in northwestern Benin at the foot and partially on the northern slope of the Atakora Mountains, the region also includes the Pendjari National Park. The municipality of Tanguiéta is made up of the smaller rural counties (*arrondissements*) of N'Dahonta, Tanongou and Cotiacou as well as the urban areas of Tanguiéta centre.

The residents earn their living primarily through agriculture, i.e. the yields of cultivation, large and small livestock herding, hunting and gathering, trade and several forms of value-added production (e.g. smoked fish, sauce additives and, in the town in particular, the production of sorghum beer). Agriculture suffers from very variable rainfall as well as a reduction in general soil attrition. Due to a great deal of rocky terrain, effectively usable agricultural land stands in relatively poor relation to population density. Peanuts and cotton are planted as cash crops. Many small, intermediate and wholesale traders, craftsmen and shop owners, as well as employees of service industries, work in Tanguiéta. From a linguistic perspective, this is a very heterogeneous region with many language groups, whereby the use of Dendi[2] (Zima 1994) as a second and common language dominates.

Towards the Definition of Social and Ethnic Relationships in Tanguiéta: the Major Socio-Economic Groups

Here I will try to reconstruct the most important levels of collective identity in the community from an etic perspective (i.e. a view that may possibly only be partially shared by the parties concerned). As a possible model, I propose a socio-economic pattern of analysis. I believe that it is possible and useful to describe certain dominant, comprehensive forms of integration of residents of Tanguiéta, without necessarily downplaying the multiple and hybrid dimensions of collective identities in this region.

Four larger units – forms of collective identification that are persistently enacted in various exchange and conflict situations – crystallize from this perspective:

- members of first settler 'farmer groups';
- members of subsequently immigrated 'trader and craftsmen groups';

- civil servants and small entrepreneurs originating from other regions or other countries;
- Fulbe 'pastoralists'.

This classification proceeds initially according to socio-economic criteria.[3] In a strict sense, the vocational categories applied here do not cover the entirety of these groups in Tanguiéta. This is why they are set in quotation marks in the text above. Nevertheless, they shape considerably the dominant self-perception of these groups and influence the public sphere within the community, independent of the actual percentage of time spent in and income earned from the respective economic activity.

This general division makes sense since these socio-economically based categories are on a par with other dominant categories (endogamy, craft guilds, religion, language, etc.) as well as dominant public discourses regarding the relationship to the colonial and post-colonial administration (on social justice, moral norms etc.), as will be elaborated below with reference to several examples.

As will be argued in the following, this is not simply about economic and social complementarity between these groups,[4] supported by and large by endogamy and other factors relevant to the creation of social distance. These differences are created by everyday practices and forms of physical and symbolic appropriation of the local environment, the modes of symbolic exchange and rhetorical separation of the self and the other, which also incorporate competing views of local history and thus generate distinctions. These can potentially break up forms of cohabitation and multiple integration into the local community and through the very articulation of various interests, difference can be politicized. We have to deal with elaborated rules of cohabitation and processes of multiple integration into the local community.[5]

Members of First Settler 'Farmer Groups'

This category includes all the members of the primarily agriculturalist, Gur-speaking groups, who share similar cultural and social characteristics, such as lineage structure, religion, settlement form, et cetera. They immigrated over the course of the last few centuries into the region of Atakora from the north and the northwest (cf. Tiando 1993; N'Tia 1993), partly in search of new settlement opportunities and partly as a result of social or military confrontations. They are linguistically different but for the most part understand and speak the language of their immediate neighbours, which is often related to their own and in many cases reveals loan words from one language to the other.[6] The Gurmancèba, Natèmba, Tankamba, Waaba, Burba (Notba) and the Bèbèlibè could be included in this category.[7] The adjacent villages of Tanguiéta are inhabited almost exclusively by members of these individual 'farmer groups' (as well as several Fulbe). In the town itself, their members dominate several quarters (Tchoutchoumbou, Yarika and Porika in particular). This is above all the result of a massive influx since the end of the 1950s. These groups maintain multifaceted social and cultural relationships, assume one another's initiation rites and often intermarry.

Members of Subsequently Immigrated 'Trader and Craftsmen Groups'

Following the colonial period, Muslim immigrants settled primarily in the centre of Tanguiéta, above all in the present-day quarters of Djindjiré-Béri and Goro-Bani. They settled there in the course of intra-African trade movements as well as in response to a demand for goods and services from the new administrative centre. Even if different forms of trade dominate here as the most important of activities, today many of these settlers also work in agriculture in combination with other forms of employment in the service sector. These immigrants can be classified into three large ethnic groups: the Hausa (emigrants from Nigeria and Niger, primarily traders and butchers); the Zerma from Niger; and further, the Mossi (or Moré) from Burkina Faso, Baatombu as well as the Yoruba, Adja and Igbo from Nigeria and from other parts of Benin (names of present-day nation-states respectively). The latter three arrived somewhat more recently. The second generation of these immigrant groups were all born here and have made Tanguiéta their home. With the exception of the Yoruba and the Igbo, they have all established themselves permanently and maintain only a limited relationship with their parents' regions of origin.

The traders arrived in the area in part via the caravan routes (Aimé 1994b; Bachabi 1980; Brégand 1998; Dramani-Issifou 1981; Kuba 1996; Lovejoy 1980). In the shadow of the *pax colonialis*, it was possible for them to found further secure settlements and stations for the caravans, the so-called *caravansérails*. In our case, this occurred along the classic east-west trade route between Nigeria and Ghana that had existed since the eighteenth century. More and more itinerant traders settled in the area, as did craftsmen who responded initially to the needs of the caravans but later also to the demands of the colonial administration and its personnel. Like in other regions of West Africa, this resulted in the establishment of a *zongo* (also *zango*), an urban centre characterized by Muslim traders and craftsmen who also worked in agriculture and horticulture.

The *zongo*, at first usually located at some distance from farming settlements, became a quarter in its own right, with its own distinct rules influenced by Islam. It was dominated by the owners of hostels and subject to religious and political authority. The *zongo* became a synonym for the settlement of strangers, characterized by Islam and a common overarching language. I will return to the meaning of the *zongo* again later. Above all, at the beginning of the period of immigration and into the 1960s, certain groups could, to a certain degree, be identified with vocational specializations and even preferred goods to be traded. Initially the Hausa were, for example, exclusively cattle traders and butchers, the Mossi barbers, the Zerma blacksmiths and the Igbo traders in spare parts.

Hausa is, as ever, a very common language in the centre of Tanguiéta, but Dendi is the most widespread and dominant language of this population throughout the whole of the region. At the same time, Dendi became a synonym for the residents of the *zongo*, even if this was in reference to residents from the most diverse of origins. Those groups that originally introduced Dendi – since been increasingly transformed – as *lingua franca* were ethnically Songhay or Zerma.

'Civil Servants' and 'Small Entrepreneurs' from Other Regions or Other Countries

Many civil servants have come to the town since the colonial period, from regions that were more advanced in terms of educational infrastructure (reading and writing) or in administrative-technical or trade related skills. This applies to ethnic groups such as the Fon, Yoruba, Baatonum, Adja et cetera. The number of local civil servants (*fonctionnaires*) is not very high. Teachers, in particular, still come from other parts of the country. Other such 'immigrants' include the small entrepreneurs, traders, et cetera. The degree of integration of this population is often limited since they initially only reckon on staying for a limited period of time. For the most part, they marry in their home region, where they also invest in building a house. Only a few of these individuals, retired civil servants, stay in the region. If they are *fonctionnaires,* they speak primarily French outside of the home. However, there are also some, small entrepreneurs in particular, with a very good knowledge of Dendi.

Fulbe Pastoralists

One of the more marginal groups in this region are the Fulbe pastoralists. They are marginal in the sense that they tend, spatially, to locate their settlements far away from others, they are barely integrated into communal activities and they demonstrate a high degree of endogamy. The Fulbe men work as paid herders and in livestock trading; the women sell milk and cheese. The Fulbe are primarily Muslims and usually speak the language of their respective neighbours very well. Their situation is characterized by their relatively low degree of formal education, since the school schedule does not always correspond well with the Fulbe work rhythm or children's herding duties. Three general categories within the Fulbe group need to be defined. First, those Fulbe, whose ancestors have immigrated from Mali and present-day Burkina Faso in search of new pastures since the end of the nineteenth century and have today become relatively sedentary, also work in agriculture and maintain close contacts to other farmers; of these, few are seasonally transhumant.

Second, a small subgroup is made up of those who have become sedentary, as craftsmen, traders and functionaries. Third, another subgroup is made up of those nomadic pastoralists who during the last thirty years used to pass through the area from the north, above all in the dry season.

The model of differentiation presented here corresponds in no way to the official ethnic classification in Benin, which bases itself on linguistic boundaries (cf. Ceccaldi 1979). It makes sense to initially highlight these units that extend beyond smaller linguistic margins. They do, however, correspond to the marked differences in settlement and economic patterns and, among other things, the strong tendency towards endogamy and other forms of inner integration among these groups. The most important criteria for my classification are marked by:

- different periods of immigration and the preferred areas of settlement;
- economic specialization and the resulting forms of complementarity and conflicts of interest;
- different forms of everyday coexistence;
- linguistic differences and marriage rules;
- references to differing religious and cultural practices as markers of difference and boundaries (Barth 1969a);
- different kinds of self-representation and distinct official norms and moral rules; and finally
- the degree to which historical references have been politicized and become a discursive resource (first settlers vs. latecomers, etc.)

The Perception of Self and Other in Relation to Religious and Cultural Practices

Stereotypes of the respective 'other' dominate, as ever, especially among the older generations. Reference is made here not only to the different religious practices but also to more general patterns of daily behaviour. Most farmers, for example, regard Islam with a great deal of suspicion. They see Islam as the religion of the former large and military expansionist empires. They also often view the increasing role of mosques and Koranic schools negatively. The daily calls to prayer are considered an annoyance. For many farmers, the traders, for example, are people who only consider their own financial gains. For the Muslim citizens on the other hand, the 'others' are those who ignore the important food taboos, drink alcohol excessively, are sexually permissive and are, from a religious perspective 'unbelievers'. Naturally, these stereotypes are maintained regardless of actual personal relationships between the residents. For the urban region of Tanguiéta, one can also speak in territorial terms of symbolic spaces that delimit daily practice and create distinctions (Bourdieu 1979). They are on the one hand given as a product of the different residential areas but go beyond those areas as well. There is, in contrast to many villages in the region, no large millet beer market as part of the weekly market in the centre of Tanguiéta. Such a market can be found further towards the periphery in the Tchoutchoumbou quarter. Most millet beer bars (*cabarets*) are established outside of the centre of the town.

Most mosques are, on the other hand, located centrally. The snack bars and cafes that dominate in the immediate vicinity of the market, along the main road and around the central bus station, are run and frequented by Muslims. These are relatively simply built stands that serve tea and coffee with bread and omelettes. Comparable kiosks can be found all over West Africa, especially at bus stations. People meet here to discuss the local business situation, observe arriving vehicles and complete smaller transactions. The dominant language here is Dendi and in some cases Hausa. Fulbe meet at some preferred stands when they come into the city to shop or visit the doctor. Alcohol is rarely served openly here. As a result, micro-spaces of cultural difference are established in the public space of the city centre (in the immediate neighbourhood of the *buvettes*) and are confirmed by the everyday rituals acknowledging belonging (through greeting rituals, preferred topics of conversation, etc.). One can observe in these public spaces the unspectacular but everyday production of difference (Desjeux 1994), the construction of levels of separation that stand in opposition to other levels of common activity and close personal relationships. Urban developments do not, however, allow for a very strict maintenance of these territorial boundaries. Some pubs built above all in the last few years find themselves in the immediate vicinity of Muslim neighbourhoods.

In terms of social alliances, one principally finds very few marriages in the region between farmers and Muslim traders. The members of both groups, and above all the elders, justify this fact not only by the incompatibility of different religious memberships and in reference to 'tradition' but speak of a certain common distrust and a general proscription in both communities. Empirically, an increasingly intensive exchange can be determined between adolescents, above all in the city of Tanguiéta and above all among those who attend school together, complete an apprenticeship together or meet in discotheques and video cinemas. Finally, some young couples do exist who do defy these normative rules. In some cases, these are civil servants who met their wives during their training or in the city in which they worked. A marriage, for example, between the daughter of a merchant and a farmer's son is, by contrast, rare.

Economic Difference, Conflicting Interests and Complementarity

Various forms of exchange between smaller groups have developed within the described larger units over the course of time, ranging from violent confrontation to complementary marriage relationships.

As already indicated, the Gur-speaking 'farmer groups', whose members today refer above all to common language and place of residence as the major factors of social and cultural difference, were marked by factors of permanent fusion and fission. This designates a double process of merging different lineages through marriage and relations to neighbours and the continuous secession of individual segments or groups of individuals in search of new settlement space. Fusion and fission includes a substantial dynamic of linguistic and cultural development of the 'farmer groups'. Languages superimpose themselves upon one another and their speakers enter into relationships with one another. It could equally well be the case that the language of the initial immigrants was adopted or that the language of the later immigrants would dominate – due often but not exclusively to demographic factors. In the individual migrations, the acquisition of land, its clearing and the ritual occupation of residential space was of great importance and is mirrored to this day in mythology and religious rites. On the one hand, in all these groups the clan, as patrilineal descent group[8] and (previously) settlement group[9] as a long time dominant point of reference, is repeatedly the focus. Nearly every such clan claims possession of a particular piece of land to this day or to be its initial settlers, even if the clan no longer occupies that area and has been dispersed or has been 'mixed' through marriage. Every clan makes reference to a mythic ancestor, often an initial settler, and abides formally by food taboos, marriage stipulations and exogamy rules. Kinship and exogamy constitute central terms of self-definition, which are, even today, confirmed symbolically by greeting formulas, joking relationships et cetera on a daily basis. On the other hand, a progressive level of mutual comprehension and exchange between the official socio-linguistically defined ethnic units (Byerebe, Natèmba, Gurmancèba) developed, above all after the colonial period. They share many original common cultural traits, especially the initiation rites (even if some of them were adopted from neighbours) and the associated age grades, marriage and ancestry rules, territorial integration and the language factor.

The thesis to be discussed here, based on the existing ethnographic descriptions, is that the most important group identities in the region of Tanguiéta are tied to the unfolding of distinct moral spaces. I mean with this term the socio-cultural frames of orientation that comprise notions (including those conflicting and discursively developed notions) about norms, and above all those regarding 'correct' behaviour in daily public exchanges and the different interpretations and assessments of these in the past and the present. These have developed above all in terms of different economic activities, but also refer to, for example, religious practices and go beyond a purely 'vocational identity', since they are tied to a whole series of different everyday rituals and rhetorical elements in public exchanges that are relatively independent of them.

My use of the term 'moral space' refers to John Lonsdale's moral ethnicity (1993, 1996; see also Lentz 1993) and to a certain extent to the work of James Scott (1976). In my definition, a moral space includes whole series of collective perceptions on modes of behaviour, norms and social values (in a specific area among a specific group of people) and which, in a broader sense, comprise the conditions for the practical mastering of daily life. It applies above all to individual behaviour, the ideal individual virtues of a group member, but also the routines and forms of social organization as well as aesthetic standards. These perceptions are, according to Lonsdale (1996: 99), never absolutely defined. They are, instead, topics of constant debate and conflict within the respective space of these moral ethnicities. Discussions of difference tied to social processes of rupture and integration are developed in public exchanges (cf. Schlee and Werner 1996a; Horstmann and Schlee 2001). In the present case, the different modes of identification acquire relevance through further factors, especially in the development of corporate vocational interest groups. They establish, simultaneously through division of labour and exchange, levels of complementarity and (for the most part economically motivated) conflict or divergence of interests.

A moral space is a social space of daily interaction in which these categories are constantly being renegotiated. Its distinctiveness lies in the conditions of social integration and the cultural markers that delimit it. These are determined by perceptions of moral behaviour.

To illustrate the emergence of such moral spaces in my case study, I will first describe the situation of the Muslim traders and craftsmen in Tanguiéta. They live, above all, in the quarters of Goro-Bani and Djindjiré-Béri. They are characterized in their everyday existence – today as in the past – by distinctive types of business activities, lifestyle, clothing, language and social rules. The example of one of their groups, the Hausa butchers, provides the best account of these features.

Case 1: The Hausa Butchers

The butchers in Tanguiéta are organized in a type of guild. Their leaders, and especially the *sarkin fawa*, the chief of the butchers, decide who receives a license to become a butcher or to sell meat, who becomes an apprentice, when a butcher will be allowed to butcher an animal and when hygiene checks are made. They also try to control prices. A different butcher has his turn in the local slaughtering house every day. He buys the respective animals (one or two per day) himself from the animal traders (some butchers are themselves animal traders) and then sells the bulk of the meat to the meat retailers, who in turn sell it at a special stand on the market.

One can only become a butcher after completing a long apprenticeship. The personal virtues of honesty and thoughtfulness and an exemplary personal history as an (ideally married) Muslim are prerequisites for acquiring the status of an independent butcher. To date, all butchers in Tanguiéta are Hausa. At the time of writing, two apprentices were originally Buruba. Both had married Hausa women, converted to Islam and live with their wives' families. They have been quasi-adopted.

Like in other comparable areas of West Africa, Islam is the most significant marker of identity, characterizing all members of the minority group of traders and craftsmen in Tanguiéta. One important element thereof are the ethical perceptions that can be considered part of a moral space. I want to use Michel Agier's (1982) category 'ethic of the zongo' (*l'éthique du zongo*) that he used to describe the Hausa traders' quarter in Lomé (Togo); a term which is also relevant in Tanguiéta, although with a different nuance.

Agier maintains that Hausa is, above all else, a synonym for a group of people who migrated from the same general region (savannah, western Sudan) and who preserve the same basic moral principles that one should follow as a resident of a traders' quarter. One can, in principle, find *zongo* quarters all over West Africa. *Zongo*[10] is the dominant term above all for the quarters of Islamic traders who have immigrated from other regions in Ghana, Benin, Togo, Niger, Nigeria and Burkina Faso. Although the residents are not exclusively traders and immigrants, they are for the most part considered the 'foreigner quarters' in opposition to the 'local' or the 'autochthonous' quarters. They go back to the first waves of immigration by Hausa traders, among them kola traders as described by Adamu (1978) and Lovejoy (1980), butchers (Cohen 1965, 1969) and soldiers (in the services of the colonial powers). *Zongo* became a synonym for:

- a community of Muslims;
- a community of traders, and a refuge for foreign Muslim traders;
- a place where the laws of Islam are respected (*shariya*);
- a place of free trade without fraud, trustfulness, brokerage and the possibility of obtaining credit etc. (Nicolas 1964);
- a place of respect for the older, established traders and the chiefs of the respective extended families (Hausa: *maigida*); and
- a place where specific marriage rules are respected.

Zongo describes a place and a community, originally of (immigrated and converted) Hausa. At the same time it is a model Islamic community, reproduced in every detail, that makes the expansion of trade possible. Warms (1994) and Launay (1982) propose a similar community model for the Djoula. In Kumasi *zongo* became a synonym for an Islamic community that became increasingly dominated by Mossi immigrants from Burkina Faso (Shildkrout 1974, 1978).

In Tanguiéta the Djindjiré-Béri and Goro-Bani quarters were actually called *zongo* in the past, and a quarter of this name can still be found in the border town of Boukombé, southwest of Tanguiéta. The *zongo* served as a meeting point for foreign Muslim traders. To this day they can find a place to sleep or to eat or to make business contacts there (cf., Shildkrout 1978); if they stay for a longer period of time, the *zongo* offers them a base for their internal integration if they conform to apparently basic rules of behaviour.[11]

The constitution and persistence of different moral spaces could also be represented as the establishment of semi-autonomous social fields.[12] By using the term semi-autonomous social field, I am making reference to Sally Falk Moore (1978) who developed the concept within legal anthropology. Following Moore, there exists in every society a degree of legal heterogeneity, i.e. coexistence or an overlapping of different formal and informal norms. These are not fully auton-omous spheres, since the state influences many of the general conditions in the development of such fields indirectly, and intervenes from time to time or is partially caught up in them. In the case of Tanguiéta several such spheres can be identified, such as the forms of collective labour organization, the organization of brewing and consumption, some of the trade, the smuggling, initiation, conflict regulation, the organization of the taxi and the bus station, the organization of trade in livestock and the butcher guild, et cetera. Those involved in these fields are interested in excluding foreign or non-conforming persons, above all where they are dealing with limited material resources.

Exclusivity is maintained by various means: endogamy, rules of admission, monopolization of knowledge, language or even latent violence. The moral space which is established in the *zongo* does not coincide with the definition of its res-idents as foreigners by accident – *les gens du zongo* or *les zongo*. These terms are being used less and less in Tanguiéta, although Dendi has become a synonym for these groups. One can speak of a kind of 'amalgamation' of partial identities, which has occurred in the last few years. Five essential factors have eased this process: (1) the moral space of a Muslim community; (2) common economic specializations; (3) Dendi as a common idiom equivalent to Hausa elsewhere, i.e. as a common language; (4) state policy (above all in the 1970s and 1980s); and (5) marriage within these groups.

Case 2: Social Integration and Differentiation in the Tchoutchoumbou Quarter

This quarter consists of an ensemble of smaller family farmsteads (*concessions*). Each includes several buildings and storehouses and is occupied by an extended family. The population density in this quarter is relatively low. There are large spaces between the individual houses, which are used for the cultivation of veg-etables, millet and tobacco. Due to the parcelling of the land, the quarter is relatively clearly subdivided and is thus different from the surrounding villages, which are marked by a relatively scattered housing situation. The quarter is occupied by members of several ethnic groups (with their respective different languages): Natèmba (who are the majority), Byerebe, and Gurmancèba, all of which are basically 'farmer groups'. This fragmentation is a result of the succes-sive waves of immigration in the last decades, above all by the Natèmba. One can find many *cabarets* (millet beer bars) in this quarter, relatively close to one another. The *cabarets* are important places for neighbourhood relationships and for daily public exchanges between people of different socio-linguistic or regional origins in Tchoutchoumbou.

Two parallel tendencies characterize the quarter. On the one hand, socio-economic and everyday cultural integration is becoming more and more important in the neighbourhood. The tendency towards mixed partnerships and marriages is increasing. On the other hand, the differences in regional origin are stressed in parts of the public discourse, above all in connection with political parties and associations.

Social integration has been on the increase since the 1960s and the massive immigration of war veterans and low-level white-collar workers (*fonctionnaires*) into the quarter. The day-to-day relations in Tchoutchoumbou are marked above all by the fact of being neighbours. More and more economic transactions are being completed between neighbours of different kinship and linguistic groups. These relationships are being shaped primarily by women who stand in numerous exchange and collaborative relationships to one another. Among these are the common of brewing beer, cultivating common fields, helping in the household and in the raising of the children, and participating in rotating savings and credit clubs (*tontines*). The men cooperate as well, for example with the harvest or in the construction of houses. The situation in the city of Tanguiéta is different from that in the smaller communities where the principles of kinship play a more important role in the moral economy. The internal integration in the quarters of Tanguiéta is intensified by the learning of the language of the respective neighbours. Nearly all the children speak the languages of their neighbours and, with Dendi, have command of three active languages. The head of the quarter (*chef de quartier*), a Natèmba man, is recognized by most residents and in the local council there are no explicit quotas for representatives of groups defined socio-linguistically. The tendency towards ethnic conversion, above all through marriage, is very strong in Tanguiéta.

The diversity of these social relationships in the neighbourhood is limited by the preference for relationships to people from the same region of origin that speak the same language (lineage membership only plays a minor role in this case). These are often relationships between men who have known one another for a longer period, worked together (for example in the army, such as the war veterans, *anciens combattants*), went to school together or have similar political points of view. The individual residents, above all the elders, naturally maintain a strong connection towards their communities of origin. But their respective frequency of contact is very variable. There are those who travel at least once a month to the villages in their region of origin and even those who tend fields there; others do this rarely, i.e. they only return for larger festivals and for the funerals of close relatives. Some few, nevertheless, above all former or active Natèmba or Gurmancèba civil servants, own houses in their home village as well as in Tanguiéta. They always return to the village for short periods of time. As influential men and organizers they could be called 'big men' (cf. Sahlins 1963; Bakel et al. 1986) and are often active in local politics. They need the support from their home region and need to foster it appropriately. They have some of their wives and children in the village and others in the city, and often own a motorcycle. The maintenance of relationships in their region of origin is a part of their personal career strategy that allows for a retreat to those villages and the use of these contacts in case of personal need (for example, in sickness, or to care for children, but also for religious ceremonies, etc.).

The increased social integration in those quarters of Tanguiéta that are occupied for the most part by farmers (Yarika, Porika) would most likely be greater if not for the tendency in the last few years to politicize the differences of linguistic and regional origin, especially as a rhetorical device for new political groups. This has several causes. On the one hand, this is generally based on the strong competition for development projects between the various neighbouring communities. In this case, the residents of the respective community turn to their emigrant relatives or other members of their communities in Tanguiéta and ask them to speak on their behalf in the relevant committees in Tanguiéta (Grätz 1998). This is especially the case in the activities of political parties, their representatives and candidates who are inclined to focus on an 'ethnic' constituency based on linguistic and regional origin. They turn first to those who see in them a 'local son' and do not refrain from making polarizing remarks against other ethnic groups, above all when there are politicians of other parties in the region looking to serve another constituency (this does not exclude the possibility that the candidates of different parties compete in the same ethnic constituency. In this case, they also throw inflammatory remarks at one another). In other circumstances, the political integration is greater, as will be shown in the following text.

The Contractual Character of Interethnic Relationships in Tanguiéta

When looking at the current communal political relationships in the community of Tanguiéta, the concept of an (unwritten) contractual relationship between larger 'we'-groups can be developed. These are, I suggest, informal regulations, which delimit physical and symbolic spaces, but also regulate potential economic exchange and access to resources and offices. It is a type of unspoken 'agreement' to not let the degrees of social difference and conflicts of interest described here become the dominant field of public discourse in the community. The informal agreement, between the members of the 'trader and craftsmen groups' and the 'farmer groups' for example, can be described in a simplified manner: the latter dominate the majority of public forums, institutions, and administrative offices in the community (even beyond the level of the quarter and the official quotas) in terms of personnel as well as institutionally (through external support, i.e. via state functionaries from the region), while the former consciously hold back in these areas. These include the administrative positions in the community, among them the mayor and the *sécretaire*, as well as those of the surrounding communities. Other important positions include those in the influential *association de développement*, as well as further communal associations, such as the parents' groups (*association des parents-elèves*), the land-grant commission and the steering committee of the community radio station *Radio Rurale Locale Tanguiéta* (Grätz 2000).

In return, there is an officially unquestioned inequality, in terms of economic influence, i.e. 'traders" access to opportunities for capital accumulation, control of capital and material flows as well as services. The wholesale traders as well as the owners of bars, video cinemas, wage labour farmers, gas station owners and other individuals with opportunities for capital accumulations are almost exclusively Dendi and Yoruba. The majority of petty traders, such as the president of the *union des producteurs*, an alliance of small entrepreneurs mainly from the cotton growing industry, also emerge out of their ranks. The cliché 'economic power vs. political power' is not simply a comprehensive, structural principle in Tanguiéta; it is the description of a tendency and is amplified by current political developments (majority elections, the numerical advantage being held by the farmers) and economic currents (growth of the domestic market for foodstuffs, reduction of cash crop production and state consumption).

Important factors here are the currently relevant comprehensive forms of political integration and common interests as well as the experiences from the past, the memories, for example, of the confrontations in the 1970s.

Conditions for Ethnic Conversion

The term 'conversion' here describes the change to the dominant identity of another group. These conversions take place on an individual basis and feature a shift in daily social, economic and cultural practices, without losing all references to origin. There are several elements in Tanguiéta that allow particular people to change from one field of reference to another or to expand the number of levels in their socio-cultural identities. In many cases, this is initially a professional strategy. These changes are tied to the negotiations between different norms: conditions that one needs to meet in order to earn the respect of others. In Goro-Bani for example, there was a case of two master butchers, who were of Bulba ancestry but converted to the Hausa. They were quasi adopted for several years by a Hausa family, married Hausa women and became Muslim. Other cases concern successful traders of Byerebe ancestry in Tanguiéta who also converted to Islam. But traders like these still maintain contact with their relatives. They often employ workers and helpers from their extended family. It is often the case that, assuming they have the choice, customers from their group of origin prefer to buy from them, and not only for language reasons. These individuals are not excluded from the social networks in the groups of origin; because of their superior financial background, one expects economic help from them. These traders will never close themselves to these requests, although they do limit them (not without problems), since they do need to reinvest their capital. On the one hand, they find themselves caught between the expectations of two reference groups. On the other hand, these small entrepreneurs extend their own range of action into a second dominant group identity, above all as a recognized Muslim, expanding their relationships in the city so as to continue their economic activities without problems. In the end, their economic success depends to a large degree on their ability to control themselves and to maintain their prestige, especially among those traders with whom they wish to complete larger transactions.

Women from the 'farmer group' who have recently established tailor shops and others who have gone into the petty trade or cereal trade need to be mentioned here as well. There are very few of these women in Tanguiéta, but they have accumulated a considerable amount of capital. They visit the weekly markets in the region of Matéri (Gouandé, Matéri, Tantéga) since there they can profit from their excellent knowledge of the Biali language. This is a relatively new development.

The different collective points of view on the socio-cultural exclusion, as well as the integration of others discussed here, are social norms that influence public exchange in Tanguiéta. They create different social spaces, in which differences in daily life are produced, perceived and filled with meaning. More simply, one can say for the case of Tanguiéta that the areas based on the mentioned principles of 'ethic of *zongo*' (Agier 1982; Shildkrout 1978; or the moral economy of the trader, cf., Evers and Schrader 1994) and the 'ethic of subsistence' (or the 'moral economy of the peasant', Scott 1976) are set in opposition to one another, even if the associated economic points of reference are being increasingly transformed.

Overarching Levels of Communal Action and Political Integration

The political transformation in Benin has been marked, since the national conference in February 1990, by a programmatic liberalization of politics and economics. The political stage in Benin is characterized by a diverse variety of parties, NGOs, new media, daily newspapers and independent radio stations. In economic terms, petty entrepreneurs and traders are being encouraged to expand their activities; in terms of state administration, things have only changed recently. The laws passed on decentralization allow for the creation of communities with elected councillors and a mayor, thus replacing the former *sous-préfet* named unilaterally by the minister of the interior.

In the last few years a particular political integration of hitherto opposed groups of local inhabitants has become, however, quite obvious. This integration is based on a common positioning against adverse politicians and a similar voting behaviour of the residents. Thus, especially in terms of politics, strategic alliances, even between groups in conflict, are made to oppose the outer world. This can also be seen in areas were the economic web of complementary relationships as a whole is endangered. This is equally true for the traders, drivers, vehicle owners and farmers, if the question is one of the state leaving the road network underdeveloped or demanding tolls that are too high, problems that affect, among other things, the functioning of the all-important weekly markets in the region. These are communal questions, which have, in the last few years, instigated common activities to enforce common interests.

Conclusions and Perspectives

A resident of Tanguiéta or someone who was born there, in the local Beninese vernacular *'fils de Tanguiéta'* (son of Tanguiéta),[13] can identify himself as a member of the 'farmer group' or the Muslim 'trader group', as resident of a quarter, where he maintains neighbourly relationships with others, or as a member of a religious community, as a member of a small linguistic group or as someone who is associated with a political party, as a member of an occupational group, et cetera. But these categories are, as was demonstrated, not arbitrary and are in some cases mutually exclusive. It is important to stress here that these forms of belonging can mean something completely different on a personal level. To be Dendi could mean, for example, finding public acceptance as a Muslim, it could be the respecting of a 'family tradition', it could be the taking up of a universal group identity as a new trader or it could mean recognizing moral principles.

Several of these collective identities come together and amplify tendencies of inclusion and exclusion. The butchers, for example, are usually Muslims as well. Dendi, like Hausa in other cases, becomes an idiom for occupational association, is tied to a work ethic and moral categories of inclusion that also allow for the definition of the criteria of conversion. The emphasis on a specific identity can also be seen among the 'farmer group' that has experienced a politicization in the last years based on (assumed) ancestry, language and above all, regional domination. The *associations de développement* are organized by politicians, based in the regional capitals, who can reorganize the cohesion of networks beyond Tanguiéta and can mobilize people. Politicians on the national stage initially look for a foundation in these individual identities; they want to be the 'in-house' candidate for the Byerebe or the Natèmba for example. But this politicization of communal social relationships is again based on successful overarching definitions: as a son of the region (*fils de terroir* or better, *fils de Tanguiéta* cf., also Bako-Arifari 1995), a civil servant or politician, who is a councillor for all the residents. They could, as a *fils de Tanguiéta*, gain acceptance as politicians despite the socio-cultural heterogeneity described. Politicians who act in this way are more successful than those who bet on an ethnic card, although they do have to balance conflicts of interest and overlapping affiliation. There is no automatic 'segmentary principle' in communal politics. Each current political issue generates its own followers and opponents as well as the respective discourse alliances.

The described dominant collective identities in Tanguiéta developed historically out of the interplay between socio-economic and social difference, delimiting perceptions of the self and the other as well as the formation of interest groups. Integration (such as conflict limitation) within the community does not follow out of common social and political cultural institutions but via communal and national factors such as elections and the intervention of an authoritarian state, but also via changes in everyday life, above all among the younger generation.

These comments were intended to support my interpretation in which the politicization of collective identities in this region is the result of historical developments and highlighted or made a public issue by outside intervention in administration, economics and culture. This occurs parallel to but partially independent of economic changes in the region. The phases of the politicization of collective identities can thus not always be seen as equal to simple conflicts over access or economic participation, even if these issues are always played upon in the argumentation of political actors. I forecast that the moral spaces described here will shift in the long term, as a result of the general social and economic transformation in the region, which is unavoidable and has already begun in the medium-sized cities and the larger seats of administration. They could become the source of new emphases on difference up to and including disintegration, if, for example, certain groups draw factually or even only rhetorically on cultural or social difference in communal conflicts over new or limited resources or decisions.

The role of institutions of conflict resolution, which tend to see the source of conflicts not as an 'ethnic' but as a legal problem, will become important. Future research has to examine the multifold changes induced by the ongoing implementation of the laws on decentralization and reform of the administration, the further establishment of the new community councils with budgetary rights and the communal elections.

Tilo Grätz studied Social Anthropology, History and African Studies in Berlin at the Free University and Humboldt University. He holds a PhD from Bielefeld University and obtained his habilitation degree (postdoctoral qualification) in social anthropology at the University of Halle-Wittenberg in 2008. He has held several research and teaching positions at various German universities and research centres. He is currently Associate Professor at the Institute for Social and Cultural Anthropology at Free University Berlin.

Notes

1. My contribution is primarily based on anthropological fieldwork in northwestern Benin between 1995 and 1997, combining participant observation, narrative interviews and the analysis of social events with oral history as well as archival research (National Archives in Porto-Novo). The setting at that time mainly corresponds to the situation just before the implementation of new laws of territorial decentralization (Grätz 2006, 2016). Various new developments have thus occurred on the municipal level since, which, nevertheless, do not jeopardize the main arguments developed here. The original essay (Grätz 2001) has been slightly revised for the present volume.
2. Dendi is related to Songhay. It has spread with the migrations of trader communities from present-day Niger and northeastern Benin and exists today with different local dialects. It is common across the whole of the Atakora and Borgou as a lingua franca. Dendi as an ethnonym is very inclusive and includes the people who speak Dendi despite their very diverse ancestry.
3. As people usually feature multiple identities, including religious, political or life-style orientations, more and more cross-cutting linguistic, economic and kinship divergences, my proposal could be considered as only one among other possible perspectives on the constitution of collective identities in that area.
4. See Müller (1989) for a case study in Mali on the development of economic complementarity and division of labour of endogamous groups.
5. Tanguiéta as a community remains a pluralist polity. In my view (and in terminological disagreement with other authors in this volume), integration along the lines of socio-economic difference occurs as integration into the (fragile) local political polity and only to a limited degree as an integration in social and cultural terms.
6. The members of the individual 'farmer groups' usually speak the language of their neighbours. The languages of the more recent immigrants, Hausa and Dendi, are spoken to a more limited degree. A simple version of Dendi is spoken in the market. The traders have a limited command of some words and numbers in the Gur languages, most often in Biali. Labour migrants and young intellectuals who have some degree of professional training usually have a better command of the version of Dendi common in the northern Atakora region. Within the city limits of Tanguiéta Dendi has become the lingua franca and is spoken by most of the youth.
7. It is justified to consider these groups (for whom a simplified spelling is used here), which for the most part belong linguistically to the Oti-Volta (Manessy 1975), votaïque- or Gur groups, as culturally related and as belonging to a continuum of socio-economic groups. This is surely only one point of view (argued by scholars such as Köhler [1958], Dittmer [1975] and Aimé [1994a]), which says little about the current group interrelationships or the self-perception of the individual groups.
8. The genealogical depth and the definition of subsegments, even between clans, can vary greatly.
9. As based on the location of the original settlement, the cemetery and the earth shrines.
10. The Hausa term *zongo* (or *zango*) is often translated into the French as *caravansérail*. The Hausa were among the first trading groups to migrate over great distances in this area of West Africa (cf. Adamu 1978). Of these, the kola trade routes are the best known (Lovejoy 1980). But it is not easy, as Adamu illustrates, to differentiate in the historical origins of these movements between 'simple' traders and Islamic scholars who in their travels also traded to earn their living.

11. The term internal integration refers here to the social cohesion within a partial group of a local community, following authors such as Elias and Scotson (1990), who use the term 'insider', and Elwert (1982).

12. Here I mean informal spheres of everyday life that have developed special norms and regulations, institutions, hierarchies, and forms of sanction, separate from 'official' state regulation or recognized ordinances.

13. To some extent, this situation seems to be similar to a public discourse in the town of Parakou, where 'locals', as representatives of the group of first arrivals (Baatombu, Fulbe, etc.), do not fully recognize 'latecomers' (especially southerners), even if the latter were born there (see Bierschenk 1999).

Chapter 6

Transnational Practices and Post-Soviet Collective Identity

Claus Bech Hansen and Markus Kaiser

Following the collapse of the Soviet Union, the question of identity in the post-Soviet space was debated intensively. Viewing the former Soviet republics as laboratories of identity formation, scholars have produced a voluminous body of studies touching, especially, on post-Soviet development of national identity (e.g. Finke 2014; Rasanayagam 2011), Soviet Nationality Policy (e.g. Martin 2001; Suny 1995), and nationalizing states (Brubaker 2011). Meanwhile, little attention has been awarded, in comparative analyses of collective identities, to the centripetal, unifying forces of the Soviet legacy. This is all the more curious since anyone who has travelled in the former Soviet countries stumbles across rather distinct similarities, such as the Kafkaesque bureaucracies, social behaviours, cultural codes and architectural traits; and scholars and inhabitants alike seem to be in broad agreement that the successor societies share not only a number of social, cultural and political practices but also a distinct sense of 'being post-Soviet', implying that the Soviet legacy continues to influence people's identities in post-Soviet space.

In this chapter we combine insights from the literature on collective identity and on spatial and structural notions and their influence on identity formation. Indeed, we presuppose that every individual has multiple dynamic identities, which serve different functions and adapt to the diverse roles and positions any individual holds. We analyse the similarities of social processes and cultural practices across the countries of the former Soviet Union and argue that these, despite the emergence of novel national identities, inform what we suggest can be understood as a post-Soviet collective identity.

Collective Identity in Post-Soviet Space

Describing the time she spent as a student abroad, Ekaterina Kalinina recalls that the majority of her friends came from 'the former Soviet Union and other socialist states', and that their friendship was facilitated partly by similar languages and partly 'by the collective memories and experiences that we shared . . . the same cultural codes' (Kalinina 2014: 16). In their view, the 'collective Eastern European experiences and memories created a very distinct identity' that brought them closer together while distancing them from Western Europeans.[1]

The sensation of difference is shared by many people of the former Soviet Union (and to some extent Eastern Europe) when encountering Western Europeans. And it is precisely this 'very distinct identity', the feeling of communality among citizens in the post-Soviet region, that stand at the heart of our interest. For want of a better term, we call it post-Soviet collective identity.[2] We want to look at what it is made up of and how it is reproduced. As a result, we hope to contribute to a growing body of literature on the colossal legacy left behind by the Soviet period.

Dating back to Lenin, Soviet policy-makers were crucially aware that social, cultural and professional interconnectedness typically facilitates and strengthens the cohesion of collectives. This resulted in a two-tiered system of official identity creation: on the one hand, the Soviet state promoted local identities to ensure political support by creating nations and buttressing local cultures and languages through the Soviet Nationality Policy (Hirsch 2005; Martin 2001; Simon 1991; Smith 1999).[3] On the other hand, the state promoted a 'supranational' Soviet identity (similar to the notion of the melting pot of US-American nation building), which encompassed all Soviet peoples and, through union-wide integrative forces, sought to generate affectional bonds between the union state and its subjects (Bennigsen 1979). Strictly speaking, the relationship between the local (e.g. Ukrainian or Latvian) and the Soviet identities was hierarchical and, given the nature of the post-Soviet collective identity as one that transgresses national borders, it is particularly the legacy of the Soviet identity that is of interest here.

The authenticity of the Soviet identity has long been a subject of interest to scholars. Both the propagandistic notion of the 'New Soviet Man' and more or less derogatory terms such as 'Homo Sovieticus' and 'sovok' were developed to capture certain aspects of Soviet collective identity, which was and remains highly politicized. Western views of the Soviet identity were further influenced by literary works, from Alexander Zinovyev's sarcastic interpretation of Soviet identity (1986) to the epic novels of Arthur Koestler (1941), George Orwell (2013) and Alexander Solzhenitsyn (1974).[4] To be sure, scholars such as Alex Inkeles and Raymond Bauer (1959) produced early notable works but, prior to 1991, limited access to sources hampered in-depth research and left a sour aftertaste of an artificial, highly constructed identity.

In hindsight, the evident constructedness of Soviet collective identity is hardly surprising. After all, Anderson (1983), Gellner (1983) and Hobsbawm (1990), to name but a few influential constructivist thinkers, have convincingly shown the 'artificial' nature of identities, while Anthony Smith (1987) has explained why they are nonetheless compelling. Unsurprisingly, then, scholars have rightfully argued that official efforts to generate a Soviet collective identity were indeed successful, albeit surely not to the extent policy-makers and supporters of the Soviet project had hoped for (e.g. Hellbeck 2006; Khalid 2007; Kotkin 1995; Yurchak 2006). This argument is based on the assumption that the duration of the Soviet period and the strong integrative forces led to an extraordinary level of interconnectedness of state, nation and population that not only impacted all arenas of everyday life but also generated emotional ties. These affective bonds are best understood as a 'communal social relationship', which, according to Max Weber (1968: 40–41), 'is based on a subjective feeling of the parties, whether affectual or traditional, that they belong together'. The majority of works are theoretically rather vague, however, and combine the study of memory, tradition, language, symbolisms and institutions (e.g. Bassin and Kelly 2012; Suny 1999).

It remains difficult to gauge whether or not the Soviet communal sense was feebler than local identities such as Russian or Uzbek. Meanwhile, it has undoubtedly waned during the post-Soviet period. The primary reason for this is, of course, the dissolution of the Soviet state, which meant that one of the preeminent forces generating collective identity in the former Soviet space has ceased to exist. In its place have stepped fifteen independent republics that each seek to actively produce their own idiosyncratic, national identity. On the western frontier of post-Soviet space these narratives often construe the Soviet period as one of repression and/or occupation, while they typically remain rather more neutral in the southern regions.

While the developments on the level of national identity formation thus pull away from a general identity comprising all nations of the former Soviet space, many political, social and cultural similarities remain in place, underlining the perseverance of the region's shared heritage (Kaiser 2001, 2003). Furthermore, the concrete experiences during the post-Soviet period have been shared by the majority of the citizens. These include the political instability of the post-Soviet period, the economic and material hardship and uncertainty resulting from successive crises as well as the ideological void left by the bygone state. Such experiences affected practically every family in the post-Soviet countries, producing further unifying elements. Moreover, one is confronted, when analysing post-Soviet collective identity, with a compound puzzle of national identities, identity conflation, provenance and entanglements which arise from a sense of shared experiences both during and after the Soviet Union was dissolved.

In order to make sense of this complex mosaic of shared identities and practices, it is helpful to look at sociological and social anthropological research on identity and identity formation. In their recent study of collective identities and corresponding processes of identification, Donahoe et al. (2009) define collective identities as variable representations containing normative appeals that serve, potentially, to orient individuals in their relations to others, to the world around them, and to themselves; while 'identification' refers to the ways in which individuals respond to or engage with collective identities. Taken together, collective identities and processes of identification 'must be analysed with reference to particular social, cultural, and historical circumstances *and* with reference to systematically outlined variables' (Donahoe et al. 2009: 31; italics in original).

The variables referred to by Donahoe et al. relate to 'dimensions of collective identity', 'markers of collective identity', and 'identity variables', including semantic relations among different identities and the significance of identities for actors in diverse social situations or under changing circumstances (Donahoe et al. 2009: 12–18). Examples of 'dimensions' include nationality, ethnicity, gender, religion, et cetera; whereas 'markers' are the sensory data that indicate an individual's orientation toward a particular collective identity, say, this or that nationality, either in their own self-understanding or in the eyes of others. 'Semantic relations' among identities may be complementary or contrasting (i.e. one may be a European black male or an Uzbek immigrant day-labourer to Russia, because these identities are complementary, while it is difficult to be Jewish, Catholic and Muslim simultaneously); or they may correspond to various levels of generality and specificity, as in the distinction between European, French and Parisian. Finally, identities may have varying significance for actors, depending on their salience in particular social situations and their pervasiveness and stability from one situation to another.

While Donahoe et al.'s (2009) study casts light on identity formation and identification processes of actors, other scholars have discussed how these processes occur in the age of globalization that is marked, particularly, by increasing mobility and information exchange. In the social sciences, the corresponding debates have led to a paradigm shift in our conceptualization of globality and locality, traditionally understood as fundamentally opposed but today conceived, rather, as interdependent and mutually constitutive. Just as we detect the local in the global, we now understand locality not as a static entity but a site of porous borders, characterized by social practice and social construction (Appadurai 1995, 1996; Freitag and von Oppen 2010). In other words, 'the social' has been relieved of its territorial component, and the concept of society as something territorially bound has gradually dissolved.

The reconceptualization of the relationship between globality and locality has had consequences for the fundamental assumptions underlying the analysis of collective identity formation by representatives of several academic disciplines. Building on a Weberian understanding[5] of the state and state authority, political scientists have long viewed nation-states as the dominant forces in organizing and controlling societies on the macro-level. The reconfiguration of 'the social', as well as mounting evidence pointing toward the importance of sub-state or 'bottom-up' factors interfering with the 'congruence between state authority, state population (demos) and state territory', have called forth critiques of state-centrism and 'methodological nationalism' (Faist 2004; Wimmer and Glick Schiller 2003). As a result of this critique, strong trends toward 'trans-isms', such as transnationalism, transregionalism, et cetera, have arisen. These seek to diminish the analytical pre-eminence of the nation-state (though by no means disavowing its central role) by recognizing the importance of networks, organizations (such as associations of political parties, trade unions, employer associations and churches) and information exchange reaching beyond (multiple) state borders and the accustomed territorial state-level memberships (Pries 1999).

The altered understanding of 'the social' has had repercussions for social and cultural anthropologists, too, working on the micro-level and researching space, interconnectedness and everyday life practices. On this level, the nation-state's limited importance, especially in states of weak institutional outreach (e.g. Afghanistan), leads scholars to write increasingly of 'translocal society' (Schetter 2012) or translocality (Hannerz 1996; Freitag and von Oppen 2010). For despite dysfunctional state institutions, for example in failed states, these societies are rarely static. In fact, the contrary is typically the case: with decreasing reliance on state institutions, local or translocal relations, organizations and institutions become increasingly important, even the dominant force in structuring everyday life, connecting communities in different localities.

The debates on collective identity, identification processes, globalization and space provide powerful tools for the analysis of identity in the former Soviet region. Indeed, the complex nature of post-Soviet collective identity is mirrored in Kalinina's description, cited above. In her experience, self-conscious identification with the post-Soviet collective identity emerged only in the confrontation with non-Soviet identities of Western Europe. This is suggestive with regard to individuals' experience of post-Soviet collective identity; for, despite the striking similarities between people, cities, structures, institutions and practices in the post-Soviet space, these in and of themselves do not guarantee the salience of a post-Soviet collective identity, i.e. an active identification with it. Indeed, with regard to all of the various identities available to individuals, identification appears to linger in a dormant state and to become salient only in certain situations, such as an encounter with sameness or difference (Schlee, Introduction in this volume; Baberowski 2006). This aspect is instructive because it suggests, first, that factors such as memories, experiences and practices generate a foundation of post-Soviet collective identity and, second, that the right stimuli can trigger a self-conscious identification of individuals as a response (e.g. Bentley 1991: 173; Bourdieu 1977). But how does this transfer take place?

In this chapter, we suggest that shared social and cultural practices constitute one way in which features of post-Soviet collective identity are transferred. We analyse various practices in post-Soviet space that have emerged through societal interconnections, encounters, exchanges, collective memory and social processes as well as experiences and established normative and behavioural codes. Today, these practices live on, transgress national borders and ensure the region's continued high level of integration (Kaiser 2001, 2003; opposing view: Tlostanova 2015: 38). Leaning on Max Weber's (1968: 40–41) understanding of communal ties, we understand such practices as transnational social and cultural practices that are not only expressions but also conveyors of a transnational communal relationship through their reproduction in the post-Soviet space. This transnational communal relationship is best understood as a cultural identity based on real or perceived experiences and memories that produce a sense of shared heritage and belonging; it is in constant negotiation, and at times in conflict with, but nonetheless complementary to, other identities (national, ethnic, professional, etc.) that individuals self-consciously identify with (Holliday 2010: 175–76). Moreover, we term this cultural identity post-Soviet collective identity and argue that shared social and cultural practices in post-Soviet space continue to generate encounters, experiences and memories that reproduce it. As a result, we hope to provide answers to several questions arising from the relationship between identity and practices: is it reasonable to apprehend the evident transnational similarities characterizing social and cultural practices in the post-Soviet countries as an indication of a post-Soviet collective identity? When do practices and corresponding identities stop being Soviet or post-Soviet and start being, say, Ukrainian, Georgian or Tajik in their own right? Is it convincing to suggest that the legacy of the bygone Soviet state induces a shared identity and, if so, for how much longer will it continue to do so?

In the sections that follow, we briefly recall, in a first descriptive part, prior debates on identity in the post-Soviet region. Then, we turn to the analysis of transnational practices in different spheres of everyday life in the former Soviet space. By no means do we attempt to provide a definitive list of features that we believe inform post-Soviet collective identity.[6] Rather, we have merely marked out, with broad-brush strokes, a number of themes, including trade, mobility, the informal economy, and socialization, rituals and tradition, where we detect transnational practices that we believe inform a post-Soviet collective identity. Reviewing these themes leads to the discovery of multiple ways in which the Soviet legacy lives on and influences current identity formation. Finally, in a third step, we discuss the possible future of post-Soviet collective identity as a perceptible phenomenon in post-Soviet space.

Expectations, Prophecies and Debates of the 1990s

Following the implosion of the Soviet Union, much ink was spilt in musing on how the newly independent former Soviet republics would develop as nations. Most had first become political entities during the Soviet period and could draw on no national precedent (Hirsch 2005; Martin 2001; Simon 1991); and many were, like Russia, multi-ethnic states potentially threatened by centrifugal forces. The right to self-determination was generally accepted, but the diverse forces at play in the former Soviet space left much room for uncertainty and debate about how collective identities would influence the trajectories of individual countries.

On the fallen giant's western frontier, few contemporaries doubted that the Baltic states would 'return' to the Western European community of stable nation-states. This narrative was based on the clear precedents that were established with nation-state formation during the period of dissolving empires following the Great War and with their violation through the Soviet invasion following the signing of the Hitler-Stalin Pact in 1939. Similarly, in western Ukraine, the grand narrative of nations found expression in a pronounced national consciousness, which observers have been swift to detect again, first in the Orange Revolution of 2004 and 2005 and then in the Maidan uprisings leading to the ousting of Janukovitch in 2014 and allowing the Ukraine to 'catch up' with the revolution of 1989 (Kappeler 2015).

Expectations for countries on the northwestern rim of the former Soviet Union were based on historical evidence of some level of national consciousness, but scholars were far less certain about the rest of the post-Soviet states. In contrast to the Baltic republics, Belarus, Moldova, and the states in Central Asia and the Caucasus had no, or hardly any, historical precedent. Consequently, even before the demise of the Soviet Union, scholars, among others, pondered the strength of pan-Turkic loyalties in Central Asia, supporting their suppositions with reference to movements of the early twentieth century (Bennigsen 1979).

Forming a large, contiguous landmass, Central Asia and Asia Minor, taken together, lie at the crossroads of ancient trade routes marked by high mobility. In these regions and along these routes, heterogeneous populations in societies, organized according to segmentary principles, developed a multitude of diverse identities. Rather than reviving pan-Turkic loyalties, however, each of the Central Asian states that gained independence in 1991 embarked on a successful process of collective identity formation, accentuating their past glories and detecting in outspokenly primordialist fashion the eternal roots of their individual national culture (see e.g. Denison 2009; Kudaibergenova 2014; Williams 2014). For example, the Uzbek government has invested heavily in legitimizing national interests by reinterpreting its regional history in order to establish a national Uzbek identity (Jacquesson 2010; Jacquesson and Beller-Hann 2012; Schatz 2014). This has included the remarkable rehabilitation of bygone rulers such as Amir Timur, or Tamerlane, who is today celebrated as the foremost Uzbek national hero (Hegarthy 1995).[7]

In hindsight, the picture that emerges is clearly one of several successful but very different nation-building processes in Central Asia based on antagonistic developmental models (import substitution, isolation, open resource-based economy, donor dependent development). Contrary to the prophecies from scholars across the world, the 'right to self-determination' was instrumentalized for the construction of individual nation-states and political elites continue to construe the 'self' through a careful ethnic reading of history. This should not lead to the flawed conclusion that the legacy of a collective Soviet identity has been vanquished by new local, regional and national identities. On the contrary, as we shall argue in the following section, these live on, interwoven, altered and reproduced by transnational cultural and social practices with the passing of time.

Transnational Practices and Post-Soviet Space

'Socialization and spatialization', Edward Soja reminds us, are 'intricately intertwined, interdependent and often in conflict' (Soja 2009). Drawing inspiration from Soja, one is tempted to suggest that the demise of the Soviet Union resulted in a conflict between the established patterns of Soviet socialization and the novel spatialization of post-Soviet territory. As noted above, however, this incongruence should not lead to the erroneous assumption that the astonishing Soviet disappearing act obliterated the tightly knit social, economic and cultural structures of the Soviet era. In fact, it is precisely the transnational social and cultural practices originating from this legacy that we analyse in the following sections.

Trade, Movement and Informality

One of the simplest ways to trace interconnectedness and corresponding practices of the post-Soviet region is by examining the movements of people and goods over time. Examining these patterns lends us insight into encounters between actors who perceive their interaction in terms of sameness and difference and sheds light on their underlying motivations, perceived opportunities and mental maps, all of which are decisive for our understanding of transnational cultural and social practices and identity formation.

Despite widespread expectations that the Silk Road would re-emerge on the southern frontier of the former Soviet Union, after having been disrupted during the Soviet interlude, trade between the post-Soviet states far outweighs trade along historical routes in the region. Russia remains the dominant regional power, as its significance for other post-Soviet republics is comparable to that of leading world economies such as China and the United States. In 2012, Kazakhstan received almost 40 per cent of its imports from Russia, while Kyrgyzstan, Ukraine and Lithuania received roughly 30 per cent. Broadening the data to include imports in each of these former post-Soviet republics not only from Russia but from all other post-Soviet republics, the figures surge further to 58, 51, 48, and 46 per cent respectively. In reverse order, i.e. in terms of exports that post-Soviet republics direct toward their post-Soviet counterparts, the numbers are similar. In 2014, almost 50 per cent of Uzbek exports went to Russia and Kazakhstan, while roughly 40 per cent of all Ukrainian exports went to the post-Soviet region at large (Observatory of Economic Complexity 2015). As of 1 January 2015, the Eurasian Economic Union, though including only Russia, Kazakhstan, Kyrgyzstan, Belarus and Armenia, is no doubt contributing to the solidification of the integration of the post-Soviet regional trading bloc, not only economically but also socially, culturally and politically.

Admittedly, the existence of a collective identity is not deducible from overall trade figures. These do, however, indicate the degree of interconnectedness within the wider region: beyond political boundaries, yet within post-Soviet space. The trade regime structure thus fosters encounters through highly modernized trade routes, which are facilitated by Soviet-era networks, traditional connections, trade treaties and not least the Russian language, which still serves as the lingua franca in large parts of the post-Soviet space. Clearly, alterations in these trade patterns are emerging. China and large regional export economies such as Turkey and Germany figure high on import scales, but the exchange of goods within the post-Soviet region mirrors patterns predating 1991.

These patterns are even more evident in the spheres of current petty trade and migration, the structures of which shed further light not only on the path-dependencies, networks and trust relations but also on mental maps, tastes and habits which emerged during the Soviet period. Today's petty trade in post-Soviet space is largely directed by established bazaar networks that function together as an extensive distribution system, especially in the southern parts of the region. Major international bazaars, such as *Barakholka* in Almaty, *Dordoi* in Bishkek and *Korvon* in Dushanbe are wholesale markets attracting suitcase traders. Goods from these markets are distributed to regional bazaars, e.g. *Altyn Orda* in Almaty, *Shanghai* in Astana and *Madina* bazaar in Bishkek, which supply the end customers (Kaminski and Mitra 2010). Admittedly, the majority of commodities at these markets originate outside the Commonwealth of Independent States (CIS). In 2001, Evers and Kaiser (2001, compare 2004) found that only about 20 per cent of petty trade goods in Uzbekistan were produced in the CIS region, while Alff and Schmidt (2011) and Alff (2013, 2014a, 2014b, 2015) recently demonstrated that commodities in Kazakh and Kyrgyz markets (including fabrics) originate predominantly from China. The point, however, is that we find a continuation of Soviet-era trade routes, indicating the interconnectedness of informal-sector trade networks within the post-Soviet space. This is the result of trade treaties and profit structures of petty trade, where wholesale markets in different areas of the post-Soviet space allow profitable import-export for traders.

Cheap goods from the Central Asian region travel north to increase the profit margin, while cheap goods in Moscow travel south for the same purpose. Thus, national boundaries, economies and their price differentials are a resource for cross-border trading.

Corresponding to the infrastructure and recurring patterns of trade within the post-Soviet space are tacit features related to taste, habits and personal networks. In the context of international and regional bazaars, for example, Kyrgyzstan has emerged as the main supplier of clothing to bazaars across Uzbekistan, Kazakhstan, Russia and Tajikistan. As Kyrgyz sewing-shop owners have reported, this is due not to profit considerations but to the superior ability of Kyrgyz buyers and sellers, in comparison to Chinese competitors, to anticipate the tastes of post-Soviet customers in commodities and fashion.

Trade relations in the post-Soviet space are thus facilitated not only by shared taste, fashion and habits, but also by enduring networks originating prior to the Soviet collapse. The relatively high mobility between the Soviet republics allowed hundreds of thousands of non-Russians to settle in Russia, while maintaining connections to their 'homeland' in one of the various republics and serving as facilitators in trade networks linking different areas. Such facilitation ranges, for example, from providing shelter to circumventing official paperwork by making available one's name or address for registration purposes.

Informal trade between post-Soviet countries does not always follow established network structures, however. In her analysis of 'shuttle trade' on the Belarussian-Lithuanian border, Olga Sasunkevich (2013) has shown convincingly that business decisions may also be based on individual spontaneity rather than established networks. For example, cross-border transportation often takes the form of day labour, as when an exporter commissions an individual who is willing and available to bring commodities across the border.

As this sort of informal trade, whether individualized or network-based, is pervasive throughout the post-Soviet space, we shall elaborate further on the structures of informality below. For now, it is important to emphasize that the particular forms of trade prevalent in the post-Soviet space, and the practices they entail, serve continuously to tie the region together. Indeed, making ends meet under dire economic conditions, adapting to the uncomfortable working conditions that capitalism has forced on them, and 'working the system' in order to succeed at trade are experiences shared by vast numbers of people in the post-Soviet space, reinforcing their sense of collective identity, at least to a degree. In short, the social processes and practices that characterize petty trade in the former Soviet region are transferred across time and space. They are based on an intimate knowledge of the established system, and they serve, in turn, to reproduce that system.[8]

Very similar patterns of continuity between the Soviet and post-Soviet periods become evident when we analyse other forms of mobility. Since

1991, migration from the southern frontier of the former Soviet Union to Russia, especially, has received a great deal of attention from scholars and policy-makers alike. Motivated by economic discontent and political conflicts at home, and made possible by the visa-free regime in the CIS region, such high levels of 'internal' migration point to the existence of mental maps and related practices which were established in the Soviet Union and which continue to direct migration flows in the post-Soviet era. Today, many Central Asians and Caucasians view Moscow, St Petersburg and Kyiv as rich, advanced cities where they can flourish by gaining access to economic advantages and education, just as they did prior to 1991. There are images and notions dating back to the Soviet period, which are reproduced and altered through interaction, travel and memory, influencing the inter-generational mental maps of vast numbers of people in the post-Soviet republics. In fact, federal universities such as St Petersburg State University or the Southern Federal University in Rostov, too, use these ties and actively recruit Russian-speaking students at Central Asian annual educational fairs as was recently the case in Almaty in February 2016. In addition, such foreign students are even granted Russian citizenship upon completion of their studies after having lived just three years in Russia as a means of addressing Russia's demographic crisis. Such practices are absolutely pivotal in ensuring the continued high level of integration between the post-Soviet countries.

Notions about life in the Russian metropolises have resulted in high migration figures, especially on a north-south axis in the post-Soviet space. From the CIS countries alone, Russia received roughly 420.000 persons in 2013 (Russian Federation Federal Statistics Service 2013), most of whom migrated because of labour shortages in Russia and promises of higher wages and education for immigrants. This is reflected in surveys conducted in Georgia before 2008 when education and work featured highest on the list of reasons for migrating (Länderanalysen 2009). It is not without reason that the rich Russian metropolises give rise to hopes of increased earnings. Polling done amongst Tajik labour migrants in 2010 show that the average income is ten times that earned in Tajikistan (Zentralasienanalysen 2010: 8). Similar numbers are seen with regard to Uzbekistan, which provided roughly 20 per cent of all labour migrants in 2014 (Russian Federation Federal Statistics Service 2013).

Unsurprisingly, migration in the Slavic regions of the former Soviet space are characterized by different patterns of movement, although these have changed, particularly since 1991. While Russia was the preferred destination for Ukrainians up until 2010, Israel, Germany and the United States combined accounted for roughly 55 per cent of Ukrainian emigrants in 2011. Despite incomplete data, similar patterns are evident for Russian emigrants, who, in 2012, preferred destinations in the United States, Israel and Germany, respectively (Migration Policy Centre 2013a and 2013b; see also on internal Russian migration Brunarska

2014). Undoubtedly, the mental maps of Russians and Ukrainians are different from those of Central Asians; but emigrants from all parts of the post-Soviet space seem to be motivated by similar hopes of prosperity, whether these have led them to Russia or beyond Russia to the United States. Moreover, this discrepancy in migration patterns does not necessarily contradict the notion that members of the former Soviet Union, from the Ukraine to Central Asia, share a sense of belonging to an interconnected region.

Migration patterns within post-Soviet space typically reflect the existence of established networks resembling those in petty trade and also dating back to the Soviet period. Based to an overwhelming degree on long-lasting ties following ethnic or kinship relations, and reaching from the Russian metropolises into the various former republics, these networks guide migrants in their movement across post-Soviet space. Once in Russia, migrants rely on their networks in their efforts to arrange employment, accommodation, documents and social lives. Ayupova (2011) and Rahmonova-Schwarz (2012) therefore speak of 'transnational migrants with kinship ties in Central Asia' or 'post-Soviet transnationalism'.[9] Moving within the trust networks encountered in Russia, migrants reconsider and negotiate the social norms, values and world-views that regulate their parallel lives both in Russia and in their home country, generating a distinct 'in-between' identity defined by the geographic binary of 'home' and country of immigration.

Given the interdependencies of Rahmonova-Schwarz's transnational communities, social and cultural practices travel across borders influencing collective identities. For, already during the Soviet period, migration for longer or shorter periods had become a vital element of the Soviet citizen's life-cycle – be it through military service, education or employment. In today's Central Asian regions, such 'rites of passage' involving migration exist in practically unaltered forms for the male members of the population. For Central Asians, migrating abroad (to Russia) for a period of time to establish oneself as economically independent, before returning to the home country to start a family, belongs to the essential steps in a young man's life on his way to adulthood. Migration and the many practices associated with it are experienced and passed on to younger generations.

With various consequences, the migration flows influence identities not only of migrants but also of people in recipient countries. In recent years, this has led to severe tensions between migrants and right-wing populists in Russia, most notably during the 2010 clashes between opposing groups in Moscow (Balmforth 2013). Whether in positive or negative ways, migration currently serves to promote the integration of the region, while ensuring the reproduction of existing migrant networks and their entanglement with society in the Russian metropolises. Transgressing borders while spanning the post-Soviet space, the migrant network not only facilitates migrants' life projects but also keeps alive and passes down through generations notions of the post-Soviet region's interconnectedness.

Now, we turn our attention briefly to informality. In its current form, informality, understood as a set of unmonitored and untaxed practices serving to increase the likelihood of achieving intended outcomes,[10] is a relic of the Soviet period where the 'lethal' combination of distrust towards official state institutions, the lack of modern bureaucratic securities, scarce resources, and reliance on patron-client relations made *blat* (personal connections) indispensable in everyday life and the basis of a huge shadow economy (e.g. Collins 2006; Fitzpatrick 1999). Needless to say, and in contrast to the migration or trade patterns discussed above, informality was not promoted or condoned officially by the Soviet state. Rather, as Timothy Johnston (2011) has argued convincingly, informality belonged to the characteristic 'tactics of the habitat', understood as a set of resources or coping strategies to which Soviet citizens in all walks of life turned in order to overcome bureaucratic obstacles or shortcomings in everyday life.

The transition from Soviet to post-Soviet statehood has done little to change this. On the contrary, the rapid and convoluted collapse of the Soviet Union in the 1990s often left bureaucracies intact, bar the Baltic countries. Coupled with rising scarcity and uncertainty, informal networks and structures survived practically unaltered with the common corollary of high corruption and dysfunctional legal structures.[11] From Dushanbe to Murmansk, and from L'viv to Vladivostok, people turn to *blat*, informal networks based on kinship, friendship or patronage, and corruption in obtaining access to the best universities, in job allocation, in food and commodity security, in earning money on the side or in successfully migrating to other countries (see, e.g. Kaiser 1998a, 1998b, 2005; Leontyeva 2013; Sik 1994a, 1994b; Nee 1992: 1–27; Wheatley 2013).

Throughout the post-Soviet space, informality thus features as a pervasive and characteristic set of practices. It also serves as a marker in discourses regarding sameness and difference among those inhabiting various areas within this space. Not infrequently, visitors from Western Europe, for example, may hear someone say that 'we do things differently here'. At the same time, commenting critically on informality may serve as a way of distinguishing among various post-Soviet peoples. A Russian, for example, will readily argue that people of the former Soviet republics on the southern frontier are far more prone to engage in informal activities than they are; while an ethnic Estonian will likely say the same about the Russians. In short, in informality we may observe an aspect of post-Soviet collective identity that also serves to distinguish between identities on both a regional level (CIS vs. Western Europe) and a national level (Russian vs. Uzbek).

Socialization, Rituals and Cultural Consumption

Over the past decade or so, a great number of scholars have investigated the surge in nostalgia for the socialist era – particularly in Russia, though one may observe this phenomenon in the formerly socialist countries of Europe too. Svetlana Boym (2001) and Maria Todorova (2010), perhaps the most prominent nostalgia researchers, have, each in different ways, provided us with a better understanding of the evolution, meaning, discursive forms and various functions of socialist nostalgia. For the vast majority of citizens in post-Soviet space, this sort of nostalgia is not defined by a wish to return to the Soviet political system but expresses a sentimental view of the past. Hence, while we acknowledge that nostalgia is a constitutive aspect of post-Soviet collective identity formation, we write more generally of rituals, norms, consumption and related practices, which include but are not restricted to nostalgia. These are best understood as the legacy of a shared culture, the result of social and cultural policies infused into society during the Soviet period but which, today, seem to be benign in nature and, therefore appealing. How, we ask, do they contribute to the production of post-Soviet collective identity and merge with local national elements, surviving in altered form?

Several scholars have rightly emphasized the importance of cultural consumption and collective action with regard to identity formation. Ekaterina Kalinina (2014), whom we cited at the outset, has convincingly shown how post-Soviet nostalgia is appropriated through media in contemporary Russia, while Stefan Kirmse (2013) has demonstrated the significance of global media for contemporary youth culture in Kyrgyzstan. Mass media provide the opportunity for what might be called ritualized consumption, denoting the entanglement of ritualized traditions, cultural consumption and established practices. Perhaps the best known example of such ritualized consumption is the annual New Year's screening of the 1976 film, *The Irony of Fate* (Ironiya Sud'by), a comedy depicting a man, who, returning home, drunk, from a bachelors' party on the eve of his wedding, unknowingly travels from Moscow to St Petersburg, where he enters a flat that he mistakes for his own but which is really occupied by a young woman. After much confusion and confrontation, he breaks his engagement to his bride-to-be and marries the young woman he met accidentally in the St Petersburg apartment.

The Irony of Fate raises themes that still bear significance for post-Soviet collective identity formation. Any inhabitant of the post-Soviet space will nod in recognition at the humoristic rendering of Soviet urban planning, architecture and interior decorating, which result in practically identical apartments in entirely different cities. As in other countries, such as Germany and Scandinavia, where *Dinner for One* is an integral part of every New Year's Eve, gathering young and old in front of the television, viewing *The Irony of Fate* is today a tradition that is passed from generation to generation, as are the practices related to it (typical food, drinks and forms of New Year's celebrations). Such movies also play a pivotal role in the waves of popular culture nostalgia that have swept across many of the former Soviet (and socialist) regions, leading to a remarkable renaissance in particular of the material culture of the socialist period (e.g. Beumers 2012; Todorova 2010). This is for the most part an urban phenomenon that is especially attractive for those born in the 1970s or later. It originated mainly in the Slavic-speaking regions, although urban centres in the Caucasus and Kazakhstan have seen similar developments, which contribute to current processes of collective identification.

Viewing specific movies on New Year's Eve is but one of the many cultural practices that persist throughout the post-Soviet space. Others include the annual celebration of Victory Day (9 May), commemorating the defeat of Nazi Germany, New Year's Day (1 January), International Women's Day (8 March) and, in most countries, International Workers' Day (1 May).[12] While only a few countries arrange parades comparable to those that take place on Red Square (indeed, most leaders of the post-Soviet republics attend the Moscow parade),[13] Victory Day gatherings or visits to monuments are part of the commemoration for many, including late-Soviet or post-Soviet generations. The celebration of International Women's Day is distinctly different from roughly comparable events in the rest of the world where few or no concrete traditions have taken hold. In post-Soviet space, however, people are appalled if a man fails to celebrate this day properly by bringing his wife or partner flowers or a present and inviting her on an elaborate date, complete with dinner and tickets to the theatre or a similar high-culture event.

Several scholars have analysed Soviet mass celebrations (Adams 2010; Rolf 2006), in particular, Victory Day, which, uniting the populations of the former Soviet space around the trauma and triumph experienced during World War II, still stands out as one of the most important holidays. Research demonstrates that Victory Day has a unique place in the collective consciousness of Russians. In Central Asia as well, it is the object of an emphatic and expressive cult; while in the Ukraine more than 70 per cent of the population think of it as a 'great day' (Nikiporets-Takigawa 2013).

In Uzbekistan, for example, Victory Day celebrations usually begin with a trip made by family members to the nearest urban centre, where they join thronging crowds on the streets decorated with ten-storey banners with holiday slogans hanging from buildings and government billboards. As if they were visiting an enormous street fair, family members stroll down the central avenues or through the major parks, as children play, parents enjoy a day off work, and the tunes of famous Russian and national pop-songs are broadcast from the hundreds of food-stands or the large speakers encircling squares and lining the streets (Adams 2007: 207–11).

Prior to 1991, celebrations of Victory Day and other Soviet holidays displayed elements of both a common Soviet culture and of the individual republics' cultural and national heritage. After 1991, both elements remain, but in different combinations and with varying emphases. Despite the ubiquity of Victory

Day throughout post-Soviet space, then, its commemoration has been subject to various post-Soviet adaptations, as some integrative signals of Soviet 'friendship of the peoples' have been replaced by national ones.

This 'nationalizing' development, which is a central feature of the post-independence era, is even more evident when one distinguishes secular and religious holidays, as Laura Adams (2007) has done with reference to Uzbekistan. There, she shows, secular holidays such as Victory Day and International Women's Day promote the formation of a civic identity, while religious celebrations nurture an ethnic-national identity. Although less pronounced in non-Muslim republics, this qualitative difference is characteristic of all post-Soviet countries and their post-independence national identity formation. Moreover, secular celebrations have remained practically identical, while non-secular rituals tend to combine Soviet and non-Soviet practices.

Research on public holidays in the post-Soviet space has been supplemented by studies of private rituals and rites of passage, which often serve to forge, express or alter local identities. For example, there has been a notable renaissance of (perceived) pre-Soviet, traditional religious practices that were formerly restricted by Soviet authorities. Scholars have persuasively argued that in Central Asia such practices may be understood as expressions of private resistance to state policies of increased control (Roche and Hohmann 2011: 119). In post-Soviet Tajikistan, this has resulted in weddings lasting several days and combining a religious wedding (*nikoh*), a traditional wedding (*tuy*) and a civil marriage ceremony (ibid.). Naturally, the specific wedding rituals depend on whether a secular or religious orientation predominates in the families in question. While some religious families meticulously 'cleanse' the religious wedding of all Soviet influences, others incorporate religious or traditional Tajik elements in wedding ceremonies more for show (ibid.: 120–22).

Despite the apparent contradiction between religious and Soviet orientations, the majority of weddings in other post-Soviet states tend to mix these orientations in non-conflictual ways. As a guest at a wedding in Almaty, Sean Roberts observed that, immediately following the imam's departure from the religious ceremony in the morning, 'several young men brought bottles of vodka and cognac to each of the tables' (Roberts 2007: 349). Such examples of coexisting secular and Muslim rituals could be multiplied; but there are several other practices that allude more subtly to the Soviet legacy. At Muslim weddings, for example, the dress code requires that the groom dresses in a Western-style suit, often wearing only a small indicator of his 'national' identity (in Uzbekistan, typically a *taqiyah* or cap). In contrast, women often wear traditional or folkloric dresses. After the civil ceremony, the newly-weds typically visit a public square of emotional importance, such as the Victory or Independence Day Square, where they pay their respects and lay some flowers, not missing the opportunity for a photoshoot. Finally, the festivities following the wedding feast often include not only traditional dances and rituals but also modern pop music, particularly from the Russian charts.

The transnational rituals and practices described above have grown out of the particular historical, cultural and social context of the Soviet Union. In the post-Soviet period they have persisted, being subject to a greater or lesser extent to change through influences from new national, cultural or social influences or formerly repressed practices. Often they undergo adaptations of content, but, structurally, they reproduce and perpetuate a sensation of being members of an interconnected region.

The few rituals and social and cultural practices that we describe above are but a small sampling of the many examples that might be cited in support of our argument. Indeed, examples could easily be expanded to include the production of norms and value systems. Contrary to the erroneous assumption that the collapse of the Soviet Union and its ideology can be equated with the vanishing of the Soviet value system, many Soviet values – for example, regarding notions of economic equality, welfare services, interpersonal behaviour and so forth – live on. Similarly, norms regarding 'proper' education and high culture have survived practically unaltered in all post-Soviet societies. In fact, the educational canon in post-Soviet countries seems to be far more resilient to change than it is in the Western European countries, which have not undergone similar upheavals. Furthermore, research on 'institutions' such as gender and sexuality, religion, child rearing practices and youth culture have yielded intriguing results and suggest that the Soviet legacy will cast a long shadow on collective identity formation in the post-Soviet regions (e.g. Wegren et al. 2010).

Quo Vadis Post-Soviet Collective Identity?

In this chapter, we have analysed various post-Soviet transnational practices that have emerged through societal interconnections, encounters, exchanges, collective memory and social processes as well as established normative and behavioural codes. We have argued that these practices keep the region highly integrated and reproduce a transnational cultural identity, with which self-conscious identification can take place. Such identification is particularly likely to occur when individuals encounter difference or sameness although such an encounter is not a prerequisite.

We have used 'post-Soviet collective identity' to denote the cultural identity growing out of the Soviet legacy. But the disappearance of the Soviet Union, arguably the pre-eminent force in generating the Soviet collective identity, raises the question of how long we can reasonably apply the attribute 'post-Soviet' to identities and practices on the territory of the former Soviet Union before other qualifiers such as Ukrainian, European or Eurasian become dominant. Obviously, this depends first and foremost on individuals' identification with it. But its applicability also depends on the perseverance of practices that originated in the Soviet era as well as on aspects of socio-cultural and political developments. The most important factor regarding the persistence of a post-Soviet collective identity is, of course, time and generational change. For, with time, generations will emerge that have no lived experience and only imaginaries of life during the Soviet era. At the same time, generational turnover does not necessarily bring to a stop identification with a post-Soviet collective identity among people inhabiting the former Soviet space. Indeed, collective identification is not merely a process that grows from within but also one that can be forced upon groups from the outside – genocidal conflicts are a grim reminder of this fact. In other words, generations completely unaffected by the Soviet past may still experience (forced) identification through encounter with sameness and difference or through Othering discourses (such as those in Western countries – see Tlostanova 2015). Ekatarina Kalinina's experience, mentioned at the outset of this chapter, is likely to be the result of such influences, at least in part.

Meanwhile, the integration of former Soviet states, as in the Eurasian Economic Union, may induce identification with post-Soviet collective identity, depending on the political rhetoric and the level of interconnectedness that accompanies it. By contrast, the integration of former Soviet republics into the European Union will presumably accelerate a process, ultimately vanquishing feelings of a post-Soviet collective identity and substituting it with a sense of belonging to the European Integration project. Similarly, political and violent conflicts as seen in Georgia or Ukraine are likely to have equally accelerating effects on identity changes. Moreover, political developments, too, will affect future collective identity formation in post-Soviet space.

Despite the importance of these factors for the maintenance or recreation of post-Sovietness, there is little doubt that, at an unspecified future time, it will cease to exist. The loss of Russian-language competencies in Central Asian provincial and rural places might be an early indicator of this process. After all, former multicultural and multi-ethnic states have lost their evocative power once enough historical layers have been deposited on them, notwithstanding their influence on later regional developments. To put it bluntly, despite the huge significance of the Roman culture, law and language for today's Europe, very few Europeans sense any form of self-conscious identification with the Roman Empire, thus, rendering debates on a 'post-Roman' identity meaningless.

Claus Bech Hansen is currently a senior researcher at the Centre for Development Research at the University of Bonn and project co-ordinator of the research network Crossroads Asia. Previous positions include a visiting professorship at Bogazici University in Istanbul and visiting postdoctoral positions at Humboldt University in Berlin and the Central European University in Budapest. He holds a PhD in History and Civilization from the European University Institute, where he wrote a thesis on Soviet power in the Central Asian periphery. His latest publication is 'Power and Purification: Violence in the Late-Stalinist Uzbek SSR', in *Central Asian Survey* 35(3), 2016.

Markus Kaiser is president of the Kazakh-German University in Almaty, Kazakhstan. In 2015 he served as scientific co-ordinator of the BMBF-financed competence network Crossroads Asia and as senior researcher at the Centre for Development Research, University of Bonn. Previous positions include visiting professorships in the Faculty of Social Sciences, Eurasian National University, Astana, the Faculty of Sociology of the State University of St Petersburg and American University of Central Asia in Bishkek. He was research fellow and senior lecturer in the Department of Sociology/Anthropology at the University of Trier and senior lecturer in Development Studies in the Faculty of Sociology and research fellow in the Institute of Global Society Studies, both at the University of Bielefeld. From 2001 until 2004, he served as director of the DAAD-funded Centre for German and European Studies at the St Petersburg State University. His latest publication is 'Stay or Return? Gendered Family Negotiations and Transnational Projects of Remigration of (Late) Resettlers to Russia' (co-author), in *Transnational Social Review* 6(1), 2016.

Notes

1. In her study, Kalinina interprets how media influence identity building, while understanding 'identity' as a dynamic, non-static process (Kalinina 2014: 35).
2. We use post-Soviet to refer not only to the period following 1991 but instead to designate the continuity between the periods before and after 1991.
3. This was a double-edged sword, for the investment in 'national' cultures, traditions and folklorization resulted in the development of national identities, which opposed the further realization of the Soviet project (Hansen 2013; Kamp 2006; Khalid 2007; Northrop 2004).
4. For an excellent critical review of the conceptual history the 'Soviet Man', with particular emphasis on the North American debate on its relation to the liberal subject, see Anna Krylova (2000).
5. Max Weber understood state and state authority as 'built upon the assumption of intergenerational continuity of the demos and a territorially fixed space within which a national political community exists' (Faist 2004: 5).
6. In researching the significance of collective identities, we encounter the problem of available empirical data. Hence, while ample data on identity is available from the Baltic countries, access to data from, for example, the Central Asian states is limited, seriously hampering research efforts.
7. As noted above, identities coexist. Though pan-Turkism is not at the forefront of political, cultural or social efforts in the Turkic language countries, the 1990s in particular saw attempts to reinvigorate some sense of pan-Turkic identity. These often originated

in Turkey and included a number of political and cultural efforts, such as strengthening ties in trade and education, resulting in the continuous funding of the Ahmet-Yesevi-University in Turkistan, the Süleyman Demirel-University in Almaty, and the Kyrgyz Turkish Manas University, as well as the International Ataturk Alatoo University in Bishkek.

8. Such networks and practices are not limited to the post-Soviet space, rather, they are indeed world-wide phenomena. For examples of networks operating across the former Soviet frontier, see Steenberg (2014) on Uyghurs in Kyrgyzstan or Kaminski and Mitra (2010: 46) on Afghans in Tajikistan.

9. There are only a few social anthropologists who have done in-depth ethnographic research on migration in Central Asia or the everyday life of Central Asian migrants in Russia and related cultural, legal or political issues (Ayupova 2011; Olimova and Bosc 2003; Reeves 2007, 2008, 2011, 2014; Rahmonova-Schwarz 2012; Röhner 2007). Instead, sociologists have produced the majority of analyses, which tend, however, to have a strong macro-economic emphasis, focusing on the economic consequences of remittance flows (Anderson and Pomfret 2005; Hill 2004; Kursad 2008; Lukashova and Makenbaeva 2009).

10. See Helmke and Levitsky (2004) and the edited volume by Giordano and Hayoz (2013a).

11. Giordano and Hayoz are quite right in reminding us that informality exists everywhere, even in highly industrialized states with high transparency. Indeed, it is the consequential shadow of formality, though the extent to which it is used to direct formal and informal institutions differs considerably depending on the object of research (Giordano and Hayoz 2013b; Giordano 2013).

12. In several post-Soviet republics, 1 May remains a holiday, but the cause of celebrating has changed, depending on national peculiarities. In Kazakhstan, for example, it has become the Kazakhstan People's Unity Day, while the Baltic countries have abolished the Victory Day celebrations which essentially sealed their loss of independence as a consequence of the Hitler-Stalin Pact of 1939.

13. For the celebration of the seventieth anniversary of victory in World War II, the Kazakh president ordered the largest parade of Kazakh history but moved it to 7 May 2015, enabling Nazerbaev to participate in the Moscow festivities on 9 May; http://www.rferl.org/content/kazakhstan-victory-day-russia-nazarbaev/26999245.html.

Chapter 7

Living Together

The Transformation of Multi-Religious Coexistence in Southern Thailand

Alexander Horstmann

Introduction

The persistence of brutal violence since the year 2000 in Thailand's southern, predominantly Muslim, border provinces has resulted in ever more deaths and has led to militarization, harassment, human rights violations, ethnic cleansing and rising numbers of refugees.[1] Relations between Buddhists and Muslims seem to be, at least in the media, characterized by deep hatred. While the media show gruesome images of burned or beheaded corpses, there is complete silence about the Songkhla Lake basin, where peaceful relations prevail. However, the violence in the Deep South provides the background to the relations between Buddhists and Muslims in the Songkhla Lake basin and raises the question of how far people at the margins of this conflict are affected by the circulation of these images.[2]

Drawing on long-term ethnographic fieldwork in the Songkhla Lake area, I attempt to explain why people are able to maintain peaceful relations. Based on my data on multi-religious dynamics in the Songkhla Lake basin, I argue that an organic solidarity is at the heart of peaceful coexistence (see Horstmann 2007a). This solidarity consists of a complex arrangement of cultural resources (oral history, customary law and religious ethics), patronage networks and the ethical commitment of the community leaders to invest positively in relations beyond the religious divide. Theravada Buddhism and Islam are embedded in a hierarchical relation with ancestor spirit worship. The article does not aim to romanticize Buddhist–Muslim neighbourhoods. I do not propose that indigenous religion in southern Thailand is a resource of peaceful relations per se; it is very well possible that political processes may be hostile. As I have explained elsewhere, peaceful coexistence is not a static and diachronic reality, but a dynamic system (and thus fragile in its synchronicity).[3]

I link the local management of cultural difference to the political positions and locations of local actors and the way that they ally themselves with external actors or resist their influence in the management of community resources. However, increased capitalist competition, the deterioration of the environment and living conditions of the peasants, dislocation and cultural fragmentation have made coexistence extremely fragile and have accentuated the notion of difference.[4] This notion of difference includes in particular the separation of cultural and social identities along religious lines, negates their multiple connections and crossovers and accentuates their political mobilization.

The dynamics of change may affect the communities in different ways. In some communities, the cultural boundaries between Buddhists and Muslims may be enhanced and the economic position of Muslims may be very marginal. In other communities, the community may be morally and physically 'exhausted', meaning that people can no longer survive in the subsistence sector anymore and are culturally uprooted, but keep some elements of exchange and flexibility in dealing with cultural difference.[5] In yet other communities, the community leaders take faith into their own hands and apply a conscious strategy to prevent conflict. In that way, the revitalization of religious ritual in no way reflects a homogeneous response in the direction of harmonious coexistence or hostility and hatred, but a very diverse and reflexive response to the same processes affecting people's livelihoods.[6]

The plan of this chapter is as follows. In the first section, I provide a brief historical and geographical background to the Songkhla Lake area before discussing some theoretical implications of conceptualizing coexistence. I argue that ethnic identities cannot be taken for granted and that ethnic categories are not an a priori determinant of identity and social coherence. Multi-religious ritual provides an arena in which traditions articulate with modernity, local and global processes are interwoven, and ethnic identities are negotiated and contested. I provide the ethnographic example of a founder's cult in Tha Sala, Nakhon Si Thammarat province, to illustrate the transformation of multi-religious ritual, which produces increasingly rigid ethnic and religious categories. I argue that the transformation of multi-religious ritual reflects the political locations of particular actors. In the second part, I analyse the political and economic structures that affect the livelihood of the people and identify transnational Islamic missionary movements, the expansion of the Thai state and the expansion of markets as major influences of change. These influences put constraints on the livelihoods of Buddhists and Muslims, but also provide enhanced opportunities and aspirations. I argue that the traditional beliefs and ritual cultures accord with modernity and coexist with standardized national ritual and transnational, globalized ritual in an uneasy relationship that produces contradictions and tensions. The result is a scattered picture in which ethnic and religious categories are differently contested in every community and in which the reinforcement of ethnic and religious identities in the rural areas divides families and generations.

The Research Context

The study area is the Songkhla Lake basin and comprises the provinces of Songkhla, Patthalung and Nakhon Sithammarat. Tambralinga was one of the oldest kingdoms in Southeast Asia (see Figure 7.1).[7] The isthmus of Kra, on the west coast of southern Thailand, was a very important trade route from mainland to insular Southeast Asia along which Buddhist influences met and crossed with Islamic ones (see Montesano and Jory 2008). With the expansion of the Thai state, the Songkhla Lake area became dominated by Theravada Buddhism, as attested by the remains of major temples. These temples played an important role in the process and narrative of state building and national representation in Southern Thailand. Muslims settled in the Songkhla Lake area as migrants and sometimes as slaves and played a marginal and peripheral role. Thus, Songkhla, Patthalung and Nakhon Srithammarat are mainly Buddhist provinces with Muslim minorities. However, in some districts, there are approximately equal numbers of Buddhists and Muslims. Here, Buddhists and Muslims live in mixed neighbourhoods and contexts of coexistence. However, with time, the communities have become more clearly separated from each other along religious lines.

Increasingly, Buddhists and Muslims distinguish themselves from each other by adopting more conspicuously religious dress and identity. In Tamot, Patthalung province, for example, Ban Tamot is a Buddhist community, Ban Hua Chang is a Muslim community. But the historical process of the communities is intertwined. The Buddhist temple is constructed on the remains of a Muslim cemetery and *surau* (Islamic prayer hall), while Ban Hua Chang used to be a Buddhist settlement with a Buddhist cave. The cemetery of Tamot used to be a Muslim cemetery, but has gradually been taken over by Buddhist villagers. Ban Tamot and Ban Hua Chang switched completely: the Buddhist villagers settled in the fertile valley, while the Muslims settled in the less fertile hills. In this sense, the religious landscape and resource use reflect the power relationships in the area. In Tamot, conversions did take place, both from Buddhism to Islam and from Islam to Buddhism. However, the noble elite in Tamot practised conversion to Buddhism during the time when the presence of the Thai state was growing. The reason may well be that conversion to Buddhism facilitated social mobility and integration into the local power elite. Today, Islam, under the influence of transnational reformist forces, no longer tolerates conversion to Buddhism.

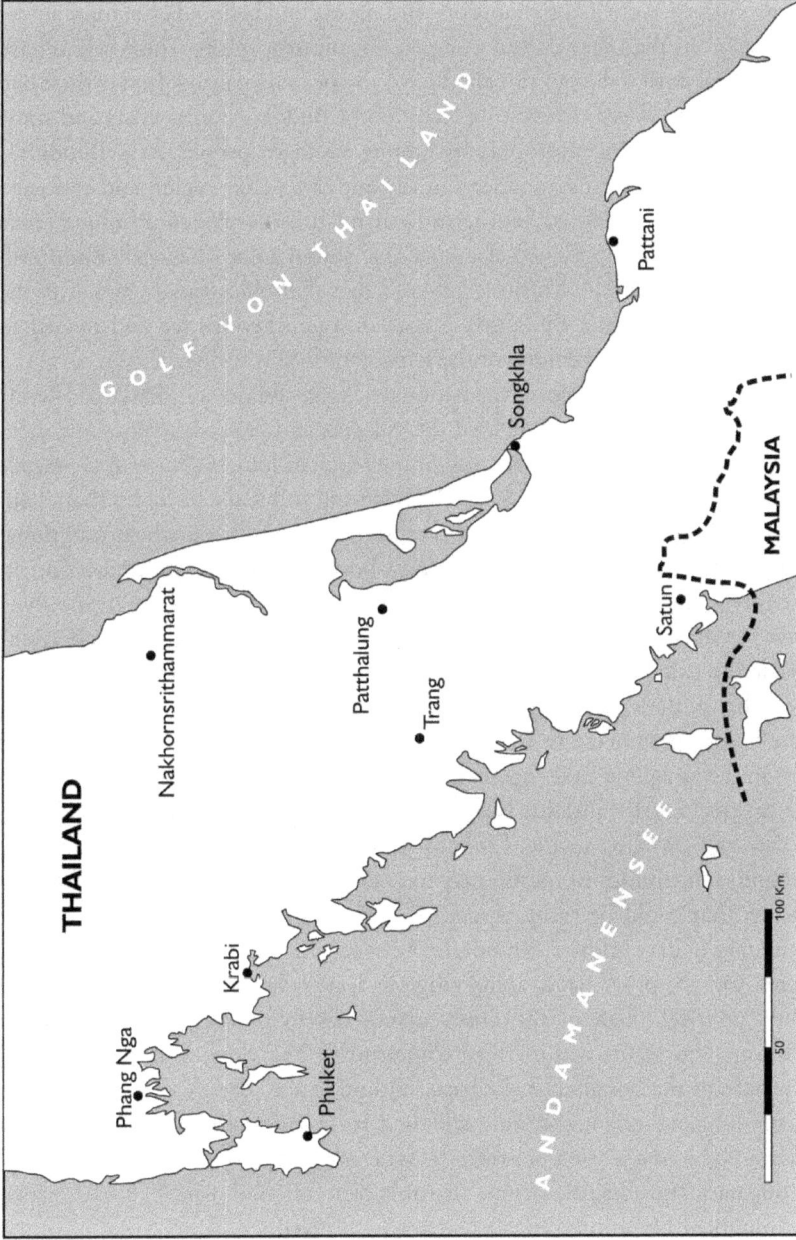

Figure 7.1 The Songkhla Lake basin, southern Thailand, bordering Songkhla and Patthalung provinces (© A. Horstmann)

Both Buddhism and Islam have been present in the Songkhla Lake region for several hundred years and can be considered indigenous religions. Both religions have syncretized with the traditional ritual and belief system. A hundred years ago, the villagers were living in unison with nature and believed even more in the power of spirits than they do today, especially ancestor spirits. These beliefs have not only held until today; spirit beliefs have also been revitalized. In the Thale Sap Songkhla region, a very interesting tradition of Buddhist saints exists and some of these saints enjoy great popularity among southern people. Both Buddhism and Islam had interesting variations in the Songkhla Lake region and coexisted with ancestor spirit beliefs. Southern Thailand thus developed a unique ritual culture and arts that combined elements of ancestral cults, Theravada Buddhism and Islam. For example, Muslims believed that their ancestors visited after the communal meals, while Buddhists prepared large offerings for and prayed to their ancestors in the ceremony of the tenth month in October.

However, the influences of the national Sangha and the transnational Islamic missionary movements have divided the villagers and have sometimes put them under pressure to drop ancestral cults. Some religious leaders continue to practise old traditions, while also being under the strong influence of forces that claim to represent modernity. People find themselves in a situation where traditional beliefs coexist with more orthodox beliefs, both from Buddhism and Islam. In more recent times, the circulation of media images of the violence in the three border provinces through television, cyberspace, video CDs and DVDs has generated a discussion on the coexistence of Buddhists and Muslims in Thailand. On the one hand, Buddhist villagers maintain solidarity with the Buddhist minority in the border provinces, as Thai Buddhists have continued to migrate to safer places in the Songkhla Lake region. On the other hand, Muslims in the Songkhla Lake region joined translocal Islamic Da'wa movements, such as the Tablighi Jama'at, and travelled to the Tabligh's centres in Yala and Bangkok. On the one hand, some Buddhist monks may have developed negative attitudes towards Muslims that could be easily tapped by anti-Muslim movements, while some imams might draw clearer boundaries between the Islamic and the Buddhist spheres. On the other hand, some religious leaders keep some form of organic civility, political alliances and cross-cutting ties to prevent hostility between Buddhism and Islam within their community. The chapter also argues that the people in the Songkhla Lake basin, although they are increasingly moving towards religious dogmatism, are still tied to traditional ancestor beliefs. The problem is thus the tension between the syncretic culture and the more orthodox and dogmatic movements. I argue that this contradiction, which characterizes a great number of locations, remains largely unresolved.

While the state has never acknowledged the diversity in the South and has preferred to talk about Thai subjects, the chapter argues that the people have developed their own strategies to think about this diversity. The state has never been interested in the multi-religious traditions of the South, but rather has seen them as Buddhist traditions and tried to incorporate the Manora tradition. In a Foucauldian perspective, the state has aimed to formalize these cultural traditions and give them a distinctive Thai character. Yet, much of southern Thai culture has kept its flexibility and has resisted appropriation by the state or the Budhhist Sangha.

Organic Civility versus Religious Hatred

The ritual tradition that developed in southern Thailand responded to the need of the multi-religious settings and initially had the potential to transcend ethnic and religious difference, although it gradually lost it. An analysis of the transformation of ritual culture helps us to understand how the people categorize diversity for themselves, question social orders or change ritual meanings. Ritual is thus seen as transformative and 'efficient', and not as stabilizing and traditional.[8] In this perspective, traditions accord with modernity. People use their belief in spirits to enchant and engage the forces of commoditization, rationalization, normalization and cultural fragmentation and thus keep modernity 'spirited'.[9]

Permanent low-scale communal violence in southern Thailand, Myanmar, Indonesia and the southern Philippines suggests an urgent need for the conceptualization of ethnically diverse forms of coexistence.[10] While much of the literature focuses on ethnically motivated conflict, we know relatively little about how ethnically different people live in sustained peace. In this context, Alberto Gomes et al. (2006) make a very important argument for the notion of organic solidarity or civility. They argue that only if we study the modus that people mobilize to peacefully coexist can we understand why in some contexts coercion and violence develop, while in others they do not, despite the tense conditions.[11] The notion of organic civility does not gloss over or negate competition and conflict, but highlights the recognition and enactment of these differences and sees ritual practices as frames for action that are related to more cosmopolitan ideas. Precisely because religion becomes politicized in the context of communal violence, community leaders have to be aware of the danger of violence and have to develop mechanisms that allow them to settle disputes before they become violent. In this context, it is worth considering how the people in contexts of coexistence conceptualize diverse neighbourhoods, through what kind of categories they describe their own identity, and how they distinguish themselves from each other. The aim is to identify different modes of differentiating, articulating and mobilizing ethnic identity, interaction and diversity. A close look at ritual traditions allows for the discovery of local modes of social participation that differs greatly from the perception of the nation-state or global religions it also offers a perspective on diversity, in which ethnic categories are not an a priori determinant of identity and social coherence. I thus welcome the proposal by Robinne and Sadan (2007: 308) to study ethnic categories 'only once the networks and their modes of articulation (between neighbourhoods, communities, villages, and transnational networks) have been identified'. In the context of the politicization of religion, networks of communities become orthodox Buddhists or Muslims and these movements and dominant discourses organize, discipline and articulate ethnic and religious positions. However, local subaltern modes of articulating identity have also been revived and may actually resist the labelling of people into fixed tables of difference and insist on a common identity of people from the 'South' in which communal ties between people and villages are not yet overridden by processes of dogmatic ethnic identification. Such a view would allow us to analyse the permanent negotiation of ethnic and religious positions in a changing world and offer a timeline in which it is possible to observe how identities and boundaries have become more rigid and what they looked like before becoming distinctively separate.

Multi-Religious Ritual in the Songkhla Lake Basin

Religious beliefs about ancestor spirits are integrated into everyday life and represent the practical order of southern Thai society. In multi-religious ritual, people reproduce their relations and reproduce themselves as a community, transcending difference. This cosmology is not restricted to the cultural sphere, but includes political and economic alliances, oral history traditions, customary law and local knowledge. Religion and traditional authority are used to prevent hostility and hatred in the community, settle disputes and prevent violence. The flexibility and fluidity expressed in the rituals allow for cross-cultural marriage between Buddhists and Muslims and prevent it from causing tension in the community. Multi-religious ritual allows for all kinds of cross-cultural encounters and cross-cutting ties, such as complex healing relations between spirit mediums, healers and patients.

It is part and parcel of a syncretic culture and an indicator that the villagers regarded both Muslim guardian spirits as well as Buddhist saints as their common ancestors. In multi-religious ritual, Buddhist and Muslim identities were subordinated to the cosmology of spirit beliefs and did not yet have the overriding function of political ideologies. The state remained largely ignorant of the local knowledge and wisdom of the community. Since the 1990s the villagers have responded to the assault on traditions by revitalizing multi-religious ritual and integrating it into a more conscious and effective strategy and tool with which to counter the cultural crisis and fragmentation of the South. The revitalization of Theravada Buddhism went hand in hand with an alternative development that envisaged nothing less than the reconstruction of the community and its traditions. In this reflexive move, the temple engages in safeguarding the environment, the watershed and the community forest, organizing prayer walks and picnics in nature. In the symbolic actions of exchanging food, gestures and money, communal relations are constantly renewed. However, the performance of multi-religious ritual, besides facilitating renewal and refreshment of social ties, also provides glimpses of the cultural and religious competition evolving in a changing community.[12]

This can be observed in the ritual of two religions in Tamot, Patthalung. The public ritual on the common cemetery of Ban Tamot has achieved some fame in the region. While the religious leaders like to present this ritual as an ideal expression of harmonious coexistence, Theravada Buddhism and Islam compete for a dominant role in the community's self-representation and have both developed a negative attitude towards ancestor spirit beliefs, for which the ritual was originally designed. While the lay people exchange food and prayer gestures, Buddhist monks and Islamic imams are committed to religious orthodoxy. Some imams may no longer participate in this multi-religious ritual with Buddhist monks, and some may be active in Islamic reformist movements, such as the Tablighi Jama'at, but still participate in order to confirm the commitment of the Muslim side to the consensus of peaceful coexistence (see Figure 7.2).

A prevalent example of multi-religious arrangements on the east coast of southern Thailand is the dance drama performance and soul-calling ritual, Manora Rongkru (dance-stage-teacher).[13] In this ritual performance, the great ancestor spirits elevated to the highest status of teachers and deities are invited

Figure 7.2 The ritual of two religions (photo: A. Horstmann)

by dancing and singing to come down to earth for a reunion with the living and family members. The Manora Rongkru has been traditionally used to settle disputes in families and in the community and included Buddhist and Muslim offerings to the deities. Lately, the Manora Rongkru has been revitalized as a prosperity cult to exhibit prestige and charisma. The state has attempted to appropriate the Manora folk tradition for its strategy of expansion in the South, and to integrate it into the national narrative as a Thai-Buddhist folk tradition, but has not been entirely successful in this attempt. The people in southern Thailand see the Manora tradition as a tradition of the South that reflects its ethnic and religious diversity and its deep commitment to the belief of ancestor spirits. The Manora has been reconfigured to meet the modern needs of the people in southern Thailand and calls to the deities to engage with the anonymous forces of the market and the insecurities of everyday life. People want to recover a vision of a peaceful past and invest money for healing.

While the modern forces of state-building and market expansion may weaken traditional authority, revitalized local movements increasingly network on a spiritual basis and coordinate their activities against the grain. These local networks are driven by local intellectuals and young activists and focus on education, health and sustainable development. However, the local movement to improve the livelihood of rural people is hindered by the exploitation of resources that is often concealed as development projects. Business people and gangsters invest in political offices to further their strategies of accumulation. In Tamot, the district head operated, in the name of 'development', a project to cut down the community forest for a reservoir of dubious utility, and the people he bought were busily buying land to sell it, as well as the timber, at high profits. The reservoir was guarded by armed thugs who threatened to kill the activists of the main monastery, Wat Tamot, if they dared to make their case public. The project, which included Muslim patronage networks, had the potential to turn Buddhists against Muslims and to threaten peaceful relations.

Patterns of Buddhist–Muslim Relations and Coexistence in Southern Thailand

In the Songkhla Lake basin, marriages between Buddhists and Muslims occur regularly and so do conversions in both directions. Sometimes, the groom converts to Islam only to return to Buddhism after staying one month at the bride's family's house. The double, or temporary, conversion is done to please the family of the bride and the ancestors of the bride's house. This kind of flexibility of course contradicts the orthodox believers who claim that the villagers live in a 'state of ignorance'. For the community, this is the smoothest way to regulate an otherwise particularly sensitive subject. Cross-cultural marriage enables the performance of a variety of multi-religious rituals: the so-called 'ritual of two religions' (Buddhism and Islam), the ordination for one day for Muslims just before circumcision, the practice of visiting a monk with a plate of rice and eggs to appease the Buddhist ancestor spirit, and the possession of a Buddhist body with a Muslim spirit during the multi-religious dance theatre and spirit possession Manora Rongkru (Horstmann 2009).

My research shows that inter-religious marriages had different social prestige at different times. Thus, 100 years ago, in Ban Tamot, Patthalung, in tandem with the intensification of state formation, grooms and brides of the highest status tended to convert to Buddhism. Conversion seemed opportune as Buddhism promised social inclusion and mobility at a time when the Thai Buddhist state was strengthening its presence. Today, only lower-class Buddhist men tend to marry lower-class Muslim women. These lower-class men mostly have to convert to Islam under the growing presence of Islamization. Thus, whereas inter-religious marriage was once associated with social prestige, it is no longer the case today. There is also a competition of religions involved. The conversion of a young Buddhist man is perceived as the loss of a soul for Buddhism. Therefore, the abbot encourages a young groom to ordain as a monk before converting to Islam. Hence, even marriage is not a sign of harmony and equality in South Thailand anymore. Buddhist–Muslim relations are not to be romanticized either. Rather, different types of plural spaces and localities can be distinguished. In the Thai-speaking Songkhla basin, Muslims have lived for centuries under the growing influence of the Thai state and Thai hegemony. Many of the characteristics of Thai-speaking Muslims are due to the tacit knowledge that social mobility and access to resources was only possible through the recognition of the key symbols of Thai nationalism. Ethnic competition was further accelerated by the dynamics of globalization in the 1990s.

Orthodoxy has grown in the Buddhist as well as in the Muslim camp and tends to weaken traditional authority. In the southern border provinces, Malay indigenous culture, especially healing rituals, are increasingly marginalized by the pressure of the reformist Islamic teachers and returnees from South Asia and the Middle East, Da'wa revivalist movements and the continuous violence. Widespread belief in the power of spirits, music, performances and the domain of healing came under strong criticism through the purifying discourse of missionaries and returnees from the Middle East, who considered Muslim traditions in the South as heretical.

Theravada Buddhism, as the dominant religion, has subordinated the power of the spirits under the authority of the Buddha and the Sangha by incorporating them in the Buddhist ritual calendar. The cultural traditions of the South are regarded as Buddhist and thus purified of their multi-religious heritage. The ancestor cult is seen as a primitive tradition, whereas Theravada Buddhism is presented as a civilization. However, the ancestor cult is intimately intertwined with the current cult and worship of Buddhists saints, such as Luang

Por Thuat. And yet, the cult of Luang Por Thuat has been actively promoted to further the consolidation of the nation-state in southern Thailand (Jory 2008: 292–303). In Nakhon Srithammarat, Songkhla and Patthalung, villagers, both Buddhist and Muslim, share the southern Thai dialect. Although many Muslims are the descendants of Malay prisoners of war, they are mostly unable to speak Malay. Although there are eighteen Islamic traditional boarding schools (*pondok*) in Patthalung, only teachers who studied in Patani are able to teach using Malay Islamic translations from Arabic (*kitab jawi*). Unlike in Patani, *pondok* in Patthalung do not represent strongholds of Malay Muslim identity (see Madmarn 1999).

Thai Buddhists call Muslim villagers in Nakhon Srithammarat, Songkhla and Patthalung '*khaek*', a term with two different meanings. First, *khaek* means nothing other than 'guest'. In southern Thailand, *khaek* is strongly affiliated with Islam, just as 'Thai' is affiliated with Buddhism. *Khaek* refers to all the immigrants who settled in Thailand from south and southwest Asia (India, Pakistan and Iran). While the term *khaek* is highly pejorative in Patani, Yala and Narathiwat, Muslims in the Songkhla Lake area call themselves *khaek* in relation to the Thais. Thus, conversion from Buddhism to Islam is called 'entering *khaek*' (*khaokhaek*). Malay-speaking Muslims have little contact with Thai-speaking Muslims, whom they regard as having been polluted by the Thai-Buddhist cosmology. It is only recently that the work of Islamic grassroots movements, whose determination to proselytize brings them to nearly every Muslim community in Thailand, including the south, has been extended from the Patani region down to the Lake basin region. This travelling culture involves a re-mapping of the territory, the heavy presence of the Tablighi Jemaat al-Dawa in all the mosques and on the streets, and a re-imagining of the Islamic landscape that is tied to the utopia of a global Islamic society. But even in the southern border provinces, there is a domain of friendly Buddhist–Muslim relations, although it is shrinking. On the local level, Buddhists and Muslims who have grown up together from an early age meet every morning in the coffee-club to exchange news. Buddhists have always been related to Muslims on a basis of friendship. In some localities, marriage does occur although there is strong pressure for the Buddhist partner to convert to Islam. Muslims are known to consult Buddhist spirit mediums and vice versa even if that practice is frowned upon by the orthodoxy. In summary, Muslim–Buddhist relations are characterized by ambiguity and fragility. On the one hand, Buddhists and Muslims seem to keep a ritual domain alive in which conflicts can be settled within the community. The community elders who are recognized by the government as community leaders do not regard the state as competent in matters of the community and keep the state outside of the ritual domain. On the other hand, there is a fundamental difference in the context influencing the Buddhist–Muslim dyad in the Songkhla basin and in the southern border provinces.

In the Songkhla basin, where the Muslim minority was exposed to Thai domination for hundreds of years, the Thai Buddhist side to a large scale dominated the rules of exchange. Muslim participation in these rules is motivated by compromise. Compromise is not characterized by harmony or equality but by certitude about the terms of power and the role of the Muslim minority. Muslims are members of an informal Buddhist temple network organized by the engaging vice-abbot, as they see the value of this network, called Buddhist parliament, where inter-confessional issues of interest can be debated. The imam participates in the ritual of two religions in honour of the first ancestor who is believed to be Muslim, because the dissolution of this ritual would have severe consequences for the relationship between Buddhists and Muslims, although the ritual is heavily dominated by the Buddhist Sangha and Buddhist participants.

The Buddhist leaders prepare donations for the renovation of the mosque or gifts for important Islamic rituals while the Muslims do prepare sweets for the Buddhist participants. The Buddhists exchange Muslim prayer gestures for the ritual of two religions while the Muslims do not exchange Buddhist gestures. Thus, the relationship is largely asymmetric and the Buddhist community in a sense imposes its exchange on the Muslims. Yet, beyond that imposed exchange, there is a lot of spontaneous interaction going on, in which ethnic or religious affiliation plays only a minor role.

Syncretism and Anti-Syncretism in the Songkhla Lake Basin

At a time when Muslims and Buddhists are drawing sharp boundaries between themselves in the Patani area, a culture developed in the Songkhla Lake region, where, although religious boundaries are not denied, difference is integrated into the local structure in an emphatic way. The most spectacular performance of a partial dissolution of these boundaries is a ritual with mixed religious elements that occurs in Songkhla.

In Songkhla and Nakhon Srithammarat there is mutual influence between Theravada Buddhism and Islam, which compete with each other in the Malay Peninsula. Malay-speaking Muslims fell under the influence of Siam in stages whereby, at the local level, villagers did not distinguish one another in public spaces. Buddhist villagers by and large shared a common and homologous social and economic structure, whereby both Buddhist and Muslim villagers used to share strong beliefs in powerful spirits that were bound to the villagers' environment, the rice fields, the ocean, the forest and the mountains. It is not always obvious which areas were settled first by Thai Buddhists and which by Muslims. In Singhanakon District, Songkhla Province, the tomb of Sultan Sulaiman indicates early settlement by a Muslim governor (*jao müang*), tolerated by Siam so long as he was loyal to the centre. The overlapping spheres are reflected in the

Figure 7.3 Peasants of Tamot form a living carpet for the monk (photo: A. Horstmann)

myths and legends concerning the foundation of these villages. In Tha Sala, on the river Klai, villagers believe that the founder of the settlements was a mighty soldier from Saiburi (formerly Kedah). He migrated to Nakhon Srithammarat, cooperated with the Thai prince, married a Thai woman, fell into disgrace and had to flee back to the Klai river, where he was pursued by Siamese troops and subsequently fell after three days of fighting, colouring the Klai red, although his body temperature remained warm. The medium of the guardian spirit is a Thai man; his mother was a Chinese woman who married the former medium's Muslim daughter and converted to Islam, even though he remains a Thai Buddhist at heart and continues to participate in Buddhist merit-making ceremonies. The medium, a wealthy trader, stated that he had renovated the small mosque and also established the first Buddhist monastery in Ban Bangsarn. His daughters, who live in Pethburi, Bangkok and Nakon Srithammarat, are being brought up as Muslims, but they are equally bound to the power of the founding spirit, who ensures the well-being of the village and protects it from misfortune. Numerous small houses (*sala*) along the river Klai are dedicated to Thuat Klai, where the spirit lives and is worshipped by all the villagers, Buddhist, Muslim and Chinese alike.[14]

The villagers hold an annual ritual in honour of the Thuat, in which they can ask for a boon that must be reciprocated after the spirit fulfils it. The offerings to the spirit, who likes cock-fighting as a pastime, betel and leaves, are included, in addition to sweets made from flour and coconut milk as well as sticky rice. Only pork must be avoided so as not to offend the Muslim spirit. The structure of the yearly ritual varies with the ethnic composition of the village and features Chinese, Muslim and Buddhist elements; the ritual calendar starts in February in Bangsarn and ends in September in the mountains. In Bangsarn, for example, the ritual is conducted in February in the Buddhist part of the village, on the beach.

After the date has been arranged, tents are set up to protect the villagers from the sun, and the women prepare a typical Chinese dish consisting of rice noodles with plenty of vegetables bought in the weekly markets. The medium summons the spirit of the Thuat with the following words: 'Dear Thuat, dear father (*por*): we have not seen you for a long time. Please come to us and share your power and strength with us and ensure that we are protected from misfortune'. On this occasion, only a few Muslims will join the ritual, the majority staying aloof. Those who attend do so not as Muslims, but as the relatives of Buddhists in a multi-faith village. I have also been told by Buddhist villagers that they perform the ritual in the Buddhist way 'for ourselves', the offerings being like those that are normally offered to Buddhist monks.

Old villagers recount that thirty years ago both Buddhist and Muslim villagers were eager participants in the ritual and that Muslims keenly worshipped the Muslim spirit. This medium, now eighty-seven years old, symbolizes the integration of diversity in this Southeast Asian society, since Chinese, Islamic and Buddhist influences are all being embodied by this medium. Still in good health, he now lives alone in a bungalow-style house in a coconut-tree garden on the beach of Bangsarn. He reflects a time in which neither Buddhist monasteries nor Islamic mosques were able to appropriate the founding cult that encompasses all villagers. However, even in the sleepy fishing village of Bangsarn, modernity has arrived with a vengeance. In the Muslim part of Bangsarn, members of the modern Da'wa grassroots movement visits the imam and the houses on a weekly basis. In the Buddhist part, the Buddhist minority of the village cannot provide enough novices to staff the monastery, the abbot and sole monk being a villager who was ordained at an advanced age. For the Buddhist Lenten festival, however, other monks from as far away as central Thailand come to join the monk in performing the ceremonies. These visiting monks therefore protect the village from the embarrassment of having a deserted temple during the tenth-month (*deun sip*) activities, when everybody living outside the village must return home to remember the ancestors and to feed the hungry ghosts. While neither the temporary monks nor the orthodox Da'wa grassroots movement have succeeded in replacing the local cosmology of the founding cult, the spirit of the Thuat has become marginal to the participating communities and, according to one medium, has vanished into the mountains, where illegal settlements are in conflict with the state. I shall return to this case study at the end of the chapter to demonstrate the appropriation of the spirit by influential representatives of the state.

Conversions take place in Nakhon Srithammarat, but they do not come from elements outside the community (for example, from proselytizing organizations), but are part and parcel of the local system of dealing with religious difference. In multi-confessional villages in Tha Sala, where Thai is the basic medium of communication among the villagers, conversion in either direction occurs after marriage, the direction being greatly influenced by the respective social environments of the husband and wife. Although conversion to Buddhism is prohibited in orthodox Islam, it does nevertheless take place, and even multiple conversions are not a rarity for 'patchwork' families. Stories of conversion upon marriage are plentiful in this society. Conversions occur because families believe that husbands and wives should be of the same religion. In the villages on the Thale Sap Songkhla, the belief in ancestors is far stronger and more explicit than in any other region of Thailand. According to Janet Carsten, who has worked on nearby Langkawi Island, just on the other side of the Thai–Malaysian border, kinship in a cognatic society tends to be projected less backwards into the past than forwards into the future. There is also a spatial and social dimension to kinship, which goes beyond 'blood': sibling relations, like kinship in general, must be produced by socializing children within the space of the house. Most of the villagers' ancestors came from the outside, and foreigners were integrated into the local society, eventually becoming 'indigenous' (Carsten 1997: 256.). Membership in the village is dependent on an acknowledgement that one is part of a system of relations that is bound to the ancestors and to the cosmological norms of the villagers, not to an individual ethnic identity.[15] It is for this reason that villagers must satisfy their ancestors when the latters' spirits possess their children. Ignoring the spirits of the ancestors would result in misfortune and illness. In this cosmological order, villagers distinguish neither the religion nor the gender of their collective ancestors. The problem begins when villagers do not acknowledge their ancestors anymore and turn to other opportunities and networks, which offer incentives for social mobility and prestige.

Some vignettes from the field may illustrate the persistence of local beliefs. In Ban Narai, Singhanakon District, Songkhla Province, I found my way to the current imam of the village. After my experiences of internal divisions in Tha Sala, I cautiously inquired into the state of Buddhist–Muslim relations in Ban Narai. The old imam told me that his mother had been a Buddhist and that nearly all the Muslim villagers in Narai had Buddhist ancestors. A large proportion of the population migrated to Hatyai when the economic situation in the Lake region became more difficult. Long ago, Muslim villagers migrated here from elsewhere, as resources were plentiful and there were 'too many temples' in their original village. At this point the young imam, the old imam's son, joined the discussion. Appeasing his Buddhist ancestors, who possessed his children and made them ill, was the only cure for them. His wife had therefore prepared a plate of sticky rice, eggs and betel leaves and brought it to the Buddhist monk, who had himself been born in the Muslim part of the village with the aid of a Muslim midwife. The imam and the monk went to school together and are related in a southern Thai form of ritual friendship known as *glö*.[16] As the first child was cured in this manner, the imam repeated the procedure for the following three children as well.

In Ban Narai, I met an old man resting after the hard work of harvesting rice. This old grandfather recounted that, in the past, he used to perform a ritual with a mixture of religious elements. To appease the ancestors' negative power, the most important Buddhist rite of passage, an ordination ceremony, had to be performed before circumcision. This ordination ceremony is the same as the Buddhist one, which means that the hair is shaved and an orange robe put on, except for a small detail: it is not performed in the temple but at the well of the private home. This is merely a temporary conversion, but it is necessary to be at peace with the spirits. Should the spirits be ignored, it is believed that the man would bleed excessively during circumcision.[17]

In Ban Narai, the villagers and I discussed their economic situation. This small village is close to vanishing, as many people have left due to the low price of rice, the high price of fertilizer and due to deteriorating environmental conditions. We met an old couple: the husband used to be a Buddhist but had converted to Islam. After some hesitation, the old lady informed us that she plays a central role in the Manora, which has been performed for hundreds of years by families living in the Lake area. The costly preparation requires a great deal of investment in both performers and costumes. On a selected day in May, the performers dance all day and night in honour of the ancestors. In the Manora, the medium-performer (*nora*) has access to the spiritual power of the ancestors and thus establishes a contact between the living and the dead (see Figure 7.4). Just like *tayai* ancestry, Manora chooses its preferred ancestors without distinguishing gender, the order of siblings or religious affiliation. Grandchildren who find

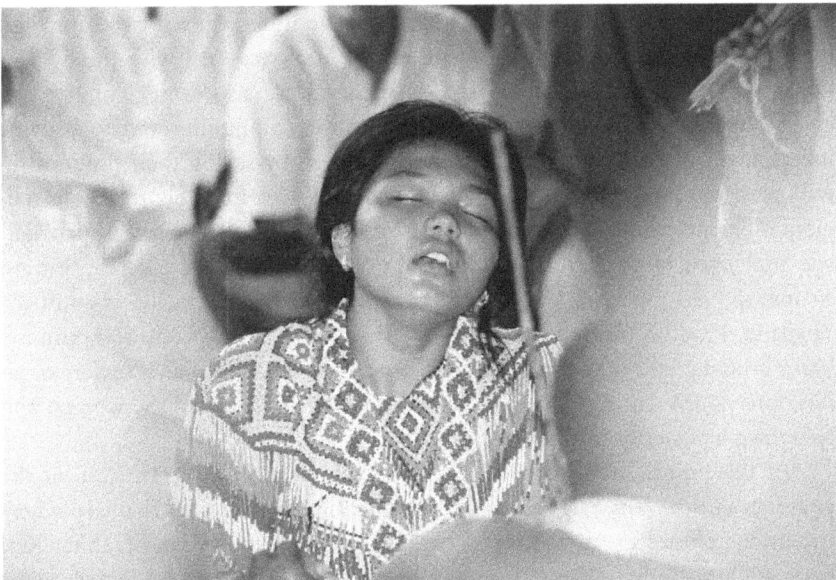

Figure 7.4 The *Manoora Rongkruu* performance (photo: A. Horstmann)

themselves ill or who have to wander long distances to places far from home can ask the *tayai* for a cure or for protection during their journey by preparing a meal for them. This principle of reciprocity with the dead is called *käbon*, 'to return merit'. In the case of the Manora, the cured person is obliged to dance for three days and three nights in honour of the ancestor-teacher, to perform the *Manoora Rongkruu*. In this ritual, the spiritual force of the *nora* performer is transferred to a higher status; the *nora* is a *khru* (teacher) or *krumor* (healer). The *nora*'s capacity to heal comes from the spiritual power of the ancestors.

This power, like the aid of the Buddhist angels, is also sought by traditional healers, who combine traditional herbs with meditation and possession. *Käbon* is the fundamental principle of reciprocal relations in the multi-religious villages of southern Thailand. Villagers are able to express a desire to the guardian spirits, Buddhist saints or teachers of the Manora performance. If their desire is fulfilled, the person is obliged to give a donation, feast or concert to honour the spirit.

Here, the stranger is bound to the self in a fascinating way. This example shows that world religion has not replaced the cosmological order; to the contrary, it has been adopted piecemeal and according to the local needs of the villagers. The power of the spirits may be a threat to a Muslim child who is possessed by a Buddhist ancestor, but it can also be a healing force that can be mobilized for help. The ancestor cult is a fundamental part of the cosmological order and provides the basis of ritual exchange in the plural spaces of peasant society.

This culture of innovation and appropriation was supported in the 1980s and 1990s by social networks among farmers who were beginning to campaign for the protection of the environment and of local resources with the help of non-governmental organizations (NGOs); they were also campaigning to be given a voice in political decision-making in the community and to become independent of economic middlemen and brokers by selling their products in ecological bio-markets. In these networks, people are often able to ignore religious differences: thus, in Nakhon Srithammarat the guardian spirit (Thuat Klai) was mobilized in an anti-dam demonstration.[18] Similarly, in a demonstration against the gas pipelines that brutally cut through the rice fields in southern Thailand, local people and (Buddhist) NGOs united in this common purpose, again bridging ethnic and religious differences. In the 1990s, civil society organizations flourished in southern Thailand, making small-scale fisherwomen and fishermen a powerful force for self-reliance.

At this point, I return to the changing significance of the worship of the guardian spirit in Tha Sala, Nakhon Srithammarat Province. In Tha Sala, where the bridge crosses the Klai River in Sa Geo district, the image of Thuat Klai now sits in a Buddha-like position in his sala, which had to be removed due to the construction of a four-lane highway, during which the main ritual was suspended for a year to avoid disturbing the guardian spirit. The monumental figure of the guardian spirit, sitting in the Buddhist fashion but still wearing Muslim clothes, was manufactured in Bangkok. Before then, Thuat Klai had just been one Thuat among many other spirits worshipped by the peasants. Village spirits in the forest temple and the rice fields protected farmers from misfortune or theft. The Thuat needed no image or ornament, and the placing of monumental but individual sculptures in the many small houses (*sala*) along the Klai is a very recent development. The main tourist attraction at Wat Sa Keo Bridge is now being organized by a self-appointed committee of influential representatives of the Thai state, including village heads, district officials and primary schoolteachers. The head of the primary school at Wat Sa Keo has revived the local cult by integrating the legend of Thuat Klai into Thai folklore, which is narrated in schoolbooks and taught to the pupils, who are encouraged to draw the heroes of the legend.

While most communities organize the ritual in their own way, most of the *sala* are in the hands of this power clique and patronage network. In addition to the image, the *sala* are being rebuilt in more lasting concrete as part of local development schemes supported by the district fund. Thuat Klai is worshipped along with his Buddhist and Chinese followers. A shelter with a tin roof has also been erected next to the Thuat's house to protect the five participating Buddhist monks from the hot sun. The myth of Thuat Klai is therefore being reinterpreted in Thai-Buddhist communities by reinforcing its non-Muslim elements. Since Thuat Klai was a mighty soldier, his image is now very popular in the Thai army in Nakhon Srithammarat. The kingdom of Nakhon Srithammarat played a conspicuous role in the expansion of Siam into southern Thailand, and this guardian spirit is said to have protected the soldiers in battle. The Thuat is now associated with attached meanings that were not relevant for the participating communities. In the remainder of this chapter, I examine the forces that undermine exchange relations between Buddhists and Muslims in the Songkhla Lake area.

The New Visibility of Da'wa Islamic Missionary Movements in Southern Thailand

Although Muslims in Nakhon Srithammarat constitute a minority, they were among the pioneer settlers in Tha Sala, including prisoners of war from Patani, Yala and Narathiwat provinces, as well as migrants. Although my Thai-Buddhist informers said that the Muslims are merely a tiny minority found mainly in coastal areas and specializing in fishing, Muslims in Tha Sala are actually involved in a large range of activities, including trading, organizing weekly markets and gardening. For those who do not own land, temporary migration to the plantations, factories or tourist facilities of Surat Thani, Phanggna and Krabi is necessary in order to make a living.

Buddhist and Muslim villagers express their reciprocal interest by preparing sweets for each other's feasts or by giving donations to a funeral ceremony. Recently, however, Tha Sala has become a showcase for the transnational Dawa movement or Tablighi Jama'at al-Dawa, a proselytizing, pietist movement that originated in India and began to spread in Southeast Asia in the early 1970s. It is active in every country where Muslims live, including England and France.[19] Tablighi Jama'at originated in 1927 in India and is closely associated with the teaching of the Deobandi School in New Delhi. Mohammad Ilyas, its founder, reinterpreted Islam by stressing the missionary Dawa character to counter the aggressive proselytizing of rightist Hindu movements at the time. Focusing on ritual rather than on educational texts, the critical aim of Tablighi Jama'at is to spread its message beyond its own community.[20]

Villagers know the Islamic network of Tablighi Jama'at as Dawa Tabligh or simply Tabligh. Many are not aware that the movement's leadership is concentrated in India and Pakistan. In Tha Sala, a missionary first introduced the message of the Tabligh from the centre (*markaz*) of Yala. The modern Dawa movement now exercises enormous pressure on the syncretic practices of the villagers, dividing communities into supporters and opponents of Islam. In Mokhalan, the transformation of Muslim society has been dramatic, as the Tablighi Jama'at is literally taking over the space of the mosque. As elsewhere in Thailand, the mosque must register with the head office of the Muslim chair (Chularajamontri) in Bangkok, which presides over all mosques in the country. However, in Mokhalan, the young Tablighi firebrands have driven the imam's assistant out of the mosque, calling him a lazy good-for-nothing who is not prepared to get up for the early morning prayers. The village includes a clan that counts senior leaders of the Tablighi among themselves, one of them having studied in a Tablighi *madrassah* or Quranic college. This *maulana* (Islamic intellectual) is a senior leader of the Tablighi Jama'at in the Yala *markaz*, where he leads the prayers for *jemaat* arriving from South Asia. The *markaz* in Yala is mainly a centre from which the leadership organizes operations and *jemaat* going abroad from Thailand. Villagers who go 'on tour' include senior leaders from the village as well as the local imam. Local villagers have become zealous Tablighi, effectively controlling the space of the mosque, especially the call for prayer, and leading the Friday prayers. The notice board at the mosque, with current news of mosque activities, includes a detailed calendar of incoming and outgoing *jemaat*, which reads like a 'Who's who' of the Tablighi Jama'at. The *maulana* in the village regularly goes to China and Cambodia, establishing strong ties with the minority Muslims there. These activities show the very cosmopolitan character of the Tablighi Jama'at. Locals who have spent long periods in Pakistan become important brokers who are able to bridge South and Southeast Asia by acting as interpreters of the spoken Urdu.

The core members of the Tablighi Jama'at are able to impose their ideological standards on the volunteers. On one occasion I travelled with the Tablighi to another village, where we based ourselves in the local mosque under the umbrella of the local imam. A young volunteer travelling for the first time badly wanted to go to the boxing match in a local town, where his small nephew was going to fight. Yet for the movement boxing, which involves gambling, is one of the evils of a secular, corrupted society, and the leader (*amir*) of the Jemaat did not allow the volunteer to go. Volunteers are socialized within the lifestyle regime of the Tablighi and consequently tend to change their lives. First, they change their appearance according to the model laid down by the *amir* (Islamic leader), wearing long white robes, beards and Muslim headwear, and sometimes add eye shadow and perfume. The most dramatic effect of the presence of the Tablighi Jama'at in the village concerns the remodelling of gender relations. Women are encouraged to veil themselves and cover themselves in a full veil (*purdah*). In the Tablighi view, women play a very modest role in the public sphere in Islam, restricting themselves to neighbourhood groups, Quran study groups and meditation groups. Women do go on tour with *jemaat*, but only in the company of male relatives for protection. Women as a rule do not stay or sleep in mosques as men do, but in pre-arranged housing. Women may be present in mass congregations, but in a hidden location. Nevertheless, women play a conspicuous role in missionary activities, persuading other women to submit themselves to the fundamentalist regime of Tablighi Jama'at. For women, the movement offers women new spaces by allowing them to join the global *umma* (community of Muslim believers). Pious women criticize the lavish expenses of wealthier women in their ceremonial lives, especially with regard to marriages.

However, Tablighi Jama'at has not yet been able to impose its norms on traditional Muslim society as a whole. Even though it enjoys the full support of the local imam, the imam does not necessarily conform to the movement's expectations. One of the major disputes concerns the treatment of the body at death: this dispute over funerals, concerning the appropriate form of commitment to the deceased, is dividing Muslim communities throughout the Malay Peninsula. Villagers insist on maintaining the tradition of staying with the dead person for seven nights and reading key passages from the Quran at the burial site in order to facilitate the deceased's passage to heaven and protect him from malevolent spirits.

During my stay in the village, the imam was suddenly informed about the death of old villager who had been ill. He decided to postpone the funeral to the following day to allow preparations to be made and to avoid burying the body in the darkness of the night. The relatives and neighbours of the deceased, some of them Buddhists, came to the house of the deceased to express their condolences. One senior elder, who is also one of the leaders of the Tablighi Jama'at at the provincial level, told me that the villagers should have buried the dead body immediately as life was no more, and that, from a Tablighi point of view, the presence of the family at the cemetery was an unnecessary expense. However, while the imam rhetorically confirmed the legitimacy of the Da'wa organization in the village, he observed the traditions of southern Thai local structure in this case.

The longer I stayed, the more I became aware that people either contradicted themselves or tried to hide their participation in traditional ritual. Only a few villagers dared to reject the new ideology openly, but they continued to practise the old traditions in secret. For the people it is just too painful to drop the deceased, to refuse food to the dead, as they fear that the spirits of the dead may wander in the village and disturb the villagers. For example, after listening to the Tablighi elder, my assistant confused me by suddenly pointing to a powerful, malevolent spirit that was thought to be that of a mother who had lost her baby in pregnancy. The imam was called once again, but in this case to exorcize the powerful spirit whom the imam pretended to see. When I asked him whether he also specializes in magic, he said that he wanted to help needy villagers without, of course, disregarding Islamic precepts. Many villagers continue to feed the dead at the cemetery, although Tablighi invest energy in encouraging villagers to cease all pre-Islamic rituals, including Malay ones. When I asked the imam and his wife if they carried out the ritual in honour of the rice goddess, they told me after some hesitation that they have stopped doing so. Yet, among the new rice I discovered the ritual items, the basket and betel leaves that are used in the ritual for the rice goddess.

Besides his qualities as a communal leader, Imam Whahab is also a specialist in magic. He used to be one of the strong men (*nakleng*) of the village, having three wives at a time and having had children with all of them, and having some talent in shadow puppet theatre, or Wayang Kulit. He reports that all young women and men had to rush, missing dinner, to join the *wayang* or *manora* whenever *manora* troupes entered the village and attracted huge Buddhist and Muslim crowds. Today, villagers in Tha Sala seem to pay less attention to traditional entertainment, although some *nakleng* in the village continue to raise lucrative cattle and cocks for bull-fighting and cock-fighting, two major pastimes of the southern Thai people. These pastimes are also pleasing to the guardian spirit of Thuat Klai, who is said to have supported them, but not to Tablighi Jama'at, for whom they represent the vices of immature Muslims.

On the other hand, not all villagers share the commitment of Dawa, and sometimes they object violently to the intruders who come from outside. As continuous travel requires long absences from home of up to six months, villagers condemn as uncivilized those men who are prepared to leave their wives and children and perhaps not even return if their children go missing or are abducted. Lengthy travel is seen as representing an attitude of escape from the responsibilities of the secular world. People complain that Tablighi youth are lazy, retreating into the easy world of nothingness. Other people, including established religious leaders, are very frustrated with the disrespect of Tablighi Jama'at for the traditional sources of the elders. One elder in Songkhla thus asked why Tablighi Jama'at, including his younger brother, had to go and 'disturb', as he put it, other communities 'who already have their imam'. This imam was so frustrated with the new ideology that others had introduced that he was building his own small mosque behind his house, where he continued to teach his disciples.

The Impact of State Policies and Thai Nationalism on Local Knowledge

The gradual takeover of the Thuat Klai ritual by state representatives is an indication of the rising influence of the state over local identities. Once the Buddhist club of influential figures in the local area had placed the image in the *sala*, it was no longer possible for Muslims to join the ceremony. The incorporation of this multi-religious ritual by the state was completed by mobilizing the village commune (*tambon*) funds as state development projects and by fully integrating the Buddhist *sangha* into a founding cult by providing a concrete shelter for the monks. The latter not only accompany the cult, chanting their verse in Pali, but are also domesticating it to the needs of Buddhist political authority.

The incorporation of the cult reflects the Buddhist *sangha*'s attitude towards local cosmologies. The pressure that the *sangha* exercises on local cosmologies is far more subtle than the Muslim one, but it is still very effective. The key change concerns the transformation of the monastery from a place of Buddhist ritual and meditation to a place of state development. The Buddhist abbot of Ban Narai was born in the Muslim part of the village and raised by a Muslim midwife. During his career as abbot of the monastery, he mobilized support to expand the monastery, build a school, lay out a sports ground and build concrete roads. The abbot travels in his private van, with his own driver, to provincial meetings of the Buddhist *sangha*. He showed me with pride photographs of visiting politicians, such as ex-prime minister Prem Tinsulanonda and Queen Sirikit, as well as his many awards for his 'development' efforts. His developmentalist approach has made the abbot popular far beyond the boundaries of his village. His monastery is firmly integrated into regional and national circuits of power and influence. Nonetheless, he sticks to caring for the spiritual development of 'his' community. Among his pupils in school are many Muslim children from poor Muslim families, who receive a Buddhist education, including learning the *dhamma* (wisdom), in addition to a cup of white rice. The abbot is a close friend of the imam of the same village, from whom he accepts offerings of eggs and betel to cure his possessed children, as he commented with a broad smile.

In Bangsarn, the ritual summoning of the spiritual force of the guardian spirit to overcome the economic problems of the villagers, who make their living from fishing, is carried out in the Buddhist manner, and the offerings are shaped according to the material needs of the Buddhist monks. As fishing does not provide the basis for a livelihood, many Buddhist villagers have left the village for good. However, all the villagers have to return to the source of their lives in the tenth month of the year, carrying photographs of their ancestors. During the tenth-month festivities, the returnees chant Buddhist verses for their ancestors, thus establishing ties between the living and the dead. Buddhist monks are known as healers throughout the Malay Peninsula. When I visited a Muslim family breaking the evening fast, the father told me that he had been very ill since leaving the Thai army. He went to the hospital, but nobody could help him. Finally, he went to a spirit doctor, who exorcized the malevolent spirit and healed him. When I inquired about the healer, he identified him as a Buddhist monk.

Despite these tolerant attitudes, however, violence in the three southern border provinces has given rise to a chauvinistic discourse that is now demonizing Islam. Buddhist monks describe Islam as a radical religion that promotes violence for its egoistical interests. Muslims who have been educated in the Middle East are suspected of being under 'terrorist' influences. 'What kind of religion', the abbot asks me, 'tells a person to kill in order to go to heaven?' Many Buddhists regard Muslims as egoists who see only themselves. Muslims are also seen as fanatics, as people who spend all their time in prayer. When I inquired about the *tayai*, a Buddhist abbot replied that of course people distinguish between the religion of their ancestors, but even for himself it is difficult to draw the line where his own family history is concerned.

The charismatic Phra Khru Ajarn Sunthorn in Tamot is leading a Buddhist initiative to raise villagers' awareness of Theravada Buddhism as well as the environment. The monastery, which is built over the remains of an Islamic cemetery, is organizing knowledge-training courses to which both Buddhist and Muslim villagers are invited. Muslim villagers from Ban Hua Chang have no problems in participating in secular activities as long as they do not have to honour the Buddhist monk or the Buddhist image (*wai phra*). Phra Sunthorn and leading Buddhist villagers teach the ordinary villagers about the importance of water and the forest and about natural herbs, performing Buddhist rituals in relation to any development project. In Tamot, Buddhist monks have a special relationship with the traditional imam of Ban Klong Nui as part of the traditional exchange systems with the dead. Thus, if there are any renovation works at either the monastery or the mosque, the monks participate and vice versa. When an Islamic kindergarten was established in Ban Hua Chang, Phra Sunthorn donated a Buddhist money-tree loaded with banknotes and handed it over to the imam. The special relationship between Buddhism and Islam is symbolically demonstrated in what might be called 'the ritual of two religions'. During the important new year rituals, on 15 April, all the descendants of Tamot come together in the ritual, in which the traditional imam and the Buddhist participate and declare that there should be no separation between the religions of Tamot. However, the influence of Tablighi Jama'at among Muslim migrants from Patani has substantially reduced Muslim participation in the ritual. In 2005, the large majority of participants were Buddhist. Whereas Buddhist converts to Islam are always welcome to attend the ritual of the Buddhist temple, Muslim villagers who have converted to Buddhism are no longer allowed into the mosque. Thus, as in Klai, Buddhism has become the dominant religion in the exchange systems, especially in the founding cult that worships the founding spirits of Islam. In Tamot, the religious leaders come together at the cemetery to worship a pre-Islamic, Hindu, Brahmanical phallus, a symbol of fertility.

Concluding Remarks

This chapter has identified a form of ritual knowledge in which the followers of Theravada Buddhism and Islam in the Songkhla Lake region acknowledge joint social membership in exchange systems with the dead. These systems can be identified as total institutions in the meaning of Marcel Mauss, because they combine religious, moral, kinship, social, emotional and legal ties. However, these institutions of ritual exchange are currently being squeezed between the forces of the Thai state from above and radical Islamization from below. Theravada Buddhism, appropriated by the Thai state, now dominates many of the ancestor rituals, including founders' cults in southern Thailand, whereas Islam has retreated into the vast Islamic networks of transnational pietist movements. While some of the rituals have survived, such as the feeding of the dead by traditional Muslims, others have disappeared, like the Buddhist ordination of Muslim villagers with Buddhist ancestors. Other rituals are being transformed, as the case study of the founders' cult in Klai or the 'ritual of two religions' in Tamot clearly shows. Obviously, then, religious difference did not always have the importance that it has today. Ancestors were perceived as collective, without religious or gender difference, and the great ancestors could be either Buddhist saints or Muslim patrons. In multi-religious ritual today, the groups involved jealously maintain and reinforce the boundaries between themselves and the religious other, rather than reproducing a communal spirit.

In my view, in the Songkhla Lake basin, we observe the coexistence of traditional beliefs and the influence of national and transnational modernizing movements. The meaning of religion – in other words, what counts as religion and why – is becoming increasingly contested. Sometimes, traditional values and modern ideologies coexist and are embodied by the same person. Thus, this chapter rejects essentialist explanations of culture that emphasize the continuity of social structures and values that deem the modernizing ideologies of national and global forces redundant, as well as post-modernist approaches that assume the withering away and disappearance of traditions in a post-modern society that only has enough space for the spirit of capitalism and the culture of mass consumerism. This study of coexistence in the Songkhla Lake basin shows that ethnic idioms are framed in specific local configurations and social networks. What emerges is a complex picture of a fragile balance between Buddhists and Muslims, who are increasingly exposed to the outside and who increasingly distinguish themselves from each other by socializing in symbolically marked milieu. In these spaces, the revitalization and reflexive transformation of multi-religious ritual and the increasing presence of orthodox religion produce all kinds of contradictions, tensions and fears. I argue that the artificial separation of the ancestors in Buddhist and Muslim constitutes a rupture, because a common belief in the power of ancestors strengthened the social ties between Buddhists and Muslims. In many communities, this process of 'religious cascading' has produced a situation of mutual distrust and fear, while in other neighbourhoods, a conscious strategy of enhancing inter-religious solidarity has kept social relationships and exchanges largely intact. The result is a context in which the networks of neighbourhoods and villages maintain the boundaries of their religious identity more clearly and more rigidly, but still participate in the institutional activities based on customary law and local knowledge in order to prevent the destabilization of their neighbourhood, community or village. In addition to the increasing separation of Buddhist and Muslim life-worlds, families and neighbourhoods in the Buddhist and Muslim milieus themselves are also deeply divided. It remains to be seen how long the remainders of organic solidarity are able to withhold this process of increasing cultural fragmentation.

Acknowledgements

The author expresses his gratitude to the Editorial Board of the *Journal of Southeast Asian Studies* for their permission to reproduce the article published in the *Journal* in 2011.

Alexander Horstmann is Associate Professor in Southeast Asian Studies at the School of Humanities, Tallinn University, Estonia, relating area studies to other teaching communities at the School of Humanities: he has held visiting positions at Tokyo University of Foreign Studies, Mahidol University and EHESS in Paris. He has published widely on the livelihood and social support networks of displaced Karen in Thailand and Burma and has published, in June 2015 (with Jin-Heon Jung), 'Building Noah's Ark for Migrants, Refugees and Religious Communities' with Palgrave. Alexander is co-editor of the Berghahn journal

Conflict and Society: Advances in Research, a new journal of qualitative research on socially organized violence.

Notes

1 This chapter was presented to the Department of Social Anthropology and Sociology at the Central University of Budapest, to the Department of Cultural Anthropology at the University of Nice-Sophia Antipolis and to the participants of a panel that Katherina Seraidari and I convened at the EASA Conference in Ljubljana, 2008. I would like to thank Prem Kumar Rajaram and Joel Candau for their invitations. A research grant from the Fritz Thyssen Foundation for Scientific Research is gratefully acknowledged. See the landmark study by Duncan McCargo (2008). For a deep ethnography on communal violence, see Marc Askew (2009). See also the informative account by Saroja Dorairajoo (2004).

2. See the special issue by Bubandt and Molnar (2004).

3. See Horstmann and Seraidari (2006).

4. See Keyes and Tanabe (2002).

5. Many communities find themselves unable to catch up with agrarian change and suffer from environmental and material deprivation. Some communities may move entirely to urban centres, such as Hat Yai.

6. For a survey of the relationships in the South, multiple connections and cross-overs, see Horstmann (2004). See the community study of Angela Burr (1974) for an earlier account of coexistence in Songkhla.

7. See Gesick (1995). Gesick provides a beautiful local history of the Songkhla Lake area. See also Jacq-Hergoualc'h (2002).

8. Accordingly, I favour a concept of ritual that emphasizes the negotiation of social order and not one that only reproduces social order, although sometimes ritual may indeed reproduce social and normative orders, and at other times challenge them. See Henn and Koepping (2008).

9. See the argument of the emergence of alternative modernities in Knauft (2002).

10. Bubandt and Molnar (2004) argue in their introduction that the quality of previous works has been hampered by simplistic arguments about essential culture or journalistic jargon. Here, I want to cite only a few works that avoid both traps: Gravers (2007); Robinne and Sadan (2007); Montesano and Jory (2008).

11. I propose that people may sometimes invest cultural resources into peace and sometimes into violence, depending on the political embeddings. Religious syncretism and conflict are not antithetical, and religious syncretism can sometimes be antagonistic. Thus, Bubandt and Molnar (2004) argue that the politics of customary law played a decisive role in the violence, not only in reconciliation. In the Thai context, see the excellent discussion of syncretism in Kitiarsa (2005).

12. For a case of intensive cultural and political competition in a syncretic ritual and pilgrimage centre in northern India, see van der Veer (1988). This case of cultural competition resulted in acute violence. Syncretism thus can presume violence.

13. On the Manora, see Horstmann (2009).

14. These observations are based on my own fieldwork in Tha Sala, Nakon Srithammarat.

15. In this line, see the (structuralist) argument by Platenkamp (2004).

16. *Glö* in southern Thailand form close social ties that bind individuals together for life. See Horstmann (2004).

17. Ryoko Nishii (1999) describes a similar ceremony in Satun, in which a Muslim must

break with his Buddhist ancestry. In this case a white shirt is placed over a cup containing water, betel and a banknote.

18. The Thuat is the guardian spirit, first ancestor and founder of the community and is believed to have made land and water available to the people.

19. *Dawa*, meaning simply the 'call to prayer', has been reinterpreted in the missionary sense as 'going out and preaching'.

20. See the contributions in Muhammad Khalid Masud (2000) for the history and ideology of the Tablighi Jama'at and for accounts of how it became a transnational movement. For a case study of the new presence of the Da'wa Tabligh in southern Thailand, see Horstmann (2007b).

Chapter 8

Three Dyads Compared

Nuer/Anywaa (Ethiopia), Maasai/Kamba (Kenya) and Evenki/Buryat (Siberia)

Günther Schlee

There is a long tradition of comparing ethnic groups, also variously called 'cultures' or 'societies', in anthropology. This has been done in small settings with limited variation in the form of relatively controlled comparisons (e.g. Nadel 1952) and world-wide using statistical methods based on the Human Relations Area Files. There are weaknesses in these approaches, as well as merits. I do not intend to discuss these works here, I simply mention them to illustrate the way in which the approach sketched in this chapter differs from them. Here I am not going to take ethnic groups as the units of comparison, but the relationships between them. I am going to compare three dyads, in particular I compare the relationship between Nuer and Anywaa with the relationship between the Maasai and the Kamba and with the relationship between the Buryat and Evenki. It goes without saying that the life-world of each of these groups goes beyond each of the dyads under discussion. The Maasai have relevant others apart from the Kamba, the social environment of the Buryat does not consist of the Evenki only, and so on. The state in particular, with its ethnic policies, acts as a third element in all these dyads and transforms them into triangles, and if we include further elements, we get polygons or multidimensional clouds of factors. I am aware that the focus on a dyad is a simplification and that we need to bring more complexity back in at a later point if we want to be able to accurately model reality. My justification for focusing on dyads is that this focus shows us something which we might not see otherwise, and that nobody should be asked to deal with more complexity than he can handle at a given moment.

The focus on dyads also suggests that the two groups interacting in each of them are given units. It must be kept in mind that the boundary between them might be drawn by a third party (e.g. the state) and that different actors hold different opinions with regard to the drawing of the boundary. The possibility of re-affiliation also needs to be kept in mind. The Buryat/Evenki divide largely coincides, as we shall learn below, with the ecological divide between steppe and taiga. Can the ethnic divide be crossed by people who move into the other ecological zone?

The use of the term 'ethnic' as an adjective suggests that there is a quality of that sort. Two 'ethnic' groups would be expected to differ according to some criteria of 'ethnic' distinction, while they would be the same at a higher level because both would qualify as 'ethnic'.

Many mutually reactive ethno-nationalisms in the modern world indeed appear very similar to each other. They tend to be territorial, they tend to comprise linguistic or some other cultural elements, they interact through well-defined diplomatic channels and when at war they become even more similar to each other, because they engage in arms races for the same types of arms, imitate each other's threatening conduct (parades, manoeuvres) and respond to each other's tactics and strategies. One would have to look closely at the emblems on their uniforms to see the difference. These co-evolving ethno-nationalisms are quite clearly phenomena of the same kind.

Anywaa and Nuer: Different Kinds of Ethnicity

In the case of Anywaa ethnicity reacting to Nuer ethnicity and vice versa, one cannot be so sure that 'ethnicity' stands for the same type of phenomenon in both cases. What makes an Anywaa more Anywaa differs so much from what makes a Nuer more Nuer that one hesitates to attach the same label 'ethnicity' to what is being intensified in either case. This emerges clearly from the PhD thesis by Feyissa (2003) entitled 'Ethnic Groups and Conflict: The Case of the Anywaa-Nuer Relations in the Gambela Region, Western Ethiopia'.

Quite plausibly, Feyissa speaks of 'two kinds' of ethnic groups, or 'two kinds' of ethnicities, rather than just two ethnic groups. The following table summarizes what can be adduced to show that the Anywaa are not just neighbours in a conflict who stress the minimal difference, but that the fundamental workings of ethnicity are rather different in both cases.

The Anywaa emphasize the fact or belief that they are of exclusively Anywaa ancestry, while the Nuer admit that their subunits, which take the form of patrilineal descent groups, are in fact of diverse origins. Descent in the patriline is perfectly sufficient for being a Nuer. It is not even a precondition, because where it is not present, it can be easily constituted by adoption. The Anywaa method of calculating descent also has a patrilineal bias, but it is distinct from that of the Nuer because of the absence of adoptions and the fact that attention is given to the patriline of the mother of a person as well in determining that person's

Table 8.1   *Differences between Anywaa and Nuer*

Anywaa	Nuer
ancestry	diversity of origins
bilateral parentage	patriliny, adoptions
specific territory	mobility
rare bridewealth beads	cattle as bridewealth
hierarchical order	'ordered anarchy'
discrimination, purity	assimilationism
particularist	universalist
Ethnogenesis	
in isolation	in a competitive setting

full status as an Anywaa. People with a non-Anywaa mother (and more so a non-Anywaa father) are not accepted as full Anywaa.

Anywaa identity is closely tied to a specific territory, where they till their fields, go hunting or have their fishing grounds. When forced to settle in a new place, they have to become one with the land by dissolving clumps of earth in the water they drink. The Nuer place a stronger emphasis on mobile pastoralism and territorial expansion. Whether one is from a lineage said to possess a given territory implies whether or not one is *diel* (member of the titular lineage, 'noble' in Evans-Pritchard's sense), but is of little practical consequence.

Bridewealth, where it exists, is always interesting to look at in interethnic relations. The Anywaa use a type of bead called *dimui* as bridewealth. No one knows where these beads originally came from, for how many centuries they have been around in Anywaa country, and where one can get a fresh supply. They can get lost but cannot increase in number. If one has a sister, one might get *dimui* for her and then be able to marry. The only people who can accumulate *dimui* are the chiefs who get them for their sisters and daughters, but who are exempt from having to pay for their brides. They can build up a following by giving *dimui* to sisterless would-be bridegrooms. Nuer expansionism and openness, on the other hand, is reflected in their use of cattle as bridewealth. Cattle populations grow just like the populations of their keepers, partly in response to the number of their keepers and the care invested in them. And if, in spite of this, a young man does not have enough cattle to marry and cannot mobilize enough help from his relatives, he can still acquire cattle through raids or by becoming a labour migrant and earning money for the purchase of cattle. Cattle are a living, flexible, expandable resource. They can also be used by Nuer to marry Anywaa brides, because the Anywaa accept cattle from Nuer bridegrooms and do not insist on *dimui* in these cases. It goes without saying that the offspring of such unions are Nuer. For an Anywaa bride, one would have to spend significantly fewer animals than for a Nuer bride. Such marriages also provide Nuer with a foothold for expansion into Anywaa territories. The mention of chiefs and the social resources they can monopolize (like *dimui*) leads us to another dichotomy: the hierarchical order of Anywaa society versus the segmentary lineage system, in Evans-Pritchard's terms the 'ordered anarchy' of the Nuer (1940). Ideas of descent and practices of marriage enhance both the contrast between the Anywaa tendency towards discrimination and purity on the one side and the expansive assimilationism of the Nuer on the other. Feyissa summarizes all this by attributing particularism to the Anywaa and a form of universalism to the Nuer. Combining scant evidence and plausible conjecture, he speculates that the Anywaa ethnogenesis must have taken place in relative isolation and that of the Nuer in a competitive setting where one had to mobilize numbers.

Primordialism and constructivism have been used as classifications of scholarly theories about ethnicity ('etic' theories, i.e. those from an analytical, non-participant perspective). Scholars tended to assume that the primordialists must be wrong if the constructivists are right and vice versa. Feyissa has shown that this dichotomy can be applied to emic theory (i.e. the views of the actors under study) and that in that domain primordialism and constructivism co-exist and share reality. He calls the ethnicity of the Anywaa primordialist and that of the Nuer constructivist (Feyissa 2003: xviii). The Nuer, he says, are aware that their system of patrilineal descent groups comprised in larger units, ultimately giving them an identity as 'Nuer' at the highest level, is a construct, and they live happily with this construct without even missing a deeper truth. They might once have had ideas of purity or descent similar to those of the Anywaa, but have given these up under the pressure of resource competition which forced them to play the numbers game: 'the bigger the group, the more powerful it becomes, the higher the chances of winning in the competition over natural resources' (ibid.). They have replaced the ideology of 'purity' with that of the 'melting pot'.[1]

The two mutually opposed ethnicities – as has now become clear – do not produce a balance or a stable boundary. Social exchanges are asymmetrical and facilitate Nuer expansion at the expense of the Anywaa.

Feyissa does not get bogged down in the usual sterile theoretical debates about whether the segmentary lineage system is just an anthropological model, or an actors' model, or whether it reflects a social reality. He simply takes it as a descriptive category and tests its adequacy empirically. He does a micro-census and counts how many members of a given settlement cluster belong to the name-giving patrilineal unit and how many others are attached to it by affinal links which develop into cognatic ties in the next generation.

Kamba and Maasai: Uneasy Coexistence

We now turn to the second dyad, that of the Maasai and Kamba in Kenya. Our source is the PhD thesis of Mutie (2003), "'In Spite of Difference": Making

Sense of the Coexistence between the Kamba and the Maasai of Kenya', published as *The Art of Interethnic Coexistence: Some Evidence from Kenya* in 2013.

The Kamba and the Maasai belong to different language families. The former are Bantu speakers, the latter Eastern Nilotes. Their languages differ as much as any two languages on Earth can. Their modes of livelihood used to be clearly distinct; before modern education and economic diversification set in, the Kamba were exclusively farmers, while the Maasai (or more precisely: those Maasai who lived in the neighbourhood of the Kamba) despised farming and were proud of their exclusive reliance on cattle. Smallstock may have had a significant economic role but was culturally downplayed.

In the two semi-arid districts in the south of Kenya where Mutie did his field research, Makueni and Kajiado, the Kamba and Maasai live side by side, the Kamba in Makueni, the Maasai in Kajiado. There are also Kamba farmers and traders who exploit opportunities in Kajiado, enjoying a precarious guest status among the Maasai.

Interethnic relationships have been examined in anthropological literature from a variety of different aspects. Leach (1954) stressed that cultural differences, especially in the visual field – frills and decorations – were used to communicate within a wider whole. Cultural differences between small-scale local societies were used by these to communicate with each other in a wider society, a society of societies or a meta-society so to speak. The current theory of ethnicity by Barth (1969a) and his followers also stresses interaction at the ethnic boundary. Boundaries are marked by cultural discontinuities and it is through these discontinuities, different standards of excellence and different values that people reduce competition and enter into a peaceful or complementary relationship at the boundary. There is no reason to romanticize complementary relations as just or equal. Often they are not. But the complementarity tends to reduce violence. Ethnic diversity can thus be seen as a factor of integration into a wider social system.

In popular theory, ethnic difference is seen as a potential source of conflict to such a degree that it is almost equated with conflict. Conflict analysts, or at least the anthropologists among them, mostly agree that ethnicity more often is something which emerges or is accentuated in the course of a conflict, rather than being its actual cause. But it is impossible to deny that the frontlines in a conflict can follow the lines of cultural discontinuities or that these lines are ethnicized, i.e. that ethnic distinctions develop along those lines of dissent. Conflict, of course, is not the opposite of integration. People communicate through their similarities and differences in hostile ways as well. Often they emulate their adversaries. War is also a social system within which it is possible to become integrated.

Rather than anchoring his analysis to this pair of concepts, integration and conflict, Mutie chooses a third term, coexistence. The concept has wide currency in politics, e.g. with reference to the Cold War. The Soviet doctrine of *Koexistenz* is the only context cited by the Brockhaus encyclopaedia. Less often it is found in the context of Israel/Palestine. It is used in an ecological context by biologists. *The International Encyclopaedia of Social and Behavioral Sciences* goes directly from 'Coeducation' to 'Cognition' and has no entry on 'Coexistence'. This history of the concept reveals that it is not a common term in the social sciences.

The utility of this rather unusual concept therefore needs to be examined. In the way Mutie uses the term, 'coexistence' implies difference but does not assume a particular form of relationship like hostility/cooperation/friendliness. It does, however, imply a certain social distance and at least partial separation (Mutie 2003: 1; see also Mutie 2013). Within this wide conceptual framework, it can comprise a whole range of contradictory forms of interaction, like armed but 'controlled' conflict, political alliances, economic exchanges, shared identities – along some features, but not along others – (ibid.: 2). Coexistence tends to be an uneasy relationship. It is close to violent conflict. In a fashion complementary to the analysis of the factors which lead to conflict (Wimmer 1997), Mutie examines the mechanisms of keeping conflicts at low levels of violence and highlights how 'tensions and conflict situations are pre-empted, avoided and precluded in other settings, despite the contested borders, competition for power, heightened degree of ethnic difference and external instigation' (Mutie 2003: 6; see also Mutie 2013).

'Coexistence' is thus characterized by ethnic distinction, social exchange, complementarity and interdependence, ethnic antagonisms and conflict below certain levels, shared territory and formative external factors, which shape the dyad under study (Mutie 2003: 10, 287, 290). Many of these phenomena have also been studied by authors who take a different key concept as their starting point, like 'integration' or 'articulation'. Another element in which Mutie is also interested, however, combines particularly well with 'coexistence' in an uneasy relationship. This is his insistence on compromises and concessions. Compromises and concessions do not really fit into those theories of ethnicity which stress the integrative workings of cultural differences, nor do they fit into those which stress their conflict potential. If the two parties make compromises and concessions, then this implies that the differences between them are neither the means of integration nor the cause of conflict. Rather, it implies that differences have a disruptive potential, and that this potential is contained by minimizing differences or by wrapping them into some sort of package deal, by adding a sweet coating to something which is otherwise hard to swallow, or by gaining acceptance for something which the other side does not like by making concessions in some other field. This accent on compromises and concessions also motivates the 'in spite of' in the title ('In Spite of Difference'). Differences are potentially disruptive, but one can handle them, tame them, mollify them, make them acceptable, and stabilize them. By these means one can coexist 'in spite of' differences.

Mutie explains that 'coexistence' is based on the maintenance of a distinction. Two things which merge into one no longer coexist, but exist as one. On the other hand, he states that 'coexistence may also take the form of commonality or sameness' (Mutie 2003: 289). What is meant is that group distinctions are marked by difference in certain features, while other features may be similar or identical, and that resort to any one of these may be made according to a particular situation. Features which are shared by Kamba and Maasai are:

- the cultural and economic focus on cattle in all their ritual and social functions, including bridewealth;
- their bilingualism which enables many of them to speak each other's language;
- female circumcision (also called FGM or female genital mutilation);
- Christianity;
- their political affiliation (in 2002 both groups voted for the National Rainbow Coalition);
- both are counted among the 'small tribes' and use similar political discourses in their struggle with larger groups for a slice of the national cake;
- their ecological vulnerability as inhabitants of semi-arid lands.

A similar list of similarities could be drawn up for Nuer and Anywaa to complement our table of differences, above. Both Nuer and Anywaa are 'black' and referred to as such by the 'red' highlanders, in addition to being abused as *barya* (slaves) by them, both speak Nilotic languages which are clearly distinct from the Afro-asiatic (Semitic, Cushitic, etc.) languages of the 'Highlanders', and both were politically marginalized by the imperial system. In the case of the Nuer and Anywaa, it seems to be the political environment of explicit ethnic politics which causes undercommunication of these commonalities and overcommunication of the differences.

Mutie perceives intermarriage as an integrating or binding force between the Maasai and the Kamba. By far the most frequent case is Maasai men marrying Kamba girls or women. Stemming from an agricultural background, the latter have the reputation of being hard working. The Kamba, however, are by no means the losers in this exchange. By becoming affinal relatives of the Maasai, they, or rather those among them who have these links, have a stronger moral right to any lands they till in the Maasai areas.

Mutie goes on to explore emic theories at some length. The most elaborate one is that of 'axes in a basket', developed by one of Mutie's interlocutors in a long conversation. The basket represents the shared territory, the wider unit, the system, the commonality to which both the Kamba and the Maasai belong. The axes are the two groups. They might hit each other and make noise as the basket is carried around. One may stop the noise by putting some insulation material between them: cloth, cotton or a lubricant. Intermarriage is among those materials that soften the contact. This is a quite elaborate emic theory, which recalls what Leach has written about associations of societies or Gluckman's writings about cross-cutting ties (1965).

Another emic theory is the one about 'eating', which resonates with recent sociological writings (Bayart 1989) and ecological theories. 'Stability is produced by "eating" with "co-eaters"' (ibid.: 16). This pattern is compared with an ecological theory by Pontin (1982) about a 'dominance ring' in which different species manage to coexist by gaining access to a resource at different times, thus avoiding direct competition. Mutie does not elaborate whether this 'dominance ring' in Kenyan politics is the result of intentional compromises or historical contiguity.

Buryat and Evenki: Ethnic Boundary Meets Ecological Boundary

The following sections are based on Sántha's[2] (2005) study on Buryat-Evenki interethnic relations in the Baikal region. The Buryats live in two different ecological zones (taiga and steppe) and the Evenki/Tungus exclusively in the taiga. Buryat livelihood largely depends on pastoralism, whereas for the Evenki/Tungus hunting plays a major role in everyday life as well as in the interpretations of their identity.

Buryats and Evenki/Tungus have been the target of various ethnic stereotypes by outsiders. Soviet social scientists have seen the Evenki as a prototype of 'primitive society', and the Buryats as representatives of a more advanced evolutionary stage. The Evenki/Tungus and the Buryat political elites have often acted as rivals in the process of 'scrambling' – seeking the favours of the Russian and Soviet state. However, in order to reduce the complexity of interethnic relations in the present analysis, let us focus on the relationships between the Buryat and Evenki, and how they describe and negotiate these.

Sántha aims to examine ethnic stereotypes (emic theories): in other words, how one ethnic group conceives of the other. His analysis comprises various spheres of activities and interaction: language; belief systems; various forms of land use and their connotations; the issue of cattle raiding; and intermarriage. What follows here deals specifically with cattle raiding and intermarriage, as well as with the question of whether and how an Evenki/Tungus can become a Buryat, and vice versa.

While cattle raiding in this region may take place on a smaller scale than in East Africa, the way it occurs reveals a certain strategic advantage of the Evenki/Tungus, which translates into stereotypes about the Tungus and the land they inhabit. The steppe-inhabiting Buryats perceive the taiga as *khatuu gazar*, as a 'hard place' in terms of cattle-herding and the prosecution of cattle thieves. Retaliation is hard to achieve not only because of the natural environment, but also because of the social environment in the taiga, where taiga-based Buryats may act as allies of the Evenki/Tungus against the Steppe Buryats. Sántha illustrates this by using the example of a group of Steppe Buryats who follow the tracks of a cattle thief through the snow. The footsteps lead them to a small village in the taiga where the trace of the criminal becomes obscured by the footsteps of the other inhabitants. The inquiries of the Steppe Buryats in pursuit of the thief remain fruitless because both the local Taiga Buryats and the Evenki/ Tungus cover up for him. Their alliance is based on a legendary female ancestor who connects the local Buryats with the local Tungus, notwithstanding the fact that the two groups see each other as ethnically different. This example implies that sometimes interethnic solidarity is stronger than shared ethnic identity. It also introduces a third (or intermediate) element into the dyadic relationship between Buryats and Evenki/Tungus, namely, the Taiga Buryats. This intermediate element, however, does not weaken the general character of interethnic relations between Buryats and Evenki/Tungus, wherein the former see the latter as unreliable, irascible, unpredictable and as the genuine 'Other' in numerous ways. The following section on intermarriage and change of ethnic identity will add further clues about this perception of the genuine 'Other'.

Is it possible for Evenki/Tungus to become Buryats, and if so, how? Here it is necessary to distinguish between how the Steppe Buryats assess this question, and how the Taiga Buryats approach it. From the Steppe Buryats' point of view, Evenki/Tungus can never become Buryats, except in very specific circumstances. Buryats will unequivocally label all individuals of mixed descent as Evenki/ Tungus (*khamnagan* in Buryat), regardless of whether his/her Evenki/Tungus ancestors are on the maternal or paternal side. An individual with any one such ancestor always has to assert his/her legitimacy and rights within the community he/she lives in, because the community never automatically accepts individuals with Evenki/Tungus ancestors as equals.

The position of women with regard to this question is less ambivalent than that of men. Whether a woman is 'Buryat' or 'Evenki/Tungus' is not important for the Steppe Buryats; what is important is the fact that women are generally 'not ours' (*kharin* = foreign), i.e. that they comply with the requirement of exogamy and patrilocal residence in order to qualify as marriage partners. Steppe Buryats perceive Evenki/Tungus as foreign, and Evenki/Tungus women as doubly so.

Similar to Steppe Buryat men, Steppe Buryat women label other women with at least one Evenki/Tungus ancestor as Evenki/Tungus (*khamnagan*). Steppe Buryats often refer to the treacherous Evenki/Tungus character and their 'blood' (*khamnagan shuhan*).

Regarding men with some Evenki/Tungus ancestry, the situation is more complex: if a man of mixed descent has a Buryat ancestor in the paternal line, he has the right to participate in communal sacrifices; he is, however, often excluded from the community's everyday activities. The individual may occupy an important niche within the community by filling a leading position in sacrifices and certain other ceremonies. His status as an outsider cannot, however, be overcome.

Exclusion is relevant not only at the level of exogamy (which in the Buryat case extends to seven generations on the paternal line), but also beyond it. Neither women (regardless of their ethnic background) nor Tungus can be 'legendary' ancestors. Exclusion works on the imaginary (spiritual) as well as on the everyday (experiential) level. In fact, Sántha's Steppe Buryat informants do not distinguish these two levels.

Steppe Buryats do not allow their children to come into close contact with Evenki/Tungus youths, as they fear that their children might engage sexually with the Evenki/Tungus and thereby cause the Buryat family to get entangled in a relation with the Evenki/Tungus.

Now we shall briefly examine the question of whether an Evenki/Tungus can become a Buryat from the Taiga Buryat point of view. While among the Buryats in general, having any one Evenki/Tungus ancestor automatically means that an individual has Evenki/Tungus ethnic features, in the eyes of the Taiga Buryats this criterion loses its importance beyond the seventh generation of forebears (since exogamy requirements do not extend beyond the seventh generation). Interestingly, there is an asymmetry not only with regard to intermarriage patterns but also with regard to the recognition of ancestors within the Taiga Buryat society. In the paternal line the threshold of clearly remembering and counting one's forebears is the seventh generation, whereas in the maternal line, the threshold is perceived in a different way. Tungus ancestors in the maternal line between the third and seventh generation are considered to be powerful and potentially dangerous ancestors – and ego inherits their power.

In short, for a Taiga Buryat it may even be expedient to have some Evenki/Tungus forebears. It may help to emphasize a person's positive characteristics and to improve his/her status within the community. Among the Taiga Buryats, Evenki/Tungus can achieve a prominent place among the community's legendary ancestors.

In addition to intermarriage and descent, another phenomenon deserves to be mentioned: spatial distance. If the wife of a Buryat originates from far away, she is often labelled as Tungus. This again highlights the connection between the quality of being 'foreign' (the genuine 'Other') and the concept of Evenki/Tungus ethnicity among the Buryats.

Complementary filiation (maternal ancestors in a patrilineal society) is thus a recurrent theme in Anywaa as well as Steppe Buryat ideology of purity of descent.

We now turn to a set of research questions and comparative points which can be applied to all three of the dyads discussed.

Forms of Resource Competition: Struggle versus Scramble

Resource competition is a widespread explanation for ethnic conflict. Not all resource conflicts, however, are ethnicized and not all ethnic discontinuities are lines of conflict. Resource conflicts in Gambela often take more severe forms on the intra-ethnic level than between ethnic groups: 'Competition over scarce resources in itself does not explain the development of mutually opposed ethnicities. In fact, competition over scarce resources has caused more deadly intra[-] than inter-ethnic conflict' (Feyissa 2003: xix). Further down Feyissa specifies that competition over natural resources is the main cause cited for intra-ethnic conflicts, namely inter-clan fights among the Nuer, and has created subethnic interest groups, some of which are strategically positioned to benefit from interethnic peace (ibid.: 211).

But also at the interethnic level a number of contested resources can be identified. This, however, does not imply that all Nuer are lined up against all Anywaa; on the contrary, there are internal cleavages within each of the groups, and in extended case studies it becomes clear that there is a buffer zone of groups with links to both sides. To speak of Nuer/Anywaa resource conflicts is therefore a simplification. Contested resources comprise riverine floodlands, which form a minimal proportion of the total surface but have an outstanding agricultural importance, and the distributive state as a resource. Especially since the introduction of a federal order in Ethiopia in 1991 which led to the foundation of the Gambela regional state, and since the ethnicization of politics at all levels, the state itself – namely political office, state revenue and facilities managed by the state such as educational and health facilities – have become hotspots of conflict. Ethnic politics in Gambela are interwoven with the civil war in Southern Sudan and the diaspora in Western countries, especially the USA (cf. Falge 2015).

The Kenyan metaphor about eating, which Mutie not only describes but takes up for his own analytical purposes, could be explored further in the field of competitive use of natural resources. Do the Kamba and Maasai scramble for resources (pasture, firewood, agricultural land) like two people eating from the same bowl, so that the one who eats faster is the winner, or do they struggle for resources (fight, litigation, arbitration) like people fighting about a bowl of food and the winner taking it? There seem to be even more forms of competition than these two. We can learn from Mutie that people sometimes hide the fact that they are eating or share what is not theirs.

The distinction between 'scramble' and 'struggle' is reminiscent of that between 'sharing' and 'dividing' resources in the usage of Dafinger and Pelican (2002: 12–15). Shared resources, if scarce, may become the object of a scramble, while divided resources (the example given is the neatly divided farming and grazing areas in North-West Cameroon) may lead to a peaceful and regulated situation if the division is accepted by both sides, or to a violent struggle if it is contested. To the extent that the ethnic divide between Buryat and Evenki coincides with the ecological divide between steppe and taiga, one can expect a peaceful division. Competition will arise in cases where the ecological divide is crossed. It then may take the form of a scramble, which might lead to the depletion of a resource (overhunting, overgrazing), or a struggle (attempts at violent exclusion).

In the Anywaa/Nuer case we seem to encounter a combination of scramble and struggle. The way in which the Nuer crowd out the Anywaa from the use of a certain resource, using their pastures or fishing in their waters, is certainly a form of scramble. Violent struggle, however, is not absent. The Nuer raid the Anywaa for their cattle. This leads us to the next section. Open Nuer violence is met by the Anywaa, so the Nuer say, by treason and clandestine murder against the Nuer in their midst.

Raiding Pressure

The literature on the Maasai attributes to them the belief that all the cattle in the world were created by God for them. In pre-colonial times, the Maasai largely restricted central Kenyan Bantu speakers to the forested highlands. To the extent that these Bantu speakers expanded into the plains and competed with the Maasai in the cattle economy, they did so by adopting Maasai military organization (the age-sets) along with Maasai weapons and ornaments. In a rather unkind way, they are referred to as '*Massai-Affen*' in the older German literature. This expression reflects their propensity to 'ape' the Maasai in that early period. By and large, however, the Maasai were in control of the low-lying open range, and they maintained this monopoly by raiding others who acquired cattle herds of a size which made the adoption of a wider ranging mobile grazing system necessary and who thus came within the reach of the Maasai warriors. The raiding pressure they exercised helped the Maasai push their grazing areas to their ecological boundaries and to maintain this advanced boundary against ethnic Others. Kikuyu and Kamba expansion into Maasai lands should be seen in the context of colonial pacification and the policies of the post-colonial state, which in these central and southern areas has managed to establish a semblance of a power monopoly.

In the case of Nuer expansion against Anywaa we see raiding pressure at work right now in the present period. Raiding people for their cattle has the side-effect, intended or unintended, of making them vacate particular areas. In these areas other resources, like agricultural lands, can then be appropriated as well.

The Buryat steppe nomads are rich in cattle and the Evenki live in an environment where cattle can easily be hidden – the taiga. The Evenki have quite a tradition in raiding the Buryat, but as their forest habitat does not offer open grazing areas to an extent that permits cattle keeping on a larger scale, they practice 'commercial raiding': they sell the cattle they have acquired as loot, unless they consume them. This form of raiding does not lead to territorial expansion, because the two groups remain in their respective habitats: the Buryat in the steppe and the Evenki in the taiga.

When comparing Siberian and East African raiding, one has to keep in mind that the contested resource (cattle) might have quite different meanings within and between the two areas. Pastoralists, especially East African ones, might ascribe more ritual and social functions to cattle than hunters who are after the meat or the money. Also, while killing human beings may be associated with rituals of status promotion in Africa, this is not the case in Siberia.

Bridewealth, Intermarriage and Ethnic Boundary Shift

Bridewealth in livestock tends to be higher in societies which are richer in livestock.[3] It is higher among the pastoral Nuer than among the agricultural Anywaa, it is higher among the pastoral Maasai than among the agricultural Kamba, and it is higher among the more pronouncedly pastoral Buryat than among the Evenki, who are predominantly hunters. In the case of interethnic marriages, this means that suitors from the first mentioned group of each dyad find brides from the second group 'cheap'.

If we compare the dynamics of expansion, however, the fact that (ex-)pastoralists marry non-pastoralist women does not always have the same implications. Among the Maasai, those who have Kamba wives stay on Maasai territory and have to face their Kamba affines encroaching on their resources. The encroachment on land, which accompanies intermarriage, takes place in the opposite direction in the Nuer/Anywaa case. It is former Nuer pastoralists who marry Anywaa women and then settle in Anywaa lands and cultivate them. Intermarriage apparently has the potential to be a means of territorial expansion to both wife-givers and wife-takers, according to circumstances which remain to be elucidated. Another dimension of comparison would be the connection between intermarriage and violent conflict. Ethnographic material from New Guinea to different parts of Africa suggests that this relationship can take a variety of forms. Often intermarriage is a de-escalating factor, but there are also cases where exogamy rules place potential marriage partners in the same categories as potential enemies, and others where intermarriage might even lead to conflict escalation, as affinal ties are the first to be cut by violent means when a war is started (Harrison 1993; Lang 1977).

The Buryat place a stronger emphasis on pastoralism and are richer in cattle than the Evenki, who are predominantly hunters. For an Evenki, it would be difficult to take a Buryat bride, because he would not be able to meet Buryat bridewealth expectations. The Buryat on the other hand regard marriage to Evenki women to be detrimental to their prestige. Therefore, intermarriage in both directions takes place on a very low scale. This may or not have always been the case. Sántha also looks into interethnic marriages in different periods to find out more about differences in social prestige of the different ethnic groups over time and whether or not there were clear ethnic hierarchies.

Conclusion

This chapter consists of six sections. The first three of them are descriptions of three couples of ethnic groups neighbouring each other, taken from three countries on two continents. In each case the description focuses on the relationship between the two groups and in cross references these relationships are compared with each other. The following three sections treat specific aspects (forms of competition; raiding; bridewealth and intermarriage) of interaction and compare these across the three dyads. The fact that (so I hope) a number of interesting things emerged from these comparisons is an indicator of a certain degree of similarity between all these cases, comprising the six groups and the three dyadic relationships they form.

Not that comparison would have been otherwise impossible. Colloquial statements like 'these things are too different to be compared with each other' are analytically not tenable. Anything can be compared with anything else. We can compare modesty with bananas. The result of the comparison would be that one is a moral attitude and the other one a tropical fruit and that the two have nothing to do with each other. Comparison between things which differ radically and in every way results in the statement of radical difference. So such a comparison is possible and does have a result, but not a very interesting one.

There are interesting comparisons to be made between components characterized by limited variation. Against a background of sameness we can discern things which vary independently of each other or co-vary with each other and get a feeling about how things are connected. In the cases under study this background of sameness which makes comparison fruitful consists (among other things I might not have noticed) of the following elements:

1. The economies of all groups are based on agriculture and animal husbandry.
2. They all have cattle.
3. They raid each other for cattle.
4. They all intermarry to various degrees.
5. They all have the institution of bridewealth payments as a constitutive part of marriage.
6. Men from the groups richer in cattle tend to marry women from the groups which have a less pastoral orientation (farmers or hunters).
7. Descent reckoning among all these groups is basically patrilineal. The child of a Nuer father is a Nuer, the one of an Anywaa father an Anywaa, of a Buryat father a Buryat et cetera.

It is against this shared background (elements 1 and 4) that we can discuss the ways in which the Nuer men marry Anywaa women and then encroach on Anywaa lands and compare our findings with the case of Maasai marrying Kamba women, where it is the kin of the wife who encroach on the lands of the group of the husband. Raiding pressure (3) results in Anywaa land being vacated and Nuer expanding into it. Evenki raiding against Buryats and Maasai raiding against Kamba does not have a marked effect of this kind. In the Evenki/Buryat case the groups are divided by an ecological boundary (taiga/steppe) while in the Kamba/Maasai case a district boundary (Makueni/Kajiado) stabilizes ethnic territories. Again, it is against the shared background (raiding) that we see the variation (territorial expansion or not). Intermarriage (4, 5, 6) results in children of ethnically mixed couples. All groups having predominantly patrilineal descent reckoning (7), we can discern the role of matrilateral ancestry from case to case. Having a non-Anywaa mother is a disadvantage for an Anywaa, while Nuer assimilate the children of mixed couples without a trace (and even adopt complete strangers). Evenki ancestry on the mother's side has different meanings for Steppe Buryats and Taiga Buryats, et cetera. Only because the general categories are the same can specific differences be discussed in a meaningful way.

The sameness described in the preceding paragraphs is sameness seen from an observer's perspective. Without having interview data to ascertain this from the six groups, I assume that none of them would find anything remarkable in having cattle, bridewealth and patrilineal descent. They would be scandalized to hear that in Europe, for example, there are people who marry without bridewealth or do not marry at all. What we perceive as similarities between them, for them is so obvious and normal that it is below the threshold of attention.

In the case of another similarity, namely the one that all six groups under study are or represent 'ethnic groups', it is not nearly as easy to answer the question of whether we are dealing with a category brought in by outside observers or categories which are or have become locally shared. Without claiming that any of these six ethnic identities is just a colonial invention,[4] there is no way to deny that colonial and post-colonial Kenya, imperial and socialist and post-socialist Ethiopia, imperial Russia, the Soviet Union and post-socialist Russia all have had ethnic policies and that the way to be an ethnic group in all these political entities has been shaped by such policies. Ethiopia since 1991 has based its entire political system on an ethnic mosaic of territorial units at all levels and representation along ethnic lines. The Nuer and Anywaa compete with each other on this field, and so do, as described by Popp (2001), the Yem and Oromo. Kenya has gone through waves of ethnic cleansing of provinces and districts and now has also come very close to a mosaic of ethnic territories which are miniaturized versions of the nation state.[5] Stalin was an influential theorist on nations and nationalities and was not a man known for hesitations in making his visions real. Russian (and

Ethiopian) concepts of ethnicity and practices of ethnic politics still owe much to him. So this element of 'sameness', that all these groups are ethnic groups in a modern, politicized sense, may have to do more with the universalization of a category than with its original universality.

Still, a recent import or not, the generalized concept of ethnicity and its political significance provide the framework in which these ethnic groups interact. The Maasai and Kamba form an ethnic coalition in an election, the Nuer and Anywaa compete for their shares of the Gambela Regional State, the Buryat and Evenki are nationalities within the Russian federation. They all play ethnic games according to rules set at the national level and informed by international discourses. Ethnicity homogenizes and universalizes because it creates ethnic units which correspond to a certain pattern. At the same time, it not only tolerates but demands differences. Ethnic units are constituted by their differences. And these differences go so far, that in the Nuer/Anywaa case, in which modes of recruitment and forms of belonging are at complete variance, Dereje raises the question of whether we are just dealing with different ethnicities or different kinds of ethnicity.

As far as sameness is concerned, we can so far point to the general features, earlier generations of anthropologists might have called them structural, which the cases under study share and which, in combination with the differences between them, give them the (medium) degree of variation from one another which makes comparison worthwhile. One may call this kind of sameness a methodological artefact, because the cases have been chosen to have such a medium degree of similarity. The artefact, however, only consists in including just these cases in our sample. The features (the above list from 1 to 7) are there and the fact that the groups compared share them can be corroborated by others.[6] Irrespective of this (i.e. also if our observations were wrong), we can state that these statements of similarity are based on an observer's perspective.

The second kind of sameness we have come across up to this point is that all cases involve 'ethnicities' which correspond to a universalized idea of what an 'ethnic group' is or should be. This makes it an 'emic' category, a category of the people under study, even if that comprises global institutions. Scholarly work on 'ethnicity' is only possible if one does not adopt the concept as one's own analytical category but keeps a critical distance to it. From an observer's point of view, we can make ethnographic observations about who shares this concept to which degree and who does not, but the concept itself belongs to the observed.

Among the authors whose work we have summarized, Dereje is most explicit about this emic perspective. The Nuer and Anywaa are both 'ethnic groups' in the perception of the Ethiopian state and they behave according to what is expected from ethnic groups by competing for influence in the Regional State, Gambela, in which many of them live. To some extent they have not chosen that.

Ethnicity, especially in Ethiopiaocus, can be seen as a kind of straightjacket into which people have to fit.[7] But what is shared between the Nuer and Anywaa (and generally Ethiopian or even global) notions of collective identity ends somewhere here. The rest is specific. Dereje's account reads as if the Anywaa and Nuer are 'playing different games' altogether, the Anywaa the purity game and the Nuer the expansion game, and that is why he chose that phrase as the title for book publication into which this thesis evolved (Feyissa 2011). A dyad is a system with two components, but contrary to what some people continue to associate with the term 'system', there is nothing balanced or stable in this particular one and its constituent parts do not obey any principle of overall system functionality. Stubbornly continuing a losing game, the Anywaa play chess. What the Nuer do is more like soccer. There is not much resistance a chess board can put up to a boot.

Günther Schlee is one of the Founding Directors of the Max Planck Institute for Social Anthropology in Halle, Germany. Prior to this appointment he was Professor of Social Anthropology at the University of Bielefeld. He conducted fieldwork in Kenya, Ethiopia and Sudan. His publications include *Identities on the Move: Clanship and Pastoralism in Northern Kenya* (Manchester University Press, 1989), *How Enemies Are Made: Towards a Theory of Ethnic and Religious Conflict* (Berghahn Books, 2008) and *Pastoralism and Politics* (with Abdullahi A. Shongolo, James Currey, 2012).

Notes

1. Expansion versus self-restriction and conservative resource use has also been discussed by Schlee (1988) in connection with the Somali and Rendille.
2. István Sántha was a member of the Siberian Studies Centre at the Max Planck Institute for Social Anthropology, Halle (Saale), Germany, from 2003 to 2004.
3. Notwithstanding this, even in purely pastoral systems there is much variation in the forms of bridewealth, from open to fixed systems, with or without delayed payments. Much of the literature on this has been reviewed by Schlee (1989). The different forms of bride-wealth were found to correlate with the kinds of relationships with affines and with the importance and the quality of stock friendships with unrelated people and with affinal relatives. This subject has also been taken up in an edited collection by Khazanov and Schlee entitled *Who Owns the Stock? Collective and Multiple Property Rights in Animals* (2012).
4. On 'invention' versus 'construction' of identities and religion and ethnicity as universal or universalized categories, see Schlee (2008a).
5. See Schlee (1989) on colonial and post-colonial policies on tribal territories in Kenya.
6. Of course, there is also an element of construction in this. The conceptual instruments used for finding these shared elements are neither natural nor universal. The term 'patrilineal' has been coined by anthropologists and also 'economy', 'agriculture' and 'bridewealth' are terms of a given language and each of them has its history. Notwithstanding that, we assume that people with the same observational methods and the same conceptual tools

would have arrived at the same findings at this pretty rough level of description. People variously refer to this kind of observation as 'objective', 'intersubjective' or 'factual'.

7.   This does not only apply to ethnicity as such, but also to specific macro-ethnic categories. Many smaller groups in southern and eastern Ethiopia now are forced to make up their minds whether they are 'Oromo' or 'Somali'. In many cases they have not regarded themselves as being part of either so far (Fekadu Adugna 2009; Schlee 2008b).

Chapter 9

Ruling over Ethnic and Religious Differences

A Comparative Essay on Empires

Günther Schlee

Introduction

Social systems do not exist in isolation but as parts of larger systems comprising interactions on various scales up to the global level. They are, however, discernible by the density of internal relationships, which justifies a special focus on them as separate subsystems of larger units. Apart from studying such subsystems in their interaction, they can be treated as separate cases and compared with each other. This chapter looks at historical materials drawn from a number of empires in both ways: as separate cases with an internal logic of rule and as historically interconnected entities, which derive models of rule from their predecessors.

Taking the Moghul Empire in northern India and its Central Asian precursors and models as its starting point, the chapter examines relations of sameness and difference among the components of empires. The other examples presented in this chapter are the Ottoman Empire and the British in the Sudan. These cases are historically interconnected. The British were part of the ethnic diversity of the Moghul Empire, acting, initially, as Moghul agents. Later, they did the same for Ottomans and their Egyptian offshoots before they managed to assume the leading role themselves. The focus of the chapter, however, is not on historical interconnections but on typological comparisons. Recurrent features of the empires under examination include, first, the levelling of ethnic differences among members of the ruling elite, i.e. the amalgamation of the leading strata often by means of individual assimilation, and second, the maintenance and even formalization and instrumentalization of ethnic difference between rulers and the ruled and within ruled populations. Maintenance of difference resonates with the famous motto *divide et impera*, and Hechter (2013: 6) is right in pointing out that 'rulers preferred to govern culturally heterogenous territory the better to divide their subjects'. But the role of ethnic and religious difference in empires goes far beyond dividing the subject population in order to diminsh the threat they might present to the rulers. Many historical empires were extremely culturalist, to give an old phenomenon a very new, somewhat post-modern name. They treated different ethnic and religious identities as simply given. They naturalized culture, they adhered to what Dereje Feyissa (2011) would call 'emic primordialism'. Ethnic difference in many empires was the basis of a societal division of labour, with such complex forms of interplay between groups that a monolineal hierarchy is not always easy to ascertain, at least not one everyone would agree on. The aim of the chapter is to open comparative perspectives and to raise questions. No final analysis of even one case is attempted.

In the following, I will go through a number of historical examples of empires, examining how ethnic diversity was handled in each case. This journey across continents and through different eras is a search for patterns. I can already promise that we are going to find several such recurring patterns.

Moghul India

Moghul or Mughal is a corruption of the word 'Mongol'. To what extent the Moghul rulers of sixteenth-century India were Mongols, however, requires some clarification.

In Central Asia, the formation of new peoples has repeatedly followed the following pattern: Turkic-speaking nomads, like the Qipchak, conquered agricultural areas inhabited by speakers of Eastern Iranian languages such as Sogdian. The modern Uzbeks were formed in this way. Their name and some elements of the population stem from a group of Turkic nomads, but modern Uzbeks descend primarily from Iranian (in the linguistic sense) agriculturalists and other oasis dwellers. Many of them still speak an Iranian language, Tajik, and the Turkic dialects of the others have undergone phonetic and lexical changes that reflect an Iranian substratum (Finke 2006a; Turaeva 2016). The Barlas, the tribe of Timur Leng or Tamerlane, the ancestor of the Indian Moghuls, are also an example of this pattern. Claiming Mongolian origin, the Barlas were bilingual in Tajik and the Chagatai dialect of Turkic.

With the expansion of the Mongols under Chinggis Khan, many Central Asian Turkic groups incorporated aristocratic elements of Chinggisid origin. For a long time, a legitimate claim to rule had to be based on Chinggisid ancestry. Unfortunately, for this purpose the ancestors of the Barlas were the wrong kind of Mongols (Finke 2006b: 112–19). They did not descend from Chinggis Khan and were not even of his clan, Borjigin.

The Timurids were defeated in Central Asia by the Uzbeks, another group of warlike Turkic-speaking ex-nomads, only partly identical with the modern nation that bears that name. Subsequently, the Timurids withdrew to what now is Afghanistan and later to India, where Babur, a fifth-generation descendent of Timur, established the Moghul Empire in the second quarter of the sixteenth century. By this time, links to Chinggisid nobility had been established by marriage and uterine descent. Intermarriage was also practiced with Persian nobility. Culturally, the Moghuls were no less eclectic than they were genealogically. They had reverted to a Persian language – not to their ancestral Sogdian but to Farsi, the flourishing modern literary language which, without the intrusion of Russian into Central Asia[1] and the quite recent spread of English in South Asia, would have developed into the unifying language for a large chunk of the Muslim world. Apart from that, they spoke less prestigious languages such as Chagatai Turkic and Hindi. Arabic was used for religious instructions (Foltz 1998: 4–5, 14).

The Moghul Empire was not only polyglot but also pluriethnic and religiously heterogeneous. There were Indian Muslims and even Hindus in the army (Foltz 1998: 5),[2] and in his budget planning Sultan Akbar (1542–1605) relied heavily on a Hindu financial wizard (Foltz 1998: 15). Hindu and other Indian merchants and money lenders were a major economic factor not only locally but all the way north to Central Asia (Foltz 1998: 62). The cultural climate was one of tolerance and debate. The Moghuls were Sunni Muslims, but the Shi'ite Persian civilization was held in high esteem (ibid.: 15). Taxation under Akbar did not distinguish between Hindus and Muslims (ibid.: 6). Even European scholars and artists were attracted by Moghul generosity: 'Portuguese priests regularly participated in religious debates, Italian doctors tended to the health of the elite, and madonnas and cherubim found their way into Indian paintings' (ibid.: 77).

Atypically for a Moghul, who would be expected to die in battle or in a succession struggle with a son or brother, one emperor, Hamayun, died falling down the steps of his library (Kulke and Rothermund 2010 [1986]: 125), reminding us of the dangers of scholarship. A cursory glance at the literature makes Moghul rulers appear rather enlightened, even as precursors of modern pluralism and multiculturalism. We will return to the question of religious plurality in the Moghul Empire below.

My sources did not reveal the extent to which ethnic and religious groups formed units of administration within the subject population, as they did in the Ottoman *millet* system. The impression I got from my limited reading was that cultural, linguistic and religious traditions mixed freely in individuals, rather than being instrumentalized for the construction of social boundaries and intergroup relations.

So, the Moghul Empire may not have been a group mosaic at all levels, as was the case with some of the other empires we are going to discuss. In its leading strata, it even had a cosmopolitan flair. But we still need a closer look in order to answer two questions:

1. Was there an ethnic core among the rulers? After all they were known by an ethnonym, Moghul or Mughal, which equals 'Mongols'.
2. How does the ethnic diversity within this empire compare with modern forms of pluralism and multiculturalism?

To answer the first question, we have to look back into history, as the Moghuls themselves did. For them, Chinggis Khan was the model ruler. Descent from Chinggis Khan conveyed legitimacy to a ruler. To compensate for the shortcoming of being Barlas by tribe, rather than being patrilineal descendants of Chinggis Khan, the ancestors of Moghul rulers, since the time of Timur Leng, had married daughters of Chinggisid princes. Thus, their descendants could claim descent from the ruler of the world at least in the way that will forever remain the second best in patrilineal and patriarchal societies, namely through their mothers or grandmothers. They did the same with Ashraaf ladies (plural of *shariif* – noble, descendant of the Prophet). They married them so that their off-spring could claim descent from the Prophet Muhammad through his daughter Fatima. Thus, the Moghuls derived their special status from descent from two personalities who would hardly have gotten along had they ever met.

Once we assume that Chinggis Khan was a role model for the Moghuls, it seems advisable to examine the significance of tribal and ethnic identities in this ruler's political system. Tamüjin, the future Chinggis Khan, was born into a seg-mentary social order of the classic type (see Evans-Pritchard 1940; Lewis 1961; Sigrist 1994) in which smaller patrilineal units are embedded in larger ones. The smallest residential and genealogical unit was called *ger*. This term means, liter-ally, 'house' or 'yurt' and in its extended genealogical sense stands for a slightly larger group occupying several yurts, namely, a man, his wife or wives, their unmarried children, and their married sons and their wives and children – i.e. a patrilineal extended family. A cluster of *ger* is called an *ayil* or village. People of the same village are assumed to be of the same clan, *oboq*, which in turn com-prises a plurality of villages sharing one clan territory.

Princes with Chinese titles worked against this structure. They demanded personal loyalty and practiced personal rule, not rule by seniority in a segmentary order. Chinggis Khan, like his father before him, started as a vassal of one of these princes (Lhamsuren 2011: 227) and, when he later assumed the status as a ruler himself, he was more successful than others in making his military organi-zation independent, to a significant degree, of this clan structure and clan-based loyalties. Leaders who submitted to him might be given command of one of the new units of a thousand (composed of hundreds and tens, with their respective leaders) into which Chinggis Khan divided his fighting force. Such units of a thousand might then be composed largely of clansmen of the commander, who had followed him prior to his submission to Chinggis Khan. Clans or tribal forces that resisted Chinggis Khan, however, were scattered, and their fragments

were recombined into other units of thousand that were not based on genealogical proximity among their members.[3] Distinguished soldiers were appointed as
leaders of such units, irrespective of their origins. In yet other cases, clan leaders
were replaced by junior members of their own lineages, if the junior members
were more willing to cooperate. Thus, old tribal aristocracies were replaced by a
new meritocracy. If, as was occasionally the case, former leaders were confirmed
in their positions, they now had to conform to new criteria (Hesse 1982).[4]

As the empire expanded, it subjected city and oasis dwellers, who had to pay
tribute to avoid annihilation, and it also incorporated more and more nomadic
warriors into the fighting force. In the east, these were Manchu, speakers of a
Tungus (Evenki) language,[5] but mostly it was speakers of Turkic languages who
became numerically dominant in the Mongol fighting force (McNeill 1997:
308). Thus, the new meritocracy came to be not only cross-clan but transeth-
nic, even non-ethnic, because the recruitment of and the modes of articulation
among its members was based not on ethnicity but on what McNeill calls – with
a very modern Weberian undertone – the 'bureaucratic principle' (ibid.: 307).
No such amalgamation took place among the sedentary subject peoples. They
had to remain distinct from the rulers, so that it was clear who had to pay tribute
to whom.

In religious matters, the Mongols appear to have been open and receptive.
Both at Chinggis Khan's residence, Karakorum, and later at his grandson Kublai
Khan's capital, just outside modern Beijing, every religion was represented in a
fashion reminiscent of the religious 'markets' in modern, pluralist societies. The
hopes of Christian missionaries to make converts, however, were disappointed.
These early Mongol rulers seemed to be interested in being on the safe side by
consulting diviners and ritual experts of all sorts, rather than putting all their eggs
in one basket by committing themselves to a particular religion.

After this big chronological leap back to the time of Chinggis Khan, we now
return to the Moghuls in India in long strides, pausing along the way to consider
an intermediary formation of power, one which was important as a 'role model
and reference point' (Foltz 1998: 22) for the Moghuls themselves:[6] the empire
of Timur Leng. Proper historians would proceed more cautiously and note more
details along the way; but my purpose is typological. Therefore, the following
dates might suffice. Chinggis Khan ruled from 1206 to his death in 1227. Timur
Leng was born roughly one hundred years later, between 1320 and 1330. In
this interval, western branches of Turko-Mongolian dynasties had converted to
Islam. Timur himself was enough of a Muslim to restrict himself, most unusu-
ally for a ruler in those days, to four wives. He died in 1404. Babur, the founder
of the Moghul Empire in India, was Timur's fifth-generation descendant. He
was the ruler of Kabul from where he set out to conquer India in 1525. The
Moghul conquest was by no means a Muslim war against Hindus. There had
been Muslims, including Muslim rulers, in India for centuries. And the category

'Hindu' would have been an anachronism in this context, anyhow. It came into use only later, during the British colonial period. Nor were the Moghuls the first Turko-Mongolians to rule in India. The most important predecessor of the Moghul Empire, the Sultanate of Delhi, which was once devastated by Timur and was lastingly conquered by Babur, was, in its final phase, ruled by another Turko-Mongolian dynasty, the Tughlaq.

Back to Timur: insofar as sons tend to succeed their fathers in high office, meritocracies develop, over time, into hereditary aristocracies. Similarly, military units start to behave like descent groups as soon as the recruitment of the sons of the aging soldiers becomes habitual. After a while they become like clans, because people are born into them. By the time of Timur Leng, the Turko-Mongolian world, including the domain of the Ulus Chaghatay, which was his immediate political environment, had become re-tribalized to a significant degree. Therefore, he had to repeat the efforts of Chinggis Khan in building up a non-tribal army loyal to him personally.

The Ulus Chaghatay comprised Transoxania (modern Uzbekistan) and much of what is today northern and eastern Afghanistan. It used to be ruled by descendants of Chinggis Khan's second son, Chaghaday, but by the fourteenth century, the time of Timur, these Chaghadayids were often puppets of men who pretended to rule in their name as 'commanders' (emirs) (Manz 1999 [1989]: 21). These real rulers were not necessarily tribal leaders who derived their legitimacy from any line of succession or order of seniority. Often, alliances with outsiders allowed pretenders to leadership to prevail over their rivals.[7] Power was based on the potential for violence. The history of internal power games in the Ulus Chaghatay is too complex to be summarized here, even in the roughest outline, as fortunes changed year by year. All this suggests, however, a higher blood toll than was actually paid. War was the day-to-day business of the steppe nomads, but they did not need to fight a battle if the outcome was clear in advance. New arrangements could be dictated by those who showed up with a larger following on the battle ground (ibid.: 63). Superficially, these power games look a bit like democracy, but the similarity does not go much beyond the importance of numbers.

The name of the game was to keep the power base non-tribal or, to the extent that tribal influences could not be ignored, to keep them carefully balanced. To maintain his position within his Barlas clan, Timur needed followers both inside and outside of it. Through the marriage of his sister or of his children as well as through marriages of his own, he secured alliances with powerful figures of other tribes (ibid.: 46). In addition to seeking allies, Timur cultivated valuable followers of an entirely different kind, namely, warriors with no power base of their own, who were entirely dependent on him (ibid.: 65). Timur's army, although it did contain Qipchak tribes and other tribes, was not an alliance of tribes that could join or quit as they chose, as had been characteristic previously of armies in the Ulus Chaghatay. It was Timur and his appointees who were in command,

and these appointees were not necessarily the leaders who had brought along their tribesmen when they joined Timur (ibid.: 104). So, in his own fashion, Timur managed to repeat Chinggis Khan's feat of creating a non-tribal army, whose members were loyal to him.

Conquest is about the acquisition of assets by force. For Timur, these assets were the sedentary peoples of the cities and oases. Not much effort was made to administer these people. The army came from time to collect tribute and then left the subject peoples alone again.

Not all subjects were sedentary, however. There were also nomads, who had not joined Timur in time and then were defeated by him. Timur's army was itself a nomad army, and his soldiers drove herds along to feed themselves and the families accompanying them; however, extensive campaigns exhausted these stocks. To replenish them, other nomads were raided. Timur caused these other nomads to be resettled across huge distances, where they had no political or military clout but were still available, should Timur's army have need of them to replenish its animal resources (Manz 1999 [1989]: 101f.).

After our excursion into the Central Asian past of the Indian Moghuls, we now move back to them to ask the same question as we have posed regarding the empires of Chinggis Khan and Timur: what was the role of ethnicity in the Moghul army and in the inner circle of power? We have already mentioned the role of Persian and Chagatai Turkic. Of these two languages, the former was dominant at the court and the latter among the army leadership. Both distinguished the rulers from the ruled, who spoke Hindi and many other Indic languages. Foltz describes one scene at the court, in which songs were invited, first in Persian and then in Turkic (Foltz 1998: 38). This seems to suggest that both languages were accorded an elevated status and treated as roughly equal, with a slight advantage for Persian. Over time, a new language developed, a variety of Hindi that incorporated many Arabo-Islamic and Persian concepts: Urdu (Kulke and Rothermund 2010 [1986]: 153). Etymologically, 'Urdu' is the same word as English 'horde', German 'Horde' and Turkish 'ordu'. It comes from the Mongolian word 'ordo', which refers to the military encampment where the language was in fact used.

This linguistic development reflects a social development. The Moghuls incorporated many Indians of all social strata, from slaves to aristocrats, into the ruling elite. But while Chinggis Khan and Timur Leng both managed to forge a homogeneous warrior class out of diverse ethnic or tribal origins and to keep this stratum distinct from the tribute-paying subjects, the Indians who had entered the ruling elite remained distinct. What is more, they frequently had a local power base of their own and could often remain semi-independent or managed to re-assert a degree of independence over time.

By the time the British East India Company (BEIC) established its footholds in India, Murshid Quli Khan, the Moghul governor of Bengal, ruled 'as if he was an independent prince' (Kulke and Rothermund 2010 [1986]: 161). He was a Brahmin, who had converted to Islam, and he established his own capital, Murshidabad, from where he ruled not only Bengal but also Bihar and Orissa, which he had conquered. He was a progressive ruler, who collected revenue in cash rather than in kind (ibid.).

In collecting revenues, he was assisted by the British. The British East India Company (BEIC), which had been established in 1600 by Queen Elizabeth, penetrated the subcontinent in the seventeenth century with a network of 'factories' (fortified warehouses), attempting in this way to monopolize trade with Europe. Apart from trade, the Company discovered another kind of income: tax farming. Moghul princes and governors, Murshid among them, often sold or rented the right to collect taxes in a certain area to tax farmers, and the BEIC entered into such arrangements with him. Subsequently, '[t]he relatively small fee that it cost to buy the right to collect revenue in the regions surrounding its factory brought substantial annual returns' (Parsons 2010: 171).

Let us pause a moment to look at the logic of tax farming. If a ruler farms out the right to collect revenues to a tax farmer, he must have a power base outside this relationship, because, inside this relationship, the tax farmer seems to be in a stronger position. The income of the ruler is the fee the tax farmer pays for the privilege to collect taxes. So, the ruler is dependent on the tax farmer for this source of revenue. The tax farmer, however, does not necessarily need the ruler, as he must obviously be able to enforce tax payments without the help of the ruler. Nor would the tax farmer expect any other services from the state to which he surrenders the taxes he has collected. Conquest states or empires are not institutions which provide services,[8] apart, maybe, from protection against other such states. Thus, if they could avoid punishment by the ruler for non-compliance, tax farmers might be better off on their own. They could keep a larger share of the revenue, even if they had to invest some of it in raising forces to protect their loot from rivals. In sum, the tax farmer, especially if he also holds other powers, such as command over a garrison, or assets, such as estates, is a potential traitor.

In itself, tax farming leaves a great deal of discretion to the tax farmer. The arrangement is typically applied in areas that are not controlled by the central bureaucracy. In areas that are within the reach of the bureaucracy, based in the capital, there is no need for it. As is the case with social distance, which we discussed earlier (Introduction to this volume), taxation follows the logic of optimization. In the case of unnecessarily low taxes, the state, the ruler or the tax farmer foregoes potential gain. If, on the other extreme, taxes are very high, tax evasion will increase, as will the costs of control. High taxes may also cause resistance and raise the costs associated with oppression. In the case of tax farming in a province on the fringe of an empire, the tax farmer can apply his own optimization strategy. He can test how much people can pay without suffering a decline in productivity, and how much he can demand without causing out-migration or rebellion. He can grant tax exemptions to his supporters or to specialists whom he needs to develop his fief and he can impose punitive taxes on undesired people or activities. So, tax collection itself provides a wide space of 'agency', to use a sociological term; it is a domain in which power is exercised and increased. It is thus also a resource of power.

The BEIC provides one example of tax farmers who turned into a threat to their overlords. The Moghuls in Bengal and other rulers all over India ended up as their puppets. Just like the Turkic rulers in Central Asia, the ancestors of the Moghuls, often needed Chinggisid, or in the Ulus Chagatay more specifically Chaghadayid rulers as puppets, the Moghuls in India now slowly turned into puppets: figure heads in whose name foreigners exerted the real power. This is an ambivalent situation for both the puppet and the puppeteer who pulls the strings attached to the puppet: by entering into such a relationship it becomes clear that legitimate rule is the prerogative of the puppet, because without this legitimacy it would not be needed as a puppet. But being a puppet also implies not having the power to actually use the right to rule, which thereby turns into something largely symbolic. For the puppeteer it is the other way round: he can only enter this relationship by wielding power, but by needing a puppet he shows his illegitimacy in his own right and the need to derive legitimacy from elsewhere. For the Moghuls the road towards becoming puppets started when British agents were entrusted with tax farming. Tax farming was, of course, not the only factor behind the rise of the British as a colonial power in India. They also had a navy and they made profits in trade, and so on. It is not my ambition to write a history of India. My modest aim here is to find some points of comparison between empires, and, indeed, we will return to tax farming in comments on the Ottoman Empire. Tax farming is merely one form of administration and revenue collection used by empires. It is a distanced, low cost, and low return form of rule. It is often the preferred option that empires take up at their fringes. It is fraught with the risk of defection, and empires use it for lack of something better.

Due, perhaps among other things, to their reliance on tax farmers of diverse ethnic origins, who did not, as agents should, identify with their principals,[9] the Moghuls did not succeed to the same extent as Chinggis Khan or Timur Leng in creating a de-ethnicized, de-tribalized elite loyal only to the ruler. Whether out of necessity or inclination, they co-opted more strangers than they could assimilate, if indeed they made efforts to do so. The result was that their rule was ended by defectors, including the British, i.e. agents of the ruler who transformed themselves into rulers in their own right and finally into rulers of rulers.

There are ways in which the British may have been different to the ideal type tax farmer I have described in the preceding paragraphs. An ideal tax farmer, like any farmer, preserves his resource. Like a farmer who takes care to restore the fertility of his land, not to overwork his mule to the point of collapse and not to let his calves starve by depriving them of too much of their dams' milk, a tax farmer (like any state or fiscal agency) would only tax the population under his sway to an extent which allows them to survive and to remain productive so that they can also be taxed next year. Taxation by the 'Company' (the BEIC) caused the Bengal famine (1769–1770) which was aggravated by speculation in rice by Company servants (Dirks 2006: 54). It caused about three million deaths (Wild 2001: 99). In normal circumstances, when the taxed population managed to survive and to produce goods, tax farming generated 'a far better return on investment than the most lucrative private trade in Bengal' (Dirks 2006: 62), but over-taxation could also have disruptive effects short of actually killing the taxpayers. In 1793, draconian measures were introduced against land owners who could not pay the full amount of the tax, which led to that '50 percent of the estates changed hands in the ensuing decades' (Dirks 2006: 152). The Company was not the only tax farmer. Private persons from Britain, including Company servants who engaged in a strange combination of representing the Company and setting other activities aside as their 'private' business,[10] gave credits to local rulers who were, like the Company, nominally under the imperial authority of the Moghul. The credits were used to finance wars which served the purpose of furthering the Company's commercial and fiscal interests. Interest rates were so high as to approximate usury, but instead of monetary repayment the creditors also accepted lavish gifts in the form of gold and diamonds and tax collection rights (Dirks 2006: 62–64). There was a positive feedback-loop between taxes and military expenses. The more oppressive taxes became, the more military power was needed to enforce their payment and the higher taxes had to become (Dirks 2006: 145f).

The British paid lip-service to Mughal sovereignty, until they formally took over, following the 'Sepoy Mutiny', the Indian Rebellion of 1857. In 1876, in her new capacity as 'Empress of India', Queen Victoria became the visible symbol of British sovereignty in India. But throughout the 'Company' period, which ended with the 'Mutiny', the identification of the British 'subjects' with their Mughal overlord was low. They were sure of their own innate superiority, out to make quick money, and to return to England to buy estates and titles. The real identity problem they had was in Britain: as upstarts who had made money by dubitable means they were despised by the old aristocracy, and they were desperate to become part of just that aristocracy (Dirks 2006). In Britain they had the same problem as in India: they were the newcomers or upstarts and lacked the legitimacy which had accrued to the old aristocracy with the passing of time, like a patina. (Although the ultimate origins of the old aristocracy might not have been nobler than the newcomers: there seems to be a law in history that the organized crime of one period is likely to turn into the aristocracy of the subsequent period.) These newcomers might buy seats in parliament[11] and marry the daughters of title-holders, but they could not quite achieve the status they aspired to as long as the methods by which they had acquired their power and fortunes remained fresh.

The concern of the British aristocracy about the dealings of the Company agents, and the rise of their social status in Britain, need to be seen against the backdrop of events next door. The French revolution and new theories about legitimacy, like the contract theory of the state, endangered their own position. Their positional identification was with the 'legitimate' Indian rulers, not with their own countrymen, the agents of the Company. It was with these rulers that they believed they shared a kind of legitimacy derived from no one lesser than God (Dirks 2006: 2000). The eighteenth-century views of the British aristocracy about legitimate rule in England and in India can be summarized in the following Figure 9.1.

Following on the discussion of sameness or difference in linguistic and ethnic terms, and examining the role of the British in what was nominally still the Moghul empire in the eighteenth century, comprising aristocratic and other class identifications, we now return to the sixteenth century to address another axis of identification: religion. Descriptions of inter-faith dialogue, as it is called, using the latest jargon, or of debates among representatives of different religions at the court of Akbar, give the impression of a tolerant or even pluralist religious attitude. Was this an early form of secularism? If so, was it the kind of secularism that we know from the French revolution, which was

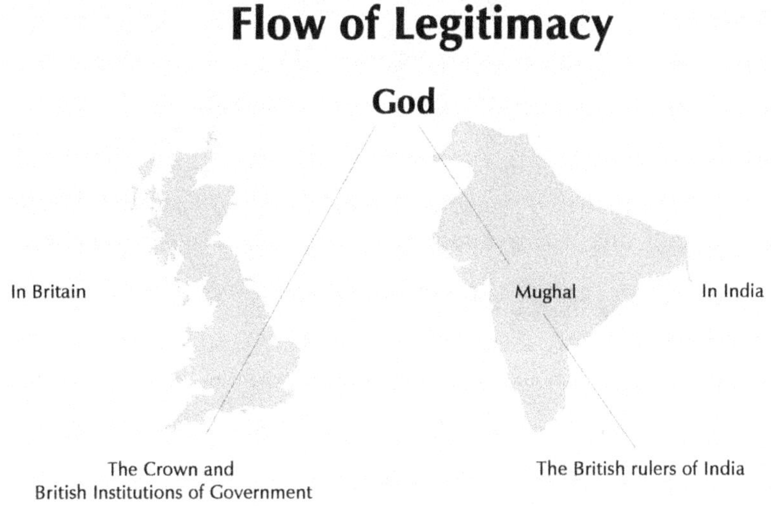

Flow of Legitimacy

God

In Britain   Mughal   In India

The Crown and   The British rulers of India
British Institutions of Government

Figure 9.1 A conservative view of the late eighteenth century about the legitimacy of power in England and India based on Dirks (2006: 200–207, simplified) (©Max Planck Institute for Social Anthropology, Halle (Saale)). This picture represents an ideological view, not meant to represent the realities of colonial domination. It is a conservative view because it comprises a figure of thought which automatically privileges the older order and protects it against change. The central idea is that God has a hand in history and therefore what has come down to us through history is sanctified by God.

anti-religious? Or was it the American type of secularism, which is an arrangement among deeply religious people who want to keep their mutually exclusive beliefs out of the sphere of politics and administration? Can it be compared to modern religious markets, where people help themselves according to personal tastes and preferences? Were the Moghuls multiculturalists and religious pluralists?

A closer look reveals that all of these questions have to be answered in the negative: none of the above. Akbar consulted the wise men of all religions in order to find the truth, the one truth. He perceived himself as the founder of *Din-ul-Lah*, the Religion of God. He wanted to overcome the division of mankind into religious communities by combining the elements of truth, which he believed every religion contains, into a unified religion.

Akbar was thus not a pluralist in the modern sense, but a 'wise ruler' similar to Alfonso the Wise of Castile. Alfonso was open to outside influences and was fascinated by things which were difficult to attain: hidden or secret knowledge and knowledge from far away that needed translation. But I think that it is safe to assume that he was looking for the one truth beneath the surface of things, and that he was not a relativist in the modern sense, believing in as many truths as there are perspectives. Foreign knowledge about topics that we, today, would call political science or natural science certainly did not shake his Christian beliefs, although stereotypes about the supposedly Jewish nature of the quest for worldly knowledge began to arise in his day – which might have left him open to attack by his adversaries (Nirenberg 2012).

To some extent, Akbar also reminds us of Chinggis Khan or Kublai Khan, who, as we have seen above, were looking for elements of the truth or something of magical or prognostic value in all religious and belief systems within their orbit. But unlike these (and unlike Alfonso), Akbar had the ambition to combine elements of heterogeneous origin into a unified religion of his own making.

In this he did not differ much from the Sikhs. Sikhism was another attempt to overcome the divide between Hinduism and Islam. Much like Martin Luther, who wanted to reform the church rather than found a new one, the founder of Sikhism, Guru Nanak (1469–1539), never intended to found a new religion. There were already too many religions, he believed, and his solution was to try to negate the difference between Hinduism and Islam: there is no Hindu, and there is no Muslim (Uberoi 1996: 61). His message was 'a common language', and his aim was to arrive at the truth, which is the unity of God, for Hindus and Muslims alike (ibid.: 62). This agenda does not sound very different from that of Akbar, 'the supposedly liberal emperor' (ibid.: 76), who, by his persecution of Sikhs, confirms that similarity breeds competition, in this case violent suppression, and that peaceful integration is sometimes more easily achieved by means of difference.

In 1715, a British mission from Calcutta to Delhi witnessed mass executions of Sikhs. The Sikhs reacted to persecution with fervour, passion and the quest for martyrdom. They

> vied with one another for precedence in death. . . . While the executions were in progress, the mother of one of the prisoners, a young man just arrived at manhood . . . pleaded the cause of her son before the [Moghul] Emperor. [The latter] pitied the woman and [issued] orders to release the youth. She arrived with the order of release just as the executioner was standing with his bloody sword upheld over the young man's head. When she showed the imperial order the youth broke out into complaints, saying, 'My mother speaketh falsely: I with heart and soul join my fellow-believers in devotion to the Guru: send me quickly after my companions.' Needless to say his request was cheerfully granted. (Uberoi 1996: 97f. citing Macauliffe 1909)

The Moghuls may have shown a kind of interest in religious ideas from far and wide, from Gnosticism to Buddhism, but when it came to a rival unifying religious project, which was thriving in their own domain, they displayed no leniency.

Synthetic religions always fail. Akbar's compromise religion, *Din-ul-Lah*, is long forgotten. Sikhism is still around and has millions of followers, but it failed as a synthesis of Hinduism and Islam. Rather than unifying the two, it became a third religion.

What was the role of the British in this system of religious plurality? How did they fit as Christians into this environment and how did they change it? In the early phase they had to accept difference. There is no way in which they could impose a religion or a way of life on their Indian environment. In demographic terms, they were a microscopic minority and they had to earn the acceptance and the respect of local people, most important among them local rulers. In circumstances in which the difference needed to be reduced, it was by them adapting to Indian custom, not the other way round. There was much intermarriage. It only became customary for British personnel to bring their wives along much later, and then only for the higher ranks. Some of the issues of mixed marriages became important figures in the early history of British colonialism in India.

It was only later, in the course of the first half of the nineteenth century, that missionaries came in increasing numbers. The general attitude of the British in India then shifted from finding local arrangements in order to make money (or from accepting the legitimacy of Indian forms of rule and Indian customs and beliefs as also sanctified by God) to missionary zeal on the side of the Church-minded and the belief of most British in the superiority of British ways and their potential benefits for the rest of the world.

The result was racial segregation with no place for mixed people, the breakdown of the system of indirect rule based on ethnic and religious differences in combination with mutual acceptance, the violent breakdown of a plural society in the bloodshed of the Mutiny, and direct colonial rule with Queen Victoria as the Empress of India.

The Ottoman Empire and Colonial Sudan

Another multi-ethnic empire with a Muslim ruling elite was the Ottoman Empire with its *millet* system. Arguably, comparative research on the *convivencia* – the period of Muslim rule in Spain and the topic of the conference where the first version of this chapter was presented – should include the Ottoman Empire as the closest parallel outside Spain. Besides displaying many parallels with the *convivencia*, the Ottoman Empire also represents a continuation of *convivencia* in the history of some population groups: Spanish Jews ended up as Ottoman subjects in Turkey, and Spanish Muslims became Ottoman subjects in North Africa.

My personal experience of the post-Ottoman world is limited to the Sudan, which is somewhat marginal in Ottoman history. As a remote province of Egypt, the Sudan was the periphery of a periphery. Rather than being under the direct control of Istanbul, the imperial capital, Egypt was a power centre in its own right. As a part of the Empire, it seemed, at times, to be a satellite on a distant circuit. At other times, however, Istanbul and Egypt came all too close to each other and clashed on hostile terms. We will return to Egypt and the Sudan after starting our account at the centre.

Historical scholarship about the Ottoman Empire focuses on the core land, the Balkans and Anatolia, and to some extent the Levante and Iraq come in. Religious and ethnic plurality was built into the Ottoman Empire from the start. The core of the Ottoman Empire coincided precisely with the core of the Byzantine Empire, a Christian empire, the eastern Rome, which had managed to survive its western counterpart by a thousand years.[12] Before and after the conquest of Constantinople, alliances, employment and trade had spanned the Muslim/Christian divide. Once established in the imperial capital, the Ottomans perceived themselves as heirs to an empire, '*Rum*', in a way reminiscent of the Franks in the west. Barkey writes about this early phase as follows: 'Under conditions of rapid expansion and lack of adequate manpower, the state that was constructed was necessarily a hybrid one in which Christians were as necessary and welcome as Muslims' (Barkey 2008: 32). There was no room for rigid or intolerant versions of Islam.[13] Despite occasional outbreaks of communal violence and the relatively rare application of state violence, long-term processes of negotiation and accommodation among religious communities seem to have resulted in a division of labour, which, though not free of hierarchical elements (political rule and military power were in Muslim hands), opened alternative routes of advancement to Christians and Jews. As payers of special taxes, Christians and Jews were given the opportunity to become economically successful. To keep or to make them poor would have been detrimental for state revenue.

Barkey's book, on which my discussion of the Ottoman Empire is largely based, bears the title *Empire of Difference: The Ottomans in Comparative Perspective*. She compares the Ottoman Empire not only to its predecessors, Rome and Byzantium, but also and especially to the contemporaneous empires of the Habsburgs and the Romanovs. Each had to find arrangements for ethnically and religiously heterogeneous populations, and each had its special way of going about it. Barkey hardly mentions Spain, but there is an implicit comparison with medieval Spain in her characterization of interreligious relationships in the Ottoman Empire as 'convivencia' (Barkey 2008: 280).

Barkey's procedure, one might note, differs from that of Foltz, to whom I referred in the preceding section about the Moghuls. By describing the continuity of the Ottoman Empire with the Roman Empire, including *Rum*, i.e. Byzantium, she does what historians mostly do: she stays in a region and describes a succession of regimes. And, in comparing the Ottomans with the Habsburgs and the Romanovs, she leaves the region but stays in the same period.[14] In contrast, the preceding section on the Moghuls restricts itself neither to a fixed regional framework nor to a fixed historical period. Instead, it traces the ancestry of a regime across a continent, having comparatively little to say about India before and after the Moghuls or about contemporaneous empires elsewhere. Both accounts, however, resemble each other in discussing the relevant models of the regimes in question: Rome and Byzantium served as models for the Ottomans, just as Chinggis Khan and Timur Leng did for the Moghuls.

As we have discussed tax farming in the Moghul Empire, it might be of comparative interest to see how taxes were collected in the Ottoman Empire. Here, direct taxation by the state administration and tax farming co-existed as parallel systems. Both had advantages. Only in the case of direct taxation could the state fine-tune taxes to changes in the productivity of an area, thus reaping the benefits of good development policy. However, the substantial down payments that were obtained, mostly in addition to annual fees, when tax farms were allocated, were quite attractive when the state was short of money, which it often was, due to wars being fought on its frontiers. Before the eighteenth century, tax farming contracts were often short-term, being allocated to the highest bidder, and thus subject to a relatively flexible and responsive market mechanism. During the nineteenth century, however, long-term allocations, often for life, became more and more common (Barkey 2008: 230). Contracts were mostly extended to members of a privileged group of high-level officers and patrons in Istanbul, and the stability of these contracts furthered the development of independent and competitive pasha and vizier households (ibid.: 233). By privileging this particular military class, however, the state solidified its links to it (ibid.: 236), thus counteracting, to some extent, the centrifugal tendency inherent in tax farming.

There are more comparative points to be made about the relative advantages of direct taxation by the state bureaucracy over tax farming. Taxes can only be used for politics – for example, by lowering them or by using them to fund popular projects – if they are under direct control of the political leadership. In Basra, the Ottomans relieved local populations of the heavy tax burden imposed by the Safavids 'to demonstrate the benefits of association with the Ottoman Empire' (ibid.: 92). In the Hijaz, the Ottomans spent funds gathered through taxation in maintaining and provisioning the Holy cities. One possible explanation for the swift expansion of Islamic rule over Christian populations in the eighth and ninth centuries is that Islamic rulers imposed lower taxes than their Christian predecessors had. Historiography, however, tends to focus on battles rather than on softer technologies of power.

High-ranking Sunni Muslims, that is, members of this state class, were not the only ones involved in the tax farming business. Greek, Armenian and Jewish bankers often helped to finance the purchase of tax farms and, as creditors of the tax farmers, had an interest in them. Some tax farms were subdivided into many small shares or were split into parts held by subcontractors (ibid.: 234). All this limits the potential of tax farmers to become lords in their own right by defection from the central government, although rich families often combined tax farming with substantial land holdings of their own and other sources of wealth and power.

Although a secure legal status was granted to Christians, albeit as citizens with limited rights, many Christians still chose to join the mainstream of imperial society by converting to Islam. On the eastern side of Anatolia's Black Sea shore, the district of Of provides an example of the extent to which this happened. This district was famous for its many religious specialists and its level of sophistication in Islamic law. Centres of Islamic learning 'were especially concentrated in the upper western valley, where Greek was more commonly spoken than Turkish. Sermons were delivered in Turkish, but also commonly in Greek (in each instance with Koranic citations in Arabic). Koranic texts were discussed in Turkish, but also commonly in Greek' (Meeker 2002: 165). The *khutba* in Greek! *Tafsir* in Greek! Greek as a language of Islamic learning? Why not! This resonates well with Bellér-Hann's (2008: 20) finding, with reference to the wider 'Turkic speaking world', 'that language is not necessarily the most important criterion of identity'.[15] For his northeast Anatolian research area, Meeker describes how an imperial nation developed out of diverse ethnic origins in Ottoman times and persisted into the modern Turkish nation-state, with certain Ottoman, rather than Kemalist, features:

> Today, in the eastern Black Sea provinces of Turkey, from Artvin to
> Ordu, the traces of ethnicity, Lazi, Armenian, Greek, and Turkic, are

easy to discover in language, stories, customs, and dress. And yet, in contrast to all these differences, the inhabitants of the rural societies still lack a strong interest in their parochial backgrounds and traditions. With the exception of a few recent authors and books, there is no developed culture of ethnicity in the eastern coastal region. Instead, social manners and relations are more or less homogenous at a certain level, a direct reflection of a local engagement in wider market and state systems, now national as once before imperial. (Meeker 2002: 108 f.)

Meeker focuses on Agha families, i.e. on the families of local dignitaries, which look as if they might be descended from earlier tribal chiefs who were co-opted into the imperial elite. But the actual history is much more complex. At least some of the founders of these distinct patrilines were, initially, officials appointed by the imperial state, without a local power base. Once in place, they forged commercial partnerships and political alliances that gave them a base of power beyond their period of appointment. In this way, they managed to secure a privileged position for their descendants. What might thus at first glance appear to be ruling lines of local tribes are actually somewhat tribalized elements of bureaucracy – a reminder that what appears to be tribal is not always older than the trappings of the modern state (ibid.: 202 ff.).[16]

This part of Anatolia, which was not located at the real periphery of the Ottoman Empire but belonged to the outer layer of its core, displayed features typical of imperial society but was not always under the full control of the Sublime Porte. Under these conditions, local bases of power could arise, as the activities of an Agha from this region indicate:

He was somehow involved in the manufacturing and shipping of flax and linen . . . He advanced villagers cash for their future produce so that they might be able to make tax payments. He collected funds to be forwarded as tax receipts to the provincial governor, taking some varying share for himself in proportion to his own position of strength. He was then, all at once, a social oligarch, an entrepreneur, a moneylender, a tax collector, and, eventually, a provincial state official. (Meeker 2002: 214)

In its core lands, the Ottoman Empire exercised mostly direct forms of rule; but, as Meeker's findings in eastern Anatolia show, the central state increasingly had to find accommodations with local powers as we move to the outer layers of the core and towards the periphery. The further we move in that direction, the more indirect the forms of rule become, as can be illustrated with reference to the literature on Syria.

Lewis characterizes Ottoman rule in Syria in the early nineteenth century as ineffective. 'Ottoman forces were weak and hardly contributed to the safety of the countryside' (Lewis 2000: 33). Power was bipolar. In the towns, there were garrisons and administrations and taxes were collected as far as their power extended. The desert and steppe rangelands were the domain of Bedouin tribes, which raided trading caravans, each other, and the peasant villages around the towns. Weaker tribes could buy 'brotherliness' (*khuwwa*) from stronger tribes. That was the way out of the raiding economy. When the power of the town expanded, people from a wider area had to pay taxes. When the power of the Bedouin expanded, peasants, villagers and townspeople also had to pay *khuwwa*: a constantly shifting boundary between two modes of extraction (Toth 2006: 49–50).

The Bedouin resisted taxation and conscription, but did not mind fulfilling military tasks under the command of their own leaders. The government paid Bedouin for the protection of the *hajj* caravan and for other tasks. Whether this was payment for a service or a tribute to a force that was perceived as a threat is a question which can only be answered on a case by case basis, taking into account the power differentials at a given moment. Often, town (=state) power could only be extended to the countryside with Bedouin help, by deals which required 'mutual recognition' of the sedentary and the nomad power.

> Tribal shaykhs would agree to such concessions as the payment of taxes, supplying fighters or camels, and agreeing to maintain security in the *bādiya*, usually against other tribes. At the same time, local authorities would present the shaykhs with semi-official titles, and acknowledge their position with payments of cash and gifts of honor such as robes, weapons and horses. (Toth 2006: 57)

Although the population increased, agriculture expanded, the sedentary sector of society grew, and statehood became stronger throughout the nineteenth century, Bedouin counterpower remained a factor to reckon with. When the French took over from the Ottomans, they first treated the Bedouins as 'a state within the state'. Later it took massive incentives in the form of private land titles, seats in Parliament, educational grants and straight cash payments to make the Bedouin sheikhs give up some of their powers (Chatty 2006: 739–40).

The history of neighbouring Iraq has been summarized by Hechter (2013: 65–74) in his comparative analysis of *Alien Rule*. Throughout much of Ottoman history, the actual penetration of the government power in what is now Iraq was weak and the form of rule indirect. City dwelling Arabs and Bedouin Arabs lived in two different worlds, and, as in Syria, the Bedouins could be ruled, if at all, only through their own sheikhs. In the towns and cities, the local rulers were Mameluks whose adherence to the Ottoman Sultan was largely symbolic. This changed in the middle of the nineteenth century, when, emulating the European nation-state model, the Ottomans deposed the Mameluk leaders at Baghdad,

Mosul and Basra and tried to establish a more direct form of rule in the region. Among the local Arabs they favoured those who were Sunni Muslims like themselves, and Hechter traces some of the hostility which marks inter-community relations in today's Iraq back to this period. Ottoman rule worked well as long as it was remote and indirect. The more it approached the nation-state model, emphasizing sameness by favouring co-religionists ('Turkification'), as the nineteenth century advanced, the more it lost acceptance. Indirect rule came with relaxed and long-term tax-farming arrangements, and as the grip was tightened and more direct forms of government attempted, terms became shorter and control closer (Ceylan 2011: 15). There are, however, no neat geographical divisions among the areas where different forms of taxation prevailed. In some areas close to the core of the empire, pre-Ottoman structures were maintained. 'Overall, in the southern Balkans and the Aegean islands of the Greek archipelago, the imperial government relied on the Byzantine and local Christians to perform administrative tasks' (Barkey 2008: 89). 'It is not surprising, therefore, that the tax system of Ottoman Anatolia and the Balkans was complex and mixed, and that scholars found elements of Islamic, Mongol, Byzantine, Armenian and Slavic tax systems in the record' (Barkey 2008: 89). Leaders of local communities, rather than the Ottoman bureaucracy or tax farmers, were given government tasks and if they were 'embroiled in violence and could not maintain calm in communities and across communities, or . . . were unable to garner enough authority to collect taxes, [they] lost their livelihoods and, more often their heads' (ibid.: 147).

My own research in the former Southern fringe of the Ottoman Empire is largely restricted to present-day society but must, necessarily, be situated in a historical context to which I now turn. Much of what is now the Sudan was conquered in 1820/1821 by the viceroy of Egypt, Muhammad Ali, and stayed under Egyptian rule until the Mahdist period (1881–1898).

In 1841, the Sublime Porte recognized Muhammad Ali as personal ruler for life of Nubia, Darfur, Kordofan and Sennar – that is roughly the territory that was to become the Sudan. Thus, the ruler of Egypt, an Ottoman dependency, was, in another function, an independent ruler of territories outside the Ottoman Empire. This, however, did not preclude the payment of tribute by the Sudan to Egypt (Gray 1961: 3). In other words, as a sovereign ruler of the Sudan, Muhammad Ali paid tribute to himself in his other capacity as an appointed (but periodically rather unruly) ruler of Egypt, that is as an Ottoman functionary.[17] The Mahdist period ended when the Sudan was occupied, nominally, by Egypt but, actually, by a largely British force. The Sudan then was an Anglo-Egyptian 'condominium' (1898–1956), in which Egypt was clearly the junior partner. Both periods, the Egyptian rule before the Mahdiyya and the Anglo-Egyptian rule after it, are known as the 'Turkish' periods – *turkiyya as-saabiqa*, 'the Turkish rule preceding [the Mahdiyya]', and *turkiyya at-taaliya*, 'the Turkish rule following [the Mahdiyya]'. In the earlier period, this term was justified by the nominal affiliation Egypt still had to the Ottoman Empire; and, at that time, much of the military personnel actually came from Albania, Bosnia or the Caucasus. In the twentieth century, however, 'Turk' had just become the habitual term for light-skinned foreigners who had come to rule. It is, to my knowledge, the only setting in which Englishmen were popularly known as 'Turks'.

Nineteenth-century Egypt was a modernizing regional power, originally with imperial designs of its own; but it later became highly indebted, internationally, and ended up as a British semi-colony. From the beginning, European officers in Egyptian service were key figures in the exercise. In 1820, the first expedition force led by Ismail Pasha, the son of Muhammad Ali, was accompanied by at least three European archaeologists and a renegade American who later joined the conquering army as an officer (Holt and Daly 2000: 43). They were surprised to find other whites: Bosnians who manned Mameluk garrisons, which had been established earlier in the Sudan. Among the first governors appointed after the conquest were a Circassian (ibid.: 51) and a Kurd (ibid.: 53). *Muʿallim* ('teacher') was the title given to Coptic Christian and Jewish administrative officials who took up their posts in the pacified areas (ibid.: 47). The ethnic core of the Mameluks was to a large degree Qipchak, the same Turkic people we mentioned above in connection with Tamerlane. Like the English, they are another ethnic element which plays a role in the imperial histories of both Asia and Africa.

There were some English among the officers who served the Ottoman/Egyptian regime in the Sudan, the best known among them being General Charles Gordon, 'Gordon Pasha', who died a soldier's death when Khartoum fell to the Mahdists in 1885. Other officers of European origin included Rudolf Slatin (still locally known as *Salatiin Baasha*, i.e. Pasha), an Austrian, and the Italian Romolo Gessi, to name just a few. Some of these international careers of the nineteenth century are not unlike those of modern development experts in their wide geographical range and the number of different appointments. The difference is that many of these nineteenth-century figures, from a European perspective, were discoverers and first explorers of the unknown parts of the globe. They wrote thick travelogues and autobiographies to meet the demands of an avid readership. To illustrate this type of career, I turn to Eduard Schnitzer, a.k.a. Emin Pasha. He was born in Oppeln, Silesia, in 1840 to a Jewish family. After the death of his father in 1845, his mother remarried and her children were baptized and raised as Protestants. After medical training, Schnitzer first entered Ottoman service in Albania. He turned up in Khartoum in 1876, practising as a medical doctor. By then, he had converted to Islam, at least nominally, and begun to use the name Mehmet Emin or, in Arabic, Muhammad Amin. Gordon made him a medical officer in the southern province of Equatoria, and later the Khedive of Egypt appointed him governor of that province.

Among the many European officers working during the first *turkiyya* period in the Sudan, Emin Pasha, a German, was probably one of the most Ottoman personalities. After all, he spoke Turkish, Albanian and a number of Slavic languages that he had acquired earlier in his career in the European part of the empire. That he also spoke Arabic goes without saying. Apparently, he picked up languages in no time. Gordon appreciated him for his fluency in Luganda,[18] which was useful in the part of Equatoria that extended into what is now Uganda. Emin Pasha also differed from other European officers in having converted to Islam, which was by no means a prerequisite for entering Ottoman service. He possibly did so for his civilian career as a doctor. Marriage is another possible explanation.[19]

Medical doctors of that period included some notorious characters. One French doctor made a flourishing business of castrating slave boys to be sold as eunuchs in Egypt. His surgical skills were worth the fee, because he significantly reduced the mortality this valuable merchandise suffered when undergoing the adjustment to market needs.[20]

The Ottoman Empire, like Tsarist Russia, offered abundant employment opportunities for Western experts. There are, however, a number of reasons why the Sudan, from a British perspective, could not just be regarded as the colony of another country (Egypt, or in terms of wider allegiance, Ottoman Turkey). Britain too had an agenda in the region, and British officers in Egyptian/Ottoman service certainly needed to combine two loyalties.

For the British, Egypt became increasingly important as a provider of cotton as a consequence of the embargo imposed by the Confederate States during the American Civil War (1861–1865). What is more, the newly opened Suez Canal (1869) was of great strategic importance for British India. And in imperialist dreams, many Britons saw everything on the map, 'From Cape to Cairo', coloured in British red. For these and other reasons, the Sudan, though nominally Ottoman, was regarded by the British as part of their sphere of interest.

In a way, the British position in nineteenth-century Sudan can be compared to their position in seventeenth-century Bengal. In Bengal, as Parsons (2010: 171) has pointed out, the British were the 'vassals' of Murshid Quli Khan, who, though officially a retainer of the Great Moghul in Dehli, was de facto an independent ruler. In a similar way, the British in the Sudan were somewhat indirect vassals of the Sublime Porte. They were in the service of the ruler of Egypt, who pledged allegiance to the Ottoman Empire, at least nominally. Thus, although the British became a colonial power in their own right, they must also be viewed, within the very same period, as one of the many ethnic groups that was ruled by the empires of others. After their decline as a colonial power in the Americas, the British were still on the rise as a colonial power in other parts of the world, where, initially, they had sometimes acted as agents of other empires.

The loss of the Sudan to the Mahdi, beginning in 1881 and culminating in the fall of Khartoum in 1885, was a serious setback and left an open wound in the British national soul. It was perceived as a humiliation, which was not avenged until fourteen years later, in 1898, when a combined British and Egyptian force advanced into the Sudan. The decisive battle was at Omdurman, which readers may know from the famous account in Winston Churchill's (1947) *My Early Life*.[21] The conquest initiated a period known as the Anglo-Egyptian Sudan or the condominium (1898–1956).

The legal justification for the conquest was the reinstallation of legitimate pre-Mahdiyya rule. So, at least nominally, the British acted in the name of Egypt, which, in turn, was still nominally affiliated to the Ottoman Empire.[22] This, however, is a rather theoretical consideration. In practice, this remote affiliation did not instil any sense of loyalty in British officers. By the time the Ottoman empire joined the Central Powers, Germany and Austria, in World War I, and Britain reacted by claiming Egypt and the Sudan for herself, a long relationship of mutual support had already cooled down. Britain and Ottoman Turkey, allies in re-taking Egypt from Napoleonic forces (1801) and allies in the Crimean war (1853), were now at war with each other after a shift of alliances. For a long time, Ottoman Turkey had received British support against stronger European empires such as Russia and Austria-Hungary as part of the British 'balance of power' politics.

Returning to the Sudan from this more global context, we now address the issue of how cultural, linguistic or religious differences were handled by two administrations, the *turkiyya* before and the *turkiyya* after the Mahdi Period. In the earlier administration, from 1821 to 1881, Kurds, Albanians, Circassians, English, Austrians and Italians all ruled the Sudan in the name of Egypt, and Egypt, at least nominally, was an Ottoman dependency. Neither '*turkiyya*' nor 'Egyptian' is an adequate name for this rule. Modern ethnic labels are misleading. Holt (1961: 37) clarifies that 'to speak of the "Egyptian conquest" is liable to call up anachronistic associations. The Arabic-speaking Egyptian nation-state with its national army did not then exist: the government of the Ottoman province of Egypt was in the hand of Turkish-speaking Ottoman subjects, a ruling *élite* linked by a complicated web of ties to the Arabic-speaking population'. The Ottoman Empire, including Egypt, in spite of all the criticism of Europeans about its backwardness, comprised an element of modernization and globalization. As in the present age, and in contrast to the more nationalist age lying between us and the modernizing empires of the nineteenth century, there was competition for the best brains from far and wide, irrespective of ethnic or religious background. The 'sick man on the Bosporus', as the critics called the Ottoman Empire, was not as sick as it/he was said to be. There was a great deal of corruption, but there were also strong forces for reform. After all, some of the Ottoman Empire's most vociferous critics were themselves on the imperial payroll. Among the governors and in the international corps of military officers and civilian administrators, there was certainly a strong element of pluralism; but this pluralism represented less a mosaic of groups than a great diversity of individual origins.

Looking at local forces, we find a different kind of pluralism. Often, local notables were simply confirmed or co-opted as rulers, and groups were incorporated with their internal structures left largely intact. Here, a few examples can be given of this form of incorporation at the group level – examples which we take from the period of the governor Khurshid.

After fighting against the Greek struggle for independence, ʿAli Khurshid Agha became governor of the Sudan in 1826 (Holt and Daly 2000: 52). He offered amnesty to those inhabitants of the Nile valley who had fought the army of conquest and taken refuge in remote areas like the hills of the Ethiopian borderlands. This helped in re-populating the villages in the fertile Nile Valley and, thus, in increasing state revenues. The Jaʿali sheikh Idris wad ʿAdlan accepted Khurshid's offer of amnesty and was even recognized by him as sheikh of the Funj Mountains. To gain the support of local notables and religious leaders, Khurshid exempted them from taxation. The ʿArakiyyin sheikh, Ahmad ar-Rayyah, was among those persuaded. He led thousands of people back to their villages along the Blue Nile. Khurshid's kind invitations were accompanied by the threat to kill all those who did not submit (ibid.: 53 f.).

In this, the holders of high office in the Ottoman Empire did not differ from conquering kings in antiquity or in medieval Europe, who often simply accepted the rulers of conquered groups as vassals. One reason for this may have been that, in such cases, to impose an alien administration would have been prohibitively costly. One may also view this system as a precursor of 'Indirect Rule', the official ideology of British rule throughout Africa, which would be applied to the Sudan in the Anglo-Egyptian period.

Whether applied in an orthodox fashion or in one of its many local applications or deviations, Indirect Rule, in the Anglo-Egyptian Sudan as elsewhere, was based on the assumption that the rulers and the ruled were substantively different groups. This certainly violates modern ideas of equality, although it resonates with other modern ideas, such as 'indigenism' and 'multiculturalism', which also allocate different rights to different groups. Indirect Rule has often been decried as a particularly perfidious trick of the colonialists, and 'colonialism' has long joined 'sin' as a member of the category of things one has to be against. All this makes it difficult to adopt an analytical attitude toward it, without exposing oneself to moral criticism. I am not going to expose myself to the wrath of all 'good' people by defending colonialism. Colonialism was not the purely humanitarian enterprise that it was portrayed to be by some colonialists. And still, one cannot deny the humanitarian motivation and the deep sense of duty on the part of many individual colonial officers. Noble motives were mixed with attitudes that appear very strange to us today, such as a clear sense of superiority and paternalistic or even racialist attitudes (Deng and Daly 1989). I will not attempt a moral evaluation of colonialism; but, whatever else one might say about British rule in the Sudan, even the sternest critic would have to admit that some aspects of it look quite clever and that, on the whole, British rule was less brutal than much of what took place before and after the British. Let us hear a Sudanese voice:

> One has to admit that the British administration was able to understand the Sudanese mentality in a very astonishing way, and that they skilfully administrated the country for more than 50 years and paralysed any organized national resistance until the end of the forties. They manipulated the influence of the local religious and political leadership and cooperated with the two groups as a counterbalanced group to control any independent domination of one group over the other or any attempt to defy the government. (Ibrahim 1979: 19)

Hayder Ibrahim sees the necessity for 'some kind of simple autonomy in which the local leaders, notables, and religious men administered the region in the name of the central government' and stresses that it had never been possible to administer this vast and heterogeneous country by other means (ibid.: 19).

Modern historians are very sceptical of Indirect Rule. They join the educated elites of the ex-colonies in describing it as a device to keep the new elites, the products of modern education, out of power. Power was based on a collusion between foreign colonialist and 'traditional' authorities. With reference to the Sudan, Daly (1991: 5) says that Indirect Rule had its heyday in the decade after 1924. It was based 'upon inexact comparisons with Northern Nigeria and on the pseudo-scientific prescriptions of Lord Lugard'.

Lord Lugard and Indirect Rule

As a colonial administrator, Lord Lugard is only a marginal figure in Sudanese history. His importance is greater in Ugandan history. As an employee of the British East Africa Company, he was very vocal in demanding the colonization of Uganda, with the result that plans to abandon that territory were revised. The Mahdists were pushed out of Wadelai, Emin Pasha's earlier headquarter on the Albert Nile, in the 1890s (Moorehead 1973 [1960]: 322). Since then, the boundary between Sudan and Uganda has shifted repeatedly.

Lord Lugard's most important impact on Sudanese history was through his writings, especially through his book *The Dual Mandate*, which presents the model of administration he later developed as a governor of Nigeria. First published in 1922, this book has appeared in many editions since then. It turned out to be the handbook of British colonialism in Africa, closely associated with the concept of Indirect Rule.

Both Direct and Indirect Rule had been tried before in India. There, some territories were administered directly,[23] while, in others, local princes were left in their positions and co-opted into the colonial administration. In northern Nigeria, the Hausa states were incorporated in accordance with the second model, that of Indirect Rule. Much of Lugard's language has a progressive ring.

> The British Empire . . . has only one mission – for liberty and self-development on no standardised lines, so that all may feel that their interests and religion are safe under the British flag. Such liberty and self-development can be best secured to the native population by leaving them free to manage their own affairs through their own rulers. . .
> (Lugard 1965 [1922]: 94)

Then, however, Lugard introduces the idea of 'advancement'. Different populations have 'advanced' on the path of development, reaching different stages, Lugard thought, in agreement with the evolutionist and modernist ideas that were unquestioned in his day. They need more guidance, or they need less, and the ultimate arbiters of such needs are the British. The passage quoted above continues as follows: 'proportionately to their degree of advancement, under the guidance of the British staff, and subject to the laws and policy of the administration' (ibid.: 94).

Appeals to 'liberty' and 'self-development' were not meant to imply that all people should mix freely; rather, developing along one's own lines required separation. One is reminded of the apartheid regime in South Africa, which, decades later, also combined a liberal language of cultural group rights, not unlike multiculturalism, with rigid racial segregation.

As a typical representative of the first half of the twentieth century, Lugard was racialist to the bone. In his view, different groups had merits, capabilities and achievements, but only as long as they remained separate. 'In matters social and racial', he argued, 'absolute equality' was possible among representatives of diverse races, if they followed 'a separate path, each pursuing his own inherited traditions, preserving his own race-purity and race-pride; equality in things spiritual, agreed divergence in the physical and material' (Lugard 1965 [1922]: 87). In other words, one should respect Africans as a different kind of beings but not socialize with them and by no means beget mixed children with them. The heading on the page that I am citing reads, 'NO RACIAL DISCRIMINATION'. I am sure that Lugard was convinced subjectively that he was not preaching or practicing racial discrimination. From a present-day perspective, we must be allowed to disagree. In Lugard and his contemporaries, however, this sort of racism was so deeply ingrained that it went unnoticed and unquestioned.

Lugard viewed Europeanized Africans – that is, the products of the schools that the colonial powers and the missionaries preceding and following them had introduced – as undesirable elements that blurred these distinctions. They were not suitable for employment, because they could not mediate between Europeans and uneducated Africans. 'The Europeanised African is indeed separated from the rest of the people by a gulf which no racial affinity can bridge' (ibid.: 81). True to his racialist perspective, Lugard regards people he dislikes, in this case educated Africans, as biologically inferior.

> The Europeanised African differs not merely in mental outlook from the other groups, but also in physique. Doctors and dentists tell us that he has become less fertile, more susceptible to lung-trouble and to other diseases, and to defective dentition – disabilities which have probably arisen from in-breeding among a very limited class, and to the adoption of European dress, which writers in the native press say is enervating and inimical to the health of the African. (Lugard 1965 [1922]: 80)

As Lugard was writing about the first generation of educated Africans, it is hard to imagine how they could have fallen victim to 'in-breeding'. These racializing ramblings must have stretched the logic even of the readers in the 1920s, when *The Dual Mandate* was first published, to the extreme, although they were used to much higher doses of racism than we are now. Also, in later decades, educated Africans probably intermarried with a wider range of people, ethnically and geographically, than uneducated ones – an observation that reduces Lugard's argument to pure fantasy.

While Africans who had been exposed to European curricula were not favoured by Lugard and his policies, traditional Muslim rulers clearly were. The resulting advancement of Islam was not due to Lugard's sympathies for this religion or for any other religion, for that matter. Rather, he viewed Islam as a necessary evil, and his tolerance of it was a by-product of Indirect Rule: 'Both the Arabs in the east and the Fulani in the west are Mohamedans, and by supporting their rule we unavoidably encourage the spread of Islam, which from the purely administrative point of view has the disadvantage of being subject to waves of fanaticism, bounded by no political frontiers' (ibid.: 210). Still, aspects of Islam were found to be useful. These included 'well understood powers of Wakils', 'educational advantages' and the Muslims' 'advanced method of disposing justice' (Lugard 1965 [1922]: 204).

Missionary interference with Islam was therefore undesirable. Generally, Lugard described missionaries, their schools, the expectations they raised, the image of Europeans they conveyed and their zeal and divisive preaching quite negatively. Indirect Rule was based on group differences, not on conversion and assimilation.

This anti-assimilationist element of Indirect Rule can be seen as a kind of allergy that British agents of Church and State had developed against their own product. Indirect Rule was established after long periods of conversion and assimilation, during which Europeanized Africans had often been highly regarded and employed as allies of their colonial masters – or, in cases where this development preceded the establishment of formal rule, their future colonial masters. Later, these Europeanized, 'trousered' Africans were rejected, largely because they were perceived as being (dangerously) close to their European masters (a case of sameness rather than difference leading to conflict). They were often ridiculed as fake Europeans, both in Europe and 'back home'. Gradually, then, in securing African allies, the British replaced Europeanized Africans with traditional rulers.[24]

Accommodating traditional authorities and local practices of law and respecting local customs was not just a British reaction against 'Europeanized' Africans. It was a necessity from the beginning. Europeans were spread thin on the ground. In Kenya they were often assisted by Goan clerks, in the Sudan by Egyptians. But, even with these allies, Europeans were never strong enough to rule alone, without regard for the ideas of rule and the social forms created by their subjects. So, Indirect Rule was not just a manipulative instrument imposed from the top down. It was a way to accommodate real power, local power, which had been there before, no matter how much it changed in the process of integration into new forms of statehood.

If one half of power stems from the rulers (their superior military technology and their effective administration), the other half stems from the ruled. They have to accept their rulers at some point, and the rulers have to seek their acceptance, because continuous violent oppression is too expensive in the long run (Spear 2003). The need to accommodate existing powers sometimes made unlikely bedfellows. Christian rulers (who, by the twentieth century, may often have been enlightened, secularized and modernist, i.e. 'soft' Christians anyhow) often felt closer to their Muslim partners in the arrangements of Indirect Rule than to Christian missionaries.

In thinking about the attitudes of European powers toward Islam, one should bear in mind that there is a radical difference between our vantage point at the beginning of the twenty-first century and the time we are dealing with in the preceding paragraphs, the early twentieth century. While European countries are now bending over backwards to please the Americans in their 'war on terror' and in fighting the 'Islamist threat',[25] a century ago, Britain and Germany were competing with each other for the hearts of Muslims. Germany was in alliance with the Ottoman sultan, the *khaliifa*, the successor of the Prophet; and the British Empire depended on the consent of the many Muslim peoples it accommodated. It is therefore no surprise that Lord Lugard perceived World War I as the crucial test of Indirect Rule by means of Muslim notables.

> The war, however, put the system to a crucial test. It was well known that Britain was fighting against Turkey, a Muslim State with whom the Senussi, whose emissaries from Tripoli find easy access to Nigeria, was in active alliance. A great rising took place in the vast regions under

French rule bordering Nigeria to the north. Reports, fully credited by the French themselves, reached the country that Agades – the desert capital—had fallen before a Muslim army well equipped with cannon. Hostile forces were said to be rapidly advancing towards Sokoto. The French asked our assistance. Half of our own forces, and most of the officers known to the natives, had already gone to East Africa [to fight the Germans]. But not for a moment there was the slightest doubt of the loyalty of the Emirs. The garrison of Kano itself was withdrawn, and replaced by police. Sokoto and Katsena, the border States, were eager to raise native levies to assist.

Each year of the war the native treasuries offered £50,000 towards its cost. The last year they submitted £11,000 to the Red Cross Fund – the Sultan of Sokoto preferring that he and his chiefs should subscribe from their private means for such a purpose rather than from the public treasury. Daily prayers in all the mosques were offered for the victory of the King's arms. (Lugard 1965 [1922]: 222 f.)

Conclusions

The presentation of material for comparison has to stop at some point. A description of examples spanning around a quarter of the globe soon runs out of time or out of space. It would have been interesting to observe how the pluriethnic and plurireligious Ottoman Empire ultimately dissolved, under the influence of the Wilsonian model, into independent nation-states – and how, in the Balkans, this had been prefigured by the formation of national churches (Hoffmann 2008, 2009).

Although our account of Sudanese history has ended abruptly, Indirect Rule has not. It has endured under the name of Native Administration until now. It has been abolished, reintroduced and reformulated several times since the independence of the Sudan in 1956.

Returning to the themes of sameness and difference as alternative modes of integration, an idea sketched at the beginning of this chapter, we may now make a basic distinction in light of our comparative findings. This distinction is between the rulers and the ruled. Among the rulers, sameness is the fundamental mode of integration, but between rulers and the ruled, and among different groups of the ruled, difference is the basis of integration. This may become clearer if we review, briefly, the cases discussed above.

Founders of empires have to transcend tribe and ethnicity to forge a loyal following and a new imperial class. The group that came to be known as the Mongols when they set out to rule the world was in fact already an amalgamation of Turkic, Mongol and Evenki speakers. Advancement was by loyalty to the ruler and by merit in the sense of usefulness to the ruler, not by virtue of representing a group. Group differences had been erased.

The ruled, however, were left alone as long as they paid tribute. Those who had escaped annihilation could keep their languages and religions. The Mongol rulers even had a friendly interest, as consumers so to speak, in the cultures and religions of their subjects. From their perspective, religious specialists of various origins might be useful for divination and magic, important techniques for the maintenance of power. The cultures of the subject people were a source of refinement for the Mongol life style.

A similar pattern of de-tribalization and de-ethnicization has been found twice again in our historical overview. Timur Leng forged a personal following out of individuals rather than tribes, thus laying the foundations of the military successes of many of his descendants, including the Moghuls in India. The Ottomans, in turn, assimilated Greeks, Serbs, Lazis and others into the ruling stratum, the imperial class, where loyalties to one's benefactors within that class and networks with other members outweighed memories of diverse ethnic origins. So, in the military class and the ruling elite, we find amalgamation or assimilation as the dominant means of integration. The result of these processes is sameness.

The mode of integration of subject peoples, however – whether they were highly valued, productive and skilled subjects who needed to be pampered, abject people in serf-like positions, or the inhabitants of slave reservoirs – was based on difference. They were kept out of core military and government functions, even if some became important figures in bureaucracy, trade or commerce.

Perhaps it was the relative lack of conformity with these basic structures of empire that brought down Moghul rule in India. The Moghuls might not have paid sufficient attention to the assimilation of strangers into the ruling Turko-Persian-Mongol stratum or their exclusion from it altogether. They may have given too much power to unassimilated strangers such as Brahmins and the British, who then dismantled the empire.

Amalgamating the ruling stratum into a culturally homogenous nation of empire, to borrow Meeker's phrase, is an ideal that is achieved to a lesser and lesser degree as we move from the centre to the periphery of empires. Here, often, Indirect Rule *avant la parole* had to be practiced, and here, often, arrangements were made with local elites who were left in place, acting nominally in the name of the centre, but remaining relatively free in practice.

Forms of taxation differed along the same line. Direct taxation was practiced in the core lands of the Ottoman Empire, as far as the arm of the bureaucracy reached. Beyond that there was the belt of tax farming. We have discussed that in the Moghul and the Ottoman cases. Throughout British colonial Africa as well, government-appointed chiefs were tax collectors, who were required to deliver a specific amount but had a lot of discretion in how they collected taxes and what they kept for themselves.

Empires have pedigrees. The Ottoman Empire saw itself as a successor to the Byzantine Empire and, thereby, to Rome. Further west, the Franks understood themselves as Rome's heirs, as did the 'Holy Roman Empire of the German Nation', until Napoleon dissolved it in 1806. The phrase, 'pax Britannica',[26] which was modelled on the Roman 'pax Imperica', indicates that the British thought of themselves as Romans of sorts. In a similar way, we could trace traditions of empire and dynastic links from the Moghuls in India back to Tamerlane and Chinggis Khan.[27]

To what extent do these chains of tradition and the concomitant derivation of prestige involve actual transfers of knowledge, law, techniques of rule, or forms of organization? This question is reminiscent of the old and unresolved debate in anthropology between diffusionists, who always find an earlier model and a connection to it, and those who believe in human inventiveness, assuming that the same devices and procedures have been invented again and again in the course of history. Some transfers among historical empires are, of course, common knowledge. Our law students still learn about Roman Law, which is mirrored in the Islamic world by bodies of law not derived from the *sharīʿa*, including, for example, *qanuun* (canon law) and *baqt* (pactum), the treaty of the Muslims with the Christian kingdoms of Nubia (until the sixteenth century). So, there is also a 'Roman' tradition of law in the Islamic world, and in the Ottoman sphere in particular. I must admit, however, that my reading of the secondary literature does not reveal much beyond these obvious links. It is here that I, as an anthropologist of contemporary northeast Africa venturing far into the fields of others, come up against my limits. No doubt, there is much evidence to be found, by people better qualified than I, of the transmission of the arts of statecraft among historically related empires.

Before closing, I return briefly to the finding that differences can be a mode of integration. This does not necessarily mean that rulers prefer difference to sameness. The early rulers of the Ottoman Empire might have preferred a purely Muslim population; but Jews and Christians happened to be there, and they were too numerous and economically too strong to be expelled or assimilated. Members of these religious communities may have learned, through an extended historical process, that it was quite profitable for them to maintain and instrumentalize their differences from the rulers. However that may be, the Ottoman Empire came to rest on a basis of interreligious arrangements. In a purely Muslim state, different forms of taxation and different ways of dividing labour would have evolved, and such an entity would have lacked the features we associate with the Ottoman Empire.

If time and space were unlimited, we could pursue our cases to the present. We would then have to listen to sad accounts of massacres and expulsions. Ethnic mixes can be unmixed, and heterogeneous populations can be homogenized by force. Such processes are part of the history of many modern nation-states. This, however, should not lead us to idealize or romanticize the pluralism of earlier periods. Systems based on different group rights have a tendency to limit individual freedom. The niche that guarantees survival or even prosperity is hard for outsiders to enter and difficult for insiders to leave. One's role is determined by one's group affiliation. Adhering to a given religion, one also ends up in a certain social role and economic niche; one speaks a particular language and must submit to a certain dress code. To become something else remains forever a dream. Secure and prosperous as they may have been, the non-Muslim groups under Muslim protection were neatly circumscribed with regard to their fields of activity. The ambition of a Christian to get into the inner circle of politics, or the dream of a Jewish boy to become a soldier, could not be realized under this kind of pluralism.

Discourses on difference and policies based on these discourses are a confusing hall of mirrors, often producing distortion. The positions of those who believe themselves to be miles apart on a scale of moral evaluation may be expressed in the same words and have the same consequences. Celebrating group identities may lead to the loss of individual liberties, as pluralism fades into segregation and multiculturalism into apartheid.

Günther Schlee is one of the Founding Directors of the Max Planck Institute for Social Anthropology in Halle, Germany. Prior to this appointment he was Professor of Social Anthropology at the University of Bielefeld. He conducted fieldwork in Kenya, Ethiopia and Sudan. His publications include *Identities on the Move: Clanship and Pastoralism in Northern Kenya* (Manchester University Press, 1989), *How Enemies Are Made: Towards a Theory of Ethnic and Religious Conflict* (Berghahn Books, 2008) and *Pastoralism and Politics* (with Abdullahi A. Shongolo, James Currey, 2012).

Notes

Part of an earlier version of this chapter has been included in a contribution to the conference 'Convivencia: Representations, Knowledge and Identities (500–1600 AD)', May 2009, Madrid, organized by the Consejo Superior de Investigaciones Científicas (CSIC) and the Max Planck Society for the Advancement of Science (MPG). Another version was presented in July 2012 at the Max Planck Institute for the Study of Religious and Ethnic Diversity, Göttingen, and yet another one at the conference 'Globalization of Knowledge in the Mediterranean World of Post-Antiquity', October 2012, at the Max Planck Institute for the History of Science, Berlin. I thank Dittmar Schorkowitz, Wolfgang Holzwarth, Jacqueline Knörr and John Eidson for comments on different versions. Burkhard Schnepel provided valuable hints to the literature on India, not all of which I managed to make full use of. His own work on *The Jungle Kings* would have been quite pertinent.

 1. Soviet language policy resulted in the promotion of Russian at the level of the Union and different Turkic languages at the level of the Republic all over Central Asia with the exception of Tajikistan.
 2. In the long history of Islam in Northern India before the Moghuls, we find earlier instances of the inclusion of non-Muslims in Muslim armies and bureaucracies, just as we find views critical of this practice. 'One of the most widely read authors of pre-Mughal

India' (Alam 2000: 220), Zia-ud-Din Barani, 'advised that non-Muslims be taken into state service to some degree. The existence of non-Muslim soldiers in the army of Mahmud, the first Muslim conqueror of Northern India, fighting the enemies of Islam, was enough of a reason for him not to abhor their presence' (ibid.: 225). These quotations show that there was incorporation as well as a segregation of non-Muslims also in pre-Moghul India, with the norm often being segregationist and purist, and the practice being more liberal. Of course, the norms themselves can be taken as an indicator of the presence of practices deviating from the norm, because otherwise the norms would not be needed. Mudabbir, another pre-Moghul author, 'recommends state offices only for religious, pious, and God-fearing Muslims' (ibid.: 219). To keep rulers and the ruled visibly apart, Mudabbir recommended, in a way reminiscent of later Ottoman practices in another part of the world, that 'The people of the *zimma* [non-Muslims living under Muslim protection] should not ride on horses, should not wear clothes like Muslims or live like Muslims' (ibid.: 219).

3. The units of thousands, composed of smaller decimal units, was an organization which followed the model of the earlier Kereyid state in the shadow of the Chinese empire (Lhamsuren 2011: 227).

4. For more detailed references to Hesse, see Schlee (2005: 39–42).

5. The languages of this family have a remarkable distribution. Their speakers are found among hunters and reindeer herders across Siberia but were also found in the Forbidden City in Beijing until 1913. The Emperor was of the Manchu Dynasty and his courtiers and concubines had to learn the Manchu language.

6. Timur himself had only briefly made conquests in India but is still of enormous importance for the Moghul self-image and legitimacy. Foltz (1998: 22) also gives iconographic examples for this.

7. See Manz (1999 [1989]: 42). In terms of patterns of conflict, this is reminiscent of New Guinea. The Manembu mistrust their co-villagers who have important links outside the village to such an extent, that killing the external ally of an internal rival is a frequent starting point of violent conflict (Harrison 1993; for a discussion see Schlee 2008a: 50f).

8. That conquest states on the whole did not provide services, that they were there to take things and not to dish out, does not mean that there were no normative ideas around that this should be otherwise. In the European tradition, the earliest formulations regarding the ideal ruler may be found in the epics, histories and philosophical works of classical antiquity. These were, in turn, important sources for the genre known as the *speculum principum* (mirror of princes), beginning in the Middle Ages (Philipp and Stammen 1996). Texts of this type contained theories about the proper behaviour of the ruler in improving the lives of his subjects or in guiding the state in the service of the common good. In this way, political theorists could suggest which tasks the ruler should perform, as can be shown with reference to an analogous genre in another region. Abul Hasan al-Marwadi (974–1058), a North-Indian writer, suggested that 'the authority of the caliph was supreme, and among his important duties were defence of the *sharïa*, dispensation of justice according to the *sharïa*, and organization of the *jihad*' (Alam 2000: 217). Even some of the most violent conquerors might have subscribed to such ideologies and claimed that they were living up to such ideals. Of course, whether or not rulers were restricted or influenced in any way by scholars who set agendas for them remains an empirical question, which may or may not be answerable, depending on available sources.

9. See Coleman (1990) on agents and principals.
10. At least one of the Company's governors of Bengal managed to acquire private tax farming rights at the expense of the Company, which had previously collected revenues in the very same territories (Dirks 2006: 57–58). Ultimately, the British taxpayer had to cover the costs of this kind of predation against the Company by its own agents, since at least once Parliament 'bailed the Company out of massive debts' (Dirks 2006: 178).
11. Back in Britain after 'serving' the Company, British agents often became agents of Indian rulers in British politics. 'Between 1763 and 1792, at least a dozen Englishmen actually sat in parliament with seats bought with nawabi money' (Dirks 2006: 64), i.e. with money given to them by Muhammed Ali, the nawab of Madras. The interests of Indian rulers in English politics comprised deferment of debt and the wish to maintain their positions.
12. Retrospectively, and seen with 'Western' eyes, both Byzantium and the Ottoman Empire have become proverbial for their social pathologies, e.g., the 'Byzantine court intrigues' and the prolonged decline and corruption of 'the sick man on the Bosporus'. Western Europeans who use this type of language, however, should not forget that most of them live in states that have not yet managed to exist nearly as long as either of the two. Both seem to have had remarkable integrative force and to have managed quite well as empires. Time has come to analyse them as success stories and to inquire into the reasons of their success.
13. On 'Purity and Power in Islamic and Non-Islamic Societies' in a different comparative framework, starting from northeast African examples, see Chapter 10 in Schlee (2008a).
14. Another promising comparison is that between the ethnic policies of Russia and China in different periods (Schorkowitz 2017).
15. For a brief typology of relations between language and collective identities in a yet wider framework, see Schlee (2008a: 99–103).
16. For a recent study of the interpenetration of patrilineal descent and clientelism in a quite different part of the Turkic world, Kyrgyzstan, see Ismailbekova (2012, 2017).
17. The situation reminds me of my native Holstein. From 1559 to 1864, Holstein belonged to the Danish king without belonging to Denmark. As a person, the King of Denmark was simultaneously Count of Holstein, which, until 1806, was nominally a part of the 'Holy Roman Empire of the German Nation' (which was then dissolved by Napoleon). I find this example to be quite illustrative and have never understood why the Schleswig-Holstein question has almost become proverbial for a complicated issue. Compare the famous quotation of the British Prime Minister, Lord Palmerstone: 'Only three people understood the Schleswig-Holstein question. The first was Albert, the Prince consort and he is dead; the second is a German professor, and he is in an asylum; and the third was myself – and I have forgotten it' (www.everything2.com/title/schleswig-Holstein+question, retrieved 15 September 2009).
18. Cf. Wikipedia: Emin Pasha, retrieved 21 May 2009.
19. With reference to 1888, Mounteney-Jephson (1891: 60) writes that 'some years before, the Pasha had married an Abyssinian lady'. He became a widower at the birth of the second and only surviving child, a daughter named Farida. Nothing is reported about the religion of the mother or the kind of marriage ceremony. As an 'Abyssinian', Emin's wife may have been of Christian origin.
20. The castration of slave boys is an interesting although somewhat gruesome example of religious division of labour. Castration – of humans and non-humans alike, since this also applies to domestic animals – is forbidden for Muslims. Yet, the demand for eunuchs

in Egypt and other parts of the Ottoman Empire was high. The buyers of eunuchs were exclusively Muslims. To satisfy their demand, non-Muslims were needed. Here Christians came in, namely the Copts of Upper Egypt, in particular their priests and monks who were famous for their medical skills (Meinardus 1969; Mowafi 1981: 16).

21. This account contains some imprecisions when it comes to the Sudan, but it gives a very vivid image of the attitudes of a young member of the English warrior aristocracy.

22. Formally, this relationship ended only when the British declared war against the Ottoman Empire in World War I. They then annexed Egypt and the Sudan. Egypt was unilaterally (by the British!) declared independent in 1922. The *Khedive,* an Ottoman appointee (at least in theory – actual power relations were changeable), thereby became 'King' of Egypt (Woodward 1990: 17).

23. As in Africa, administration in India was first in the hands of a company, the East India Company, and only later in the hands of the Colonial Office.

24. I owe these considerations, which seem to apply to much of British rule in Africa, to Jacqueline Knörr (personal communication), who was thinking, primarily, of the Upper Guinea Coast. On educated Africans who speak European languages or a European-language based Creole and on the 'lack of indigeneity and ethnic authenticity' (Knörr 2010: 745) of which they are often accused in colonial and post-colonial power games, see also Cohen (1981), the by now classic reference.

25. See Schlee (2008a: 107–69) for some of the paradoxical effects of the 'war on terror' and the fight against the 'Islamist threat' in Somalia.

26. See Schlee with Shongolo (2012) for the use of this metaphor in Kenya.

27. Comparisons across wide spaces are also possible. Lhamsuren (2010: 272) compares the Great Code of the Mongols (1640) to the Peace of Westphalia (1648) and the prior political order of the Mongols to the Holy Roman Empire.

Epilogue

Günther Schlee, Alexander Horstmann and John Eidson

This volume aims to deconstruct some very familiar and powerful assumptions about ethnicity, ethnic relations and ethnic identity. Its precursor in German (Horstmann and Schlee 2001), and many works by others, have tried to do the same. It is a long and uphill struggle. One such assumption, deserving of critical examination, is that ethnic identity is long-lasting and based on cultural traditions and values.

We are currently (February 2017) witnessing a huge push for populist, hyper-nationalist and, ultimately, fascist policies and discourses that promise the redistribution of wealth to the white inhabitants of mono-ethnic European nation-states or white-settler states, who are in their own opinion solely entitled to the wealth of the nation. The new wars in the Middle East (that are impossible to win), the (self-produced) humanitarian crises, and the radicalization of some excluded spectrum of Muslim immigrants have produced a backlash against multiculturalism and introduced the promise of a protected welfare paradise for the white majority inside the heavily militarized borders of Europe and the US. This process is dangerous, as it leads directly to the introduction of heavy-handed security measures that will put pressure on human rights and marginalize civil society. It will have dramatic consequences for our education system as well, as budget cuts in the humanities show. Not only the far right but also German chancellor Angela Merkel has declared multiculturalism dead.

Significantly, ethnographic and historical examples of conditions approximating today's understanding of multiculturalism do exist. In his classic study, *Political Systems of Highland Burma* (1954), which we refer to in the introduction and discuss in more detail elsewhere (Schlee 2008a), Leach already showed that diversity does not necessarily work against integration; rather, there are processes in the societies he studied that achieve integration through or by diversity.

Leach demonstrated, in his analysis of the relationship of the Shan and the Kachin of Highland Burma, that both of these categories were colonial inventions or re-interpretations introduced in the context of colonial surveys and related control technologies in the occupied territories. This shows that categories may be imposed on actors in a given local setting from the outside. Imperialist states, both capitalist and communist, select (essentialized) identities to suit their purposes. For example, the creation of the new 'socialist' man in the communist system intensified the pressure on ethnic minorities, rather than lessening it. This volume shows, however, that the selection of social identities is often more complex than is initially apparent, as the corresponding processes, being based on local connections and local support, are often hidden from the outsider observer.

Especially before the introduction of the plural society (Furnivall 1931), identities in Burma were quite flexible. They could be changed by marriage or simply by assimilating to a new clan. Society in upper central Burma has always been extremely heterogeneous, although it was in the interest of the immigrants not to appear to be outsiders. More recently, however, the Buddhist nationalism of the modern extremist spectrum around the *Ma Ba Tha* has incited hatred against Burmese Muslims, who used to intermarry with Buddhists in Mandalay and who were visually indistinguishable from them – who were, in short, well integrated.

Clearly, authoritarian governments and modernization programmes have induced ethnic majority discourses and religions and thus exerted great influence on the border-work of local societies, i.e. on the local negotiation of ethnic boundaries and resources (e.g. Reeves 2014). From this, however, one need not conclude that local societies have been corrupted by outside forces; rather, local actors are also able to negotiate and manipulate the policies that affect them, and they also participate in the 'public transcript' much more than Scott, in the nostalgic vision of *The Art of Not Being Governed* (2009), concedes.

As Horstmann's contribution to this volume illustrates, local societies have their own tools and their own recipes for dealing with difference. Often, these recipes are not well-known to outsiders for the simple reason that the participants have their own deals and have no interest in being visible. In a context of hatred and violence, as in the region bordering on Horstmann's fieldsite, Patani, where the state is clashing with violent nationalist secessionist movements, the open display of these local ways of achieving integration would lead to unnecessary tensions and clashes, and may even be suicidal, especially when local elite interests are involved.

In modern immigrant societies, governments set strong directives by defining the identities (and obligations) of migrants and refugees, and by controlling their movement. For their part, the migrants, often organized in migrant associations and assisted by sympathetic NGOs or organizations in the cultural sphere, try to achieve greater mobility and freedom of movement by re-defining their identity. Integration through difference counters assimilation.

It is important to ask how strategies and processes such as those described in this volume have come about. Are they planned by anyone? By leaders or ordinary people? Are they conscious? Are they based on learning? Do they somehow 'evolve'? And, if so, how? In order to contest perceptions that social identities are simply given, it is necessary to examine their evolution and the evolution of systems based on the coexistence or even interaction of such identities. If we assume that social identities are simply given, we might treat them as independent variables, i.e. we are tempted to explain what people do by who they are. That is how popular prejudice works: Gypsies steal because they are Gypsies; Africans are lazy because they are Africans – that is their 'culture'. Armenians fight Azeris because they have always done so. Factional violence is part of the Balkan 'mentality' – it is the essence of 'Balkanization', etc. To overcome such culturalism, we have to treat 'culture', 'identity' and political agencies that refer to identities as dependent variables. We have to examine what causes them to change, how they evolve. 'Evolution' immediately evokes two other concepts: variation and selection.

One of the questions raised in the introduction to this volume was that of the unit of selection. Starting from a generalized Darwinian model, which can be applied not only to biological evolution but to all kinds of evolution by focusing on variation and selection, we found that earlier models of system selection (in the sense of the selection of entire social systems) were probably inadequate in accounting for the speed of development that we find in actual history. These models, inspired as much by yet earlier functionalist assumptions as by evolutionism, took medium-scale to large-scale associations of people, referred to as 'cultures' or 'societies', as internally coherent or even equilibrated self-regulating systems, which, according to their degree of 'fit' with their environment and their capacity to reproduce, either survived to fill the present ethnographic record or were selected against and are no longer with us.

Social development is too fast for such a model. To account for its speed, we need smaller units of selection which die faster. Contested ideas and practices on a religious or political 'market' can be such units, as can individuals as well. Individuals can spread their beliefs and practices by living longer than others and having more children who resemble them to some degree, due to biological and cultural processes of transmission or the interplay of the two. Alternatively, or in addition, they can be models for others who observe them, or they can actively propagate what they believe and what they do. The multiplicity of beliefs and practices here stands for variation, and the fact that some are passed on, and others not, is selection.

There is even variation and selection on the sub-individual level. The oldest of the three of us has the habit of starting his day in a warm bath tub. There his mind wanders off and spontaneously produces a lot of sense and a lot of non-sense. Out of the bath tub, he rushes to his computer to write down some of his ideas and not others. Later, and through communication which also involves selection and modification by others, some of these ideas make it into the class-room or into publications. Thus they become part of the social sphere, of collec-tive knowledge, which can be accessed by many people in many ways, though not by everyone from everywhere with the same ease. Some of these ideas may have a noticeable or unnoticeable influence on the course of scholarly developments or on a political decision, others not. This is variation and selection at many different levels.

Selection in favour of one type or category influences the selection of other types or categories. An obvious example is gender discrimination. Selective abor-tion of female embryos, motivated by a preference for sons who are expected to 'continue the [male] line', is practiced in several Asian countries. The result, in the next generation, is that many young men will not find a bride. The sought-after young women will have the choice, or, in more patriarchal societies, their elders will make strategic choices for them. They can reject less attractive partners and can make use of chances of upward social mobility. A large proportion of men will remain childless. There is high selective pressure on men as a consequence of selecting against female embryos. Under a one-child policy, as in China, some parents will start to understand that the safest way to enhance one's chances of having any grandchild at all is to raise a daughter. If so, then selective abortion may thereby come to an end or even be reversed in terms of its gender bias.

Other selection processes lead not to responses which reverse them but to an acceleration in the same direction. Take the choice of a language. In a setting with a majority language A and a minority language B, we may have a fairly stable situation as long as B is spoken by a fairly large minority. But if more and more people give up language B and, after a bilingual phase, speak only language A, eventually, a tipping point will be reached, and the remaining speakers of B will learn A quickly, because speakers of language B no longer form a self-sufficient linguistic community. In other words, there will no longer be enough people of the different kinds one needs in the course of the day who respond to language B.

Today, many languages are approaching this tipping point. Of the 6,909 languages spoken on Earth, according to one count, 20 to 50 per cent are in danger of disappearing within the next 100 years. By 1999, 50 of them had only one remaining speaker; 500 had fewer than 100 speakers; and 1,000 were spoken by 100 to 1,000 people (Ngure 2015: 46–47). The world is losing linguistic diversity as fast as it is losing biodiversity. In the present volume, we have come across some factors that accelerate this process and others that slow it down. The standardization and unification of language in the nation-state framework has been discussed in general terms in the introduction and in the Nepalese case in Pfaff-Czarnecka's contribution. More recently, the globalization of the Anglosphere has accelerated this process of the loss of diversity. As late as the 1970s, it was quite usual to publish volumes like this one with some chapters in German with a French summary and others in French with a German summary. The present volume is exclusively in English, although none of the authors is English.

In West Africa, the choice of acquiring or maintaining a minority language is, no doubt, facilitated by the link between language and ethnicity, on one hand, and the ethnic monopolization of economic niches, on the other (see, in this volume, both Diallo and Grätz). The minority language offers its speakers an internal sphere occupied by those who share not only a language but also a status and an economic specialization – things that are valuable and worth defending together. It also structures the external relations of specialists with their clients, partners or customers. One's language (as in the case of other ethnic markers) advertises the fact that the speaker is, for example, a pastoralist who interacts with farmers or townspeople, or a craftsman who depends on customers from various ethnic groups, and so on.

Multiple and interrelated selection processes lead to the distribution, on the ground, of languages and cultural features, and to a chorus of collective identities expressed through these and responding to each other.

Although the various ways of organizing difference and sameness in medium-sized and large aggregates of human beings, such as tribes, nations and empires, may not have come about by system selection, they represent a range of variation which may be the base of future processes of selection. In other words: nations, supra-national organizations and economies may succeed or fail as a consequence of the role difference and sameness play in them. The world has changed a great deal not only in our individual lifetimes but even in the time it may take for a book project to mature. Since the predecessor volume to this one was published in German (Horstmann and Schlee 2001), the role that difference plays in our lives has changed greatly. We used to hope that being a Muslim or a Christian (or a Buddhist or an agnostic for that matter) would play a lesser and lesser role in civic or civilized conviviality in modern nation-states and supranational units – for example, that it would be normal to be a Muslim and a German, that the two features would be easy to combine in our grammar of identification (Eidson et al. 2017). Since the terrorist attacks on the World Trade Center, the subsequent wars, declared or undeclared, which rightly or wrongly were depicted as reactions to these attacks, and the terrorist responses to these wars, history has changed its course, at least for the time being. The trend towards secularism and pluralism has been reversed. The majority of Muslims who think that democracy is the perfect instrument for organizing relationships among Muslims and between them and others has been side-lined and has disappeared from public perception. Theocracy (a euphemism for autocracy and arbitrariness at the expense of God, whose name is misused) has taken over. On the other side, tens of thousands of post-Christians, whose very actions show that they do not have the faintest idea of Christianity, call out for the defence of the Christian Occident against Islam. The noisiest of these movements calls itself PEGIDA, the German acronym for 'Patriotic Europeans against the Islamization of the Occident'. Since the financial crisis in 2008, nationalism and disruptive tendencies have been revived in the European Union; and, most recently, in 2016, the leading nation of the 'free world', the United States, so far the spearhead of capitalist globalization (not an unmixed blessing either), has elected a president who preaches xenophobia and protectionism.

We have the chance to make good use of the samenesses and the differences between us. Within a nation-state, for example, we may agree on a language (or two in more complicated cases) and a constitutional order, and agree to differ along other features and make productive use of our diversity. On the global level we still have to learn to grasp our humanity as a universally shared identity and to take it seriously. Our common humanity is the collective identity most difficult to mobilize. All others can be mobilized against someone else; but against whom do we proclaim our shared identity as human beings? Yet the interdependence of the world and the fragility of our environment demand it.

Large-scale human aggregates, understood as ways of organizing sameness and difference, have not come about by selection of such systems in their entirety, but they may yet fail at that level because of insufficiencies in the way in which they organize difference and sameness.

Günther Schlee is one of the Founding Directors of the Max Planck Institute for Social Anthropology in Halle, Germany. Prior to this appointment he was Professor of Social Anthropology at the University of Bielefeld. He has conducted fieldwork in Kenya, Ethiopia and Sudan. His publications include *Identities on the Move: Clanship and Pastoralism in Northern Kenya* (Manchester University Press, 1989), *How Enemies Are Made: Towards a Theory of Ethnic and Religious Conflict* (Berghahn Books, 2008) and *Pastoralism and Politics* (with Abdullahi A. Shongolo, James Currey, 2012).

Alexander Horstmann is Associate Professor of Southeast Asian Studies at the School of Humanities, Tallinn University, Estonia, relating area studies to other teaching communities at the School of Humanities. He has held visiting positions at Tokyo University of Foreign Studies, Mahidol University and EHESS in Paris. He has published widely on social protection strategies of displaced Karen in Myanmar and is author (with Jin-Heon Jung) of *Building Noah's Ark for Migrants, Refugees and Religious Communities* (Palgrave, 2015). Alexander Horstmann is co-editor of *Conflict and Society: Advances in Research*, a Berghahn journal of qualitative research on socially organized violence.

John Eidson is Senior Research Fellow in the 'Integration and Conflict' Department at the Max Planck Institute for Social Anthropology in Halle, Germany. He is editor of *Das anthropologische Projekt: Perspektiven aus der Forschungslandschaft Halle/Leipzig* (Leipziger Universitätsverlag, 2008) and author, most recently, (with Günther Schlee and others) of 'From Identification to Framing and Alignment: A New Approach to the Comparative Analysis of Collective Identities', in *Current Anthropology* 58(3) (June 2017): 340–359.

Bibliography

Adams, Laura. 2007. 'Uzbekistan's National Holidays', in Jeff Sahadeo and Russell Zanca (eds), *Everyday Life in Central Asia: Past and Present*. Bloomington, IN: Indiana University Press, pp. 198–212.

——. 2010. *The Spectacular State: Culture and National Identity in Uzbekistan. Politics, History, and Culture*. Durham, NC: Duke University Press.

Adamu, Mahdi. 1978. *The Hausa Factor in West African History*. Zaria: Ahmadu Bello University Press.

Agier, Michel. 1982. *Commerce et sociabilité: les négociants soudanais du quartier zongo de Lomé (Togo)*. Paris: Orstom.

Aimé, Marco. 1994a. 'Frontiera ed etnie nell'Atakora (Nord Benin)', *Africa* 49(1): 54–74.

——. 1994b. 'Djougou, una chefferie sulla rotta della cola', *Africa* 49(4): 481–97.

Alam, Muzzaffar. 2000. 'Sharīʿa and Governance in the Indo-Islamic Context', in David Gilmartin and Bruce B. Lawrence (eds), *Beyond Turk and Hindu: Re-Thinking Religious Identities in Islamicate South Asia*. Gainsville: University Press of Florida, pp. 216–45.

Alff, Henryk. 2013. 'Basarökonomie im Wandel: Postsowjetische Perspektiven des Handels in Zentralasien', *Geographische Rundschau* 65(11): 20–25.

——. 2014a. 'Embracing Chinese Modernity? Articulation and Positioning in China-Kazakhstan Trade and Exchange Processes', *Crossroads Asia Working Paper Series no. 21*. University of Bonn: Centre for Development Research.

——. 2014b. 'Post-Soviet Positionalities: Relations, Flows and the Transformation of Bishkek's Dordoy Bazaar', in Henryk Alff and Andreas Benz (eds), *Tracing Connections – Explorations of Spaces and Places in Asian Contexts*. Berlin: WVB, pp. 71–90.

——. 2015. 'Profiteers or Moral Entrepreneurs? Bazaars, Traders and Development Discourses in Almaty, Kazakhstan', *International Development Planning Review* 37(3): 249–67.

Alff, Henryk and Mathias Schmidt. 2011. 'Seidenstraße 2.0? Handel und Mobilität im Grenzraum Kasachstan-Kirgistan-Xinjiang', *Osteuropa* 61(11): 63–76.

Amborn, Hermann. 2009. 'Mobility, Knowledge and Power: Craftsmen in the Borderlands', in Günther Schlee and Elizabeth E. Watson (eds), *Changing Identifications and Alliances in North-East Africa, vol. 2, Ethiopia and Kenya.* Oxford and New York: Berghahn Books, pp. 113–31.

Amselle, Jean-Loup. 1985. 'Ethnies et espaces: pour une anthropologie topologique', in Jean-Loup Amselle and Elikia M'Bokolo (eds), *Au coeur de l'ethnie: ethnies, tribalisme et Etat en Afrique.* Paris: Editions La Découverte, pp. 11–48.

Anderson, Benedict. 1983. *Imagined Communities: Reflections on the Origin and Spread of Nationalism.* London: Verso.

Anderson, Kathryn H. and Richard Pomfret. 2005. 'Spatial Inequality and Development in Central Asia', in Anthony Venables, Ravi Kanbur and Guanghua Wan (eds), *Spatial Disparities in Human Development: Perspectives from Asia.* Tokyo and New York: United Nations University Press, pp. 233–70.

Appadurai, Arjun. 1995. 'The Production of Locality', in Richard Fardon (ed.), *Counter-Works: Managing the Diversity of Knowledge.* London and New York: Routledge, pp. 205–25.

———. 1996. *Modernity at Large: Cultural Dimensions of Globalization.* Minnesota, MN: University of Minneapolis Press.

Arditi, Claude. 1990. 'Les Peuls, les Senufo et les vétérinaires: pathologie d'une opération de développement dans le nord de la Côte d'Ivoire', *Cahiers des sciences humaines* 26(1–2): 137–53.

Asad, Talal. 1970. *The Kababish Arabs: Power, Authority and Consent in a Nomadic Tribe.* London: Hurst.

Askew, Marc. 2009. 'Landscapes of Fear, Horizons of Trust: Villagers Dealing with Danger in Thailand's Insurgent South', *Journal of Southeast Asian Studies* 40(1): 59–86.

Ayupova, Shakhnoza. 2011. 'Uzbek Labor Migration to Russia and Its Impact on Gender Relations'. MA thesis. OSCE Academy.

Ba, Ahmadou Mahmadou. 1932. 'L'émirat de l'Adrar mauritanien de 1872–1908', *Bulletin de Géographie et d'Archéologie de la province d'Oran* 53: 83–119 and 263–98.

Baberowski, Jörg. 2006. 'Selbstbilder und Fremdbilder: Repräsentation Sozialer Ordnungen Im Wandel', in Jörg Baberowski, Hartmut Kaelble and Jürgen Schriewer (eds), *Eigene und fremde Welten.* Frankfurt am Main: Campus, pp. 9–13.

Bachabi, Awaou. 1980. *La constitution du groupe Dendi de Zougou-Wangara: approche historique.* Mémoire de Maitrise. Porto-Novo: Université Nationale du Benin, École Nationale Supérieure.

Baier, Stephen and Paul E. Lovejoy. 1977. 'The Tuareg of the Central Sudan: Gradations in Servility at the Desert Edge (Niger and Nigeria)', in Suzanne Miers and Igor Kopytoff (eds), *Slavery in Africa, Historical and Anthropological Perspectives.* Madison, WI: University of Wisconsin Press, pp. 391–410.

Bakel, Martin A., Renée R. Hagesteijn and Pieter van de Velde. 1986. '"Big-man": From Private Politics to Political Anthropology', in Martin A. Bakel, Renée R. Hagesteijn and Pieter van de Velde (eds), *Private Politics: A Multi-Disciplinary Approach to 'Big-Man' Systems.* Leiden: E.J. Brill, pp. 211–15.

Bako-Arifari, Nassirou. 1995. 'Démocratie et logiques du terroir au Bénin', *Politique Africaine* 59: 7–24.

Balmforth, Tom. 2013. 'Moscow Police Arrest 1,200 Migrant Workers after Murder of Ethnic Russian', *The Guardian*, 14 October. Retrieved 2 March 2015 from http://www.theguardian.com/world/2013/oct/14/russia-police-arrest-migrants-nationalist-rioting.

Banton, Michael. 1992. *Racial and Ethnic Competition.* Aldershot: Gregg Revivals.

———. 2015. *What We Know about Race and Ethnicity.* Oxford and New York: Berghahn Books.

Barbier, Maurice (ed.). 1984. *Trois Français au Sahara occidental en 1784–1786*. Paris: Harmattan.

Barbour, Bernard and Michelle Jacobs. 1985. 'The Mi'raj: A Legal Treatise on Slavery by Ahmad Baba', in John Ralph Willis (ed.), *Slaves and Slavery in Muslim Africa, vol. 1: Islam and the Ideology of Enslavement*. London: Frank Cass, pp. 125–59.

Barkey, Karen. 2008. *Empire of Difference: The Ottomans in Comparative Perspective*. Cambridge: Cambridge University Press.

Barnett, Steve. 1977. 'Identity Choice and Caste Ideology in Contemporary South India', in Janet L. Dolgin, David S. Kemnitzer and David M. Schneider (eds), *Symbolic Anthropology: A Reader in the Study of Symbols and Meaning*. New York: Columbia University Press, pp. 270 –91.

Barnett, Steve, Lina Fruzzetti and Akos Ostor. 1976. 'Hierarchy Purified: Notes on Dumont and his Critics', *The Journal of Asian Studies* 35(4): 627–46.

Barry, Boubacar. 1972. *Le royaume du Waalo, le Sénégal avant la conquête*. Paris: Maspéro.

Barth, Fredrik (ed.). 1969a. *Ethnic Groups and Boundaries*. Bergen and Oslo: Universitetsforlaget.

Barth, Fredrik. 1969b. 'Introduction', in Fredrik Barth (ed.), *Ethnic Groups and Boundaries*. Bergen and Oslo: Universitetsforlaget, pp. 9–38.

Bassin, Mark and Catriona Kelly. 2012. 'Introduction: National Subjects', in Mark Bassin and Catriona Kelly (eds), *Soviet and Post-Soviet Identities*. Oxford and New York: Oxford University Press, pp. 3–16.

Bayart, Jean-François. 1989. *L'Etat en Afrique: la politique du ventre*. Paris: Fayard.

Bazin, Jean. 1985. 'A chacun son Bambara', in Jean-Loup Amselle and Elikia M'Bokolo (eds), *Au coeur de l'ethnie: ethnies, tribalisme et Etat en Afrique*. Paris: Editions La Découverte, pp. 87–127.

Bellér-Hann, Ildikó. 2008. 'Introduction', in Ildikó Bellér-Hann (ed.), *The Past as Resource in the Turkic Speaking World*. Würzburg: Ergon, pp. 9–22.

Bennigsen, Alexandre. 1979. 'Several Nations or One People? Ethnic Consciousness among Soviet Central Asians', *Survey – A Journal of Soviet and East European Studies* 24(3): 51–64.

Bennigsen, Alexandre and Marie Broxup. 1984. *The Islamic Threat to the Soviet State*. London: Croom Helm.

Bentley, G. Carter. 1991. 'Response to Yelvington', *Comparative Studies in Society and History* 29(1): 24–55.

Berger, Peter. 2012. 'Theory and Ethnography in the Modern Anthropology of India', *HAU – Journal of Ethnographic Theory* 2(2): 325–57.

Bernus, Edmond. 1960. 'Kong et sa région', *Etudes éburnéennes* 8: 239–324.

Besteman, Catherine. 2005. 'Why I Disagree with Robert Kaplan', in Catherine Bestemen and Hugh Gusterson (eds), *Why America's Top Pundits Are Wrong: Anthropologists Talk Back*. Berkeley, CA: University of California Press, pp. 83–101.

Beumers, Birgit. 2012. 'National Identity through Visions of the Past: Contemporary Russian Cinema', in Mark Bassin and Catriona Kelly (eds), *Soviet and Post-Soviet Identities*. Oxford and New York: Oxford University Press, pp. 55–72. Retrieved 23 July 2015 from http://www.cambridge.org/de/academic/subjects/literature/european-literature/soviet-and-post-soviet-identities.

Bhattachan, Krishna Bahadur. 1995. 'Ethnopolitics and Ethnodevelopment: An Emerging Paradigm in Nepal', in Dhruba Kumar (ed.), *State Leadership and Politics in Nepal*. Kathmandu: Tribhuvan University, Centre for Nepal and Asian Studies, pp. 124–47.

———. 1996. 'Induced and Indigenous Self-Help Organizations in the Context of Rural Development: A Case Study of the GTZ Supported Self-Help Promotion Programs in Nepal', in Madan K. Dahal and Horst Mund (eds), *Social Economy and National Development Lessons from Nepalese Experience*. Kathmandu: NEFAS.

———. 1998. 'Review Article: Making No Heads and Tails of the Ethnic "Conundrum" by Scholars with European Head and Nepalese Tail', *Contributions to Nepalese Studies* 25(1): 111–30.

Bierschenk, Thomas. 1999. 'Herrschaft, Verhandlung und Gewalt in einer afrikanischen Mittelstadt (Parakou, Bénin)', *Africa Spectrum* 34(3): 321–48.

Binger, Louis G. 1892. *Du Niger au golfe de Guinée par le pays de Kong et le Mossi 1887–1889*. Paris: Hachette.

Bista, Dor Bahadur. 1991. *Fatalism and Development: Nepal's Struggle for Modernization*. Calcutta: Orient Longman.

Bloch, Maurice. 1992. 'What Goes without Saying: The Conceptualization of Zafimaniry Society', in Adam Kuper (ed.), *Conceptualizing Society*. London: Routledge, pp. 127–46.

Bluestain, Harvey S. 1977. 'Power and Ideology in a Nepalese Village', unpublished manuscript. Yale University.

Bonte, Pierre. 1986. 'Une agriculture saharienne: les grâyr de l'Adrar mauritanien', *Revue de l'occident musulman et de la Méditerranée* 41/42: 378–96.

———. 1988. 'Krieger und Reuige: Die Towba und die politische Entwicklung der Maurischen Emirate', in Édouard Conte (ed.), *Macht und Tradition in Westafrika, französische Anthropologie und afrikanische Geschichte*. Frankfurt: Campus, pp. 175–202.

Botte, Roger, Jean Boutrais and Jean Schmitz (eds). 1999. *Figures peules*. Paris: Éditions Karthala.

Bourdieu, Pierre. 1972. *Esquisse d'une théorie de la pratique: précédé de trois études d'ethnologie kabyle*. Geneva: Librairie Droz.

———. 1977. *Outline of a Theory of Practice*. Cambridge: Cambridge University Press.

———. 1979. *La distinction*. Paris: Éditions de minuit.

Bourgeot, André (ed.). 1999. *Horizons nomads en Afrique sahélienne: sociétés, développement et démocratie*. Paris: Karthala.

Boym, Svetlana. 2001. *The Future of Nostalgia*. New York: Basic Books.

Brass, Paul (ed.). 1985. *Ethnic Groups and the State*. Totowa, NJ: Barnes and Noble.

Braukämper, Ulrich. 1992. *Migration und ethnischer Wandel: Untersuchungen aus der östlichen Sudanzone*. Stuttgart: Franz Steiner.

Brégand, Denise. 1998. *Commerce caravanier et relations sociales au Bénin: les Wangara du Borgou*. Paris: L'Harmattan.

Brhane, Meskerem. 1997. 'Narratives of the Past, Politics of the Present Identity, Subordination, and the Haratines of Mauritania', PhD dissertation. Chicago, IL: University of Chicago.

———. 2000. 'Histoires de Nouakchott: discours des *hrâtîn* sur le pouvoir et l'identité', in Mariella Villasante-de Beauvais (ed.), *Groupes serviles au Sahara: approche comparative à partir du cas des arabophones de Mauritanie*. Paris: CNRS, pp. 195–234.

Bringa, Tone. 2005. 'Haunted by the Imaginations of the Past: Robert Kaplan's *Balkan Ghosts*', in Catherine Besteman and Hugh Gusterson (eds), *Why America's Top Pundits Are Wrong: Anthropologists Talk Back*. Berkeley, CA: University of California Press, pp. 60–82.

Brown, Richard H. 1993. 'Cultural Representation and Ideological Domination', *Social Forces* 71(3): 657–76.

Brubaker, Rogers. 2011. 'Nationalizing States Revisited: Projects and Processes of Nationalization in Post-Soviet States', *Ethnic and Racial Studies* 34(11): 1785–1814.

Brunarska, Zuzanna. 2014. 'Regional out-Migration Patterns in Russia', *Working Paper no. 56*, European University Institute: Migration Policy Center. Retrieved 3 August 2015 from http://cadmus.eui.eu/handle/1814/31382.

Bubandt, Niels and Andrea Molnar. 2004. 'On the Margins of Conflict: An introduction', *Antropologi Indonesia* (special vol.): 1–6.

Burghart, Richard. 1984. 'The Formation of the Concept of Nation State in Nepal', *Journal of Asian Studies* 64(1): 101–25.

Burkert, Claire. 1997. 'Defining Maithil Identity: Who is in Charge?' in David Gellner, Joanna Pfaff-Czarnecka and John Whelpton (eds), *Nationalism and Ethnicity in a Hindu Kingdom: The Politics of Culture in Contemporary Nepal*. Amsterdam: Harwood, pp. 241–74.

Burnham, Philip. 1991. 'L'ethnie, la religion et l'Etat: le rôle des Peuls dans la vie politique et sociale du Nord-Cameroun', *Journal des Africanistes* 61(1): 73–102.

———. 1996. *The Politics of Cultural Difference in Northern Cameroon*. Edinburgh: Edinburgh University Press.

Burr, Angela. 1974. 'Buddhism, Islam and Spirit Beliefs and Practices and Their Social Correlates in Two Southern Thai Coastal Fishing Villages', PhD dissertation. London: University of London.

Caillié, Rene. 1830. *Journal d'un voyage de Temboctou à Jenné dans l'Afrique centrale*, vol. 1. Paris: Imprimerie Royale.

Calhoun, Craig. 1994. 'Social Theory and the Politics of Identity', in Craig Calhoun (ed.), *Social Theory and the Politics of Identity*. Oxford: Blackwell, pp. 9–36.

Campbell, Ben. 1997. 'The Heavy Loads of Tamang Identity', in David Gellner, Joanna Pfaff-Czarnecka and John Whelpton (eds), *Nationalism and Ethnicity in a Hindu Kingdom: The Politics of Culture in Contemporary Nepal*. Amsterdam: Harwood, pp. 205–35.

Capron, Jean. 1973. *Communautés villageoises bwa (Mali-Haute-Volta)*. Paris: Institut d'Ethnologie.

Caratini, Sophie. 1989. *Les Rgaybât (1610–1934), tome II, territoire et société*. Paris: L'Harmattan.

Carsten, Janet. 1997. *The Heat of the Hearth: The Process of Kinship in a Malay Fishing Community*. Oxford: Clarendon Press.

Catley, Andy, Jeremy Lind and Ian Scoones. 2013. 'Development at the Margins: Pastoralism in the Horn of Africa', in Andy Catley, Jeremy Lind and Ian Scoones (eds), *Pastoralism and Development in Africa: Dynamic Change at the Margins*. Abingdon and New York: Routledge, pp. 1–25.

Ceccaldi, Pierrette. 1979. *Essai de nomenclature des populations langues et dialectes de la république populaire du Bénin*. Paris: Centre d'études africaines.

Ceylan, Ebubekir. 2011. *Ottoman Origins of Modern Iraq: Political Reform, Modernization and Development in the Nineteenth-Century Middle East*. London and New York: I.B. Tauris.

Chatty, Dawn. 2006. 'Assumptions of Degradation and Misuse: The Bedouin in the Syrian Bādiya', in Dawn Chatty (ed.), *Nomadic Societies in the Middle East and North Africa*. Leiden and Boston: Brill, pp. 737–58.

Churchill, Winston. 1947. *My Early Life: A Roving Commission*. London: Odhams Press.

Clark, Andrew F. 1998. 'The Ties that Bind: Servility and Dependency among the Fulbe Bundu (Senegambia), 1930s to 1980s', *Slavery and Abolition* 19(2): 91–108.

Cleaveland, Timothy. 1995. 'Becoming Walata: A Study of Politics, Kinship, and Social

Identity in Pre-Colonial Walata', PhD dissertation. Evanston, IL: Northwestern University.

Cohen, Abner. 1965. 'The Social Organization of Credit in a West African Cattle Market', *Africa* 35(1): 8–19.

———. 1969. *Custom and Politics in Urban Africa: A Study of Hausa Migrants in Yoruba Towns*. London: Routledge and Kegan Paul.

———. 1981. *The Politics of Elite Culture: Explorations in the Dramaturgy of Power in a Modern African Society*. Berkeley, CA and Los Angeles: University of California Press.

Coleman, James S. 1990. *Foundations of Social Theory*. Cambridge, MA: Belknap Press of Harvard University Press.

Colin, G.S. 1960. 'Hartani', in *Encyclopedia of Islam*. Leiden: Brill, pp. 230–31.

Collins, Kathleen. 2006. *Clan Politics and Regime Transition in Central Asia*. Cambridge and New York: Cambridge University Press.

Conte, Édouard. 1991. 'Entrer dans le sang: perceptions arabes des origines', in Pierre Bonte, Édouard Conte, Constant Hamés and Abdel Wedoud Ould Cheikh (eds), *Al-Ansâb: la quête des origines, anthropologie historique de la société tribale arabe*. Paris: Édition Maison de la science de l'homme, pp. 51–100.

Cooper, Frederik. 1977. *Plantation Slavery on the East Coast of Africa*. New Haven, NJ: Yale University Press.

Cremer, Jean. 1924. *Les Bobo*. Paris: Geuthner.

Cunnison, Ian. 1966. *Baggara Arabs: Power and the Lineage in a Sudanese Nomad Tribe*. Oxford: Clarendon Press.

Dafinger, Andreas and Michaela Pelican. 2002. 'Land Rights and the Politics of Integration: Pastoralists' Strategies in a Comparative View', *Max Planck Institute for Social Anthropology Working Paper no. 48*. Halle (Saale): Max Planck Institute for Social Anthropology.

Dahal, Dilli Ram. 1993. 'Anthropology of the Nepal Himalaya: A Critical Appraisal', in Charles Ramble and Martin Brauen (eds), *Anthropology of Tibet and the Himalaya*. Ethnologische Schriften 12. Zurich: Völkerkundemuseum der Universität Zürich, pp. 49–59.

Daly, Martin W. 1991. *Imperial Sudan: The Anglo-Egyptian Condominium 1934–1956*. Cambridge: Cambridge University Press.

Darwin, John 2013. *The Empire Project: The Rise and Fall of the British World System 1830–1970*. Cambridge: Cambridge University Press.

Davis, Robert W. 1997. *The Evolution of Risk Management Strategies in a Hanging Social and Economic Environment: The Case of the Assaba Region of Mauritania*. Baltimore, MD: Johns Hopkins University.

De Waal, Alex. 1997. 'Exploiter l'esclavage: droits de l'homme et enjeux politiques', *Politique Africaine* 66: 49–60.

Deng, Francis M. and Martin W. Daly. 1989. *Bonds of Silk: The Human Factor in the British Administration of the Sudan*. East Lansing, MI: Michigan State University Press.

Denison, Michael. 2009. 'The Art of the Impossible: Political Symbolism, and the Creation of National Identity and Collective Memory in Post-Soviet Turkmenistan', *Europe-Asia Studies* 61(7): 1167–87.

Desjeux, Dominique. 1994. *Le sens de l'autre: stratégies, réseaux et cultures en situation intercul-turelle*. Paris: L'Harmattan.

Diallo, Youssouf. 1996a. 'Paysans sénoufo et pasteurs peuls du Nord de la Côte d'Ivoire: les questions de l'accès à la terre et de l'ethnicité', in Thomas Bierschenk, Pierre-Yves Le

Meur and Matthias von Oppen (eds), *Institutions and Technologies for Rural Development in West Africa*. Weikersheim: Margraf Verlag, pp. 223–32.

———. 1996b. 'Bauern, Viehzüchter und staatliche Intervention im Norden der Elfenbeinküste', in Günther Schlee and Karin Werner (eds), *Inklusion und Exklusion: die Dynamik von Grenzziehungen im Spannungsfeld von Markt, Staat und Ethnizität*. Cologne: Köppe Verlag, pp. 87–105.

———. 1997. *Les Fulbe du Boobola: genèse et évolution de l'Etat de Barani (Burkina Faso)*. Cologne: Köppe Verlag.

———. 1999. 'Les dimensions sociales et politiques de l'expansion pastorale dans les savanes ivoiriennes', in Victor Azaria, Mirjam de Bruijn, Anneke Breedveld and Han van Dijk (eds), *Pastoralists under Pressure? Fulbe Societies Confronting Change in West Africa*. Leiden: Brill, pp. 211–36.

Diallo, Youssouf, Martine Guichard and Günther Schlee. 2000. 'Quelques aspects comparatifs', in Youssouf Diallo and Günther Schlee (eds), *L'ethnicité peule dans des contextes nouveaux*. Paris: Karthala, pp. 225–55.

Diallo, Youssouf and Günther Schlee (eds). 2000. *L'ethnicité peule dans des contextes nouveaux*. Paris: Karthala.

Dirks, Nicholas B. 2006. *The Scandal of Empire: India and the Creation of Imperial Britain*. Cambridge, MA: The Belknap Press of Harvard University Press.

Dittmer, Kunz. 1975. 'Die Obervolta-Provinz', in Hermann Baumann (ed.), *Die Völker Afrikas und ihre traditionellen Kulturen*, 2 vols. Wiesbaden: Franz Steiner, pp. 495–542.

Donahoe, Brian, John Eidson, Dereje Feyissa, Veronika Fuest, Markus Virgil Höhne, Boris Nieswand, Günther Schlee and Olaf Zenker. 2009. 'The Formation and Mobilization of Collective Identities in Situations of Conflict and Integration', *Max-Planck-Institute for Social Anthropology Working Papers no. 116*. Retrieved 14 July 2015 from http://www.eth.mpg.de/pubs/wps/pdf/mpi-eth-working-paper-0116.pdf.

Dorairajoo, Saroja. 2004. 'Violence in the South of Thailand', *Inter-Asia Cultural Studies* 5(3): 465–71.

Dramani-Issifou, Zakari. 1981. 'Routes de commerce et mise en place des populations de nord du Bénin actuel', in J.P. Chrétien et al. (eds), *Le sol, la parole et l'écrit: 2000 ans d'histoire africaine. Mélanges en hommage à Raymond Mauny*, 2 vols. Paris: Société Française d'Histoire d'Outre-mer and l'Harmattan, pp. 655–72.

Dumont, Louis 1979 [1966]. *Homo Hierarchicus: le système des castes et ses implications*. Paris: Gallimard.

———. 1980. *Homo Hierarchicus: The Caste System and its Implications*. Complete revised English edition. Chicago, IL: University of Chicago Press.

Durkheim, Emile. 1998 [1893]. *De la division du travail social*. Paris: Quadrige.

Eidson, John R., Dereje Feyissa, Veronika Fuest, Markus V. Hoehne, Boris Nieswand, Günther Schlee and Olaf Zenker. 2017. 'From Identification to Framing and Alignment: A New Approach to the Comparative Analysis of Collective Identities', *Current Anthropology* 58(3): 340–59.

El Hamel, Chouki. 1999. 'The Transmission of Islamic Knowledge in Moorish Society from the Rise of the Almoravids to the 19th Century', *Journal of Religion in Africa* 29(1): 62–87.

Elias, Norbert and James L. Scotson. 1990. *Etablierte und Außenseiter*. Frankfurt am Main: Suhrkamp.

Elwert, Georg. 1982. 'Probleme der Ausländerintegration: Gesellschaftliche Integration durch Binnenintegration?', *Kölner Zeitschrift für Soziologie und Sozialpsychologie* 34: 717–31.

———. 1997. 'Boundaries, Cohesion and Switching: On We-Groups in Ethnic National and

Religious Forms', in Hans Rudolf Wicker (ed.), *Rethinking Nationalism and Ethnicity*. Oxford: Berg, pp. 251–71.

Elyas, Khalda. 2014. 'Sudan Allocates 100,000 Acres for Egyptian Farmers', *Sudan Vision. An Independent Daily*, 7 December. Retrieved 24 December 2014 from http://news.sudanvisiondaily.com.

Ennaji, Mohamed. 1994. *Soldats, domestiques et concubines: l'esclavage au Maroc au XIX siécle*. Paris: Balland.

Ensel, Remco. 1998. *Saints and Servants: Hierarchical Interdependence between Shurfa and Haratin in the Moroccan Deep South*. Amsterdam: University of Amsterdam.

Esman, Milton J. (ed.). 1977. *Ethnic Conflict in the Western World*. Ithaca, NY: Cornell University Press.

Evans-Pritchard, Edward Evan. 1940. *The Nuer: A Description of the Modes of Livelihood and Political Institutions of a Nilotic People*. Oxford: Clarendon Press.

Evers, Hans-Dieter and Markus Kaiser. 2001. 'Two Continents, One Area: Eurasia', in Peter Preston and Julie Gilson (eds), *The European Union and Pacific Asia: Inter-Regional Linkages in a Changing Global System*. Cheltenham: Edward Elgar Publishing House, pp. 65–90.

Evers, Hans-Dieter, and Markus Kaiser. 2004. 'Eurasische Transrealitäten – Das Erbe der Seidenstrasse', in Markus Kaiser (ed.), *Auf der Suche nach Eurasien: Politik, Religion und Alltagskultur zwischen Russland und Europa*. Bielefeld: transcript, pp. 36–78.

Evers, Hans-Dieter and Heiko Schrader (eds). 1994. *The Moral Economy of Trade: Ethnicity and Developing Markets*. London: Routledge.

Faist, Thomas (ed.). 2000. *Transstaatliche Räume: Politik, Wirtschaft und Kultur in und zwischen Deutschland und der Türkei*. Bielefeld: transcript.

———. 2004. 'Towards a Political Sociology of Transnationalization: The State of Art in Migration Research', *Archives Européennes de Sociologie* 45(3): 331–66.

Falge, Christiane. 2015. *The Global Nuer: Transnational Life, Religious Movements and War*. Cologne: Köppe Verlag.

Fekadu, Adugna. 2009. 'Negotiating Identity: Politics of Identification among the Borana, Gabra and Garri around the Oromo-Somali Boundary in Southern Ethiopia', PhD dissertation. Halle (Saale): Martin Luther University Halle-Wittenberg.

Fergusson, Niall. 2004. *Empire: How Britain Made the Modern World*. London: Penguin.

Feyissa, Dereje. 2003. 'Ethnic Groups and Conflict: The Case of the Anywaa-Nuer Relations in the Gambela Region, Western Ethiopia', PhD dissertation. Halle (Saale): Martin Luther University Halle-Wittenberg.

———. 2011. *Playing Different Games: The Paradox of Anywaa and Nuer Identification Strategies in the Gambella Region, Ethiopia*. Oxford and New York: Berghahn Books.

Finke, Peter. 2006a. 'Variations on Uzbek Identities: Concepts, Constraints and Local Configurations', habilitation thesis. Leipzig: University of Leipzig.

———. 2006b. 'Competing Ideologies of Statehood and Governance in Central Asia: Turkic Dynasties in Transoxania and Their Legacy in Contemporary Politics', in David Sneath (ed.), *States of Mind: Power, Place and the Subject in Inner Asia*. Bellingham, WA: Western Washington University, pp. 109–28.

———. 2014. *Variations on Uzbek Identity: Strategic Choices, Cognitive Schemas and Political Constraints in Identification Processes*. Oxford and New York: Berghahn Books.

Finley, Moses I. 1968. 'Slavery', *International Encyclopaedia of the Social Sciences* 14: 307–13.

Fitzpatrick, Sheila. 1999. *Everyday Stalinism: Ordinary Life in Extraordinary Times: Soviet Russia in the 1930s*. New York: Oxford University Press.

Foltz, Richard C. 1998. *Mughal India and Central Asia*. Karachi: Oxford University Press.

Förster, Till. 1997. *Zerrissene Entfaltung*. Cologne: Köppe Verlag.

Fortes, Meyer. 1969. *Kinship and the Social Order*. London: Routledge.

Fox, Kate. 2004. *Watching the English*. London: Hodder and Stoughton.

Freitag, Ulrike and Achim von Oppen (eds). 2010. *Translocality: The Study of Globalising Processes from a Southern Perspective*. Leiden and Boston: Brill Academic Publishers.

Furnivall, John. S. 1931. *An Introduction to the Political Economy of Burma*. Rangoon: Burma Book Club.

———. 1944. *Netherlands India: A Study of Plural Economy*. With an introduction by A.C.D. De Graeff. Cambridge: The University Press.

Gaenszle, Martin. 1997. 'Changing Conceptions of Ethnic Identity among the Mewahang Rai', in David Gellner, Joanna Pfaff-Czarnecka and John Whelpton (eds), *Nationalism and Ethnicity in a Hindu Kingdom: The Politics of Culture in Contemporary Nepal*. Amsterdam: Harwood, pp. 351–73.

Garlinski, Majan and Albin Bieri. 1991. *Review of Makai*, Film. Zurich: Makai Connection, Zurich TV UNI Zurich.

Geertz, Clifford. 1973. *The Interpretation of Cultures*. New York: Basic Books.

———. 1980. *Negara: The Theatre State in Nineteenth-Century Bali*. Princeton, NJ: Princeton University Press.

Gellner, David. 1999a. *From Cultural Hierarchies to a Hierarchy of Multiculturalisms: The Case of the Newars of Kathmandu Valley*. New Delhi: Oxford University Press.

———. 1999b. *From Group Rights to Individual Rights and Back: Nepalese Struggles over Culture and Equality*. Cambridge: Cambridge University Press.

Gellner, David and M.B. Karki. 2007. 'The Sociology of Activism in Nepal: Some Preliminary Considerations', in H. Ishii, David Gellner and K. Nawa (eds), *Political and Social Transformations in North India and Nepal*. New Delhi: Manohar, pp. 361–97.

Gellner, David, Joanna Pfaff-Czarnecka and John Whelpton (eds). 1997. *Nationalism and Ethnicity in a Hindu Kingdom: The Politics of Culture in Contemporary Nepal*. Amsterdam: Harwood.

Gellner, Ernest. 1983. *Nations and Nationalism*. Ithaca, NY: Cornell University Press.

Gesick, Lorraine M. 1995. *In the Land of Lady White Blood: Southern Thailand and the Meaning of History*. Ithaca, NY: Southeast Asia Program Publications, Cornell University Press.

Giordano, Christian. 2013. 'The Social Organization of Informality: The Rationale Underlying Personalized Relationships and Coalitions', in Christian Giordano and Nicolas Hayoz (eds), *Informality in Eastern Europe: Structures, Political Cultures and Social Practices*. Bern: Peter Lang, pp. 357–78.

Giordano, Christian and Nicolas Hayoz. 2013a. *Informality in Eastern Europe: Structures, Political Cultures and Social Practices*. Bern: Peter Lang.

———. 2013b. 'Introduction', in Christian Giordano and Nicolas Hayoz (eds), *Informality in Eastern Europe: Structures, Political Cultures and Social Practices*. Bern: Peter Lang, pp. 9–24.

Glaze, Anita. 1981. *Art and Death in a Senufo Village*. Bloomington, IN: Indiana University Press.

Glazer, Nathan and Daniel P. Moynihan. 1963. *Beyond the Melting Pot: The Negroes, Puerto Ricans, Jews, Italians, and Irish of New York City*. Cambridge, MA: MIT Press.

Gluckman, Max. 1965. *Politics, Law and Ritual in Tribal Society*. Oxford: Blackwell.

Gomes, Alberto, Timo Kaartinen and Timo Kortteinen. 2006. 'Introduction: Civility and

Social Relations in South and Southeast Asia', *Suomen Antropologi: Journal of the Finnish Anthropological Society* 32(3): 4–11.

Grätz, Tilo. 1998. 'Staat, Macht und Gewalt in Tanguiéta: Zur Interpretation gewaltsamer Auseinandersetzungen in Tanguiéta (Nordbenin)', in Sonja Heyer and Jan Köhler (eds), *Anthropologie der Gewalt*. Berlin: Verlag für Wissenschaft und Forschung, pp. 119–30.

———. 2000. 'New Local Radio Stations in African Languages and the Process of Political Transformation in the Republic of Benin: The Case of *Radio Rurale Locale Tanguiéta* (Northern Benin)', in Richard Fardon and Graham Furniss (eds), *African Broadcast Cultures*. London: James Currey, pp. 110–27.

———. 2001. '*Les fils (divers) de Tanguiéta*: Politische Geschichte und Identitätsprozesse in einer afrikanischen Kleinstadt', in Alexander Horstmann and Günther Schlee (eds), *Integration durch Verschiedenheit: Lokale und globale Formen interkultureller Prozesse*. Bielefeld: transcript, pp. 297–32.

———. 2003. 'Administration étatique et société locale à Tanguiéta (Nord du Bénin): une analyse politique suite à des interprétations des événements de février 1996 à Tanguiéta', *Working Paper of the Institute of Social Anthropology and African Studies* no. 20. Mainz: Johannes Gutenberg University.

———. 2006. *Tanguiéta: facettes d'histoire et de la vie politique d'une commune béninoise à la veille de la décentralisation*. Cotonou and Paris: Les Éditions du Flamboyant.

———. 2016. *Tanguiéta: facettes d'histoire*. Sarrebruck: Editions universitaires européennes.

Gravers, Mikael. 2007. *Exploring Ethnic Diversity in Burma*. Copenhagen: NIAS Press.

Gray, Richard. 1961. *A History of the Southern Sudan 1839–1889*. London: Oxford University Press.

Gregory, Joseph R. 1996. 'African Slavery 1996', *First Things* 63: 37–39.

Guignard, Michel. 1975. *Musique, honneur et plaisir au Sahara, étude psycho-sociologique et musicologique de la société maure*. Paris: Geuthner.

Haberland, Eike. 1993. *Hierarchie und Kaste: Zur Geschichte und politischen Struktur der Dizi in Südwest-Äthiopien*. Stuttgart: Franz Steiner Verlag.

Hamès, Constant. 1979. 'L'évolution des émirats maures sous l'effet du capitalisme marchand européen', in Equipe Ecologie (ed.), *Pastoral Production and Society/Production pastorale et société*. Cambridge: Cambridge University Press, pp. 375–98.

Hangen, Susan. 2005. 'Boycotting Dasain: History, Memory, and Ethnic Politics in Nepal', *Studies in Nepalese History and Society* 10(1): 105–33.

Hannerz, Ulf. 1996. *Transnational Connections: Culture, People, Places*. London: Routledge.

Hansen, Claus Bech. 2013. 'The Ambivalent Empire: Soviet Rule in the Uzbek Soviet Socialist Republic, 1945–1964', PhD dissertation. European University Institute.

Hanson, John H. 1990. 'Generational Conflict in the Umarian Movement after the Jihad: Perspectives from the Futanke Grain Trade at Medine', *Journal of African History* 31(2): 199–215.

Harris, Marvin. 1974. *Cows, Pigs, Wars and Witches: The Riddles of Culture*. New York: Random House.

Harrison, Simon J. 1993. *The Mask of War: Violence, Ritual and the Self in Melanesia*. Manchester: Manchester University Press.

Hechter, Michael. 2013. *Alien Rule*. New York: Cambridge University Press.

Hegarthy, Steve. 1995. 'The Rehabilitation of Temur: Reconstructing National History in Contemporary Uzbekistan', *Central Asia Monitor* 1: 28–35.

Hellbeck, Jochen. 2006. *Revolution on My Mind: Writing a Diary under Stalin*. Cambridge, MA: Harvard University Press.

Helmke, Gretchen and Steven Levitsky. 2004. 'Informal Institutions and Comparative Politics: A Research Agenda', *Perspectives on Politics* 2(4): 725–40.

Henn, Alexander and Klaus-Peter Koepping. 2008. *Rituals in an Unstable World: Contingency–Hybridity–Embodiment*. Frankfurt: Peter Lang.

Hesse, Klaus. 1982. *Abstammung, Weiderecht und Abgabe: zum Problem der konsanguinalpolitischen Organisation der Mongolen des 13. bis zum 17. Jahrhundert*. Berlin: Dietrich Reimer Verlag.

Hill, Fiona. 2004. 'Eurasia on the Move: The Regional Implications of Mass Labour Migration from Central Asia to Russia', unpublished paper presented at the Kennan Institute, Washington, 27 September 2004. Retrieved 14 July 2015 from http://www.wilsoncenter.org/event/eurasia-the-move-the-regional-implications-mass-labor-migration-central-asia-to-russia.

Hirsch, Francine. 2005. *Empire of Nations: Ethnographic Knowledge and the Making of the Soviet Union. Culture and Society after Socialism*. Ithaca, NY: Cornell University Press.

Hirschman, Albert Otto. 1992. *Denken gegen die Zukunft: die Rhetorik der Reaktion*. Munich: Hanser.

Hobart, Mark. 1978. 'The Path from the Soul: The Legitimacy of Nature in Balinese Conceptions of Space', in G. Milner (ed.), *Natural Symbols in South East Asia*. London: School of Oriental and African Studies, pp. 5–28.

Hobsbawm, J. Eric. 1990. *Nations and Nationalism since 1780: Programme, Myth, Reality*. Cambridge and New York: Cambridge University Press.

Hobsbawm, Eric and Terence Ranger (eds). 1983. *The Invention of Tradition*. New York: Columbia University Press.

Höfer, András. 1979. *The Caste Hierarchy and the State in Nepal: A Study of the Muluki Ain of 1854, in Khumbu Himal*. Innsbruck: Universitätsverlag Wagner.

Hoffmann, Clemens. 2008. 'The Balkanization of Ottoman Rule', *Cooperation and Conflict* 43: 373–96.

———. 2009. 'Nationalism and the State: Historical Lessons from the Greek Secession from the Ottoman Empire', *Presentation at European Science Foundation Conference on Post-Crisis States Transformation: Rethinking the Foundations of the State*. Linköping, 1–5 May 2009.

Holas, Bohumil. 1966. *Les Sénoufo (y compris les Minianka)*. Paris: PUF.

Holliday, Adrian. 2010. 'Complexity in Cultural Identity', *Language and Intercultural Communication* 10(2): 165–77.

Holt, Peter Malcolm. 1961. *A Modern History of the Sudan: From the Funj Sultanate to the Present Day*. London: Weidenfeld and Nicolson.

Holt, Peter Malcolm and Martin W. Daly. 2000. *A History of the Sudan from the Coming of Islam to the Present Day*. Harlow: Pearson Education Limited.

Horstmann, Alexander. 2004. 'Ethnohistorical Perspectives on Buddhist–Muslim Relations and Coexistence in Southern Thailand: From Shared Cosmos to the Emergence of Hatred?', *Sojourn* 19(1): 76–99.

———. 2007a. 'Violence, Subversion and Social Creativity in the Thai–Malaysian Borderscape', in Prem Kumar Rajaram and Carl Grundy-Warr (eds), *Borderscapes: Hidden Geographies and Politics at Territory's Edge*. Minneapolis, MN: University of Minnesota Press, pp. 137–57.

———. 2007b. 'The Inculturation of a Transnational Islamic Missionary Movement: Tablighi Jamaat al-Dawa and Muslim Society in Southern Thailand', *Sojourn* 22(1): 107–30.

———. 2009. 'The Revitalization and Reflexive Transformation of the Manoora Rongkruu

Performance and Ritual in southern Thailand: Articulations with Modernity', *Asian Journal of Social Sciences* 37(6): 918–34.

Horstmann, Alexander and Günther Schlee (eds). 2001. *Integration durch Verschiedenheit: Lokale und globale Formen interkultureller Kommunikation*. Bielefeld: transcript.

Horstmann, Alexander and Katherina Seraidari. 2006. *Intimacy and Violence: Fragile Transitions in Southeast Asia and Southeast Europe*. Oxford and New York: Berghahn Books.

Howe, Leo. 1987. 'Caste in Bali and India: Levels of Comparison', in Leo Holy (ed.), *Comparative Anthropology*. London: Blackwell, pp. 135–52.

Huntington, Samuel P. 1993. 'The Clash of Civilizations?', *Foreign Affairs* 72(3): 22–49.

Hunwick, John O. 1992. 'Black Slaves in the Mediterranean World: Introduction to a Neglected Aspect of the African Diaspora', in Elizabeth Savage (ed.), *The Human Commodity: Perspectives on the Trans-Saharan Slave Trade*. London: Frank Cass, pp. 5–38.

Ibrahim, Hayder. 1979. *The Shaiqiya: The Cultural and Social Change of a Northern Sudanese Reverain People*. Wiesbaden: Franz Steiner Verlag.

Inkeles, Alex and Raymond Bauer. 1959. *The Soviet Citizen: Daily Life in a Totalitarian Society*. Cambridge, MA: Harvard University Press.

Institut National de la Statistique et de l'Analyse Economique (INSAE). 2014. 'Recensement Général de la Population et de l'Habitation au Bénin. Resultats definitifs'. Retrieved 15 May 2016 from http://www.insae-bj.org/recensement-population.html.

Ismailbekova, Aksana. 2012. '"The Native Son and Blood Ties": Kinship and Poetics of Patronage in Rural Kyrgyzstan', PhD dissertation. Halle (Saale): Martin Luther University Halle-Wittenberg.

———. 2017. *Blood Ties and the Native Son: The Poetics of Patronage in Kyrgyzstan*. Bloomington, IN: Indiana University Press.

Jacq-Hergoualc'h, Michel. 2002. *The Malay Peninsula: Crossroads of the Maritime Silk Road (100 BC–1300 AD)*. Leiden: Brill.

Jacquesson, Svetlana. 2010. 'A Power Play among the Kyrgyz: State versus Descent', in Isabelle Charleux, Gregory Delaplace, Roberte Hamayon and Scott Pearce (eds), *Representing Power in Modern Inner Asia*, vol. 2. Bellingham, WA: Center for East Asian Studies, Western Washington University Press, pp. 221–44.

Jacquesson, Svetlana and Ildiko Beller-Hann. 2012. 'Introduction: Local History as an Identity Discipline', *Central Asian Survey* 31(3): 239–49.

James, Wendy. 1988. 'Perceptions from an African Slaving Frontier', in Leonie J. Archer (ed.), *Slavery and Other Forms of Unfree Labour*. London: Routledge, pp. 130–41.

Jarvie, Ian C. 1984. *Rationality and Relativism: In Search of a Philosophy and History of Anthropology*. London: Routledge.

Jensen, Jürgen. 1999. 'Probleme und Möglichkeiten bei der Bildung Kulturen übergreifender Begriffe im Vergleich kultureller Phänomene', in Waltraut Kokot and Dorle Dracklé (eds), *Wozu Ethnologie?* Berlin: Dietrich Reimer, pp. 53–73.

Joas, Hans. 2000. *Kriege und Werte: Studien zur Gewaltgeschichte des 20. Jahrhunderts*. Weilerswist: Velbrück.

Johnston, Timothy. 2011. *Being Soviet: Identity, Rumour, and Everyday Life under Stalin 1939–1953*. Oxford and New York: Oxford University Press.

Jory, Patrick. 2008. 'Luang Pho Thuat and the Integration of Patani', in Michael J. Montesano and Patrick Jory (eds), *Thai South and Malay North: Ethnic Interactions on a Plural Peninsula*. Singapore: NUS Press, pp. 292–303.

Kaiser, Markus. 1998a. 'Reopening of the Silk Road: International Informal Sector Trade in Post-Soviet Uzbekistan', PhD dissertation. Bielefeld University.

———. 1998b. 'Informal Sector Trade in Uzbekistan', *Journal of Central Asian Studies* 2(2): 2–19.

———. 2001. 'Formen der Transvergesellschaftung als gegenläufige Prozesse zur Nationsbildung in Zentralasien', in Günther Schlee and Alexander Horstmann (eds), *Integration durch Verschiedenheit*. Bielefeld: transcript, pp. 113–42.

———. 2003. 'Forms of Transsociation as Counter-Processes to Nation Building in Central Asia', *Central Asia Survey* 22(2/3): 315–31.

———. 2005. 'Cross-Border Traders as Transformers', in Raj Kollmorgen (ed.), *Transformation als Typ sozialen Wandel: Postsozialistische Lektionen, historische und interkulturelle Vergleiche*. Münster: LIT, pp. 191–214.

Kalinina, Ekaterina. 2014. 'Mediated Post-Soviet Nostalgia', *Södertörn Doctoral Dissertations*, vol. 98. Elanders: Södertörn University. Retrieved 14 July 2015 from http://sh.diva-portal.org/smash/get/diva2:746181/FULLTEXT01.pdf.

Kaminski, Bartlomiej and Saumya Mitra. 2010. *Skeins of Silk: Borderless Bazaars and Border Trade in Central Asia*. Washington, DC: World Bank.

Kamp, Marianne Ruth. 2006. *The New Woman in Uzbekistan: Islam, Modernity, and Unveiling under Communism*. Seattle and London: University of Washington Press.

Kaplan, Robert D. 1996. *Balkan Ghosts: A Journey through History*. New York: St. Martin's Press.

Kappeler, Andreas. 2015. 'Im Schatten Russlands: Wie die Ukraine aus dem europäischen Bewusstsein verschwand', *Frankfurter Allgemeine Zeitung*, 10 June. Retrieved 14 July 2015 from http://www.faz.net/aktuell/feuilleton/debatten/warum-wir-die-ukraine-noch-im-mer-unterschaetzen-13636172.html?printPagedArticle=true#pageIndex_2.

Keyes, Charles F. and Shigeharu Tanabe. 2002. *Cultural Crisis and Social Memory: Modernity and Identity in Thailand and Laos*. London: Routledge Curzon.

Khalid, Adeeb. 2007. *Islam after Communism: Religion and Politics in Central Asia*. Berkeley, CA: University of California Press.

Khazanov, Anatoly M. and Günther Schlee. 2012. *Who Owns the Stock? Collective and Multiple Property Rights in Animals*. Oxford and New York: Berghahn Books.

Kirmse, B. Stefan. 2013. *Youth and Globalization in Central Asia: Everyday Life Between Religion, Media, and International Donors*. Frankfurt and New York: Campus Verlag.

Kitiarsa, Pattana. 2005. 'Beyond Syncretism: Hybridization of Popular Religion in Contemporary Thailand', *Journal of Southeast Asian Studies* 36(3): 461–87.

Klein, Martin A. 1983. 'Women in Slavery in the Western Sudan', in Claire C. Robertson and Martin A. Klein (eds), *Women and Slavery in Africa*. Madison, WI: University of Wisconsin Press, pp. 76–94.

Knauft, Bruce. 2002. *Critically Modern: Alternatives, Alterities, Anthropologies*. Bloomington and Indianapolis, IN: Indiana University Press.

Knörr, Jacqueline. 2010. 'Contemporary Creoleness; or, The World in Pidginization?', *Current Anthropology* 51: 731–48.

Koestler, Arthur. 1941. *Darkness at Noon*. New York: Macmillan Co.

Köhler, Florian. 2016. 'Transhumant Pastoralists, Translocal Migrants: Space, Place and Identity in a Group of FulBe WoDaaBe in Niger', PhD dissertation. Halle (Saale): Martin Luther University Halle-Wittenberg.

Köhler, Oswald. 1958. 'Zur Territorialgeschichte des östlichen Nigerbogens', *Baessler-Archiv* 6(2): 229–60.

Kotkin, Stephen. 1995. *Magnetic Mountain: Stalinism as a Civilization*. Berkeley, CA: University of California Press.

Kraft, Claudia, Alf Lüdtke and Jürgen Martschukat. 2010. *Kolonialgeschichten: regionale Perspektiven auf ein globales Phänomen.* Frankfurt am Main and New York: Campus.

Krämer, Karl-Heinz. 1996. *Ethnizität und nationale Integration in Nepal: Eine Untersuchung zur Politisierung der ethnischen Gruppen im modernen Nepal.* Stuttgart: Franz Steiner.

Krauskopff, Gisèle and Marie Lecomte-Tilouine (eds). 1996. *Célébrer le pouvoir: Dasai, une fête royale au Népal.* Paris: Éditions CNRS.

Krylova, Anna. 2000. 'The Tenacious Liberal Subject in Soviet Studies', *Kritika: Explorations in Russian and Eurasian History* 1(1): 1–28.

Kuba, Richard. 1996. *Wasangari und Wangara. Borgu und seine Nachbarn in historischer Perspektive.* Hamburg: LIT.

Kudaibergenova, T. Diana. 2014. 'National Identity Formation in Post-Soviet Central Asia: The Soviet Legacy, Primordialism, and Patterns of Ideological Development since 1991', in Sevket Akyildiz and Richard Carlson (eds), *Social and Cultural Change in Central Asia: The Soviet Legacy.* London and New York: Routledge, pp. 160–73.

Kulke, Hermann and Dietmar Rothermund. 2010 [1986]. *A History of India.* London and New York: Routledge.

Kursad, Aslan. 2008. 'Labour Migration and its Potential Consequences for Central Asia', *Central Asia-Caucasus Analyst* 10: 13–16.

Labov, William. 2006. *The Social Stratification of English in New York City,* 2nd edn. Cambridge: Cambridge University Press.

Lachenmann, Gudrun. 1992. 'Frauen als gesellschaftliche Kraft im sozialen Wandel in Afrika', *Peripherie* 12(47/48): 74–93.

Lang, Hartmut. 1977. *Exogamie und interner Krieg in Gesellschaften ohne Zentralgewalt.* Hohenschäftlarn: Kommissionsverlag Klaus Renner.

Launay, Robert. 1982. *Traders Without Trade: Responses to Change in Two Dyula Communities.* Cambridge: Cambridge University Press.

———. 1995. 'The Dieli of Korhogo: Identity and Identification', in David C. Conrad and Barbara E. Frank (eds), *Status and Identity in West Africa.* Bloomington, IN: Indiana University Press, pp. 153–69.

Le Moal, Guy. 1980. *Les Bobo: nature et fonction des masques.* Paris: ORSTOM.

———. 1990. 'De la brousse au village: autels de fondation et code sacrificiel chez les Bobo', in Marcel Détienne (ed.), *Traces de fondation.* Paris: Bibliothèque de l'EPHE, pp. 69–84.

Leach, Edmund. 1954. *Political Systems of Highland Burma.* London: Athlone Press.

Lentz, Carola. 1993. *Ethnizität und 'Tribalismus' in Afrika: Ein Forschungsüberblick.* Berlin: Das Arabische Buch.

Leontyeva, Elvira. 2013. 'Corruption Networks in the Sphere of Higher Education: An Example from Russian Mass Universities', in Christian Giordano and Nicolas Hayoz (eds), *Informality in Eastern Europe: Structures, Political Cultures and Social Practices.* Bern: Peter Lang, pp. 357–78.

Levinson, Stephen C. 2006. 'On the Human "Interaction Engine"', in N.J. Enfield and Stephen C. Levinson (eds), *Roots of Human Sociality: Culture, Cognition and Interaction.* Oxford: Berg, pp. 39–69.

Levtzion, Nehemia and J.F.P. Hopkins (eds). 1981. *Corpus of Early Arabic Sources for West African History.* Cambridge: Cambridge University Press.

Lewis, Bernard. 1990. *Race and Slavery in the Middle East: A Historical Enquiry.* New York: Oxford University Press.

Lewis, Ioan M. 1961. *A Pastoral Democracy: A Study of Pastoralism and Politics among the Northern Somali of the Horn of Africa.* London: Oxford University Press.

Lewis, Norman. 2000. 'The Syrian Steppe During the Last Century of Ottoman Rule: Hawran and the Palmyrena', in Martha Mundy and Basim Musallam (eds), *The Transformation of Nomadic Society in the Arab East*. Cambridge: Cambridge University Press, pp. 33–43.

Lhamsuren, Munkh-Erdene. 2010. 'The 1640 Great Code: An Inner Asian Parallel to the Treaty of Westphalia', *Central Asian Survey* 29(3): 269–88.

———. 2011. 'Where Did the Mongolian Empire Come From? Medieval Mongol Ideas of People, State and Empire', *Inner Asia* 13: 211–37.

Lonsdale, John. 1993. 'Staatsgewalt und moralische Ordnung: Die Erfindung des Tribalismus in Afrika', *Der Überblick* 29(3): 5–10.

———. 1996. 'Ethnicité morale et tribalisme politique', *Politique Africaine* 61: 98–115.

Lovejoy, Paul E. 1980. *Caravans of Kola: The Hausa Kola Trade*. Zaria: Ahmadu Bello University Press.

———. 1989. 'The Impact of the Atlantic Slave Trade on Africa: A Review of the Literature', *Journal of African History* 30: 365–94.

Lugard, Lord F.D. 1965 [1922]. *The Dual Mandate in British Tropical Africa*. Hamden, CT: Archon Books.

Lukashova, Irina and Irina Makenbaeva. 2009. 'Impact of the Global Financial Crisis on Labour Migration from Kyrgyzstan to Russia: Qualitative Overview and Quantitative Survey', Report by OSCE, ACTED and European Commission. Retrieved 14 July 2015 from http://www.osce.org/bishkek/40540.

Lukes, Steven M. 1974. *Power: A Radical View*. Houndmills and London: Macmillan.

Macauliffe, Max A. 1909. *The Sikh Religion: Its Gurus, Sacred Writings and Authors*. Oxford: Clarendon Press.

Macfarlane, Alan. 1997. 'Identity and Change among the Gurungs (Tamu-mai) of Central Nepal', in David Gellner, Joanna Pfaff-Czarnecka and John Whelpton (eds), *Nationalism and Ethnicity in a Hindu Kingdom: The Politics of Culture in Contemporary Nepal*. Amsterdam: Harwood, pp. 185–204.

Madmarn, Hasan. 1999. *The* Pondok *and* Madrasah *in Patani*. Bangi: Penerbit University Kebangsaan Malaysia.

Makris, G.P. 1996. 'Slavery, Possession and History: The Construction of the Self among Slave Descendants in the Sudan', *Africa. Journal of the International African Institute* 66(2): 159–82.

Manessy, Gabriel. 1975. *Les langues Oti-Volta: classification généalogique d'un groupe de langues voltaiques*. Paris: SELAF.

Manz, Beatrice Forbes. 1999 [1989]. *The Rise and Rule of Tamerlane*. Cambridge: Cambridge University Press.

Martin, Terry. 2001. *The Affirmative Action Empire: Nations and Nationalism in the Soviet Union, 1923–1939*. Ithaca, NY: Cornell University Press.

Masud, Muhammad Khalid (ed.). 2000. *Travellers in Faith: Studies of the Tablighi Jama'at as a Transnational Islamic Movement for Faith Renewal*. Leiden: Brill.

McCargo, Duncan. 2008. *Tearing Apart the Land: Islam and Legitimacy in Southern Thailand*. Ithaca, NY: Cornell University Press.

McDougall, E. Ann. 1985a. 'The View from Awdaghust: War Trade and Social Change in the Southwestern Sahara from the Eighth to the Fifteenth Century', *Journal of African History* 1: 1–30.

———. 1985b. 'Camel Caravans of the Saharan Salt Trade: Traders and Transporters in the Nineteenth Century', in Catherine Coquery-Vidrovitch and Paul E. Lovejoy (eds), *The Workers of African Trade*. Beverly Hills: Sage, pp. 99–122.

——. 1988. 'A Topsy-Turvy World: Slaves and Freed Slaves in the Mauritanian Adrar 1910–1950', in Suzanne Miers and Richard Roberts (eds), *The End of Slavery in Africa*. Madison, WI: University of Wisconsin Press, pp. 362–88.

McNeill, William Hardy. 1997. *A History of the Human Community: Prehistory to the Present*. Upper Saddle River, NJ: Prentice Hall.

Meeker, Michael E. 2002. *A Nation of Empire: The Ottoman Legacy of Turkish Modernity*. Berkeley, CA: University of California Press.

Meillassoux, Claude. 1977. *Terrains et théories*. Paris: Édition Anthropos.

——. 1986. *Anthropologie de l'esclavage, le ventre de fer et d'argent*. Paris: Presses Universitaires.

Meinardus, Otto. 1969. 'The Upper Egyptian Practice of the Making of Eunuchs in the XVIIIth and XIXth Century', *Zeitschrift für Ethnologie* 94: 47–58.

Menashri, David (ed.). 1998. *Central Asia Meets the Middle East*. London: Frank Cass.

Mercer, John. 1982. *Slavery in Mauritania Today*. London: Anti-Slavery-Society.

Middleton, John. 1979. *The Central Tribes of the North-eastern Bantu*. London: International African Institute.

Miers, Suzanne and Igor Kopytoff. 1977. 'Introduction: African "Slavery" as an Institution of Marginality', in Suzanne Miers and Igor Kopytoff (eds), *Slavery in Africa: Historical and Anthropological Perspectives*. Madison, WI: University of Wisconsin Press, pp. 3–81.

Migration Policy Centre. 2013a. 'Russia Migration Profile'. Retrieved 2 August 2015 from http://www.migrationpolicycentre.eu/docs/fact_sheets/Factsheet%20Russia.pdf.

——. 2013b. 'Ukraine Migration Profile'. Retrieved 2 August 2015 from http://www.migrationpolicycentre.eu/docs/fact_sheets/Factsheet%20Ukraine.pdf.

Ministère de l'Agriculture et des Ressources Animales. 1994. *Terre et Progrès*. Abidjan.

Mohammadou, Eldrige. 1976. *L'histoire des Peuls Férôbé du Diamaré Maraoua et Petté*. Tokyo: ILCAA.

Mohammed. 2014. 'Sudan Offers Egypt 100,00 Acres of Farmland', *Africa Review*, 8 December. Retrieved 24 December 2014 from http://www.africareview.com/News/Sudan-offers-Egypt-farmland/-/979180/2549114/-/46mtbq/-/index.html#.

Montesano, Michael J. and Patrick Jory (eds). 2008. *Thai South and Malay North: Ethnic Interactions on a Plural Peninsula*. Singapore: NUS Press.

Moore, Sally Falk. 1978. 'Law and Social Change: The Semi-Autonomous Social Field as an Appropriate Subject of Study', in Sally Falk Moore, *Law as a Process: An Anthropological Approach*. London: Routledge and Kegan Paul, pp. 54–81.

Moorehead, Alan. 1973 [1960]. *The White Nile*. Harmondsworth: Penguin Books.

Mounteney-Jephson, Arthur J. 1891. *Emin Pasha and the Rebellion at the Ecquator: A Story of Nine Month's Experiences in the Last of the Soudan Provinces*. New York: Charles Scribner's Sons.

Mowafi, Reda. 1981. *Slavery, Slave Trade and Abolition Attempts in Egypt and the Sudan 1820–1882*. Lund: Lunds Universitet.

Müller, Franz-Volker. 1989. 'Ethnizität und gesellschaftliche Arbeitsteilung in Westafrika: Beispiele aus der Ethnographie Malis', in Georg Elwert and Peter Waldmann (eds), *Ethnizität im Wandel*. Saarbrücken: Breitenbach, pp. 169–86.

Munier, Pierre. 1952. 'L'Assabe, essai monographique', *Études Mauritaniennes* 3: 1–72.

Münster, Daniel. 2007. *Postkoloniale Traditionen: Eine Ethnographie über Dorf, Kaste und Ritual in Südindien*. Bielefeld: transcript.

Muriuki, Godfrey. 1974. *A History of the Kikuyu: 1500–1900*. Nairobi: Oxford University Press.

Mutie, Pius Mutuku. 2003. '"In Spite of Difference": Making Sense of the Co-Existence between the Kamba and the Maasai Peoples in Kenya', PhD dissertation. University of Bielefeld, Faculty of Sociology: Sociology of Development Research Centre.

———. 2013. *The Art of Interethnic Coexistence: Some Evidence from Kenya.* Saarbrücken: LAP Lambert Academic Publishing.

N'Tia, Roger. 1993. 'Géopolitique de l'Atakora précolonial', *Afrika Zamani* 1: 107–24.

Nadel, Siegfried F. 1952. 'Witchcraft in Four African Societies: An Essay in Comparision', *American Anthropologist* 54(1): 18–29.

Nader, Nada. 2014. '10,000 Sudanese Acres Ready for Egyptian Farmers: Sudanese Investment Minister. Sudan Is Now Adopting the Open Door Policy for Investments', *Daily News Egypt*, 13 December. Retrieved 24 December 2014 from http://www.daily newsegypt.com/2014/12/13/10000-sudanese-acres-ready-egyptian-farmers-sudanese-investment-minister/.

Nee, Victor. 1992. 'Organisational Dynamics of Market Transition: Hybrid Forms, Property Rights, and Mixed Economy in China', *American Sociological Quarterly* 37(1): 1–27.

Ngure, Kenneth Kamuri. 2015. *From Rendille to Samburu: A Consequence of Compromised Linguistic Fidelity.* Cologne: Köppe Verlag.

Nicolas, Guy. 1964. *Étude de marchés en pays Hausa (Rep. du Niger).* Bordeaux: Documents ethnographiques, Université de Bordeaux.

Nikiporets-Takigawa, Galina. 2013. 'Memory Events and Memory Wars: Victory Day in L'viv, 2011 through the Prism of Quantitative Analysis', in Ellen Rutten, Julie Fedor and Vera Zvereva (eds), *Memory, Conflict and New Media: Web Wars in Post-Socialist States.* London: Routledge, pp. 48–62.

Nirenberg, David. 2012. 'Worrying about Cultural Excange in the Court of Alfonso X "the Wise"', [Preliminary] *Reader.* [Conference on] Globalization of Knowledge in the Mediterrean World of Post-Antiquity. Mechanisms of Transfer and Transformation. Organized by the Max Planck Institute for the History of Science at the Ethnological Museum, Berlin-Dahlem, 26–27 October 2012, pp. 115–24.

Nishii, Ryoko. 1999. 'Coexistence of Religions: Muslim and Buddhist Relationship on the West Coast of Southern Thailand', *Tai Culture: International Review on Tai Cultural Studies* 4(1): 77–92.

Northrop, Douglas. 2004. *Veiled Empire: Gender and Power in Stalinist Central Asia.* Ithaca, NY: Cornell University Press.

Observatory of Economic Complexity. 2015. 'OEC: Russia (RUS) Profile of Exports, Imports and Trade Partners', *Observatory of Economic Complexity*, 7 July. Retrieved 14 July 2015 from https://atlas.media.mit.edu/en/profile/country/rus/.

Olimova, Saodat and Igor Bosc. 2003. 'Labor Migration from Tajikistan', *Tajikistan International Organization for Migration (IOM).* Dushanbe.

Orwell, George. 2013. *Nineteen Eighty-Four: The Annotated Edition.* London: Penguin Books.

Ould Ahmed, Mohamed Lemine. 1983. 'L'abolition de l'esclavage en Mauritanie', Master thesis. Dakar University: Faculté des Sciences Juridiques et Economiques, 1982–1983.

Ould Cheikh, Abdel Wedoud. 1991. 'La tribu comme volonté et comme représentation: le facteur religieux dans l'organisation d'une tribu maure: les Awlad Abyayri', in Pierre Bonte, Édouard Conte, Constant Hamès and Wedoud Ould Cheikh (eds), *Al Ansâb: la quête des origines, anthropologie historique de la société tribale arabe.* Paris: Édition Maison de la science de l'homme, pp. 201–38.

Ould Hamidoun, Mokhtar. 1952. 'Précis sur la Mauritanie', *Études Mauritaniennes* 4: 1–71.

Ould Khalifa, Abdallalii Ould Youba. 1991. *Les aspects économiques et sociaux de l'oued Tijigja: de la fondation du ksar l'indépendance (1600–1960).* Paris: Université de Paris I.

Ould Mohand, Hussein. 1993. 'El Med'h, gospels des haratines', *Al Bayane* 64(9).

Oxby, Clare. 1978. *Sexual Division and Slavery in a Tuareg Community*. London: University of London Press.

Park, Robert E. 1930. 'Assimilation, Social', in Edwin R. Seligman and Alvin Johnson (eds), *Encyclopedia of the Social Sciences*, vol. 2. New York: Macmillan, pp. 281–83.

Parkin, David. 1987. 'Comparison as Search for Continuity', in Ladislaw Holy (ed.), *Comparative Anthropology*. London: Blackwell, pp. 52–69.

Parsons, Timothy H. 2010. *The Rule of Empires: Those Who Built Them, Those Who Endured Them, and Why They Always Fall*. Oxford: Oxford University Press.

Patterson, Orlando. 1982. *Slavery and Social Death: A Comparative Study*. Cambridge, MA: Harvard University Press.

Paul, Robert A. 1989. *The Sherpas of Nepal in the Tibetan Cultural Context*. New Delhi: Motilal Banarsidass Publishers.

Pautz, Hartwig. 2005. 'The Politics of Identity in Germany: the *Leitkultur* Debate', *Race & Class* 46(4): 39–52.

Peleikis, Anja. 2003. *Lebanese in Motion: Gender and the Making of a Translocal Village*. Bielefeld: transcript.

Pfaff-Czarnecka, Joanna. 1989. *Macht und Rituelle Reinheit: Hinduistisches Kastenwesen und ethnische Beziehungen im Entwicklungsprozess Nepals*. Grüsch: Rüegger.

———. 1997. 'Vestiges and Visions: Cultural Change in the Process of Nation-Building in Nepal', in David Gellner, Joanna Pfaff-Czarnecka and John Whelpton (eds), *Nationalism and Ethnicity in a Hindu Kingdom: The Politics of Culture in Contemporary Nepal*. Amsterdam: Harwood, pp. 419–70.

———. 1998. 'A Battle of Meanings: Commemorating Goddess Durgā's Victory over Demon Mahisā as a Political Act', *Asiatische Studien* 52(2): 575–610.

———. 1999. 'Debating the State of the Nation: Ethnicization of Politics in Nepal – A Position Paper', in Joanna Pfaff-Czarnecka et al. (eds), *Ethnic Futures – The State and Identity: Politics in Asia*. New Delhi: Sage Publications, pp. 41–98.

———. 2012. 'F®ictions, Frames and Fragments: Belonging and Ethnic Boundary Making in Nepal's Contested Ritual Communication', in Gabriela Kiliánová, Christian Jahoda and Michaela Ferencová (eds), *Ritual Conflict and Consensus: Case Studies from Asia and Europe*. Vienna: Verlag der Österreichischen Akademie der Wissenschaften, pp. 15–30.

Pfaff-Czarnecka, Joanna, Christian Büschges, Friso Hecker and Olaf Kaltmeier. 2007. 'Ethnisierung und De-Ethnisierung des Politischen: Aushandlungen um Inklusion und Exklusion im andinen und im südasiatischen Raum', in Christian Büschges and Joanna Pfaff-Czarnecka (eds), *Die Ethnisierung des Politischen: Identitätspolitiken in Lateinamerika, Asien und den USA*. Frankfurt am Main: Campus, pp. 19–63.

Philipp, Michael and Theo Stammen. 1996. 'Fürstenspiegel', in Gert Ueding (ed.), *Historisches Wörterbuch der Rhetorik*, vol. 3. Tübingen: Max Niemeyer Verlag, pp. 495–507.

Platenkamp, Josephus M. 2004. 'From Partial Persons to Completed Societies', *Zeitschrift für Ethnologie* 129: 1–28.

Pontin, A.J. 1982. *Competition and Coexistence of Species*. Boston: Pitman Advanced Publication Programm.

Popp, Wossen Marion. 2001. 'Yem, Janjero oder Oromo? Die Konstruktion ethnischer Identität im sozialen Wandel', in Alexander Horstmann and Günther Schlee (eds), *Integration durch Verschiedenheit*. Bielefeld: transcript, pp. 367–403.

Pries, Ludger. 1999. 'New Migration in Transnational Space', in Ludger Pries (ed.), *Migration and Transnational Social Spaces*. Aldershot: Ashgate, pp. 1–35.

Quigley, Declan. 1997. 'Deconstructing Colonial Fictions? Some Conjuring Tricks in the Recent Sociology of India', in Alison James, Jenny Hockey and Andrew Dawson (eds), *After Writing Culture*. London: Routledge, pp. 103–21.

Rahmonova-Schwarz, Delia. 2012. *Family and Transnational Mobility in Post-Soviet Central Asia: Labor Migration from Kyrgyzstan, Tajikistan and Uzbekistan to Russia*. Baden-Baden: Nomos.

Ramble, Charles. 1997. 'Tibetan Pride of Place; or, why Nepal's Bhotiyas are not an Ethnic Group', in David Gellner, Joanna Pfaff-Czarnecka and John Whelpton (eds), *Nationalism and Ethnicity in a Hindu Kingdom: The Politics of Culture in Contemporary Nepal*. Amsterdam: Harwood, pp. 379–413.

Rapport, Nigel. 2012. *Anyone: The Cosmopolitan Subject of Anthropology*. Oxford and New York: Berghahn Books.

Rasanayagam, Johan. 2011. *Islam in Post-Soviet Uzbekistan: The Morality of Experience*. Cambridge: Cambridge University Press.

Redfield, Robert, Ralph Linton and Melville J. Herskovits. 1936. 'Memorandum for the Study of Acculturation', *American Anthropologist (New Series)* 38(1): 149–52.

Reeves, Madeleine. 2007. 'Unstable Objects: Corpses, Checkpoints and "Chessboard Borders" in the Ferghana Valley', *Anthropology of East Europe Review* 25(1): 72–84.

———. 2008. 'Materializing Borders', *Anthropology News* 49(5): 12–13.

———. 2011. 'Staying Put? Towards a Relational Politics of Mobility at a Time of Migration', *Central Asian Survey* 30(3–4): 555–76.

———. 2014. *Border Work: Spatial Lives of the State in Rural Central Asia*. Ithaca, NY: Cornell University Press.

Regmi, Mahesh Chandra. 1972. *A Study in Nepali Economic History, 1768-1846*. New Delhi: Manjusri Publishing House.

———. 1978. *Thatched Huts and Stucco Palaces: Peasants and Landlords in 19th-Century Nepal*. New Delhi: Vikas Publishing House.

Roberts, Richard. 1988. 'The End of Slavery in the French Soudan, 1905–1914', in Suzanne Miers and Richard Roberts (eds), *The End of Slavery in Africa*. Madison, WI: Wisconsin University Press, pp. 282–307.

Roberts, Sean R. 2007. 'Everyday Negotiations of Islam in Central Asia: Practicing Religion in the Uyghur Neighborhood of Zarya Vostoka in Almaty, Kazakhstan', in Jeff Sahadeo and Russell Zanca (eds), *Everyday Life in Central Asia. Past and Present*. Bloomington, IN: Indiana University Press, pp. 339–54.

Robinne, François and Mandy Sadan. 2007. *Social Dynamics in the Highlands of Southeast Asia: Reconsidering Political Systems of Highland Burma by E.R. Leach*. Leiden: Brill.

Roche, Sophie and Sophie Hohmann. 2011. 'Wedding Rituals and the Struggle over National Identities', *Central Asian Survey* 30(1): 113–28.

Röhner, Irene. 2007. 'National and International Labour Migration: A Case Study in the Province of Batken, Kyrgyzstan', *NCCR North-South IP6 Working paper no. 8*. University of Zurich: Development Study Group.

Rolf, Malte. 2006. *Das sowjetische Massenfest*. Hamburg: Hamburger Edition, HIS Verlag.

Rothman, Jay. 2000. 'The "Aria" Approach to Conflict', *Pegasus Communications*. Retrieved 17 April 2013 from http://www.pegasuscom.com.

Roussel, Louis. 1965. *Région de Korhogo: étude de développement socio-économique*. Rapport sociologique.

Ruf, Urs Peter. 1995. *Mobil Sesshafte, Sedentarisierung und Geschichte der Nomaden in*

Mauretanien. Bielefelder Studien zur Entwicklungssoziologie 61. Saarbrücken: Verlag für Entwicklungspolitik.

———. 1999. *Ending Slavery: Hierarchy, Dependency and Gender in Central Mauritania.* Bielefeld: transcript.

Russell, Andrew. 1997. 'Identity Management and Cultural Change: The Yakha of East Nepal', in David Gellner, Joanna Pfaff-Czarnecka and John Whelpton (eds), *Nationalism and Ethnicity in a Hindu Kingdom: The Politics of Culture in Contemporary Nepal.* Amsterdam: Harwood, pp. 325–50.

Russian Federation Federal Statistics Service. 2013. 'Demograficheskiyi Ezhegodnik Rossii 2013'. Saarbrücken: LAP LAMBERT Academic Publishing. Retrieved 7 July 2015 from http://www.gks.ru/wps/wcm/connect/rosstat_main/rosstat/ru/statistics/publications/catalog/doc_1137674209312.

Sahlins, Marshall. 1963. 'Poor Man, Rich Man, Big Man, Chief: Political Types in Melanesia and Polynesia', *Comparative Studies in Society and History* 5: 285–303.

Sántha, István. 2005. 'Somewhere in Between: Social Ties on the Borderland between Taiga and Steppe to the West of Lake Baikal', in Erich Kasten (ed.), *Rebuilding Identities: Pathways to Reform in Post-Soviet Siberia.* Berlin: Reimer, pp. 173–96.

Sardan, Jean-Pierre Olivier de. 1976. *Quand nos pères étaient captifs.* Paris: Nubia.

Sasunkevich, Olga. 2013. '"Business as Casual". Shuttle Trade on the Belarus-Lithuanian Border', in Jeremy Morris and Abel Polese (eds), *The Informal Post-Socialist Economy: Embedded Practices and Livelihoods.* London and New York: Routledge, pp. 135–51.

Saugnier, F. and Pierre-Raymond de Brisson 1969 [1792]. *Voyages to the Coast of Africa.* Reprinted edition. New York: Negro University Press.

Schatz, Edward. 2014. *Modern Clan Politics: The Power of 'Blood' in Kazakhstan and Beyond.* Seattle, WA and London: University of Washington Press.

Schatz, Merle. 2014. *Sprache und Identität der Mongolen Chinas heute.* Cologne: Köppe Verlag.

Schetter, Conrad. 2012. 'Translocal Lives: Patterns of Migration in Afghanistan', *Crossroads Asia Working Paper no. 2.* University of Bonn: Centre for Development Research.

Schlee, Günther. 1988. 'Camel Management Strategies and Attitudes towards Camels in the Horn', in Jeffery C. Stone (ed.), *The Exploitation of Animals in Africa.* Aberdeen: University African Studies Group, pp. 143–54.

———. 1989. 'The Orientation of Progress: Conflicting Aims and Strategies of Pastoral Nomads and Development Agents in East Africa. A Problem Survey', in Elisabeth F. Linnebuhr (ed.), *Transition and Continuity in East Africa and Beyond: In Memoriam David Miller, Bayreuth African Studies Series: Special Issue.* Bayreuth: E. Breitinger, pp. 397–450.

———. 1994a [1989]. *Identities on the Move: Clanship and Pastoralism in Northern Kenya.* Nairobi: Gideon S. Were.

———. 1994b. 'Ethnicity Emblems, Diacritical Features, Identity Markers', in David Brokensha (ed.), *A River of Blessings: Essays in Honour of Paul Baxter.* Syracuse, NY and New York: Maxwell School of Citizenship and Public Affairs, Syracuse University, pp. 129–43.

———. 1998. 'Gada Systems on the Meta-ethnic Level: Gabbra/Boran/Garre Interactions in the Kenyan/Ethiopian Borderland', in Eisei Kurimoto und Simon Simonse (eds), *Conflict, Age & Power in North East Africa.* Oxford: James Currey, pp. 121–46.

———. (ed.). 2004. *Ethnizität und Markt.* Cologne: Köppe Verlag.

———. 2005. 'Forms of Pastoralism', in Stefan Leder and Bernhard Streck (eds), *Shifts and Drifts in Nomad-Sedentary Relations.* Wiesbaden: Reichert, pp. 17–54.

———. 2008a. *How Enemies are Made.* Oxford and New York: Berghahn Books.

——. 2008b. 'Ethnopolitics and Gabra Origins', *Max Planck Institute for Social Anthropology Working Paper no. 103*. Halle (Saale): Max Planck Institute for Social Anthropology.

——. 2009. 'Tackling Ethnicity from Different Sides: Marc Howard Ross' Work on Culture and Conflict', *Anthropos* 104: 571–78.

——. 2010. 'The Information Economics of Identification', *Max Planck Institute for Social Anthropology Report 2008–2009*, vol. I. Halle (Saale): Max Planck Institute for Social Anthropology, pp. 19–25. www.eth.mpg.de.

——. 2013. 'Why States Still Destroy Pastoralism and How They Can Learn That in Their Own Interest They Should Not', *Nomadic Peoples* 17(2): 6–19.

Schlee, Günther with Abdullahi A. Shongolo. 2012. *Islam and Ethnicity in Northern Kenya and Southern Ethiopia*. Woodbridge: James Currey.

Schlee, Günther and Abdullahi A. Shongolo. 2012. *Pastoralism and Politics in Northern Kenya and Southern Ethiopia*. Woodbridge: James Currey.

Schlee, Günther and Karin Werner (eds). 1996a. *Inklusion und Exklusion: Die Dynamik von Grenzziehungen im Spannungsfeld von Markt, Staat und Ethnizität*. Cologne: Rüdiger Köppe.

Schlee, Günther and Karin Werner. 1996b. 'Inklusion und Exklusion: Einführung', in Günther Schlee and Karin Werner (eds), *Inklusion und Exklusion*. Cologne: Köppe Verlag, pp. 9–36.

Schorkowitz, Dittmar. 2015. 'Imperial Formations and Ethnic Diversity: Institutions, Practices, and *longue durée* Illustrated by the Example of Russia', *Max Planck Institute for Social Anthropology Working Paper no. 48*. Halle (Saale): Max Planck Institute for Social Anthropology.

——. 2017. 'Dealing with Nationalities in Imperial Formations: How Russian and Chinese Agencies Managed Ethnic Diversity in the 17th to 20th Centuries', in Dittmar Schorkowitz and Chia Ning (eds), *Managing Frontiers in Qing China: The Lifanyuan and Libu Revisited*. Leiden: Brill, pp. 389–434.

Scott, James C. 1976. *The Moral Economy of the Peasant: Rebellion and Subsistence in Southeast Asia*. New Haven, NJ: Yale University Press.

Scott, James. 1998. *Seeing Like a State: How Certain Schemes to Improve the Human Condition Have Failed*. New Haven, NJ: Yale University Press.

——. 2009. *The Art of Not Being Governed: An Anarchist History of Upland Southeast Asia*. New Haven, NJ: Yale University Press.

Sharma, Prayag Raj. 1992. 'How to Tend this Garden', *Himal* 5(3): 7–9.

Sharma, Ursula. 1994. 'Berreman Revisited; Caste and the Comparative Method', in Mary Searle-Chatterjee and Ursula Sharma (eds), *Contextualising Caste*. Oxford: Blackwell, pp. 72–91.

Shildkrout, Enid. 1974. 'Ethnicity and Generational Differences Among Urban Immigrants in Ghana', in Abner Cohen (ed.), *Urban Ethnicity*. London: Routledge, pp. 187–222.

——. 1978. *People of the Zongo: Transformation of Ethnic Identities in Ghana*. Cambridge: Cambridge University Press.

Sigrist, Christian. 1994. *Regulierte Anarchie: Untersuchungen zum Fehlen und zur Entstehung politischer Herrschaft in segmentären Gesellschaften Afrikas*. Hamburg: Europäische Verlagsanstalt.

Sik, Endre. 1994a: 'Network Capital in Capitalist, Communist and Post-Communist Societies', *International Contributions to Labour Studies* 4: 73–93.

——. 1994b: 'From Multicoloured to Black and White Economy: The Hungarian Second Economy and the Transformation', *International Journal of Urban and Regional Research* 18(1): 46–70.

Simon, Gerhard. 1991. *Nationalism and Policy Toward the Nationalities in the Soviet Union: From Totalitarian Dictatorship to Post-Stalinist Society*. Boulder, CO: Westview Press.

Smith, D. Anthony. 1987. *The Ethnic Origins of Nations*. Oxford and New York: Blackwell.

Smith, Jeremy. 1999. *The Bolsheviks and the National Question, 1917–23*. Studies in Russia and East Europe. New York: St. Martin's Press.

Soja, W. Edward. 2009. 'Taking Space Personally', in Barney Warf and Santa Arias (eds), *The Spatial Turn: Interdisciplinary Perspectives*. London and New York: Routledge, pp. 11–35.

Solzhenitsyn, Alexander I. 1974. *The Gulag Archipelago, 1918–1956: An Experiment in Literary Investigation*. New York: Harper and Row.

Sørbø, Gunnar M. 1985. *Tenants and Nomads in Eastern Sudan – A Study of Economic Adaptations in the New Halfa Scheme*. Uppsala: The Nordic Africa Institute.

Spear, Thomas. 2003. 'Neo-Traditionalism and the Limits of Invention in British Colonial Africa', *Journal of African History* 44: 3–27.

Steenberg, Rune. 2014. 'Network or Community? Two Tropes for Analysing Social Relations among Uyghur Traders in Kyrgyzstan', *Crossroads Asia Working Paper Series no. 18*. University of Bonn: Centre for Development Research.

Stichweh, Rudolf. 1992. 'Der Fremde – Zur Evolution der Weltgesellschaft', *Rechtshistorisches Journal* 11: 295–316.

Suny, Ronald Grigor. 1995. *The Revenge of the Past: Nationalism, Revolution, and the Collapse of the Soviet Union*. Stanford, CA: Stanford University Press.

———. 1999. 'Provisional Stabilities: The Politics of Identities in Post-Soviet Eurasia', *International Security* 24(3): 139–78.

Sureau, Timm. 2016. '"The Last Bullet": South Sudan's Emerging State', PhD dissertation. Halle (Saale): Martin Luther University Halle-Wittenberg.

Tauzin, Aline. 1984. 'Statuts féminins dans une société pastorale: les Maures de Mauritanie', *Production pastorale et société* 14: 79–91.

———. 1993. *Contes arabes de Mauritanie*. Paris: Karthala.

Taylor, Raymond M. 1996. *Of Disciples and Sultans: Power, Authority and Society in the Nineteenth Century Mauritanian Gebla*. Urbana, IL: University of Illinois at Urbana-Champaign.

Tiando, Emmanuel. 1993. 'L'historiographie de l'Atakora', *Afrika Zamani* 1: 95–106.

Tilly, Charles. 1985. 'War Making and State Making as Organized Crime', in Peter Evans, Dietrich Rueschemeyer and Theda Skocpol (eds), *Bringing the State Back In*. Cambridge: Cambridge University Press, pp. 169–87.

Tlostanova, Madina. 2015. 'Postcolonial Post-Soviet Trajectories', *Balticworlds*. Retrieved 20 May 2015 from http://balticworlds.com/postcolonial-post-soviet-trajectories/.

Todorova, Maria. 2010. 'Introduction: From Utopia to Propaganda and Back', in Mariia Nikolaeva Todorova and Zsuzsa Gille (eds), *Post-Communist Nostalgia*. Oxford and New York: Berghahn Books, pp. 1–12.

Tonah, Steve. 1993. 'The Development of Agropastoral Households in Ghana: Policy Analysis, Project Appraisal and Future Perspectives', *Bielefelder Studien zur Entwicklungssoziologie* 56. Saarbrücken: Verlag für Entwicklungspolitik.

Toth, Anthony B. 2006. 'Last Battles of the Bedouin and the Rise of Modern States in Northern Arabia: 1850–1950', in Dawn Chatty (ed.), *Nomadic Societies in the Middle East and North Africa*. Leiden and Boston: Brill, pp. 49–77.

Toupet, Charles. 1958. 'La vallée de Tamourt en Naaj (Tagant), problèmes d'aménagement', *Bulletin de l'IFAN* série B 20(1–2): 68–110.

Trimingham, J. Spencer. 1970. *A History of Islam in West Africa*. Oxford: Oxford University Press.

Tule, Philipus. 2004. *Longing for the House of God: Dwelling in the House of the Ancestors*. Sankt Augustin (Studia Instituti Anthropos 50): Academic Press Fribourg Switzerland.

Turaeva, Rano. 2016. *Migration and Identity in Central Asia: The Uzbek Experience*. London and New York: Routledge, Taylor and Francis Group.

Uberoi, J.P. Singh. 1996. *Religion, Civil Society, and the State: A Study of Sikhism*. Delhi and Oxford: Oxford University Press.

van der Veer, Peter. 1988. *Gods on Earth: The Management of Religious Experience and Identity in a North Indian Pilgrimage Centre*. London and Atlantic Highlands, NJ: The Athlone Press.

Vertovec, Steven. 2007. 'Super-Diversity and Its Implications', *Ethnic and Racial Studies* 30(6): 1024–54. doi:10.1080/01419870701599465.

Walsh, Lorena S. 1997. *From Calabar to Carter's Grove: The History of a Virginia Slave Community*. Colonial Williamsburg Studies in Chesapeake History and Culture. Charlottesville, VA: University Press of Virginia.

Warms, Richard L. 1994. 'Commerce and Community: Paths to Success for Malian Merchants', *African Studies Review* 37(2): 97–120.

Weber, Eugen. 1976. *Peasants into Frenchmen: The Modernization of Rural France; 1870–1914*. Stanford, CA: Stanford University Press.

Weber, Max. 1968. *Economy and Society: An Outline of Interpretive Sociology*, edited by Günther Roth and Claus Wittich. New York: Bedminster Press.

Wegren, Stephen et al. 2010. 'Rural Reform and the Gender Gap in Post-Soviet Russia', *Slavic Review* 69(1): 65–93.

Werbner, Pnina. 1997. 'Essentialising Essentialism, Essentialising Silence: Ambivalence and Multiplicity in the Constructions of Racism and Ethnicity', in Pnina Werbner and Tariq Modood (eds), *Debating Cultural Hybridity*. London and New Jersey: Zed Books, pp. 226–54.

Wheatley, Jonathan. 2013. 'Informal and Formal Institutions in the Former Soviet Union', in Christian Giordano and Nicolas Hayoz (eds), *Informality in Eastern Europe: Structures, Political Cultures and Social Practices*. Bern: Peter Lang, pp. 319–35.

Whelpton, John, David N. Gellner and Joanna Pfaff-Czarnecka. 2008. 'New Nepal, New Ethnicities: Changes since the mid-1990s', in David N. Gellner, John Whelpton and Joanna Pfaff-Czarnecka (eds), *Nationalism and Ethnicity in Nepal*. Kathmandu: Vajra Publishers, pp. i–xxxiii.

Wild, Anthony. 2001. *The East India Company: Trade and Conquest from 1600*. London: Harper Collins Illustrated.

Wilk, Richard R. and Lisa C. Cligget. 2007 [1996]. *Economies and Cultures: Foundations of Economic Anthropology*. Boulder, CO: Westview Press.

Williams, H. James. 2014. *(Re)Constructing Memory: School Textbooks and the Imagination of the Nation*. Rotterdam: Sense Publishers.

Wimmer, Andreas. 1995. 'Interethnische Konflikte: Ein Beitrag zur Integration aktueller Forschungsansätze', *Kölner Zeitschrift für Soziologie und Sozialpsychologie* 47(3): 464–93.

———. 1997. 'Who owns the State? Understanding Ethnic Conflict in Postcolonial Societies', *Nations and Nationalisms* 3(4): 631–65.

Wimmer, Andreas and Nina Glick Schiller. 2003. 'Methodological Nationalism, the Social Sciences, and the Study of Migration: An Essay in Historical Epistemology', *International Migration Review* 37(3): 576–610.

Witsenburg, Karen and Fred Zaal. 2012. *Spaces of Insecurity: Human Agency in Violent Conflicts in Kenya*. Leiden: African Studies Centre.

Woodward, Peter. 1990. *Sudan, 1898–1989: The Unstable State.* Boulder, CO: Lynne Rienner Publishers.

Yurchak, Alexei. 2006. *Everything Was Forever, Until It Was No More: The Last Soviet Generation.* Princeton, NJ: Princeton University Press.

Zahir, Musa Abdal-Kareem. 2016. 'Group Identification and Resources Conflicts in Gedaref State, Eastern Sudan', PhD dissertation. Halle (Saale): Martin Luther University Halle-Wittenberg.

Zentralasien-Analysen. 2010. *Arbeitsmigration* 29. Retrieved 1 June 2016 from http://www.laender-analysen.de/zentralasien/pdf/ZentralasienAnalysen29.pdf.

Zima, Peter. 1994. *Lexique Dendi (Songhay).* Cologne: Köppe Verlag.

Zinovyev, Aleksandr. 1986. *Homo Sovieticus.* London: Paladin.

Zitelmann, Thomas. 1999. 'Des Teufels Lustgarten: Themen und Tabus der politischen Anthropologie Nordostafrikas', habilitation thesis. Berlin: Free University of Berlin.

Index

Integration and Conflict Studies

Published in Association with the Max Planck Institute for Social Anthropology, Halle/Saale

Series Editor: Günther Schlee, Director of the Department of Integration and Conflict at the Max Planck Institute for Social Anthropology

Editorial Board: Brian Donahoe (Max Planck Institute for Social Anthropology), John Eidson (Max Planck Institute for Social Anthropology), Peter Finke (University of Zurich), Joachim Görlich (Max Planck Institute for Social Anthropology), Jacqueline Knörr (Max Planck Institute for Social Anthropology), Bettina Mann (Max Planck Institute for Social Anthropology), Stephen Reyna (Max Planck Institute for Social Anthropology)

Assisted by: Cornelia Schnepel and Viktoria Zeng (Max Planck Institute for Social Anthropology)

The objective of the Max Planck Institute for Social Anthropology is to advance anthropological fieldwork and enhance theory building. 'Integration' and 'Conflict', the central themes of this series, are major concerns of the contemporary social sciences and of significant interest to the general public. They have also been among the main research areas of the institute since its foundation. Bringing together international experts, *Integration and Conflict Studies* includes both monographs and edited volumes, and offers a forum for studies that contribute to a better understanding of processes of identification and inter-group relations.